AMC

Massachusetts Trail Guide

8th Edition

AMC Guide to Hiking Trails
in Massachusetts

Compiled and edited by
Charles W. G. Smith

APPALACHIAN MOUNTAIN CLUB BOOKS
BOSTON, MASSACHUSETTS

Cover design: Kala Sabel
Front cover photograph: Hikers on Appalachian Trail, Mt. Greylock, MA
© Kindra Clineff, www.kindraclineff.com
Back cover photographs (l-r): Hikers on Old Indian Trail, Wachusett Mtn. State
Reserve, MA © Kindra Clineff
View from Metacomet-Monadnock Trail by Marny Ashburne
Hikers at sunset © David Brownell
Book design: Amy Winchester
Map cartography: Larry Garland

AMC Massachusetts Trail Guide, 8th edition
Copyright © 2004 by the Appalachian Mountain Club. All rights reserved.

Distributed by The Globe Pequot Press, Guilford, CT.

Library of Congress Cataloging-in-Publication Data
Smith, Charles W. G.
Massachusetts trail guide / Charles W.G. Smith.—8th ed.
p. cm.
Rev. ed. of: Massachusetts and Rhode Island trail guide. 7th ed. c1995.
Includes bibliographical references and index.
ISBN 1-929173-44-X (alk. paper)
1. Hiking—Massachusetts—Guidebooks. 2. Trails—Massachusetts—Guidebooks.
3. Massachusetts—Guidebooks. I. Appalachian Mountain Club. II. Massachusetts
and Rhode Island trail guide. III. Title.

GV199.42.M4S55 2004
917.4404'4—dc22
2004003999

**Due to changes in conditions, use of the information
in this book is at the sole risk of the user.**

10 9 8 7 6 5 4 3 2   06 07 08

Contents

Key to Maps

Map 1: Northern Berkshires
Map 2: Southwestern Massachusetts
Map 3: Wachusett Mtn. State
       Reservation

Map 4: Blue Hills Reservation
Map 5: Mt. Tom State Reservation
Map 6: Mt. Holyoke Range

Introduction

Robert Frost wrote of two roads diverging in a yellow wood. In Massachusetts hundreds of trails diverge in woods and fields, climb ridges and mountaintops, and wind across the breadth of the state. You can explore lakes and waterfalls, cliff-top vistas, forests, fens and bogs, old stone walls and cellar holes—and that's just the start. Whether you're looking for a day hike up a mountain or a weeklong trek on the Appalachian Trail, Massachusetts is the place to be.

With so many paths to explore, it can be challenging to find a desired trail or determine the best route to a preferred destination. That's what this guide is all about. This book provides extensive trail information for each of the state's six regions: the Berkshires, the Pioneer Valley and Vicinity, Central Massachusetts, North and West of Boston, Boston and Vicinity, and Southeast Massachusetts and the Islands. In addition, updated and comprehensive information is provided for every one of the state's 10 distinctive long-distance trails, including, of course, the Robert Frost Trail. No matter where you are in Massachusetts, a diverse and interesting trail awaits nearby. To help you find your way, accurate topographic maps are included that cover six major hiking areas. Finally, the book's easy-to-use format and size make it convenient to carry on every adventure.

As you peruse this collection of trails and destinations you will see a unique diversity emerge that is unmatched by other regions. Massachusetts is the nexus of a complex of geology, soils, climate, latitude, and a host of other factors that have combined to create scores of fascinating yet completely different natural places. The state also has a national reputation for protecting substantial amounts of land and opening these resources to recreation such as hiking. These things combine to create not only hiking opportunities, but an array of hiking opportunities found nowhere else.

Acknowledgments

This is a book for everyone who enjoys the pleasure of walking in the woods in Massachusetts. It is also such a large undertaking that it seems as if everyone has had an active part in revising it. The help I received from myriad outdoorspeople who hiked the trails and collected data was self-sacrificing, excellent, and deeply appreciated. Foremost is my wife, Susan, who spent countless hours orchestrating this revision at the outset. She is wonderful in every way.

I also extend my heartfelt thanks to the many volunteers and dedicated organizations from Cape Cod to the Berkshires who assisted in the updating effort. I appreciate all your help: Becky Barnes, Dave Boone, Dr. Rob Bristow, Cosmo Catalano, the Clark Art Institute, Dave Conna, Janet Di Mattia, Wes and Teri Dunn, Alan French, Larry Garland, Beth Goettel, Jim Goyea, Cindy Gray, Don Hoffses, Kevin Hollenbeck, the Housatonic Valley Association, Patrick Kimball/CC Trails, René Laubach, the Laurel Hill Association, Mary Ann Leekley, Mark Levine, Mary Malmros, Mass Audubon, the Massachusetts Department of Conservation and Recreation (DCR), Mass Wildlife, Steve McMahon, The Nature Conservancy, Bob Quay, Chris Ryan, Bill Shearer, Liz Tentarelli, The Trustees of Reservations, Bob Vogel, Ted Weber, and Leslie Reed-Evans and Rebecca of the Williamstown Rural Lands Foundation.

How to Use This Book

This book is designed to fulfill the needs of all hikers, from beginners to backcountry experts. To help you prepare, the following chapters contain information essential for a safe, responsible hiking experience. First, read and review the chapter on Safety and Trip Planning. Hikers unfamiliar with all that Massachusetts has to offer can learn more about the state's mountains, valleys, and shores in the Natural History chapter. This chapter is also valuable for hikers who have explored one region thoroughly and are interested in finding new areas to visit. Of course all the beauty that you'll encounter on the trail is a resource that every hiker is responsible for maintaining. We go into the wild seeking adventure, but conscious of the fact that we are always stewards of the creation around us. The Stewardship and Conservation chapter outlines ways to minimize impact on the landscape we all enjoy. After all this careful reading and planning, simply flip through the descriptions of each region's parks, forests, preserves, and sanctuaries to locate the perfect destination for your next outdoor adventure.

This guide divides the state into six regions, organized west to east from the Berkshires to the offshore islands. Each part begins with comprehensive descriptions of that region's long-distance trails. Following are entries that describe trails and trail systems in area parks, forests, and other protected spaces. In general major trails are described before major paths in the trail system or network.

Massachusetts has a rich tradition in land conservation and as a result contains an extensive number of trails, far more than the size of the state might imply. A description of every one of these trails is beyond the scope of this book. What this guide does provide is a broad selection of the state's best paths and trails. Because of space limitations some trails that appear on the maps included with this guide do not appear in the text. For information on additional hiking opportunities, many agencies (including The Trustees of Reservations, Massachusetts Audubon Society, and Massachusetts Department of Conservation and Recreation) have literature and maps that are excellent supplements to this guide. Many parks, forests, and preserves also have booklets or other information on short trails designed as interpretive nature walks. Contact information for these agencies can be found in the appendix at the back of the book.

TRAIL DESCRIPTIONS

Each trail description provides an overview of the route, concise directions for following the trail, and mileage points along the way; many include information on the surrounding natural history. Driving directions to the trailhead are included, usually with the destination introduction. Following most trail descriptions, distances and estimated times to key landmarks are listed.

Mileage information was obtained from a variety of sources, including ground measurement, computer topographic map programs, and posted trail signs. Hiking times are estimates for an average hiker traveling under normal weather conditions. Your hiking speed may be faster or slower. After you have done a few hikes and compared your hiking times to those listed in the book, you will get a sense for the necessary correction factor for your physical condition. Carrying a heavy pack or traveling in a large group adds time. Remember that going up slows you down, but going down can often slow you down even more, especially in unfavorable conditions.

SUGGESTED HIKES

In our continued effort to make the *Massachusetts Trail Guide* more useful and helpful to readers, a feature called "Suggested Hikes" has been added to this edition. At the end of each part of this guide is a list of suggested hikes designed to supply readers with a number of options for easy, moderate, and strenuous hikes within a region. While there are no strict criteria for these classifications, in general a short (easy) hike can be completed in about an hour or less, a moderate hike in one to three hours, and a longer (strenuous) hike in three to eight hours. The numbers in brackets indicate distance and estimated time; "ow," "rt," and "lp" mean "one way," "round trip," and "loop" respectively. Remember that the time allowances are merely a rough estimate—many parties will require more time, and many will require less—and they do not include time for extensive stops for scenery appreciation or rest.

MAPS

The 8th edition of the *Massachusetts Trail Guide* includes six computer-designed topographic maps, created using a variety of digital data to ensure the highest degree of accuracy. They provide coverage of the state's most popular hiking regions, and clearly indicate trails, campgrounds, backcountry shelters and tentsites, parking areas, visitor centers, and other available facilities. Land ownership and general use guidelines are indicated as well, but it is the responsibility of the individual to be aware of current land-use restrictions for both public and private lands. The maps are sufficient for navigation in all of the featured regions.

The regions covered are: the Northern Berkshires, including Mt. Greylock (Map 1); Southwestern Massachusetts and its large complex of interconnected parklands (Map 2); Wachusett Mtn. State Reservation in central Massachusetts (Map 3); Blue Hills Reservation just south of Boston (Map 4); and Mt. Tom State Reservation (Map 5) and the Mt. Holyoke Range (Map 6), both located in the Connecticut River Valley.

Due to the broad distribution of hiking opportunities in Massachusetts, not every trail described in this book appears on these maps. For areas not covered, the US Geological Survey produces a series of detailed topographic maps. Most areas in Massachusetts are now covered by the recent, more detailed 7.5-minute quads, which have largely replaced the old 15-minute quads. While topography on the newer maps is excellent, some are inaccurate in showing the location of trails. These maps can be obtained at a number of local outlets and from USGS Map Sales, Federal Center, Box 25286, Denver, CO 80255 (800-USA-MAPS, www.usgs.gov). Index maps showing the available USGS quads in any state and an informative pamphlet titled *Topographic Maps* are available free on request from the USGS. USGS maps are now also available on compact disc from a number of sources, including TOPO! and Maptech.

Many state parks and forests also provide useful trail maps; they may be more accurate than the USGS quad for the area. They are usually available at park entrance stations and visitor centers, or can be downloaded from the MassParks website (www.state.ma.us/dem/forparks.htm). Lastly, many of the organizations listed in the back of the book produce maps for their respective areas; contact information is provided.

CAMPING

Overnight trips are as much a part of hiking in Massachusetts as day hikes. Some locations offer backcountry camping, but most overnight opportunities involve staying at one of the dozens of designated campgrounds found across the state. Some drive-in campgrounds require reservations, while space in others is on a first-come, first-served basis. Massachusetts state parks and forests provide the most campgrounds, but nearly every land-management agency offers at least one campground somewhere in the state. For in-depth information on camping opportunities, use the appendix to locate contact information for the appropriate management agency. Their websites are usually loaded with updated information for all types of camping, from extremely rustic to drive-it-up-and-plug-it-in RV camping sites.

Backcountry camping is mostly limited to the Berkshires region in the western part of the state. Overnight shelters and camping areas are established along the length of the Appalachian Trail, and several other parks provide excellent backpacking opportunities. Parks and forests that offer backcountry camping include Mt. Washington State Forest, Mt. Everett State Reservation, October Mtn. State Forest, Mt. Greylock State Reservation, Monroe State Forest, and Dubuque Memorial State Forest.

OTHER RECREATIONAL OPPORTUNITIES

The trails in this guide are first and foremost hiking trails, yet many of them are also open to other recreational opportunities such as cross-country skiing, mountain biking, and horseback riding. What types of recreation a trail is open for often changes, and sometimes these changes occur frequently. When in doubt about the legal uses of a trail, check with the managing agency either via the Internet, by phone, or by visiting the property headquarters.

Some trails provide excellent opportunities for mountain biking, yet hiking and mountain biking are different enough to demand the tolerance and patience of both bikers and hikers. Mountain bikers must observe trail-use restrictions. Where biking is permitted, riders should yield to hikers on the trail, and suspend biking during wet weather in areas where trail erosion is a problem.

Lately much debate has centered on the use of ATVs and dirt bikes on forest trails. At present the solution has been to open selected areas of some state forests to motorized recreation. This limits erosion and other damage to the environment but also concentrates the machines in a smaller area, and thus increases the environmental damage. Trails that have been designated as ATV and dirt bike trails are largely not compatible with a pleasant hiking experience. In some areas hikers are specifically requested not to use these multiuse trails at all. As a result trails that are open to motorized recreational use are not described in this guide.

Abbreviations

The following abbreviations are used for the major trail maintenance organizations in this region:

AMC	Appalachian Mountain Club
ATC	Appalachian Trail Conference
BCAMC	Berkshire Chapter, Appalachian Mountain Club
BNRC	Berkshire Natural Resources Council
DCR	Massachusetts Department of Conservation and Recreation
FOW	Friends of the Wapack
HVA	Housatonic Valley Association
LHA	Laurel Hill Association
MAS	Massachusetts Audubon Society
NETC	New England Trail Conference
PAOC	Phillips Academy Outing Club
SEAMC	Southeastern Massachusetts Chapter, Appalachian Mountain Club
THC	Taconic Hiking Club (Troy, NY)
TTOR	The Trustees of Reservations
WOC	Williams Outing Club
WRLF	Williamstown Rural Lands Foundation

Trip Planning and Safety

Hiking is a sport of self-reliance. A hiker relies on physical ability, unaided by motorized or nonmotorized technology, to reach the goal and return. This aspect of the sport often provides as much satisfaction as the beautiful views or visions of wildlife encountered along the way. As with any worthwhile skill, learning self-reliant hiking takes time and experience. Part of that process is proper preparation.

Plan your trip schedule with safety in mind. Consider the strength of your party and the general strenuousness of the trip: the overall distance, the amount of climbing, and the roughness of the terrain. Knowing the latest weather information is essential to safe hiking. Get a weather report, but be aware of the fact that most forecasts are not intended to apply to higher elevations; a day that is sunny and pleasant in the lowlands may well be inclement higher up. Keeping in mind the vagaries of New England weather ("if you don't like the weather, wait a minute"), prepare for the worst possible conditions. During your hike, constantly reassess the weather forecast by observing clouds and wind, and be prepared to change the itinerary as necessary.

Plan to start your hike as early in the day as possible. Know what time sunset will be, and start early enough to allow for a return while there is still plenty of daylight. Remember that dusk and darkness come quickly in the woods, and seem to descend even faster in winter. Hiking after dark, even with flashlights (which may fail), makes finding trails more difficult and crossing streams hazardous. For longer hikes in more remote areas, it is also important to let someone know your route and when you expect to be back.

With appropriate clothing you can hike all the trails in this book safely and comfortably during spring, summer, and fall. For spring hikes be alert for lingering patches of ice and to the possibility of difficult brook crossings due to runoff from melting snow. In fall the trail may be covered with fallen leaves that can be slippery or hide rocks, roots, or other impediments that can trip you up. Winter hiking, with the additional hazards of snow and extreme cold, requires special skills and preparation (see Winter Concerns, later in this section). Under such conditions novice hikers should always hike with more experienced trekkers.

BACKCOUNTRY HAZARDS

Safe hiking means knowing how to avoid dangerous situations as well as being prepared to deal with problems when they do occur. The following section outlines the common hazards encountered in the Massachusetts outdoors and discusses how to approach them.

Falls and Injuries

The remoteness of the backcountry makes any injury a potentially serious matter. Be alert to places where the footing might be poor, especially on steep or wet sections of trail. In autumn wet leaves are a particular hazard. Remember that carrying a heavy pack can affect your balance. Rock climbing should be attempted only in areas where it is permitted and only with proper training and equipment.

In case of serious injury, apply first aid and keep the injured hiker warm and comfortable. Then take a minute to assess the situation before going for help. Backcountry evacuation is usually measured in hours, not minutes, so don't rush. Write down your location, the condition of the injured person, and any other pertinent facts. At least one person should stay with the injured hiker while two others go for help. (For this reason it is safest to hike in the backcountry in groups of four or more.)

Hypothermia

Hypothermia is the loss of ability to preserve body heat because of injury, exhaustion, lack of sufficient food, or inadequate or wet clothing. The result is a dangerous lowering of the body's core temperature. Our bodies lose heat all the time, but we don't suffer hypothermia because the loss of heat is buffered by insulation. Most often this comes in the form of clothing made of fabrics that help retain body heat. Many fabrics are good insulators when dry, but when some get wet the insulating ability drops so drastically that they become very efficient at cooling the body just when you need warmth.

In hiking circles the phrase *Cotton kills* is as accurate as it is serious. Most cases of hypothermia occur in temperatures above freezing (between 32 and 50 degrees F) on windy, rainy days. Some fabrics, such as wool, polypropylene, and polyester fleece, retain much of their insulating ability even when wet. Others, most notably cotton, do not. Even in dry weather, cotton clothing can become quickly saturated with perspiration, which at the least is uncomfortable and at the worst can lead to hypothermia in cooler conditions.

Symptoms of hypothermia include uncontrolled shivering, impaired speech and movement, lowered body temperature, and drowsiness. The ultimate result is death, unless the victim (who may not understand the situation, due to impaired mental function) is rewarmed. In mild cases the victim should be given dry clothing and placed in a sleeping bag if available (perhaps with someone else in it to provide body heat), then provided quick-energy food and something warm (not hot) to drink. In severe cases only prompt hospitalization offers reasonable hope for recovery. It is not unusual for a victim to resist treatment and even combat rescuers. It should therefore be obvious that prevention of hypothermia is the only truly practical course. Uncontrollable shivering should be regarded as a sure sign of hypothermia; this shivering will eventually cease on its own, but that is merely the sign that the body has given up the struggle and is sinking toward death.

For those interested in more information, a thorough treatment of the subject is contained in *The Basic Essentials of Hypothermia* (2nd ed., 1999) by William W. Forgey, MD, published by The Globe Pequot Press, P.O. Box 480, Guilford, CT 06437, www.globe-pequot.com.

Heatstroke

The opposite of hypothermia, heatstroke occurs when the body is unable to control its internal temperature and overheats. Usually brought on by excessive exposure to the sun and accompanying dehydration, symptoms include cramping, headache, and mental confusion. In Massachusetts the hot, humid days of summer pose the greatest risk of heatstroke, because the high humidity reduces the amount of sweat that can evaporate from the skin. This consequently limits the body's ability to cool itself through evaporative heat loss and can lead to a dangerous rise in core body temperature. Treatment entails rapid, aggressive cooling of the body through whatever means are available—cooling the head and torso is the most important—and drinking lots of fluids. Stay hydrated and have some type of sun protection for your head if you expect to travel a hot, shadeless section of trail.

Lightning

Lightning can be a serious hazard in open areas, particularly on any bare ridge or summit. The best course of action is to avoid dangerous exposed places when thunderstorms are likely, and to seek shelter in thick woods as quickly as possible if an unexpected "thumper" is detected. Most thunderstorms occur when a cold front passes, or on very warm days; those produced by cold fronts are typically more sudden and violent. Weather forecasts that mention cold fronts or predict temperatures much above 80 degrees in the lowlands and valleys should arouse concern.

Brook Crossings

Rivers and brooks are often crossed without bridges, and it is usually possible to jump from rock to rock; a hiking staff or stick is a great aid to balance. Use caution; several fatalities have resulted from hikers (particularly solo hikers) falling on slippery rocks and suffering an injury that rendered them unconscious, causing them to drown in relatively shallow streams. If you need to wade across (often the safer course), wearing boots, but not necessarily socks, is recommended. Note that many crossings that may be only a nuisance in summer may become a serious obstacle in cold weather when feet and boots must be kept dry. Higher waters, which can turn innocuous brooks into virtually uncrossable torrents, come in spring as snow melts, or after heavy rainstorms, particularly in fall when trees drop their leaves and take up less water. Avoid trails with potentially dangerous stream crossings during these high-water periods. If you are cut off from roads by swollen streams, it is better to make a long detour, even if you need to wait and spend a night in the woods. Rushing current can make wading extremely hazardous, and several deaths have resulted. Floodwaters may subside within a few hours, especially in small brooks. It is particularly important not to camp on the far side of a brook from your exit point if the crossing is difficult and heavy rain is predicted.

Wildlife

Black bears have made a strong comeback after having been nearly eradicated from Massachusetts by the mid–19th century. In recent decades the state's black bear population has been increasing at a rate of nearly 8 percent per year, and today an estimated 2000 bears roam the state's forests. They can be found nearly everywhere west of the Connecticut River (approximately one bear per square mile of forest), but are less common in central Massachusetts and rare in the eastern part of the state. Black bears live mostly on nuts, berries, and other plants, and dead animals, and rarely kill anything larger than a mouse. They almost never attack humans and will usually flee at the first sight of an approaching hiker. Nevertheless, the black bear is a large and unpredictable animal that must be treated with respect. Several serious incidents have been unnecessarily provoked by deliberate feeding of bears, or by harassment by a dog.

The philosophy of dealing with bears has undergone some modification in recent years. Formerly the usual advice was that, if approached by a bear, you should throw down your pack and back away slowly. This advice works, but unfortunately it teaches the bear that people have food and that very little effort or risk is required to make them part with it. The result is a bear that is likely to be more aggressive toward the next visitor, which may result in injury to the human (who may be you) and frequently results in a death sentence for the bear. Many hikers regard bears as an indispensable feature of wild country in New England, and preservation of the bears requires us to make sure that they remain wild, so feeding them either deliberately or through carelessness should be regarded as tantamount to bringing about their execution. Thus the current advice is that a hiker confronted by a bear should attempt to appear neither threatening nor frightened, and should back off slowly but not abandon food unless the bear appears irresistibly aggressive. A loud noise, such as one made by a whistle or by banging metal pots, is often useful. Careful protection of food at campsites is mandatory; it must never be kept overnight in a tent, but should be hung between trees well off the ground.

The state's moose population also has been on the increase in recent years, and today numbers between 500 and 1000 animals. This has added a significant new hazard for hikers driving to the trailhead. Indeed, the state's first-ever moose–car fatality occurred in the summer of 2003, when a driver was killed in a collision on the Mass Pike. Motorists need to be aware of the seriousness of the problem, particularly at night when these huge, dark-colored animals are both active and very difficult to see. Instinct often causes them to face an auto rather than run from it, and they are also apt to cross the road unpredictably as a car approaches. It is thus safest to assume that moose will behave in the most inconvenient manner possible. Otherwise they probably constitute little threat to hikers on foot, though it would be wise to give bulls a wide berth during the fall mating season.

Two poisonous snakes exist in Massachusetts—the timber rattlesnake and northern copperhead—but they are extremely rare and infrequently encountered by hikers. Although once widespread across the region, both snakes today are found only in isolated locations. If threatened, the two species can deliver painful, but nonfatal, bites. If bitten, try to remain calm, and remove any constricting items (rings, watches, etc.) from the soon-to-be-swollen extremity. Do not apply ice to the bite; this can cause further damage to the surrounding tissue. Seek medical attention as quickly as possible.

Mosquitoes and black flies are the woodland residents most frequently encountered by hikers. Mosquitoes are worst throughout the summer in low, wet areas, and black flies are most bloodthirsty in June and early July; at times these winged pests can make life in the woods virtually unbearable. Head nets can be useful for maintaining sanity at these times. The most effective repellents are based on the active ingredient diethyl-meta-toluamide, generally known as DEET, but there are concerns about its safety. Hikers should probably apply repellents with DEET to clothing rather than skin where possible, and avoid using them on small children. There are other effective repellents available. There is also a good deal of folklore and tradition on the subject: People who seek true solitude in the woods often employ the traditional creosote-scented recipes, reasoning that anything that repels fellow humans might have the same effect on insects.

Ticks have been an increasing problem in recent years, becoming common in woods and grassy or brushy areas at lower elevations. Countermeasures include using insect repellent, wearing light-colored long pants tucked into socks, and making frequent visual checks of clothing and skin. Ticks wander for several hours before settling on a spot to bite, so they can be removed easily if found promptly. If you find a tick attached to you, do not try to pull it out with your fingers or pinch the body; this can inject tick juices under your skin and increase the risk of infection. Using an appropriate tool, gently pull the tick out by lifting upward from the base of the body where it is attached to the skin. Pull straight out until the tick releases; do not twist or jerk, which may break the mouthparts off under your skin. A small V-cut in the side of a credit card works well for this operation.

Lyme disease is present throughout Massachusetts, but only one species of tick is capable of transmitting it—the diminutive black-legged tick (also known as the deer tick). Caused by a spirochete, this potentially life-threatening disease can be hard to diagnose in its early phases. Common early symptoms include fatigue, chills and fever, headache, muscle and joint pain, swollen lymph nodes, and a blotchy skin rash around the bite site that clears centrally to produce a characteristic ring shape 3 to 30 days after exposure. If you fear that you have been exposed to Lyme disease, consult a doctor immediately; it can be easily treated in its early stages.

Poison Ivy

If you learn only one plant in Massachusetts, it had better be this one. Easily recognized by its characteristic clusters of three shiny leaves, poison ivy can appear either as a low-lying shrub or a climbing vine. It can be seen winding up trees in open woodlands, or growing close to the ground along fencerows, in thickets, and in disturbed areas. Yellowish white clusters of flowers appear in late spring and early summer, and the leaves turn red in fall. When not eaten by birds, the plant's small white fruit can remain through winter. Both the leaves and stems contain an oil that causes a strong allergic reaction in most people, creating a maddening and long-lived rash that can spread across the body. Wash thoroughly after any exposure. Avoidance is of course the best form of prevention: "Leaves of three, let them be."

Hunting Season

Hunting is permitted in season in all state wildlife management areas, as well as in most state parks and forests. Most hunters stay fairly close to roads, and, in general, the harder it would be to haul an animal out of a given area, the lower the probability that a hiker will encounter hunters there. During hunting season avoid wearing brown or anything that might give a hunter the impression of the white flash of a white-tailed deer running away. Wearing hunter-orange clothing is recommended.

Various hunting seasons occur from September through the winter months. In Massachusetts the primary deer-hunting season (with guns) does not occur until late November or early December, but archery hunting is permitted beginning in mid-October. Bear hunting is permitted in the eastern regions of the state for a few weeks in September and then again in November. The main hunting season for birds (pheasant, quail, grouse) runs from mid-October through November. Hunting is prohibited on Sunday and at night from half an hour after sunset until half an hour before sunrise. Exact dates and regulations vary from year to year. Contact the Massachusetts Department of Fish and Game for current information (617-626-1590; www.state.ma.us/dfwele).

Winter Concerns

Snowshoeing and cross-country skiing have steadily become more popular in the last decade. Increasing numbers of hikers have discovered the beauty of the woods in winter, and advances in clothing and equipment have made it possible for experienced winter travelers to enjoy great comfort and safety. The greatest danger is that it begins to look too easy and too safe, while snow, ice, and weather conditions are constantly changing, and a relatively trivial error of judgment may have grave, even fatal, consequences. Conditions can vary greatly from day to day, and from trail to trail; therefore, much more experience is required to foresee and avoid dangerous situations in winter than in summer. Days are very short, particularly in early winter when darkness falls shortly after 4 p.m. Trails are frequently difficult or impossible to follow, and navigation skills are hard to learn in adverse weather conditions (as anyone who has tried to read a map in a blizzard can attest). "Breaking trail" on snowshoes through new snow can be strenuous and exhausting work. The most dangerous aspect of winter in New England, however, is the extreme variability of the weather: It is not unusual for a cold, penetrating, wind-driven rain to be followed within a few hours by a cold front that brings sub-freezing temperatures and strong winds.

Winter on the most trails in Massachusetts trails may require only snow-shoes or skis and some warm clothing. Even so, summer hiking boots are usually inadequate, flashlight batteries fail quickly (a headlamp with battery pack works better), and water in canteens freezes unless carried in an insulated container or wrapped in a sock or sweater. The winter hiker needs good physical conditioning from regular exercise, and must dress carefully in order to avoid overheating and excessive perspiration, which soaks clothing and soon leads to chilling. Cotton clothes are useful only as long as they can be kept perfectly dry (an impossible task); only wool and synthetics retain insulating value when wet. Fluid intake must increase, because dehydration can be a serious problem in the dry winter air.

No book can begin to impart all the knowledge necessary to cope safely with the potential for such brutal conditions, but helpful information can be found in *Winterwise: A Backpacker's Guide* by John M. Dunn (1996, Adirondack Mountain Club) and *AMC Guide to Winter Camping* by Stephen Gorman (2nd ed., 1999, AMC Books), which despite their titles are also quite useful for those primarily interested in day hiking. Hikers who are interested in extending their activities into the winter season are strongly advised to seek out organized parties with leaders who have extensive winter experience. Each year the AMC and Adirondack Mountain Club operate a weeklong winter school that exposes participants to techniques and equipment for safe winter travel. The AMC and several of its chapters also sponsor numerous workshops on evenings and weekends, in addition to introductory winter hikes and regular winter schedules through which participants can gain experience. Information on such activities can be obtained from the AMC at 5 Joy St., Boston, MA 02108 (617-523-0636; www.outdoors.org).

DRINKING WATER

The pleasure of quaffing a cup of water fresh from a pure mountain spring is one of the traditional attractions of the outdoors. Unfortunately the presence of cysts of the intestinal parasite *Giardia lamblia* in water sources throughout the region is probably pervasive. It is impossible to be completely sure whether a given source is safe, no matter how clear the water or remote the location. The symptoms of giardiasis are severe intestinal distress and diarrhea, but such discomforts can have many other causes, making the disease difficult to diagnose accurately. The safest course for day hikers is to carry their own water, allowing 2 quarts per person for a full-day hike, more in hot weather. If it is necessary to use sources in the woods, the water must be treated. The traditional methods of boiling or treating water with iodine are effective but somewhat inconvenient. A popular choice today is one of the newer, lightweight filtering units, which produce tasty, safe drinking water. Although somewhat expensive, these filters are durable and easy to use.

DOGS

Dogs are permitted on many of the trails described in this book, but regulations vary widely by region and managing agency. Dogs are permitted in Massachusetts state parks and forests but must be leashed at all times; they are prohibited at Walden Pond State Reservation and Boston Harbor Islands State Park. In state wildlife management areas dogs may run unleashed but must be under voice control at all times. In order to protect wildlife, dogs are prohibited in all national wildlife refuges and Massachusetts Audubon Society locations. For other areas, call beforehand to check regulations.

When hiking with your dog, please respect other visitors. Barking dogs disrupt the peacefulness of the forest and detract from the wilderness experience—keep your pet quiet or leave it at home. Clean up after your dog and do not leave unpleasant surprises on the trail for the next hiker. Carry out your dog's waste in a plastic bag or bury it as you would your own. When another hiker approaches, keep your dog close and do not let it go bounding toward the other person; some people may misinterpret the dog's behavior as aggressive, while others may dislike dogs in general (no matter how friendly). And always, both for its safety and for the comfort and safety of others, keep your dog under control at all times.

PRIVATE PROPERTY

Some trails described in this book cross private property and exist only with the consent of the landowners. Hikers must respect the rights of these owners and observe all the customary rules of courtesy if the privilege of trail walking on private property is to continue. In particular, respect No Trespassing signs, do not bend or break fences, and leave gates open or closed as you found them. Never camp on private land without permission.

WHAT TO CARRY

Adequate equipment for a hike varies greatly according to the length of the trip and the difficulty of getting to the nearest trailhead if trouble arises. If you are only strolling to a pond or waterfall a mile or so from the road in good weather, then perhaps a light jacket, a candy bar, and a bottle of water will suffice. If, however, you are going on an extended hike and are not inclined to turn back at the first sign of questionable weather, you will need a good pack filled with plenty of warm clothing, food for emergency use, and other equipment. No determination of what should be taken along can be made without considering the length of a trip and the hazards of the terrain it will cross.

Good things to have in your pack for a day hike include guidebook, maps, water bottle (ordinary plastic soft-drink bottles, with or without original contents, work well), compass, pocketknife, rain gear, windbreaker, a warm synthetic or wool pullover, wool hat and mittens, waterproof matches, enough food for your usual needs plus high-energy foods (such as dried fruit or candy) in reserve, first-aid supplies (including personal medicines; a nonprescription painkiller such as aspirin, acetaminophen, or ibuprofen; adhesive bandages; gauze; and antiseptic), lightweight plastic tarp, whistle, sunscreen, sunglasses, insect repellent, needle and thread, safety pins, nylon cord, trash bag, toilet paper, and a (small) flashlight or headlamp with extra batteries and a spare bulb. For groups hiking on longer day trips in remote areas, one sleeping bag can provide an additional element of safety, as it can be used to keep an injured hiker warm while awaiting assistance.

For all but the shortest hikes, hiking boots are much preferred over sneakers or walking shoes, because they provide better traction and ankle support and help reduce foot fatigue. Both leather and synthetic boots are available. Leather boots must be properly broken in before being worn on an extended hike. For younger children, hiking boots are not always practical for financial reasons. If it is necessary for children to hike in sneakers, choose shorter trails with smoother footing.

Blue jeans, sweatshirts, and other cotton clothes are popular but, once wet, dry very slowly and may be uncomfortable; in adverse weather conditions they often seriously drain a cold and tired hiker's heat reserves. While such clothes are worn by many hikers on summer trips, people who are planning to travel to remote places or on exposed summits should seriously consider wearing (or at least carrying) wool or synthetics (such as fleece) instead. These fabrics keep much of their insulation value even when wet, and are indispensable for hikers who want to visit places from which return to civilization might require substantial time and effort if conditions turn bad. Not only do hats, mittens, and other such gear provide safety in adverse conditions, but they also allow you to enjoy the summits in comfort on those occasional crisp, clear days when the views are particularly fine, when the other hikers who snickered at your bulging pack are driven from the magnificent vistas with terse greetings forced through chattering teeth.

FOLLOWING TRAILS

Getting lost is probably the novice hiker's single greatest fear. Basic navigational skills are not difficult to learn, and with them even the beginning hiker should have the confidence to complete a hike successfully. But to be a true expert requires not only learned skills but also a "woods sense" that can only be acquired through experience.

Most of the time a trail can be followed simply by alert observation. Look for worn footing or footprints, evidence of trail maintenance (such as water bars or sawn logs), or gaps in the undergrowth. But keep in mind that many of the trails described in this book are not heavily traveled or regularly maintained, so the pathway may not always be obvious. At unmarked junctions it helps to know the general direction in which the trail should be heading.

Blazes, typically geometric shapes painted on trees, are used to mark some trails. In some cases the blaze might be a metal cutout attached to a tree or a mark painted on the rocks underfoot. If you have been following a well-blazed trail and the blazes suddenly stop or change color, you might have taken a wrong turn. Stop walking and look all around. If you cannot see a blaze, mark the spot with something obvious that you'll easily recognize—a rock, or a stick stuck in the ground. Now retrace your steps to the last blaze you saw and look around again. Trails are usually marked so that three blazes can be seen at all times: the immediate blaze, one up the trail, and one down the trail. Not every path conforms to this pattern, but most do. Pay particular attention to a double blaze mark, which indicates a change in trail direction.

Trail descriptions in a guidebook are an important source of information, but they are not perfect. Trails may be rerouted, abandoned, or closed by landowners; signs may be stolen or fall from their posts; bridges can get washed away; storms may cause blowdowns or landslides, which can obliterate a trail for an entire hiking season or longer. Trail guides are an aid to planning, not a substitute for careful observation and good judgment.

Maps are another important navigational tool, but as with trail guide descriptions, they cannot be relied upon blindly. They are especially useful in trip planning and in visualizing the overall lay of the land. Be prepared to find discrepancies between a trail's plotted location and its actual location. This book includes trail maps for some of the major hiking areas in the region.

A compass, and knowledge of how to use it, are important complements to trail maps. The best compass for hiking is the protractor type: a circular, liquid-filled compass that turns on a rectangular, clear plastic base. Excellent compasses of this type, with leaflets that give ample instructions for their use, are available for about $10. Novice hikers in the woods sometimes forget which is the north end of the compass needle. It is therefore helpful to scratch a reminder somewhere on the case. If in doubt remember that the sun in Massachusetts runs from east to west along the southern portion of the sky, so if your compass needle is pointing at the sun it is the south end of the needle you're looking at, not the north. Compass directions in the text and on the maps give true north rather than magnetic north. On most hikes in Massachusetts the difference, or declination, in these two values isn't enough to make a difference in your hike. In Massachusetts the compass will point about 13 degrees west of true north.

One common source of confusion in trail navigation arises from crossings of other trails and streams. Because most of this region was settled at one time, many small paths and woods roads cross most hiking trails. Many of these are not documented in trail descriptions or on maps. Conversely, intersecting paths that are mentioned may become so overgrown as to be missed entirely. A brook crossing might be deemed too small to be mentioned in the trail guide. At the same time, a documented watercourse might happen to be dry and therefore go unnoticed by the hiker.

The careful hiker will use all sources of information—visual observation, guidebook descriptions, and maps—to chart progress. Try at all times to have at least a general sense of your location, which can be confirmed or corrected when reaching major, unmistakable landmarks such as bridges, signed trail junctions, or summits.

IF YOU'RE LOST

Even the most experienced hiker will occasionally lose a trail. This is not necessarily a serious matter, even in remote areas. First, stop. Go back over your route slowly, marking it clearly, until you pick up a sure indication of the trail. The point of your first mistake will usually be evident then. If, after a careful and deliberate search, you are still unable to find the trail, your course of action will depend on whether you are on a mountain. If so, you can usually reach a road in a few hours or less simply by going downhill until you reach a brook or stream and then following it downward. If you are in comparatively level woodland, you can take a compass bearing and follow it until you reach a road. If you know your general position on the map, your selection of the direction to travel will be easier.

When traveling with a group on a hard-to-follow trail, each hiker should stay within sight of the next person. If the group becomes too spread out, it is almost inevitable that at least one person will take a wrong turn. In no event should slower hikers be allowed to lag behind. If you do become separated from your group, do not wander. Stay in one place and signal your location from time to time by three blasts on a whistle or three loud shouts.

Natural History of Massachusetts

Geography

Though one of the smallest states, Massachusetts has a wonderfully diverse geography. The variety of terrain not only is exciting to hike but also holds exceptional biodiversity. The six parts in this guide encompass 13 regions, called ecoregions, that take into account the area's topography, climate, and biology. (These areas are defined in the BioMap report issued by the Massachusetts Division of Fisheries and Wildlife through the Executive Office of Environmental Affairs in 2001.)

Part I: The Berkshires

The Berkshires is a largely mountainous region located at the extreme western edge of the state. It is bounded by Connecticut to the south, New York to the west, Vermont to the north, and the Pioneer Valley to the east. The Berkshires contains four ecoregions: the Taconic Mtns., the Western New England Marble Valleys, the Lower Berkshire Hills, and the Berkshire Highlands. Three long-distance trails cross the region: the Appalachian Trail (AT), South Taconic Trail (STT), and Taconic Crest Trail (TCT). In addition, a large trail network (including portions of the AT) covers the Mt. Greylock massif.

Taconic Mtns. This ecoregion comprises the Taconic Mtns., a range that largely follows the Massachusetts and New York border, but also includes Mt. Greylock (at 3491 ft., the tallest peak in the state). Elevations from 1500 to more than 2000 ft. are common. Weather conditions in the higher elevations can be severe. This area has abundant swift-running streams and an array of interesting plants and animals that live in the cool forests cloaking the mountains. Notable habitats include the pitch pine–scrub oak plant community of the southern Taconics, seen along the AT and the STT; and the spruce-fir plant community, seen along the AT in the Mt. Greylock area.

Western New England Marble Valleys. This ecoregion is sandwiched between the Taconic Mtns. to the west and the Berkshire Highlands to the east, and contains the watersheds of the Housatonic and Hoosic Rivers. The area is underlain with limestone and marble bedrock, which creates one of the most unusual natural regions in the northeastern United States. Calcareous fens, rare in New England, host more than 30 rare species. Lakes, rivers, and streams are plentiful and support species such as bald eagles and ospreys. Elevations are often well below 1000 ft. The AT passes through many miles of these marble valleys.

Lower Berkshire Hills. This ecoregion consists of forested hills ranging from 1000 to about 1700 ft. tall in the southeastern Berkshires. The area offers numerous lakes, streams, and hiking trails scattered throughout state forests and parks. The terrain is usually fairly level, but often covered with hummocks that inhibit drainage and create numerous wetlands and vernal pools. The AT passes through the northern edge of this region. When compared to the Berkshire Highlands just to the north, the Lower Berkshire Hills are lower in elevation and have a slightly less severe climate. Northern hardwood forests and cool upland hemlock forests are common.

Berkshire Highlands. The Berkshire Highlands contain the southernmost spur of Vermont's Green Mtns. where they creep over the border into Massachusetts as a high-elevation plateau. The high average elevation (approximately 2000 ft.) helps produce a cool climate more like northern New England, which is evident in the abundance of transition forest (hardwoods with balsam fir and red and black spruce) and spruce-fir forests. The forests are often extensive and unbroken, allowing for large populations of animals such as black bears.

Part II: Pioneer Valley and Vicinity

This large area is a grab bag of climates and terrain, and one of the state's most diverse and beautiful regions. The area runs from the Berkshires on the west to the Worcester Highlands to the east, and from the Vermont border to the Connecticut line. Within the Pioneer Valley and Vicinity region are three ecoregions: the Vermont Piedmont, Berkshire Transition, and Connecticut Valley. Three long-distance trails are found here: the Metacomet–Monadnock Trail, Robert Frost Trail, and Pocumtuck Ridge Trail.

Vermont Piedmont. This region is found along the Vermont border, between the Berkshire Highlands and the Connecticut Valley, and is typified by hilly terrain from about 500 to 1500 ft. in elevation. The area sports energetic streams and rivers (such as the Deerfield River) as well as a few ponds and lakes. The bedrock is a mix of many rock types that produce rich, deep soils. The soils in turn support a wonderfully rich array of wildflowers, ferns, shrubs, and trees. The forest primarily consists of northern hardwoods, including sugar maple, basswood, hickory, and elm. Many forests, parks, and preserves are in the area, though no long-distance trails pass through this region.

Berkshire Transition. This area acts as a buffer between the harsh, high-elevation Berkshire Hills and the milder, lower-elevation Connecticut Valley. It is bounded to the south by the Connecticut border near Southwick and extends north to include the DAR State Forest in Goshen. The eastern boundary runs roughly north-northeast following the western edge of the flat Connecticut Valley plain. This area has a lower elevation than the Vermont Piedmont to the north, and similar geology allows forests of northern hardwoods to mix with warmer-climate hickories and oaks. One notable feature of the Berkshire Transition is the abundance of high-energy rivers and streams. These have flow rates that rise quickly in storms and during spring thaws—stream crossings can be difficult and dangerous during these times. Portions of the Metacomet–Monadnock Trail pass through this region.

Connecticut River Valley. This distinctive valley follows the magnificent Connecticut River from the Connecticut line near Springfield to the Vermont border near the Vernon Dam. In shape the region is triangular, with a broad base to the south that tapers to a sharp point in the north. The Connecticut River Valley typically has flat topography and fertile, deep soils. In certain areas, notably the south, a number of basalt hills (including the Mt. Holyoke Range and Mt. Tom) jut up from the plains and offer excellent hiking. Portions of the Metacomet–Monadnock Trail, the Robert Frost Trail, and the Pocumtuck Ridge Trail pass through this region.

Part III: Central Massachusetts

This large region runs from the New Hampshire border south to Rhode Island and Connecticut, and is largely defined by the borders of Worcester County. The area is roughly divided into two ecoregions: the Worcester–Monadnock Plateau and the Lower Worcester Plateau. The area has three long-distance trails: the Tully Trail, the Wapack Trail, and the Midstate Trail. The dominant feature is Wachusett Mtn., which is crossed by the Midstate Trail.

Worcester–Monadnock Plateau. This small ecoregion covers the area south of the New Hampshire border and north of the Quabbin Reservoir. It incorporates areas just east of the Connecticut Valley, including Mt. Grace. The region is very hilly and ranges in elevation from about 500 to more than 1800 ft. atop Mt. Watatic. The climate is cool, though not as severe as in the mountains of the Berkshires. The Metacomet–Monadnock Trail, the Wapack Trail, and the Tully Trail pass through this region.

Lower Worcester Plateau. This region is southern sibling to the Worcester Plateau and extends from the Connecticut border north and east of the Quabbin Reservoir area. It is less hilly than the Worcester Plateau and has a milder climate. There are many streams and rivers, such as the Brookfield and Quaboag, and abundant swamps, marshes, and bogs. The Midstate Trail runs through a portion of this region.

Part IV: North and West of Boston

This area consists of low rolling hills interspersed with wide, flat wetlands. It runs from the Atlantic coast north of Boston west along the New Hampshire border to the Worcester–Monadnock Plateau. There are many hiking opportunities, as the region contains an abundance of forests, parks, and preserves from barrier beaches to forests. Its proximity to the metropolitan area makes reaching these destinations easy to get to.

Southern New England Coastal Plains and Hills. On and near the Atlantic coast miles of salt marsh and protected beach environments offer many hiking opportunities. Portions of the Bay Circuit Trail pass through this region. The area has generally acidic soils that support thickets of highbush blueberry and a wide array of plant and animal species. Notable destinations include Parker River National Wildlife Refuge and Crane Beach Reservation.

Part V: Boston and Vicinity

This area encompasses metropolitan Boston and the off-shore waters near the city, including Boston Harbor. The Boston Basin ecoregion comprises most of the area.

Boston Basin. This ecoregion doesn't have vast acres of protected space, but its parklands host a variety of plants and animals, some found nowhere else in Massachusetts. Within its borders the Blue Hills Reservation trail network offers a seemingly endless variety of routes within easy access of Boston. Another special treasure are the Boston Harbor Islands.

Part 6: Southeast Massachusetts and the Islands

This region covers the large area south of Boston and offers a nearly unequaled variety of habitats and terrain. Glacial features make up a large portion of the landscape in places, from moraines to kettle ponds. A variety of trails is available, including challenging walks through miles of loose sand.

The Warner Trail and the Bay Circuit Trail run through this region. Cape Cod National Seashore, Cape Poge Wildlife Refuge, and Sandy Neck Barrier Beach can all be found in this area.

Bristol Lowlands, and Cape Cod and the Islands. These ecoregions incorporate all the area east of Rhode Island, including Cape Cod and the islands of Martha's Vineyard and Nantucket. Created largely during the last ice age, the landscape is a mix of wide outwash plains, moraines, and other glacial features. The dry, largely infertile soils support large tracts of pitch pine–scrub oak forests. Cranberry bogs are common, as are extensive tidal flats and marshes. This area has long been recognized as an area of global ecological importance and offers a lifetime of exciting recreational opportunities.

LONG-DISTANCE TRAILS

This book provides comprehensive coverage of the 10 major long-distance trail systems found in Massachusetts. As outlined in the preceding part, most travel through several of the state's ecoregions.

Appalachian Trail. Perhaps the nation's most famous footpath, the AT travels more than 2100 mi. from Springer Mtn. in Georgia to Katahdin in Maine. Eighty-five mi. of the trail are located in Massachusetts, running north–south through the Berkshires. It reaches many of the highest summits in the region, including Mt. Greylock, the highest point in Massachusetts.

South Taconic Trail. The 16-mi. South Taconic Trail and a network of connecting trails provide access to the southern end of the Taconic Range in the southwest corner of Massachusetts. These trails extend into New York and Connecticut.

Taconic Crest Trail. The northern end of the Taconic Range, straddling the Massachusetts–New York border, has a network of more than 100 mi. of hiking trails, including the 29-mi. Taconic Crest Trail.

Metacomet–Monadnock Trail. This 98-mi. trail follows the ridges bordering the Connecticut River Valley, including the exceptionally scenic Mt. Holyoke Range and Mt. Tom. It begins on the Connecticut state line (where it connects with the Metacomet Trail) and ends on the summit of Mt. Monadnock in southern New Hampshire (where it connects with the Monadnock–Sunapee Greenway Trail).

Midstate Trail. The 92-mi. Midstate Trail runs north–south across Massachusetts through the woodlands, open fields, and isolated hills of Worcester County. It traverses Wachusett Mtn., the highest peak in eastern Massachusetts. At its northern terminus in Ashburnham, just south of the New Hampshire border, it connects with the Wapack Trail leading into New Hampshire.

Robert Frost Trail. A scenic trail stretching over 40 mi. of countryside from Mt. Holyoke Range State Park in Granby to Wendell State Forest in Wendell. The path coincides with the Metacomet–Monadnock Trail over some portions of its route.

Pocumtuck Ridge Trail. One of the newest additions to the Massachusetts trail system, the Pocumtuck Ridge Trail runs from Mt. Sugarloaf Reservation to the Poet's Seat Tower, a distance of about 15 mi.

Warner Trail. The 30-mi. Warner Trail stretches from Canton, Massachusetts, just south of Boston, through the woodlands of Norfolk County to Diamond Hill State Park in Rhode Island.

Tully Trail. This 18-mi. loop trail in north–central Massachusetts was completed in 2001 and is maintained by The Trustees of Reservations. It connects three Trustees properties—Doane's Falls, Jacob's Hill, and Royalston Falls—as well as Tully Lake Campground and the Tully Dam. It also travels through both Tully Mtns. and Fish Brook Wildlife Management Areas, managed by MassWildlife.

Bay Circuit Trail. Still under construction, the Bay Circuit Trail will eventually extend in a 200-mi. arc around the Boston metropolitan area, from Newbury and Ipswich on the North Shore to Duxbury and Kingston on the South Shore. Presently about 150 mi. of trail are open.

CLIMATE AND SEASONS

Part of the beauty and charm of Massachusetts is its changing seasons. They rejuvenate any trail you choose to walk, making a familiar path new and different each time you visit. Radiant spring wildflowers, the lush green of a summer forest, and the brilliant mosaic of changing autumn leaves provide ever-changing backdrops for the hiking experience. The seasons produce spectacular sights, but they also produce weather conditions that can make trails more challenging and sometimes hazardous.

Rain

On average, 41.7 in. of rain falls on the eastern and central portions of the state each year, while a little more, about 44.6 in., falls in the Berkshires. A very wet year may have 10 in. more than the average, while a dry year might have 10 in. less. Annual percipitation is remarkably even throughout the year, with 3 to 4 in. of (melted) precipitation falling each month across the state.

Snow

Snowfall is fairly uniform across the state, with most regions averaging somewhere between 76 and 115 in. per year. Regions closer to the ocean—and its warming effect—receive less annual snowfall. The southeast region receives only 38 in. on average, while the Cape and the islands get even less (0 to 38 in.). The golden shovel award, however, goes to the northern Berkshires, where 115 to 153 in. fall each year. The earliest snow on record fell on July 10, 1955, while the latest occurred on December 16, 1973. On average the first flakes fall in the first week of November. The last snowfall in spring ranges anywhere from late March to mid-June, with the average being April 20. The year with the most snowfall, as recorded at the Boston station, was 1995–96, with nearly 108 in.

While rain can make the trail slick, snow and ice make it even more dangerous. On many trails in winter, snowshoes, crampons, and other winter equipment will be necessary for a safe trip. South-facing slopes melt out earliest in spring, with north slopes and areas shaded by pines and other evergreens the last to warm up. Exactly when a snow-free hike can be undertaken varies considerably from year to year and location to location. Generally March is the key month to watch as the weather turns from winter to spring, and snow and ice melt from all but the coolest places. In the high country, such as the Worcester Plateau, the Berkshires, and Taconics, a storm will dump heavier amounts of precipitation on the upwind slopes. For example, a winter storm approaching from the coast with strong easterly winds will drop more snow on the eastern slopes as it is forced up and over the mountains. The western slopes will receive less snow and be somewhat easier for traveling.

Temperature

Massachusetts temperatures run from summer highs in the upper 90s to winter lows reaching –30 degrees. Generally spring is cool and moist, summer warm to hot, and fall pleasantly cool and dry. Freezing temperatures can be encountered as early as late August in the highest elevations, but will generally hold off until late October to early November in most other locations. Winter is frustratingly variable, with some winters being warm and others bone chilling—expect anything from arctic cold and blizzards to mild snow-free conditions.

Storms

In Massachusetts, thunderstorms—affectionately called "boomers" or "thumpers"—are most often associated with cold fronts, but do occur occasionally with warm fronts. Thunderstorms can occur during any month of the year but are most numerous from April to October. The months to be extra alert are May, June, and July. Fronts most often move in from the west to northwest, but also can come from the southwest, north, or south. Thunderstorms can drop a torrential amount of precipitation in a short period, but are usually short lived and pass through quickly.

Weather Reports

For the most up-to-date weather information log onto the website of the National Weather Service (National Oceanic and Atmospheric Administration) at www.weather.gov. Reports are available for anywhere in the state—when the map of the United States appears select the portion of Massachusetts you are interested in. The Pioneer Valley and Berkshires forecast is through the Albany, NY, office while the remainder of the state is forecast through Boston.

GEOLOGY

As you hike across Massachusetts the landscape that surrounds you is the product of a nonstop process that has been molding and forming this area for the last half-billion years. Over that time the region has undergone scores of personality changes, from tropical island to ice cap, from mountain range to ocean floor to volcano. Every transformation has built on the previous manifestation until today we walk upon a conglomerate of different histories stratified in rock and glacial drift.

Human history spans only a small fraction of this time. To illustrate, if a book that represented this span of time contained 100,000 pages, the entire account of human history would contain just a single page. But do we need to know about things that happened even before people were here? Does it matter if Massachusetts was the seabed of a tropical ocean hundreds of millions of years ago? It matters because the rocks that formed from the sediment on that seafloor turned into the limestone that is now the bedrock of a river. And that bedrock makes the water of the river more alkaline, and alkaline water allows the soil of the riverbank to release just the right combination of nutrients to support rare plants. And those unusual plants are growing beside the interpretive trail at the wildlife sanctuary. Everything, even something as seemingly remote as a long-extinct ocean, has an effect on the landscape today. Change doesn't stop, and to appreciate the landscape we hike over, neither should our curiosity.

Geology is often defined as the study of rocks. But geological history isn't just about rocks, but about how they got here and what happened to them after they arrived. It is one thing to know that the Taconic Mtns. were once a great range 15,000 ft. high, but another to ask, Where did the mountains go?

The current working theory in geology is called plate tectonics. Most of the Earth is molten rock and minerals, with only the top few miles cooled rock. This zone of cool rock is called the earth's crust and is where we live. The crust is cracked into dozens of pieces, called plates, that float on the hot rock layer (called the mantle) beneath. The plates are of two basic varieties, continental and oceanic crust. Continents are typically formed from the less dense continental crust; ocean beds and some islands are made of more dense oceanic rock. The hot rock of the mantle flows in currents, and the currents move the plates above them. As the plates move slowly over geological time, collisions occur between them and cause mountain-building events called orogenies. Elsewhere plates are split apart; this is known as rifting. Evidence of past orogenic and rifting events can be seen in the rocks of New England.

The practical geological history of Massachusetts begins at the bottom of a warm tropical ocean 500 million years ago. The only nearby land was a large island with its western shore consisting of what are now the Adirondack Mtns. and Hudson Highlands. Because of plate tectonics this island and seabed weren't anywhere near present-day New England at this time, but rather in the Southern Hemisphere where Brazil now lies. Sediments from the land settled to the bottom of the sea, as did the remains of sea creatures such as trilobites and small aquatic arthropods. Over millions of years this ocean began to shrink, and there occurred the first major event whose remnants are still visible today.

While the shores of what would become North America and Europe drew closer, an island arc of tall volcanoes formed near shore and lifted the seabed around them. As the tectonic plates continued to collide, this arc of islands was joined to the shore and the surrounding land uplifted into a range of mountains perhaps 15,000 ft. high. Today the remains of this range are found in the Taconic Mtns. along the border of New York and Massachusetts. This was not one event, but rather a series of mountain-building episodes that started about 460 million years ago, ended about 440 million years ago, and coincided with appearance of the first land plants. The upper portions of the mountains were sedimentary rocks (sandstones and shales), while the core of the mountains was composed of metamorphic rocks (schist and gneiss) formed miles below the surface by immense pressures and temperatures.

For the next 40 million years rain and wind wore down the Taconics until Massachusetts was reduced to one great plain. Approximately 400 million years ago another major event began—the Acadian Orogeny. As this event unfolded, another island mass off the coast, called Avalonia, advanced toward and then collided with the continent. The geological remains of Avalonia can be found today from southeastern Connecticut, Rhode Island, and southeastern Massachusetts northward into coastal Maine and Newfoundland. These unusual remains also appear in the Carolinas and parts of England and Wales, but nowhere else in the world. Geologists call Avalonia a "suspect terrane," a term that means its geographic origins prior to collision are unknown.

As the closing continents finally crushed into each other, much of what is now western Massachusetts heaved skyward to create yet another mountain range, this one east of the Taconics. Intense metamorphism occurred, creating high-temperature rocks in the western region and granite intrusions elsewhere. The sea, which until now had still covered portions of the land, drained away as the land rose. The roots of this great range are now the mountains of the Berkshire Plateau. Many of New England's granites were formed as compressed rocks deep beneath the surface melted under the extreme heat and pressure.

Another equally immense erosion of the landscape followed this mountain-building event. A huge fan of eroded sediment, called the Catskill Delta, formed to the west of the mountains. East of the mountains in Massachusetts, other smaller deltas formed. A number of specialized plants thrived in these flat, swampy deltas. From approximately 360 to 290 million years ago swamplands covered much of the region. Immense lycophyte trees, giant horsetails, ferns, and conifers dominated the swamps. Flowering plants evolved during this period. As swampland plants died and decayed, thick deposits of organic material accumulated.

The region's final mountain-building event, the Allegheny Orogeny, had minimal impact on Massachusetts but was felt much more intensely elsewhere in the East. Beginning about 290 million years ago, it created the folded ridges and mountains typical of the central Appalachian Range farther south. Among its effects in Massachusetts were granite intrusions in the southeast. It also helped turn the swamp sediments into beds of coal; a few small coal deposits can be found today in southeastern Massachusetts and the southern Berkshires. At the end of the Allegheny Orogeny sediments carried down from the towering mountains in the west to the lowland swamps were buried, and eventually formed the rocks that we see in these areas today.

By the late Triassic and middle Jurassic periods of the Mesozoic era (220 to 180 million years ago) the continents of the world had collected together into one supercontinent called Pangea. They then began to break up, creating the present-day Atlantic Ocean as the plates separated. As the land pulled itself apart, great wounds in the crust, called rifts, opened up and allowed molten rock to rise toward the surface. One such tear in the earth created the Connecticut Valley, pulling apart the bedrock as it formed and causing massive faulting. Molten rock poured outward from these fissures and formed distinctive basaltic lava flows. The cliffs of Mt. Tom and the Mt. Holyoke Range are spectacular remnants of these flows.

Other rocks of the Connecticut Valley have a very different origin. The characteristic red sedimentary rocks of the region, often seen interbedded between the lava flows, are a result of erosion from other rocks that created sand beds across flat areas. These sandstones have a rich red color, are often high in feldspar, and contain dinosaur footprints and other fossils that can be observed at many locations along the Connecticut River.

After the catastrophic episodes of volcanic activity and faulting during the Triassic and Jurassic periods, New England entered a period of relative quiescence. Significant tectonic activity ceased and erosional forces began to dominate, a state of geological affairs that continues to this day. The towering mountains of earlier times have been mostly eroded away to a relatively flat plain, while more resistant rocks—such as those of Mt. Greylock and Wachusett Mtn.—form the highlands of today.

The last major geological event to shape the landscape of southern New England began approximately 3 million years ago, during a time of global climate change. Around the world temperatures dropped, precipitation patterns changed, and a long cycle of glaciation began. Glaciers and ice sheets have since advanced and retreated across Massachusetts 18 to 20 times. In New England the last and greatest glacial advance began about 70,000 years ago, reached its greatest extent approximately 20,000 years ago, and ended abruptly, sometimes catastrophically, 10,000 years ago. At the peak of this ice age 5 million sq. mi. of ice covered Canada, much of the Northeast, and large areas of the Plains and Northwest. So much of the earth's water was locked up in the glaciers that the sea level in northern Europe and North America was at least 350 ft. below present levels.

A glacier changes the landscape in many ways. The enormous weight of a mile-thick continental ice sheet presses the earth downward, causing the land to sink. As the glaciers retreat in warmer times, seas and lakes inundate the depressed land. Gradually the land rebounds upward, draining the water away and creating earthquakes as it rises.

Evidence of the glaciers' advance and retreat can be seen throughout New England. Existing valleys were widened by the glaciers and became U-shaped. Scouring of the bedrock left linear marks—called striations—throughout the region. Formed as the glaciers dragged rocks beneath it over the bedrock surface, striations are indicators of the localized flow direction of the ice.

Rocks fell from the downslope side of hills and mountains as the glaciers overrode them. This can be seen in the asymmetrical profile of bedrock hills. Many hills and mountains in New England have gradual, smooth sides facing north-northwest and steep rugged sides to the south-southeast.

The immense weight of glaciers keeps their bases above freezing, and streams of meltwater run under the ice. These streams travel through tunnels beneath the glacial ice, depositing long sinuous lines of gravel and cobbles. Once the glacier melts, these lines form distinctive raised landforms known as eskers. Eskers are common in much of eastern and central New England, but rare in Connecticut and Rhode Island. In the Boston area you can see esker deposits in the Auburndale section of Newton, to the east of the Charles River near the intersection of the Massachusetts Turnpike and MA 128.

The tons of soil and rock left behind as a glacier melts is called till. If it is washed down streams and deposited in layers it is called stratified till. As the glaciers overrode the countryside they deposited streamlined, oblong hills of till known as drumlins. These hills are common in Massachusetts; notable examples include Bunker Hill, Breed's Hill, Dorchester Heights, and many of the Boston Harbor islands. Generally drumlins are aligned in the same direction (often northwest to southeast) and indicate the local direction of ice flow.

Beyond the glacier's edge stretched the outwash plain where streams of water carried finer-grained materials from the melting ice. Often, large chunks of ice would break off as the glacier retreated and become buried in the outwash. As these isolated chunks melted they formed holes called kettles. Today kettles typically remain as ponds or bogs. They are particularly common on Cape Cod and in southeastern Massachusetts. One well-known example is Thoreau's Walden Pond in Concord, Massachusetts.

Boulders left behind as the glaciers melted and receded are known as glacial erratics. It is important to realize that glaciers advanced as the weight of additional ice and snow pushed them downhill and southward. They retreated by merely melting away as the climate began to warm. Some erratics traveled hundreds of miles, carried by the glaciers. These boulders are common throughout New England. Well-known examples include Plymouth Rock; Cradle Rock in Barre, Massachusetts; Doane Rock near Eastham on Cape Cod; and the boulder fields of Cape Ann.

Moraines are piles of boulders and debris deposited at a glacier's edge. Terminal moraines mark the farthest extent of glaciation. Southeastern New England provides classic examples of terminal moraines. The glaciers' farthest extent is marked by an undulating line of moraine deposits running east to west through Nantucket, Martha's Vineyard, and Long Island. From this line an unbroken sheet of ice extended 2000 mi. northward. As the glaciers retreated they stopped temporarily, forming a second line located farther north through Cape Cod, the south side of Buzzards Bay, and westward through southwestern Rhode Island. The Mid-Cape Highway (US 6) follows the crest of the Sandwich Moraine from Sagamore to Dennis.

As the ice receded, moraines often functioned as dams, and temporary lakes formed. One of the largest in New England was Lake Hitchcock, which lasted about 4000 years. Lake Hitchcock filled the Connecticut River Valley from Rocky Hill, Connecticut, northward well into Vermont and New Hampshire. Over the millennia deep beds of glacial sediment accumulated at the bottom of Lake Hitchcock. When the spillway at Rocky Hill finally eroded and the lake drained away, the present Connecticut River took form. Over the years it has carved the river channel through old lakebeds, the layered soils still evident in the riverbanks along many locations. Many other locations also hosted glacial lakes, including the Housatonic Valley and Lake Bascom in the Hoosic River Valley.

How quickly the ice receded is still in question, but there seems to be growing evidence that the retreat was faster than first supposed. Evidence of great floods implying rapid melting have come to light, but just when or how powerful these floods were is still a mystery.

Postglacial Forests

When a glacier recedes, it doesn't leave much in its wake but rock and earth. However, it doesn't take much time for plants to begin colonizing the seemingly barren landscape again.

The climate at the edge of the dying glaciers was tundra, a treeless landscape with permanently frozen subsoil. Pollen evidence indicates that the first plants to claim this habitat were low-growing grasses and sedges; dwarf willows, alders, and birches; shrubby perennials; and a variety of mosses and lichens. Some of these plants continue to grow on New England's highest mountaintops where alpine tundra still exists.

Approximately 12,500 years ago, as the climate warmed, larger trees of the boreal forest began to displace the tundra species. Conifers, primarily spruce and pine, dominated, but cold-tolerant deciduous trees, such as alder, birch, poplar, and arctic willow, were also present. As more diverse plant species came north the herbivores that ate them followed. Grazing animals such as bison, elk, and moose entered the region, and birds, bears, and numerous small mammals also returned.

A dramatic change occurred approximately 9,500 years ago, as the climate grew significantly warmer over a short period. Spruces and other conifers that had long dominated the forests gave way to the deciduous hardwoods and the pines of the temperate forest. The northern hardwood forest took shape, with species such as beech, hickory, oak, pine, and hemlock expanding. By about 6000 years ago the spectrum of habitats and range of species found today in Massachusetts were established.

Today's Forestlands

The forests of Massachusetts can be roughly divided into three major areas—transition forest, mixed deciduous forest, and scrub oak–pitch pine forest.

The transition forest, like the boreal forest of cooler climates, has numerous lakes and bogs. This forest is sometimes referred to as the white pine–hemlock–northern hardwood forest. The most common conifers are the eastern white pine and the eastern hemlock. Other less abundant conifers include eastern aborvitae, balsam fir, and a variety of spruce species. Deciduous trees are also abundant in the transition forest, including beech and a variety of birch (paper and yellow) and maple species (red, sugar, striped, and mountain). This forest is the northern range limit for hickories and most oaks.

Common understory trees found in the transition forest include American mountain ash, hop hornbeam, witch hazel, and a variety of viburnums including hobblebush. Highbush blueberries thrive in swamps, boggy areas and moist woodlands; lowbush blueberries are found in bogs and in open mountainous areas called blueberry barrens often found at the edge of transitional forests. Shadbush, or serviceberry, is found from wetlands to ridges, producing white flowers early in spring when anadromous fish such as the alewife and shad (herring) run. Ferns and club mosses are common. A small sampling of the herbaceous plants of this region includes starflower, milkwort, wood lily, twinflower, baneberry, violet, trillium, and clematis.

The transition forest is home to a wide variety of animal species. Mammals include the white-tailed deer, moose, black bear, beaver, bobcat, fox, raccoon, opossum, porcupine, mink, muskrat, fisher, squirrel, and numerous small rodents. There are more than a dozen species of raptors, including eagles, owls, falcons, and hawks. Songbirds and grouse, sparrows and waterfowl, all inhabit these forests. Diverse insects can be found in the soil, on the vegetation, and in the air and waters of this region.

In the warmer regions of the state the mixed deciduous or oak-hickory forest is dominant. This forest type predominates in eastern Massachusetts and the lowland valleys in western Massachusetts. Its major tree species are oaks, cherries, hickories, maples, and ashes. Other common deciduous trees include beech and tulip tree. Conifers are less common in the mixed deciduous forest than in the transition forest, with the adaptable white pine being the most abundant.

Understory plants include dogwood, American holly, magnolia, and rosebay rhododendron in the eastern part of the state. Mountain laurel, striped maple, wild azalea, and hop hornbeam are common in the western region. Hundreds of species of wildflowers exist in the mixed deciduous forest including trout lily, lady's slipper, bloodroot, wood poppy, larkspur, spring beauty, trillium, violet, and mint. Ferns and club mosses are also abundant here.

The mixed deciduous forest zone is also marked by extensive wetlands, both coastal and inland. Some notable examples are the Ipswich River Wildlife Sanctuary, with its extensive estuary and salt marshes; Belle Island Marsh, a salt marsh just north of Boston; and Ponkapoag Pond in the Blue Hills and Halfway Pond at October Mtn. State Forest, both with quaking sphagnum bogs.

Many of the same animal species occur in both the transition forest and the mixed deciduous forest. Fewer large mammals, such as bear, deer, and moose, are found in the mixed deciduous forest of southern New England, while the human population is generally more dense. Birds and smaller mammals are abundant, and many species of amphibians, including frogs and salamanders, exist in the mixed deciduous forest.

The scrub oak–pitch pine forest is a plant community that exists in two very different locations in the state. The sand plain community, found on the south shore of Cape Cod and the islands, is dominated by extensive dune fields, barrier beaches, sand spits, and salt marshes. Although the sand plain community is primarily a coastal environment, it also exists inland in areas of southeastern Massachusetts.

While this region has the mildest climate in New England, poor soils provide a substrate for only the hardiest plant species. Forested areas are dominated by scrub forest of oak and pitch pine. Pitch pine has a deep root system, which allows it to obtain water from the dry, sandy soils and stand up to the strong winds of the Cape and the islands. Trees of the sand plain forests are also adapted to survive frequent fires; the pitch pine has excellent postfire, stump-sprouting ability. Bear oak occurs as a shrub or small tree and is the most common oak across much of Cape Cod. Post oak reaches its northern range limit on the Cape and is present here as a smaller tree than in the heart of its range farther south. American holly is an understory tree on the sand plain that reaches the northern limit of its range in Quincy, Massachusetts. Other trees of this community include dwarf chestnut oak, black oak, scarlet oak, and white oak. In localized areas the soil is better and a wider variety of trees is present, including species of birch, sassafras, maple, locust, and beech.

Huckleberry, lowbush blueberry, sheep laurel, and wintergreen are all shrubs found in the sand plains. Bearberry is one of the most common shrubs on Cape Cod. Sweet fern, inkberry, and broom crowberry are also found here. One of the more unusual plants found in the southern New England sand plain community is the prickly pear cactus, the only cactus found in the East.

Scotch heath and heather—introduced by settlers—now dominate Nantucket's moorlands. This area was cleared of its natural forest for use as pastureland. When the pastures were abandoned, the poor soils failed to support reforestation, and the heath and heather, well adapted to the difficult environment, spread.

Another scrub oak–pitch pine community survives in the harsh environment atop the southern Taconics and nearby mountains in the Berkshires. These forests survive on thin ledgy soils with roots that grasp at fractures in the rock. Wind, freezing fog, and fire are frequent elements that shape the forest. Despite the extreme conditions, these mountains host hundreds of acres of old-growth pine.

Cranberry bogs are abundant in southeastern Massachusetts and on the Cape, and produce the region's chief agricultural crop. The largest and best cranberries are harvested from the American cranberry, which is found only in North America. American cranberries grow in many other regions of the state, such as the Berkshires, but in nowhere near the numbers found in the eastern bogs. Cape Cod National Seashore, known for its magnificent sand dunes and beaches, also encompasses salt marshes, heath swamps, red maple swamps, and an American white cedar swamp.

The sand plain community is home to diverse groups of wildlife. White-tailed deer, raccoon, beaver, skunk, fox, and small mammals inhabit the forests. The many types of wetlands provide habitats for waterfowl, amphibians, insects, fish, turtles, and snakes. The beaches and marshes are home to a wide variety of seabirds, including a number of threatened and endangered species.

Civilization and Its Impacts

People began making a marked impact on the environment during the Woodland Period, from about 3000 years ago to the time of European colonization. During this period there was great diversification among Native cultures. People established semipermanent villages and developed both pottery and agriculture. They used fire to clear the fields, and cultivated corn, beans, squash, and gourds. They gathered roots, herbs, berries, and nuts. They developed trade routes between the highlands and coast. During this period the post-glacial coastlines stabilized, and shellfish beds became another food resource.

Woodland Indians were the first to encounter the Europeans as they reached the eastern shores of North America. Europeans were first drawn to the Grand Banks fisheries in the early 16th century. Then came the fur traders, whose influence had devastating effects on the Native populations, bringing disease as well as economic and moral changes and challenges.

Although the indigenous peoples had cleared some land for planting, the European colonists greatly accelerated the agricultural process. When agriculture reached its peak in the mid–19th century, approximately 23 million acres (slightly more than half) of New England's land area was cleared.

By the late 1800s demographics began to shift as the Industrial Revolution attracted more people to the cities and towns. In 1840 less than one-fifth of New England's population resided in towns; by 1880 more than half of the population lived in towns and cities of 2500 or more people. The great economic depression in the last half of the 19th century caused the rocky New England fields to be largely abandoned. Slowly these fields and pastures began to grow back to forest again. It will take hundreds of years for the previously cleared forests to reach full maturity, and in some areas, such as the moorland of Nantucket, the forest has not yet returned.

Clearing of the forests resulted in the destruction of one habitat and the creation of another. At one point the white-tailed deer was nearly wiped out of Massachusetts, and with it the bears and wolves and cougars. Bounties on most predators left humans as the only significant predator by the early 20th century.

The settlers altered the landscape not only by clearing trees, but also by introducing nonnative species of plants, animals, and disease. Although the introduced species included cultivated plants and domesticated animals that provided some benefit to the people of New England, the unintentional (and sometimes intentional) introduction of diseases such as smallpox, typhoid fever, diphtheria, measles, tuberculosis, and chicken pox devastated indigenous populations. Until the early 1900s the American chestnut was a dominant tree species in southern New England, composing up to 25 percent of the forest. Beginning in 1904 the effects of a fungal disease accidentally brought into New York started a blight that destroyed all the big trees. But the American chestnut isn't gone from the woods—it survives as stump sprouts. Another introduction is the gypsy moth, which seriously threatens the white oak; the woolly adelgid, which blew into the state on the winds of Hurricane Gloria in 1985, threatens the hemlock.

The latest chapter is still being written. The pressures of suburban sprawl and unregulated development in the late 20th and early 21st centuries have caused the loss of much forestland and open space throughout the region. At the same time, more than a century of industrial and postindustrial pollution has taken its toll on the health of the region's natural resources. The future holds promise for the Massachusetts outdoors, but careful stewardship and conservation efforts are required to protect the state's natural places for future generations.

Stewardship and Conservation

It is part of human nature to one day admire and cherish something that is the next day taken for granted. A trail through the woods allows us the freedom to explore the natural areas where we live, but is also representative of our responsibility to care for these places and paths. Hikers are by nature independent, relying completely on their own ability to walk their chosen path and reach their goals. This produces a sense of accomplishment and confidence that is different from any other outdoor pursuit. An even greater feeling, richer and more lasting, comes from building and maintaining the paths others walk.

Think about getting more involved in caring for trails near you. There are many organizations that are presently doing a huge amount of work maintaining trails with very few hands. When you help build a bog bridge or install rock cribbing on a trail that slabs a ridge you not only improve the trail, but also protect the environment and strengthen yourself physically and emotionally. Volunteering is a wonderfully unselfish way to make a positive difference to something you already love—the outdoors. Many of the organizations mentioned in this book, including the AMC, need your help and will welcome you as a volunteer. For information about getting involved with the AMC, turn to the back of this book.

HIKING ETHICS

Every hiker has an obligation to respect and care for the outdoor environment, so that it may be enjoyed by all who follow. As you hike, try to adhere to these rules of the outdoors:

- Carry out everything you carry in. Go a step further: Carry out any litter that you find.

- Don't pick the flowers, and avoid gathering wood. Even dead trees have their place in the ecosystem and should be left undisturbed. Do not light a campfire unless it is an emergency. If you are using a backpacking stove, do not leave it unattended.

- Stay on the trail, and try to avoid muddy places where foot traffic can cause erosion.
- Bury human waste at least 200 ft. from the trail and any water sources. The careless disposal of human waste is probably the principal cause of the spread of giardiasis.
- If you wish to listen to music, wear headphones. But it's much more interesting to listen to the sounds of the forest. Preserve the forest sounds for others to enjoy.
- Where dogs are permitted it is often with the stipulation they be leashed at all times. Respect and follow the rules regarding pets when hiking and be sure to control your pet so it won't be a nuisance to other hikers.
- On overnight trips, travel in small groups and practice low-impact camping. Use established campsites if available; if not, camp well away from trails and streams and avoid using sites that have been used previously by campers.

Part I

The Berkshires

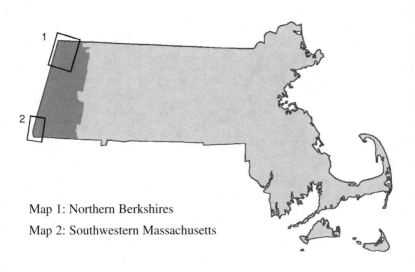

Map 1: Northern Berkshires

Map 2: Southwestern Massachusetts

LIST OF TRAILS

LIST OF TRAILS

LIST OF TRAILS

Appalachian Trail (BCAMC, DCR)

In 1676, at the close of King Philip's War, Major John Talcott lead his company of Connecticut Militia into the Berkshires in pursuit of Native American refugees. The major was one of the first Europeans to see the westernmost region of Massachusetts now called the Berkshires. And he despised the place. It was a land of wild animals, rugged mountains, raging rivers, and steep ravines draped in impenetrable forest. However, all the things that Talcott scorned make the Berkshires a paradise for today's hikers. The tallest mountains in the commonwealth, from Mt. Everett in the south to Mt. Greylock in the north, overlook unique marble river valleys that host some of the most treasured ecosystems in the nation. Many long-distance trails, including the Appalachian Trail, weave past the majesty of waterfalls and ridgetop views, ravines, river walks, and woodland ponds.

Approximately 90 mi. of the 2167-mi. Appalachian Trail (AT) are located in Berkshire County. The trail enters Massachusetts from Connecticut near Sages Ravine, passes over Mt. Race, Mt. Everett, and Mt. Bushnell, and then goes east across the Housatonic Valley. Passing over June Mtn., the trail climbs steeply to East Mtn. State Forest and descends to MA 23. After skirting Benedict Pond in Beartown State Forest it ascends to the headwaters of Swan Brook and descends through Tyringham Valley. Beyond Tyringham the trail skirts the eastern edge of Upper Goose Pond, crosses the Massachusetts Turnpike (I-90) at Greenwater Pond, and enters October Mtn. State Forest, where it leads over Becket Mtn. and Bald Top. After climbing Warner Hill the trail runs through continuous woods, except for the towns of Dalton and Cheshire, ascends Saddle Ball Mtn. and Mt. Greylock, passes over Mt. Fitch and Mt. Williams, and again descends. After crossing the Hoosic Valley at North Adams, the AT reaches the Vermont line, where it continues north as both the AT and the Long Trail.

For day hikers the AT serves as an access route to a number of Berkshire summits. It can be entered at numerous highway crossings, usually marked with signs. There are parking areas at most of the high-use trail crossings. Long-distance hikers should consult the Appalachian Trail Conference's *Appalachian Trail Guide to Massachusetts–Connecticut.* A number of shelters are located on or near the trail, between 7 and 10 mi. apart. Off-trail accommodations are within easy reach. Note that the times indicated in the mileage summaries are approximate, and your hiking time may vary from them—especially on the longer sections. If you are new to hiking or backpacking, be conservative in your time estimates until you have a better idea of your actual pace.

The AT Committee of the Appalachian Mountain Club's Berkshire Chapter maintains the Appalachian Trail in Massachusetts. Hikers interested in participating in these maintenance efforts are always welcome; contact the AMC for more information.

White rectangular paint blazes, 2 in. by 6 in., indicate the trail route; double blazes warn of abrupt changes in direction. Most side trails are blue-blazed. The exact trail routing is always subject to change, as a result of ongoing efforts to run the trail through protected corridors and to avoid paved road sections. Relocations are always well marked in the field.

Section 1. Massachusetts–Connecticut Line to Jug End Rd. (12.3 mi.)

The southern end of the Massachusetts section of the AT, about 0.7 mi. south of Sages Ravine, is accessible by side trails from the east and west. On CT 41 just south of the Connecticut–Massachusetts border is the heavily used parking area for the blue-blazed Undermountain Trail. Follow the Undermountain Trail 0.9 mi. to the intersection with the blue-blazed Paradise Lane Trail. Turn onto the Paradise Lane Trail, constructed in 1954 by the AMC, and hike 2.1 mi. to the intersection with the AT. The west access is from East St. (seasonal) in the town of Mt. Washington. A pull-off is just south of a stone state boundary marker. From the pull-out an unmarked woods road travels east 1.0 mi. to the AT.

Immediately north of Bear Mtn. the AT crosses into Massachusetts and begins the descent into scenic Sages Ravine. The trail follows the south side of Sawmill Brook, passing Sages Ravine Campsite on the left. (A caretaker is on duty May–October; tent platforms, privy, spring except in dry times.)

At 1.0 mi. north of the state line, the trail turns sharp left, crosses the brook (high water, most often in spring, can make crossing difficult), and begins a gradual ascent up the ridge leading to Mt. Everett. At the output from a spring, and before crossing Bear Rock Stream, a sign and path on the left lead to Laurel Ridge Campsite (five dirt tent pads, three tent platforms, a water source, and a composting privy—read the instructions). The trail continues north through an open hemlock grove in a gradual ascent of the ridge.

Emerging from the woods, the trail traverses open cliffs of Race Mtn. that offer outstanding views sweeping from northeast to southeast. For 0.3 mi. the trail closely follows the edge of the cliff and reaches the summit of Race Mtn. (2365 ft.). From the summit the trail traces the backbone of the ridge past many great views before dropping to the saddle between Race Mtn. and Mt. Everett. Here the blue-blazed Race Brook Falls Trail enters on the right. (The Race Brook Falls Trail leads east about 0.4 mi. to Race Brook Falls Campsite with tent platforms and privy, then continues another 1.5 mi. to MA 41 and the parking area.) *Caution: Access to MA 41 from the AT as it traverses the southern Taconics is limited to the Undermountain/Paradise Lane Trails, Race Brook Falls Trail, and Elbow Trail. Several hikers have lost their lives, and others have been seriously injured, attempting to bushwack down the cliffs to the highway. Stay on the trail!*

From the Race Brook Falls Trail junction the AT begins to ascend the south slope of Mt. Everett. This ascent is rocky and fairly steep, climbing into a pitch pine–scrub oak plant community that contains some of the largest unbroken tracts of old-growth forest in Massachusetts.

The summit of Mt. Everett (2602 ft.) offers extensive views in all directions: Monument Mtn. and Mt. Greylock to the north, and East Mtn., Warner Mtn., and the Housatonic Valley to the east. To the south are Race Mtn. and Bear Mtn., while to the west are Mt. Frissell, Alander Mtn., Mt. Darby, and, in the distance, the Catskills.

The fire tower that was atop the summit for many years was removed in May 2003. Near the concrete footings of the old fire tower the AT turns sharp right and begins to descend on a narrow path that widens into an abandoned service road. The trail quickly leaves the road and continues straight ahead down an embankment, and into the woods. (About 100 yd. down the service road is a poorly maintained stone shelter and parking area. The service/access road has been closed to vehicles since about 2001 due to the poor condition of the road. The closure is indefinite. Camping is not permitted at the shelter, which leaks during a heavy rain.) The AT continues through woods and briefly follows a gravel road before turning right and reentering the woods.

As the descent moderates, the trail enters Guilder Pond picnic area (2042 ft.). The trail bears right at the picnic area past an outhouse. This picnic area is accessible on foot via the access road from the gate on Mt. Washington Rd. (approx. 1 mi.). The AT crosses a small stream, then the blue-blazed Guilder Pond Loop Trail enters from the left. The AT descends a short pitch, crosses another small brook, and turns left, descending on log steps. A side trail on the right leads 0.1 mi. to Hemlocks Shelter (privy and water source). The shelter area also has a composting privy—read the directions before using. At 100 ft. after the Hemlocks side trail, a brook is crossed, then a side trail to Glen Brook Shelter and Campsite (privy and water source) exits to the right.

Continuing north, the AT begins a gentle descent along the east slope of Mt. Undine (2203 ft.) and then snakes sharp right, then left. At this point the blue-blazed Elbow Trail intersects from the right. The Elbow Trail, the last access to MA 41, leads 1.5 mi. southeast to the Berkshire School and MA 41. Soon the AT begins a gradual ascent to reach the wooded summit of Mt. Bushnell (1834 ft.). The trail crosses two intermediate peaks and reaches Jug End summit at the north end of the ridge, where there is a spectacular view. After a gradual descent from Jug End summit, the AT reaches a crest of rock, the "jug's end," with steep outcrops and extensive open views to the northwest and southeast. Mt. Greylock is clearly visible on the horizon to the north. The trail turns sharp right and shortly begins a steep zigzag descent over rock ledges. Use caution when the trail is wet. The descent moderates as the trail approaches Jug End Rd. (a.k.a. Curtiss Rd.), where there is parking space for 1–2 cars. A spring is located on the south side of the road, approx. 0.1 mi. east of the trail.

Appalachian Trail: Massachusetts–Connecticut Line to Jug End Rd.

Distances from the Undermountain Rd. parking area in CT

> *to* Sages Ravine and Campsite: 2.2 mi., 1 hr., 15 min.
>
> *to* Laurel Ridge Campsite: 4.1 mi., 2 hr.
>
> *to* Race Brook Trail: 7 mi., 3 hr., 30 min.
>
> *to* summit of Mt. Everett: 7.7 mi., 4 hr.
>
> *to* Hemlocks Shelter and Glen Brook Shelter and Campsite: 8.9 mi., 4 hr., 45 min.
>
> *to* Elbow Trail: 9.5 mi., 5 hr., 15 min.
>
> *to* summit of Jug End: 11.2 mi., 6 hr., 15 min.
>
> *to* Jug End Rd.: 12.3 mi., 7 hr., 15 min.

Section 2. Jug End Rd. to US 7 (4.5 mi.)

To reach the south trailhead, from the junction of MA 41 and 23 take MA 41 south to Jug End Rd. (a.k.a. Curtiss Rd.) on the right. The trail crosses Jug End Rd. at a small roadside turnout. At 0.1 mi. east of the trail crossing of Jug End Rd., a spring is piped to the roadside.

Proceeding north of Jug End Rd., the AT soon crosses a stone wall in the middle of a mature white pine forest. Upon reaching an open pasture, the trail crosses another stone wall and traverses 100 yd. of wet pasture before coming to MA 41. At 1.1 mi. the trail passes along a fenced pasture and crosses a farm brook. A gradual ascent brings the trail into the trees along a woods road atop a ridge. It crosses a series of bog bridges at 1.6 mi. on the way to higher ground and another ridge. The trail drops off this hemlock ridge to the east and travels through the next swampy area on bog bridging (bring the bug spray). At 2.4 mi. it crosses Hubbard Brook on a large bridge, then arrives at South Egremont Rd., a small parking area, kiosk, and across the street a stone monument commemorating the last battle of Shays' Rebellion in 1798.

Passing the monument on the left, the trail travels on a grassy farm road through active farm fields, then enters the woods to climb a small hill. Descending the hill and crossing West Sheffield Rd. at 3.9 mi., the trail follows the edge of a swamp along a sidehill trail, then crosses the swamp on a long set of bog bridges and at 4.4 mi. crosses railroad tracks. Use caution approaching and crossing this active railway. Descend the embankment and cross the field to US 7 at 4.5 mi.

Appalachian Trail: Jug End Rd. to US 7

Distances from Jug End Rd.

> *to* MA 41: 0.9 mi., 20 min.
>
> *to* US 7: 4.5 mi., 2 hr.

Section 3. US 7 to MA 23 (8.4 mi.)

The trail crosses US 7 about 3 mi. south of Great Barrington. (Parking is not allowed on US 7.) Leaving the east side of the highway, the trail follows a grassy trail through an overgrown field; it soon curves right past a small pond and over a stream on a bridge at 0.2 mi. The trail immediately enters an active farm field and goes left, then right, along the bank of the Housatonic River. The trail follows the river south through a series of fields and open woodlands. At 0.9 mi. the trail takes a left onto Kellogg Rd. The AT follows the road across the Housatonic. At 1.1 mi. the trail enters another active field and turns right along the edge of the field, then left following Kellogg Rd. to its intersection with Boardman St. at 1.3 mi. Crossing Boardman St., the AT enters the woods and begins to ascend June Mtn. (1206 ft.). Coming off the height-of-land, at 2.9 mi. the trail crosses Holmes Rd. (Brush Hill Rd.). Reentering the woods, the trail reaches a rounded rock ledge at 3.3 mi., then crosses a deep fissure in the rock spanned by a wooden bridge at 3.6 mi. The trail then descends sharp around a split glacial boulder before beginning a moderate-to-steep ascent to attain the top of a ridge. At 3.8 mi. the junction with the blue-blazed Bad Weather Bypass is reached. This 1.5-mi.-long bypass affords a route over the western portion of East Mtn. that is away from the ledges and cliffs and is mostly sheltered by thick mountain laurel and mature forest.

From the bypass junction the AT runs along the edge of East Mtn. and for the next 0.4 mi. passes several exposed ledges that afford fine views to the south and west. The Catskills are clearly visible, and the Taconic Range, with Mt. Everett (2602 ft.) dominating, lies west across the Housatonic Valley.

The trail passes a small spring in a gully at 4.2 mi. and, climbing again, soon reaches a viewpoint among large boulder at the south end of East Mtn. This exposed location offers more good views, especially to the south. At the viewpoint the AT makes a sharp turn left, passing an obscure woods road leading left. At 5.8 mi. the northern end of the Bad Weather Bypass is reached on the left in an area that is often wet. The AT continues over undulating terrain, never getting far from the rim of a steep slope on the right. At 6.4 mi. a short side trail leads to Tom Leonard Shelter (shelter, privy, and one tent platform). Water is available from a small creek in the ravine below the shelter area.

The trail then follows along the edge of ledges with views into Ice Gulch, a rocky chasm of boulders and a buried stream. The path snakes through hemlocks as it descends to flatter land, crossing paved Lake Buel Rd. at 7.5 mi. A signed parking area with a kiosk is located 50 yd. west of the trail crossing.

From Lake Buel Rd. the walking is easy as the trail crosses numerous horse trails and Shore Camp Rd. The path crosses a broken dam across an outlet of Lake Buel Swamp at 8.0 mi. then passes through an area ravaged by the Memorial Day tornado of 1995. MA 23 and a fairly large parking area are reached at 8.4 mi.

Appalachian Trail: US 7 to MA 23

Distances from US 7

   to Boardman St.: 1.3 mi., 30 min.

   to Holmes Rd.: 2.9 mi., 1 hr., 30 min.

   to Tom Leonard Shelter: 6.4 mi., 4 hr.

   to MA 23: 8.4 mi., 5 hr., 30 min.

Section 4. MA 23 to Tyringham (12.1 mi.)

To reach the MA 23 trailhead, follow US 7 to the north intersection with MA 23 at Belcher Square. Take MA 23 east 5 mi. toward Monterey. The parking area is on the left and very close to the Monterey town line. The northern trailhead pull-off (parking for 2–3 cars) is on Tyringham Main Rd., approximately 5 mi. south of the MA 102 and 23 junction in Lee, very close to Exit 2 of the Mass Turnpike.

From MA 23 on the Monterey–Great Barrington line the trail crosses an open field and parking area, then enters the woods and climbs steeply to the top of a height-of-land. The trail now gradually descends to a red maple swamp at 1 mi., crosses the wetland on bog bridges and steppingstones, and arrives at Blue Hill Rd. (Stony Brook Rd.). From the road the path steeply weaves up rock outcrops and boulders to the top of a cliff in Beartown State Forest. Crossing through open woods, the trail soon crosses a paved service road, then a blue-blazed side trail left (Benedict Pond Loop Trail) that leads to the Benedict Pond boat launch, parking area, phone, privies, public camping area, and showers (use fee required). These facilities are part of Beartown State Forest. The AT continues and skirts the eastern end of Benedict Pond on bog bridging. At 2.2 mi. it crosses a stone bridge then turns right onto a wide trail and begins a sharp ascent of stone steps to a formation known as The Ledges and turns sharp right to cross below the outlet of a beaver dam.

The trail follows along The Ledges, a run of exposed cliffs that offer fine views of East Mtn., Warner Mtn., Mt. Everett, and the distant Catskills. The path turns left away from the ridge and begins a moderate-to-sharp descent, crossing a series of brooks and a woods road before climbing again at a power-line crossing. At 3.3 mi. a side path (on the right) leads uphill 200 ft. to the Mt. Wilcox South Shelter. Water can be obtained from a spring off the shelter access trail. The AT continues sharp uphill and after a steady climb reaches a plateau with open woods at 4 mi. At 4.5 mi. the trail crosses the outlet to an abandoned (2003) beaver pond before coming to the blue-blazed, 0.25-mi. access trail to Mt. Wilcox North Shelter. Water can be obtained from the brook at the shelter, though this source is uncertain during dry periods.

At the Wilcox North junction the trail turns sharp left and heads north, descending steadily off the ridge to Beartown Mtn. Rd. at 5.8 mi. The trail crosses Beartown Mtn. Rd. (dirt), passes through some swampy areas, and ascends a ridge of white pine. From the ridge crest the path makes a steep zigzag descent and meets Fernside Rd. (dirt) at 8.5 mi. The trail continues across the road and reaches Shaker Campsite on the right at 9.2 mi. Water is located at a stream crossing 0.1 mi. beyond the campsite. At 9.5 mi. the AT crosses an open field at a buried gas pipeline and continues along the edge of other open fields. It follows Hop Brook for a short distance before crossing a barbed-wire fence onto the Tyringham Cobble Reservation (The Trustees of Reservations). The trail slabs around the south side of the cobble, a steep, picturesque hill that is the centerpiece of Tyringham, and at 10.7 mi. a side trail leads left to the summit and viewpoint. The AT descends Cobble Hill through scrubby open fields and crosses Jerusalem Rd. at 11 mi. After crossing an active pasture, the AT enters hemlock woods, crosses Braided Brooks at 11.3 mi. and shortly thereafter crosses the pipeline right of way again. The trail follows hedgerows and a boardwalk around a wet field, crosses Hop Brook, and reaches Tyringham Main Rd. at 12.1 mi.

Appalachian Trail: MA 23 to Tyringham

Distances from MA 23

to Benedict Pond: 2 mi., 1 hr., 15 min.

to The Ledges: 2.6 mi., 1 hr., 30 min.

to Mt. Wilcox South Shelter: 3.3 mi., 2 hr., 15 min.

to Mt. Wilcox North Shelter: 5.1 mi., 3 hr., 30 min.

to Beartown Mtn. Rd.: 5.7 mi., 4 hr., 45 min.

to Shaker Campsite: 9.2 mi., 5 hr., 30 min.

to Cobble Hill side trail: 10.7 mi., 6 hr., 15 min.

to Tyringham: 12.1 mi., 7 hr.

Section 5. Tyringham to US 20 (Jacob's Ladder Highway) (8.6 mi.)

From Tyringham Main Rd. in Tyringham (0.9 mi. east of the village center) the trail climbs, steeply at times, over a knoll and through an overgrown field near the wooded summit of Baldy Mtn. At 1.9 mi. it descends steeply over cobbles to unpaved Webster Rd. Continuing across the road, the trail crosses an inlet to Knee Deep Pond at 2.2 mi. After going through a hemlock grove, pass a short side trail at 3.4 mi. (this side trail leads 0.1 mi. to a spring). At 4.3 mi. the trail crosses Goose Pond Rd., where there is room to park 3–4 cars. MA 8 can be reached by following Goose Pond Rd. east 3 mi. US 20 is 3 mi. to the west in Lee, MA.

Crossing Goose Pond Rd., the AT passes by a stone wall and soon crosses a small brook. The trail parallels another stone wall with abundant ferns and ground pines, leading to a marsh and pond on the right. The path enters a stand of hemlock, crosses a long bridge over the outlet of the pond, and moderately ascends through a deciduous forest. It climbs over some large rocks and at 5.4 mi. reaches a sign marking the boundary of the Upper Goose Pond Management Area (no fires, no camping except at the Upper Goose Pond Cabin area). Paralleling the ridge top to the right, the trail turns left and descend a series of stone steps, then continues easily downslope, passing the narrow east end of Upper Goose Pond, which is intermittently visible through the trees. A spring, reached via a short unmarked side trail, is reached at 5.9 mi. The trail now bears left at a double blaze (do not walk straight up the hill) and crosses the inlet to Upper Goose Pond at 6.2 mi. At 6.7 mi. the path passes an old chimney, all that remains of the old Mohhekennuck fishing club. The club sold its land to the National Park Service, a transaction that protected much of the shoreline of Upper Goose Pond.

At 7 mi. the trail turns sharp right and briefly ascends to the junction with a blue-blazed side trail left that leads in 0.5 mi. to the Upper Goose Pond Cabin and Campsite. A caretaker is on duty, and the cabin is open from Memorial Day to mid-October. After passing the side trail the path soon steeply descends through attractive woods and crosses the Massachusetts Turnpike (I-90) on a skywalk footbridge at 8.2 mi. After a short, level walk US 20 is reached at 8.6 mi. Lee, MA, and Exit 2 of the Massachusetts Turnpike (I-90) can be reached by traveling 5 mi. west. Bus connections to Boston, Pittsfield, and other destinations are available there. Parking for a few cars is available 0.2 mi. west of the US 20 crossing. Please do not park on the adjacent private property.

Appalachian Trail: Tyringham to US 20 (Jacob's Ladder Highway)

Distances from Tyringham

to trailhead on Goose Pond Rd.: 4.2 mi., 2 hr., 30 min.

to side trail to Upper Goose Pond Cabin and Campsite: 7 mi., 3 hr., 45 min.

to US 20: 8.6 mi., 4 hr., 45 min.

Section 6. US 20 to Pittsfield Rd. (9.4 mi.)

The trailhead is located on US 20, 5 mi. east of Exit 2 of the Massachusetts Turnpike and the town of Lee. There is limited parking on the south side of US 20 approx. 0.2 mi. west of the trail crossing. Please respect the adjacent private property.

From the north side of US 20 the trail climbs steeply, passing under a high-tension line at 0.2 mi. The trail briefly levels off, turns right, and continues to ascend, passing some ATV trails along the way. At 0.7 mi. it crosses paved Tyne Rd., which leads in 3.5 mi. to Becket (right) and in 0.9 mi. to US 20 (left). The trail now climbs to the wooded summit of Becket Mtn. (2178 ft.), where a register box (1.3 mi.) is nailed to a tree. The concrete footings are all that remains of the tower that once stood here. From Becket Mtn. the AT descends to a col before climbing to the crest of Walling Mtn. (2220 ft.) at 2.3 mi. After a moderate descent via some switchbacks, the descent steepens over rocky trail. After crossing another ATV trail the western shore of Finerty Pond (in October Mtn. State Forest) is reached at 3.1 mi. The trail skirts the pond, then turns north away from the water and moderately ascends through open woods, crossing several small streams.

At 4.4 mi. the trail passes close by a fast-moving brook on the right that often makes the trail bed wet. Skirting some beaver ponds and squeezing through some rocky clefts, the AT then intersects unpaved County Rd. at 5.4 mi. This road is rough, but passable by automobile. There is some limited space for day-use parking. Overnight parking is not recommended. (A right turn leads 5 mi. to Becket and MA 8.) The trail turns right, briefly follows the road, and then heads left into the woods. It begins a steep ascent of a washed-out trail to the overgrown summit of Bald Top Mtn. (2040 ft.) at 5.6 mi. The trail soon crosses another ATV trail, and at 6.9 mi. it crosses an underground cable right of way. After crossing a small brook, there is a short side trail to the left for October Mtn. Shelter at 7.2 mi.

West Branch Rd. is crossed at 7.9 mi. adjacent to another beaver pond. (Right leads 0.6 mi. to Pittsfield Rd. and old Washington Town Hall.) From here to Pittsfield Rd. the trail is mostly level. At 9.3 mi. the trail intersects an unpaved service road for the Pittsfield Water Company, turns right, and travels on the road a short distance to Pittsfield Rd. (paved). Pittsfield is 8 mi. down the road to the left. Cars can be parked along Pittsfield Rd.

Appalachian Trail: US 20 to Pittsfield Rd.

Distances from US 20

   to Tyne Rd.: 0.7 mi., 30 min.

   to summit of Becket Mtn.: 1.3 mi., 1 hr.

   to summit of Walling Mtn.: 2.3 mi., 1 hr., 30 min.

   to Finerty Pond: 3.1 mi., 1 hr., 45 min.

   to County Rd.: 5.4 mi., 3 hr., 15 min.

   to summit of Bald Top Mtn.: 5.6 mi., 3 hr., 30 min.

   to October Mtn. Shelter: 7.2 mi., 4 hr., 30 min.

   to Pittsfield Rd.: 9.4 mi., 5 hr., 45 min.

Section 7. Pittsfield Rd. to Dalton (9.6 mi.)

The trail begins on Pittsfield Rd., 5 mi. from Becket and 8 mi. from Pittsfield.

From Pittsfield Rd. the trail enters the woods. The terrain is generally flat with long runs of bog bridges that pass through a boggy transitional forest of balsam fir and red spruce. This land is part of the Pittsfield Watershed Lands, and the trail crosses on a 50-ft.-wide easement. No camping or fires are permitted. The AT crosses a small stream at 0.6 mi. At 1.6 mi. it passes over a stone wall to cross a bridge over a sandy stream at 2.1 mi. Descending gradually, the trail comes to an active beaver pond and crosses the outlet stream below several beaver dams. After ascending beside an impressive overhanging 30-ft. cliff, the trail turns sharp left at the top. At 3.0 mi. it crosses Blotz Rd. (Left leads 6 mi. to Pittsfield; right leads 1.3 mi. to MA 8.) There is parking for 3–4 cars in a small lot. Overnight parking is not recommended.

From Blotz Rd. the trail continues to the top of Warner Hill (2050 ft.) at 3.9 mi., with views to the west and north including Mt. Greylock. The AT now turns sharp left, passing the summit, which is a rock outcrop a few feet off the path to the right. The trail then descends through a beautiful area of ferns and reenters the forest. Turning left, it traverses an abandoned woods road for a short distance, then at 6.5 mi. crosses under high-tension lines, where there is a view to the west. The AT now passes over rocky terrain and reaches the side trail to the Kay Wood Shelter at 6.6 mi. At 6.9 mi. the trail crosses Grange Hall Rd., follows a stream, then crosses it before slabbing steeply to the summit of Day Mtn. at 7.7 mi. The subsequent descent begins steeply, following along a mossy ledge before becoming more gradual as it proceeds through open woods. Railroad tracks are reached at 9.0 mi. Use caution crossing as these are active tracks, there is limited sight distance, and trains approach quickly. Follow the trail down the dirt driveway with a lumberyard to the right. Cross Housatonic St. and continue down Depot St. to the intersection with MA 8 at 9.4 mi. Turn left onto MA 8 and at 9.6 mi. reach the junction of MA 8 and 9.

Appalachian Trail: Pittsfield Rd. to Dalton

Distances from Pittsfield Rd.

  to Blotz Rd.: 3 mi., 1 hr., 30 min.

  to summit of Warner Hill: 3.9 mi., 2 hr.

  to Grange Hall Rd.: 6.9 mi., 3 hr., 30 min.

  to MA 8–MA 9 (Dalton): 9.6 mi., 5 hr., 15 min.

Section 8. Dalton to Cheshire (9.3 mi.)

Cross MA 9 and follow High St. west 0.9 mi. to Park Ave. Cross the street onto Gulf Rd. At 1.0 mi. reach a parking area and kiosk. The trail now turns right into the woods and ascends ridges as it follows along the Dalton–Lanesboro line, passing beneath a power line at 4.3 mi. At 4.7 mi. there is a blue-blazed side trail that leads to Crystal Mtn. Campsite, with an outhouse. The trail comes to a hemlock grove on the west side of Gore Pond, where significant illegal ATV activity is common. At 5.6 mi. the AT passes over the outlet of Gore Pond and ascends to an overgrown summit pasture. After crossing a number of old logging roads, the trail passes near the Dalton–Cheshire granite boundary marker on the left. The path climbs gently and at 7.5 mi. reaches a USGS bronze marker on Cheshire South Cobble. From here the trail briefly descends steeply over rocks before intersecting a blue-blazed side trail that presses through dense mountain laurel to the North Cobble, a rocky overlook with a dramatic view of Mt. Greylock.

From the side trail the AT descends somewhat steeply, crossing more old woods roads before leveling out and reaching Furnace Hill Rd. The trail turns right and follows the road downhill to a T-intersection at the bottom of the hill. The trail turns left, soon crossing the Hoosic River and the new (2003) Ashuwillticook Rail Trail. Hikers may park in the rail-trail parking lot. Parking is not permitted on Furnace Hill Rd.

Continue from the rail-trail toward the center of Cheshire, then turn right onto School St., directly across from the post office. On the corner there is a concrete replica of the giant press used to make the famous "Cheshire Cheese" sent to Thomas Jefferson in the early 1800s. Continuing along School St., turn left just past the senior citizens center onto a grassy path leading across active farm fields and MA 8 at 9.3 mi.

Appalachian Trail: Dalton to Cheshire

Distances from MA 8–MA 9 (Dalton)

   to Gulf Rd.: 1.0 mi., 30 min.

   to Gore Pond: 5.6 mi., 2 hr., 45 min.

   to side trail to North Cobble: 7.6 mi., 3 hr., 45 min.

   to Furnace Hill Rd.: 8.4 mi., 4 hr., 15 min.

   to MA 8 (Cheshire): 9.3 mi., 4 hr., 30 min.

Section 9. Cheshire to MA 2 (North Adams) (14.0 mi.)

This section traverses the Mt. Greylock Reservation and the summits of the two highest mountains in Massachusetts. There is significant elevation gain and loss. Weather on the summits can be significantly more severe than weather in the valleys. Be prepared with proper clothing, footwear, and plenty of water. Bascom Lodge on the summit of Mt. Greylock is open from mid-May to mid-October. Day parking at the summit is available for a $2 fee.

From a small parking area on MA 8, the trail ascends to open fields with views of Cheshire. It soon enters the woods and at 0.6 mi. crosses a stile over barbed wire into an active pasture. At 0.8 mi. Outlook Ave. is crossed just north of the interesting rock formation called Reynolds Rock. Another stile crosses the fence adjacent to Outlook Ave. (no parking available). The AT enters a field beside a stone wall and follows hedgerows and fence lines into the woods. Crossing a muddy area, the trail begins to ascend, soon crossing a power line. Climbing steeply along the north side of the Kitchen Brook ravine, the path offers occasional views down into the ravine. The trail now turns away from the brook and travels through mixed woods often on a rocky footbed. At 3.5 mi. the trail crosses unpaved Old Adams Rd. in a grove of red spruce.

Leaving the spruce grove, the trail weaves between some huge boulders and arrives at the bottom of a steep, short pitch of stone steps. At the top of the steps a short side trail offers a view back down Kitchen Brook ravine. Use caution, as the ground is steeply sloped. At 4.4 mi. a blue-blazed side trail leads 0.2 mi. right to Mark Noepel Shelter where water, tentsites, and an outhouse are available.

From the shelter the AT gradually ascends through a beech forest and passes another short side trail to a small viewpoint on the right. At 5.0 mi. the AT meets the blue-blazed Jones Nose Trail, where the path enters the cool balsam forest that caps the ridges of Saddle Ball Mtn. The Jones Nose Trail leads 1 mi. down the south side of Saddle Ball Mtn. to the Jones Nose day-use parking area on Rockwell Rd. Some excellent southerly views are 0.3 mi. down the Jones Nose Trail. The AT then turns right, bypassing a balsam swamp, and comes to a small view to the east from a knoll on Saddle Ball Ridge.

Continuing to traverse the ridge through dense balsam and spruce, the trail passes over beautiful, undulating terrain. Leaving Saddle Ball Ridge, the AT descends toward the topmost hairpin curve on Rockwell Rd., the southern access road up Mt. Greylock. From here is a fine view of the Mt. Greylock summit on the right.

At 7.2 mi. the AT crosses Rockwell Rd. and intersects two side trails, the blue-blazed Cheshire Harbor Trail that leads 6 mi. east (right) to Adams, and the Hopper Trail (also blue-blazed) that leads 1.1 mi. west (left) to a campground and then continues down the mountain to Hopper Rd. in Williamstown. The trail joins the Hopper Trail and climbs easily past a small pond to the tri-junction of Notch Rd., Summit Rd., and Rockwell Rd. The Gould Trail leaves this intersection to the east and descends steeply for 1.0 mi. to Peck's Brook Shelter and Falls. The AT crosses the intersection and climbs over ledge and stunted conifers toward the summit, emerging into the open in a parking lot by a communications tower (restrooms on the right here), then proceeds to the open summit area. A bronze model of the Greylock Range is passed as the trail approaches the War Memorial Tower on the crest of the summit. The summit of Mt. Greylock (3491 ft.) is the highest point in Massachusetts. Bascom Lodge, also on the summit, provides meals and lodging from mid-May to mid-October. During winter there are no services at the summit.

Continuing north from the tower, the trail skirts the far end of the parking area and passes a winter ski shelter before dropping sharply and crossing Summit Rd. The AT levels off as it begins to trace the ridgeline. The blue-blazed Robinson's Point Trail leaves left, crossing Notch Rd. and descending about 0.75 mi. to a spectacular western view of the Hopper. Immediately after the Robinson's Point junction, two other side trails go off to the east (right). The first side trail is the blue-blazed Thunderbolt Trail, once used for Olympic training in the 1930s. The second path is the blue-blazed Bellows Pipe Trail that leads steeply down about 1 mi. to Bellows Pipe Shelter.

The AT passes an outcrop of milky quartz, coming to the tree-covered top of Mt. Fitch (3110 ft.). Along the way a few short side trails offer views of the Bellows Pipe and Ragged Mtn.

Descending from Mt. Fitch, a four-way intersection is reached at 9.8 mi. To the right (east) the blue-blazed Bernard Farm Trail descends about 3 mi. to Notch Rd. To the west (left) the blue-blazed Old Summit Rd. Trail bypasses the Mt. Williams summit and rejoins the AT near Notch Rd. After the junction the AT climbs briefly and reaches the register box on top of Mt. Williams (2951 ft.) at 10.0 mi. Turning sharp left, the trail descends via switchbacks, passing over some badly eroded footbed to meet Notch Rd at 10.9 mi. Just before reaching Notch Rd. a side trail leaves left to a day-use parking area and kiosk. From Notch Rd., the parking area is about 200 yd. down the road to the left (south).

The AT passes through spruce forest and bears right as the blue-blazed Money Brook Trail bears left (0.3 mi. to Wilbur Clearing Shelter: tent platforms, privy, and water supply). The Money Brook Trail continues down to the Hopper Rd. trailhead and the beginning of the Hopper Trail. Leaving the red spruce grove, the AT ascends steeply over ledge to a spectacular view of Williamstown, the Taconic Range, and the southern Green Mountains. The blue-blazed Mt. Prospect Trail leaves south for 2.0 mi. to its junction with the Money Brook Trail in the Hopper.

The AT turns sharp right at the overlook and descends very steeply at times through a northern hardwood forest. The slope moderates as the trail leaves Mt. Greylock Reservation and crosses a logging road. There is a police firing range to the left of the trail, and although gunfire may be heard, there is no danger to hikers. After passing through a spruce plantation and over a bridge, the trail reaches Pattison Rd. at 13.1 mi. Parking is available for 3–4 cars but is recommended for day use only. The trail descends through the woods past the North Adams Water Treatment Plant to the Phelps Ave. extension. It then goes left downhill, crosses Catherine St., and continues along sidewalks on Phelps Ave. until it reaches MA 2 at 14.0 mi. Long-term and overnight parking is available at the Greylock Community Club approx. 0.1 mi. east (right) of the trail crossing. Park near the AT signboard behind the building. A small donation is requested.

Appalachian Trail: Cheshire to MA 2 (North Adams)

Distances from MA 8 (Cheshire)

> *to* Outlook Ave.: 0.8 mi., 30 min.
>
> *to* Old Adams Rd.: 3.5 mi., 2 hr.
>
> *to* side trail to Mark Noepel Shelter and outhouse: 4.4 mi., 3 hr.
>
> *to* Saddle Ball Mtn. and side trail to Jones Nose: 5.0 mi., 3 hr., 15 min.
>
> *to* Notch Rd.–Rockwell Rd. junction: 7.2 mi., 4 hr., 15 min.
>
> *to* summit of Mt. Greylock: 7.6 mi., 4 hr., 30 min.
>
> *to* summit of Mt. Williams: 10.0 mi., 5 hr., 30 min.
>
> *to* Notch Rd.: 10.9 mi., 6 hr.
>
> *to* Money Brook Trail Shelter: 11.0 mi., 6 hr.
>
> *to* Mt. Prospect Trail: 11.2 mi., 6 hr., 30 min.
>
> *to* Pattison Rd.: 13.1 mi., 7 hr., 30 min.
>
> *to* MA 2 (North Adams): 14.0 mi., 8 hr.

Section 10. MA 2 (North Adams) to the Massachusetts–Vermont Line (4.1 mi.)

North Adams offers gas stations and fast-food outlets just 0.7 mi. east of the MA 2 trailhead; all-night supermarkets are located 0.7 mi. east and west of the trailhead.

On the north side of MA 2, by the traffic light, a steel-and-concrete footbridge passes over the B&M Railroad and the Hoosic River to Massachusetts Ave., where the trail turns right (east). Just before Sherman Brook goes under Massachusetts Ave. through a stone culvert, the trail departs the paved road and turns north (left) up a driveway along the west side of Sherman Brook, following it for 50 yd. Please respect the private property of trail abutters in this area.

At 0.4 mi. the trail enters the woods at the end of the driveway, passes over two well-built footbridges, then runs along an old spillway from the city of North Adams' waterworks. A high-voltage power line crosses the trail at 0.6 mi. The trail climbs steadily through separate hemlock groves for the next 0.4 mi., then zigzags left then quickly right on and off a logging road. At 1.8 mi. Pete's Spring is reached and a blue-blazed side trail leads left to Sherman Brook Campsite, with tent platforms and an outhouse. The campsite access trail rejoins the AT about 0.25 mi. farther along as the AT ascends a long, gradual ridge covered with patches of laurel. At 2.4 mi. the trail turns sharp toward the west and travels on an old roadbed until it heads steeply uphill through a rockfall of granite, marble, and quartz. A blue-blazed bad-weather bypass trail branches off on the left just before the rockfall and rejoins the AT at the top of the cliff.

After climbing the rockfall and a couple of steep, narrow switchbacks, the trail tops an eastern-facing bluff overlooking the Hoosac Range. On a wide section of East Mtn. ridge, the trail passes around the north side of a fragile mossy pond and arrives at an area of quartzite cobbles. A short distance across the cobbles at 2.8 mi. is the intersection of the Pine Cobble Trail (blue blazes). The Pine Cobble descends 0.5 mi. to an overlook of Williamstown to the west and North Adams to the east. Mt. Prospect and Mt. Williams dominate the horizon directly south. Turning right just before the overlook, the Pine Cobble Trail descends somewhat steeply at times 2.1 mi. to Cole Ave. in Williamstown. Limited parking is available at the trailhead.

Turning right at the junction with the Pine Cobble Trail, the AT goes up through azalea, sheep laurel, and pink lady's slipper. Out of the woods again, the trail passes the Class of '98 Trail, which descends to join the Pine Cobble Trail farther down the mountain. The AT comes to the overgrown Eph's Lookout at 3.3 mi. (Off the trail to the east about 0.3 mi. is Bear Swamp Brook in Clarksburg State Forest.) The AT rises sharp then travels partly on an old woods road to the Massachusetts–Vermont line and the Long Trail register at 4.1 mi. The next trail junction is with the Broad Brook Trail. Go left on County Rd. (dirt) for approx. 0.25 mi. to blue blazes leading left 4.1 mi. back to White Oaks Rd. in Williamstown. County Rd. is just before the Seth Warner Shelter at 2.8 mi.

This is the end of the Massachusetts section. The trail continues into Vermont, where it is maintained by the Green Mountain Club. (See the *Guide to the Appalachian Trail in New Hampshire and Vermont*, published by the Appalachian Trail Conference.)

Appalachian Trail: MA 2 (North Adams) to the Massachusetts–Vermont Line

Distances from MA 2 (North Adams)

   to Sherman Brook Campsite: 1.8 mi., 1 hr.

   to Pine Cobble Trail: 2.8 mi., 1 hr., 45 min.

   to Eph's Lookout: 3.3 mi., 2 hr.

   to Massachusetts–Vermont line: 4.1 mi., 2 hr., 20 min.

Jug End Reservation

Jug End Reservation and Wildlife Management Area covers 1158 acres in Egremont. It is a joint acquisition of the Massachusetts Department of Conservation and Recreation and the Massachusetts Department of Fisheries and Wildlife. The reservation is on the site of an old resort; the foundations and landscaping are still present around the trailhead on Jug End Rd. The trail that leaves from the parking area on Jug End Rd. is 2.0 mi. long, forming an elongated north–south loop that explores the Fenton Brook ravine sandwiched between Mt. Bushnell (1834 ft.) to the east and Mt. Darby (2030 ft.) to the west.

To reach Jug End Reservation from MA 23 in Egremont, turn onto MA 41 south, skirt Mill Pond on the right, then turn immediately right (west) onto Mt. Washington Rd. Travel west 1.7 mi. and turn left (south) onto Jug End Rd. Drive past the brown Jug End sign at about 0.3 mi., cross Fenton Brook, and turn right into the parking area 0.8 mi. from Mt. Washington Rd.

Jug End Loop Trail (DCR)

At the south end of the parking area is a kiosk. The trail (marked by DCR brown trail stakes) leaves from the eastern end of the parking lot, passing through an overgrown field and into the woods. The trail continues south and ascends the lower slopes of Jug End, keeping roughly parallel to Fenton Brook. At about 1 mi. the path bends west and descends to the brook. Crossing the brook, the trail now swings north along the western bank of Fenton Brook Ravine. The trail then begins to closely parallel the brook at 1.6 mi. for about 0.2 mi. before crossing the stream and returning to the parking area.

Jug End Loop Trail

Distance from parking area

> *to* parking area (circuit): 2.0 mi., 55 min.

Mt. Everett State Reservation

To reach Mt. Everett State Reservation, from the intersection of MA 23 and 41 in South Egremont follow MA 41 south 0.2 mi. Turn right onto Mt. Washington Rd. (this becomes East St.) and travel 7.4 mi. to the reservation entrance on the left. The auto access road from the parking facility on East St. in Mt. Washington to Guilder Pond and other areas of the mountain was closed indefinitely in 2001 due to disrepair. It will open again when funds for the repair work become available.

Mt. Everett (2602 ft.) is the highest mountain in the southern Berkshires but has earned rank and status for much more than its height. The mountain, as well as many other areas along the south Taconic Ridge, is home to priceless and fragile ecosystems. Along the ridge, traversed by the Appalachian Trail, are pitch pine and scrub oak plant communities that harbor old-growth forests sheltering rare plant and animal species. In spring 2003 the fire tower was removed from the summit, restoring the mountain's natural profile. From the rounded, breezy summit, distant peaks are visible: from Mt. Race and Bear Mtn. to the south to the rugged Catskills to the west.

Guilder Pond Trail (DCR)

On the north shoulder of Mt. Everett is picturesque Guilder Pond (2042 ft.) surrounded by mountain laurel and hemlock. The blue-blazed Guilder Pond Trail traces a course around the western, northern, and eastern shores of this scenic mountain pond, joining the AT briefly before ending at a picnic area near the south side of the pond. From the southern trailhead on the closed auto access road, the path crosses the outlet to the pond on a wooden bridge and enters a hemlock grove. It then wanders through thick laurel that blooms in June. Winding around the sometimes wet northern shore, the path goes through brushy spots and joins the AT near a picnic area and privy.

Guilder Pond Trail

Distances from East St. parking area

   to southern trailhead along access road: 0.8 mi., 30 min.

   to AT junction: 1.4 mi., 50 min.

   to picnic area: 1.6 mi., 1 hr.

   to Mt. Everett summit via AT: 2.2 mi., 1 hr., 20 min.

Elbow Trail (Berkshire School)

From the intersection of MA 23 and 41 in South Egremont, travel south on MA 41 for 3.5 mi. Turn right onto the paved entry road to Berkshire School and travel west along the road through the school's broad lawn. Take the first right, then turn left and pass between Memorial Hall on the left and Stanley

Hall on the right. Bear right, traveling uphill past a house and onto a dirt road (200 yd.). Park behind the gymnasium.

From the parking area the blue-blazed Elbow Trail makes an initially steep ascent up the eastern flank of Mt. Everett. Soon the grade of the well-worn path moderates and the trail becomes a moderately easy hike up the forested mountain. A small brook is crossed on rocks before reaching the junction with the white-blazed Appalachian Trail at 1.5 mi. From the AT junction the summit of Mt. Everett can be reached by following the AT approximately 1.8 mi. south, while the summit of Mt. Bushnell (1834 ft.) is about 0.5 mi. north on the AT.

Elbow Trail (Berkshire School)

Distances from Berkshire School parking area

   to AT: 1.5 mi., 1 hr.

   to summit of Mt. Everett (via AT): 3.3 mi., 2 hr., 45 min.

Appalachian Trail (BCAMC & DCR)

See Section 1, Appalachian Trail, Massachusetts–Connecticut Line to Jug End Rd., for a complete description.

Race Brook Trail (BCAMC & DCR)

From the junction of MA 41 and Berkshire School Rd. continue south on MA 41 for 1.4 mi. to a parking area on the right. Traveling north from the Massachusetts–Connecticut state line, the parking area is 2.9 mi. north of the border.

Race Brook Trail is a rugged, spectacular path that accesses the Appalachian Trail in the saddle between Mt. Race and Mt. Everett. Along the way this blue-blazed trail passes some excellent views as well as the five cataracts that make up Race Brook Falls. From the parking area the path immediately crosses a small stream, skirts a field, and enters hemlock woods. At a junction (signed AT 2 Miles) turn left into thick laurel and reach the brook at 0.4 mi. *Caution: At high water this crossing can be difficult.* The path now begins a steep ascent along Race Brook, passing a side trail to an overlook atop the lower falls at 0.6 mi. The base of another waterfall is reached at 0.8 mi. as the trail crosses the brook and continues steeply up the mountain. *Caution: At high water this crossing can be difficult.* The path reaches the ridge crest and easily descends to the brook, which it crosses on a log bridge and follows upstream through flat open woods. After passing many bedrock outcrops, at 1.6 mi. the trail reaches the Race Brook Falls Campsite, with tent platforms and privy. The junction with the white-blazed AT is at 1.9 mi. From here the summit of Mt. Everett is 0.8 mi. north along the AT. To the south 1.1 mi. on the AT is the narrow summit ridge of Mt. Race (2365 ft.), from which there are fine views.

Race Brook Trail

Distances from MA 41

> *to* first brook crossing: 0.4 mi., 15 min.
>
> *to* second brook crossing: 0.8 mi., 45 min.
>
> *to* Race Brook Falls Campsite: 1.6 mi., 1 hr., 05 min.
>
> *to* AT: 1.9 mi., 1 hr., 30 min.
>
> *to* summit of Mt. Everett: 2.7 mi., 2 hr., 15 min.

Mt. Washington State Forest

Mt. Washington State Forest and adjacent Bash-Bish Falls State Park protect about 3300 acres of mountains, valleys, wilderness, and waterfalls in the rugged southwestern corner of the state. Taconic State Park in New York borders this area and adds additional hiking opportunities. Principal summits include Mt. Frissell (2453 ft.) and Alander Mtn. (2239 ft.). Just to the east of the state forest are Mt. Ashley (2390 ft.) and Mt. Plantain (2088 ft.). Bash-Bish Falls, the signature cascade of the Berkshires, is another well-known landmark.

Backcountry camping opportunities are available; it's a 1.5-mi. hike from the park headquarters. Overnight campers must register at the Mt. Washington State Forest headquarters on West St. in Mt. Washington.

Reach the area via Mt. Washington Rd., off MA 41 in the village of South Egremont near the junction of MA 23 and MA 41. Mt. Washington Rd. becomes West St. in the town of Mt. Washington and passes the forest headquarters, where trail information is available.

Mt. Frissell Trail

Mt. Frissell (2453 ft.) stands on the Southern Taconic Highland, its summit being in Massachusetts and the highest point of Connecticut lying on its southern slope at the Massachusetts–Connecticut line. The scenic Mt. Frissell Trail, lying in three states and marked with red-painted blazes, travels over the mountain. It extends 2.2 mi. from Mt. Washington Rd. on the Massachusetts–Connecticut line to the South Taconic Trail.

The trailhead is on East St. in Mt. Washington (on the MA–CT state line). From the road the red-blazed path briefly heads northwest on a woods road and turns left up a narrow path through dense growth. The path then travels into Connecticut, climbing moderately then steeply up Round Mtn. The trail reaches Round Mtn.'s broad, open summit (2296 ft.) at 0.7 mi., then descends northwest, reentering Massachusetts and reaching a notch where a side path descends right to a shallow pond (dry in summer). The trail now enters Mt. Washington State Forest and begins to ascend the very steep east face of Mt. Frissell. At 1.2 mi. the trail reaches a stone pile at the summit and a register box maintained by the New Haven Hiking Club.

From the summit the path heads south down the brushy ridge to an overlook, then turns right into dense laurel and a nearly anonymous pile of rock and a survey marker designating the highest point in CT. The trail then continues over rocky terrain to a stone post that marks the tristate boundary of NY, MA, and CT. At the time the boundary was set CT didn't agree with the survey line, and so the marker only has MA and NY chiseled into the stone. The blue-blazed Ashley Hill Trail enters right (1.9 mi.) in a flat spot before the Mt. Frissell Trail scrambles the short distance to its junction with the white-blazed South Taconic Trail at 2.2 mi.

Mt. Frissell Trail

Distances from East St.

> *to* summit of Round Mtn.: 0.7 mi., 45 min.
>
> *to* summit of Mt. Frissell: 1.2 mi., 1 hr., 15 min.
>
> *to* CT high point: 1.3 mi., 1 hr., 25 min.
>
> *to* tristate marker: 1.8 mi., 1 hr., 45 min.
>
> *to* Ashley Hill Trail: 1.9 mi., 1 hr., 50 min.
>
> *to* South Taconic Trail: 2.2 mi., 2 hr., 10 min.

Alander Brook Trail

To reach the trailhead of this strenuous trail, located in the area of Boston Corners in New York's Harlem Valley, take NY 344 to NY 22 in Copake Falls.

Follow NY 22 south about 4 mi. to unpaved Undermountain Rd. Drive on this road 0.8 mi. to the blue-blazed Alander Brook Trail, which exits left as a woods road. Park at the trailhead.

The trail goes north past the intersection of the red-blazed Robert Brook Trail, which exits right (east). At 0.75 mi. the trail crosses Alander Brook, turns right, and ascends through mountain laurel. It then turns right again onto another woods road. The trail ascends east and northeast along the deep, hemlock-clad ravine of Alander Brook to where the blue blazes end (this is the end of the Alander Brook Trail) and the white blazes of the South Taconic Trail begin.

To ascend Alander Mtn., turn left onto the South Taconic Trail, which climbs steeply north up the mountain to the western summit of Alander Mtn.

Alander Brook Trail

Distances from Undermountain Rd.

to South Taconic Trail: 1.45 mi., 1 hr.

to western summit of Alander Mtn. via STT: 2.25 mi., 2 hr.

Robert Brook Trail

Follow the Alander Brook Trail from its trailhead north about 150 yd. The strenuous red-blazed Robert Brook Trail, a woods road, turns right and ascends rather steeply along the Robert Brook ravine. The trail reaches an 1898 New York–Massachusetts boundary monument and climbs north as a footpath along the state line to a second such monument. It continues north to the junction with the white-blazed South Taconic Trail, where the Robert Brook Trail ends.

Going left (north) on the South Taconic Trail, proceed to the intersection of the blue-blazed Alander Loop Trail at 0.5 mi. Hikers can continue along the South Taconic Trail another 0.2 mi. to the upper end of the blue-blazed Alander Brook Trail, then follow the white-blazed South Taconic Trail up Alander Mtn. as described in the preceding section. Alternately, ascend the blue-blazed Alander Loop Trail northeast into Massachusetts to a notch at the height-of-land, then follow the trail north along the crest as a narrow path through thick scrub growth, with good views over the highland from open areas, to the eastern summit of Alander Mtn. This has the same elevation as the western summit (2240 ft.) and has a nice view eastward over the highland in Massachusetts. The Alander Loop Trail continues a short distance west, climbing over a small

HARVARD COOPERATIVE SOCIETY

6889 CASH-1   6711 0300 057

978192917344 TRADE
Massachusetts Trai   MDS 1   19.95
              SUBTOTAL   19.95
        5% SALES TAX   1.00
              TOTAL   20.95

ACCOUNT NUMBER   XXXXXXXXXXXX5644
  Visa/Mastercard   20.95
Expiration Date   XX/XX
  Authorization   155619

Please visit us on the web thecoop.com

                          6/13/08 4:53 PM

intervening rise and descending into a final small notch in which a state forest cabin is on the right. It then merges with the Alander Mtn. Trail immediately prior to reaching just north of the summit and old fire tower footings.

Robert Brook Trail

Distances from Undermountain Rd.

> *to* South Taconic Trail: 1.2 mi., 1 hr.
>
> *to* Alander Loop Trail via STT: 1.7 mi., 1 hr., 20 min.
>
> *to* summit of Alander Mtn. via Alander Loop and Alander Mtn. Trails and STT: 2.8 mi., 2 hr., 10 min.

Ashley Hill Trail

This moderate blue-blazed trail leads to the heart of Mt. Washington State Forest. The trail starts with the Alander Mtn. Trail at the trailhead from the Mt. Washington State Forest parking area on East St. in Mt. Washington MA. It leads west across a field and into the forest and soon emerges into another field. The trail descends past a ruined house on the right and crosses Lee Pond Brook on a wooden bridge. The Charcoal Pit Trail, a short blue-blazed connector trail that rejoins the Ashley Hill Trail, leaves left at 0.6 mi. Following a woods road for about 0.25 mi., the Ashley Hill Trail branches left at the intersection with the blue-blazed Alander Mtn. Trail. The Ashley Hill Trail ascends gradually along a woods road and always keeps Ashley Hill Brook to the right, never crossing the brook.

After about 2.5 mi. of easy climbing, the Ashley Hill Trail exits the woods road on the left and continues as a less well-defined trail uphill at a slightly steeper grade. (A blue-blazed connector trail continues straight through this intersection, crosses Ashley Hill Brook, and ascends on a less well-defined path for about 1 mi. to intersect with the white-blazed South Taconic Trail.) The Ashley Hill Trail is well marked and generally follows another woods road to the Massachusetts–New York line, where it intersects and ends at the red-blazed Mt. Frissell Trail (see the description of the Mt. Frissell Trail from the west). Straight ahead the path continues onto private land.

Ashley Hill Trail

Distances from Mt. Washington State Forest parking area (East St.)

> *to* connector trail: 2.5 mi., 1 hr., 30 min.
>
> *to* Mt. Frissell Trail: 3.4 mi., 2 hr., 10 min.

Alander Mtn. Trail

Alander Mtn. (2240 ft.), with its twin summits, stands on the western escarpment of the Southern Taconic Highland. The blue-blazed trail starts in conjunction with the Ashley Hill Trail at the Mt. Washington State Forest parking area on the western side of East St. in the town of Mt. Washington MA. The trail proceeds west across a field and then through the woods. It descends through another field, crosses a brook by a vacant house (do not turn left on the woods road before the brook), and at 0.6 mi. intersects the blue-blazed Charcoal Pit Trail, which branches left. At 0.8 mi. the blue-blazed Ashley Hill Trail forks left. The Alander Mtn. Trail forks right, first descending to cross Ashley Hill Brook and then climbing westward. At 1.5 mi. a side trail ascends left to a primitive camping area of the state forest. The main trail continues west and southwest, ascending as it narrows, and reaches a state forest cabin in a small notch just below the summit of Alander Mtn. The cabin has wooden bunks and a wood stove, and backpackers can stay here overnight at no charge on a first-come, first-served basis. The nearest water supply is back down the Alander Mtn. Trail about 400 yd. A few yards beyond the cabin the blue-blazed Alander Loop Trail enters left. The Alander Mtn. Trail quickly joins the white-blazed South Taconic Trail a short distance north of the summit and old fire tower footings.

Alander Mtn. Trail

Distances from Mt. Washington State Forest parking area (East St.)

  to primitive camping area: 1.5 mi., 45 min.

  to cabin: 2.7 mi., 1 hr., 30 min.

  to western summit of Alander Mtn.: 2.8 mi., 1 hr., 35 min.

Alander Loop Trail

This short, 0.9-mi.-long, blue-blazed trail functions as a bypass of the South Taconic Trail on Alander Mtn. and provides a faster means of ascent from the south than following the South Taconic Trail exclusively. The south trailhead is 0.5 mi. north of the junction of the Robert Brook Trail at an elevation of about 1700 ft. It climbs moderately up a swale before angling northwest through thick scrub. The trail joins the Alander Mtn. Trail about 200 ft. before the intersection with the South Taconic Trail just north of the summit and old fire tower footings.

Charcoal Pit Trail

The Charcoal Pit Trail begins 0.6 mi. from the Mt. Washington State Forest Headquarters on the combined Alander Mtn. Trail and Ashley Hill Trail. The blue-blazed path leaves Lee Pond Brook and heads southwest, easily climbing through woods. After 0.7 mi. it rejoins the Ashley Hill Trail.

Bash-Bish Falls State Park

The centerpiece for this 200-acre state park is the magnificent gorge and waterfall created by Bash-Bish Brook. The clear waters of the stream tumble down almost 150 vertical ft. through a dizzying chasm of cliffs with whitewater cascades on the canyon floor. The gorge abruptly ends at a waterfall where the waters drop from an 80-ft.-tall cliff in an unforgettable waterfall into the pool below. The falls have long been called the signature landmark of the Berkshires.

Bash-Bish Falls State Park is within Mt. Washington State Forest, a preserve of 4169 acres offering 30 mi. of trails and wilderness camping experiences. Trails along the rim of the gorge offer spectacular views, but the gorge itself is a restricted area and entrance is not permitted. Swimming in the pool beneath the falls and rock climbing are also not permitted. Leashed pets are allowed. To reach the park, from the intersection of MA 41 and MA 23 turn onto MA 41 South and travel 0.2 miles to Mount Washington Road. Turn right (west) onto Mount Washington Road and proceed 7.7 miles to Cross Road (Mount Washington Road becomes East Street upon entering Mount Washington). Turn right onto Cross Road and follow Cross Road then West Street a total of 3.2 miles to the Upper Bash-Bish Falls parking area on the left.

Bash-Bish Gorge Trail (DCR)

This short but rugged blue-blazed trail begins at the gate at the south end of the parking area on Falls Rd. in Mt. Washington. The trail descends easily along a gravel road, then follows Bash-Bish Brook the short distance to the mouth of the gorge and crosses the brook. *Caution: This crossing can be dangerous. Cross as far upstream of the gorge as possible. Avoid crossing when current is strong.* The trail climbs extremely steeply along the metal fence to an overlook above the gorge. It then heads away from the gorge, climbing steeply through hemlocks to the junction with the white-blazed South Taconic

Trail at 0.6 mi. From here Mt. Alander is about a 2.2-mi.-long hike southbound (left and uphill). A loop hike back to the upper parking area can be made by turning northbound (right and downhill) and descending to the parking area on NY 344. Walk the gravel road back into MA and the Bash-Bish Falls parking area, then continue up the wide gravel road to the falls viewing area. The Bash-Bish Falls Trail leaves from the grassy area near the viewing area and climbs to the upper lot. Total mileage for loop is 2.6 mi.

Bash-Bish Gorge Trail

Distances from Bash-Bish Falls upper lot

   to junction with South Taconic Trail: 0.6 mi., 45 min.

   to summit of Alander Mtn. via STT: 2.8 mi., 3 hr.

Bash-Bish Falls Trail (DCR)

To reach the trailhead, follow the directions to the Bash-Bish Gorge Trail. The blue-blazed Bash-Bish Falls Trail leaves the parking area near the north side of the paved lot (signed), descending in a serpentine pattern steeply down the ravine. The path passes numerous boulders and ferns, emerging from the woods a few yards from the viewing area for Bash-Bish Falls.

Bash-Bish Falls Trail

Distances from Bash-Bish Falls upper lot

   to falls viewing area: 0.3 mi., 20 min.

South Taconic Trail

The white-blazed South Taconic Trail (STT) runs 15.7 mi. in a north–south direction along the western escarpment of the South Taconic Mtns., a range that roughly follows the border of New York and Massachusetts in the southern Berkshires. The trail traverses portions of Taconic State Park (NY), Mt. Washington State Forest (MA), and Bash-Bish Falls State Park (MA). The nearby Appalachian Trail runs atop the eastern range of the southern Taconics about 4 mi. away.

   The trail is maintained by volunteers from the Berkshire Chapter of the Appalachian Mountain Club, members of the Mid-Hudson Chapter of the Adirondack Mountain Club, the NY–NJ Trail Conference, and the Sierra Club.

The STT runs the western ridge of the southern Taconics, an area that is distinctly more remote and lesser known than its twin range to the east (traversed by the AT) but arguably has a greater abundance of spectacular views. The STT is especially scenic because it runs over large areas of open ridges and summits, such as South Brace Mtn., Brace Mtn., and the nearly 0.75 mi. of almost continuous open ridge on Alander Mtn. The views over New York's Harlem Valley and on to the Catskills are stunning and unob-structed. A public campground accessed by the STT is located in Taconic State Park (NY) at the Copake Falls Campground, very near the lower Bash-Bish Falls parking area on NY 344.

The trail's southern trailhead is at Rudd Pond Farms off Rudd Pond Rd. just north of Millerton in New York's Harlem Valley. The northern end is at the Catamount Ski Area on MA 23 in Egremont MA, just east of the New York–Massachusetts line. Thru-hikers can traverse the trail in a weekend using the state forest cabin at Alander Mtn. as an overnight stop. The cabin is located at about the halfway point, can accommodate 12 persons, and is open free of charge on a first-come, first-served, basis.

Section 1. Rudd Pond Farms to NY 344 (9.7 mi.)

To reach the southern end of the trail, drive 5.5 mi. north on NY 22 from the traffic light at Millerton. Take a right onto White House Crossing Rd. and fol-low it to the end. Turn left onto Rudd Pond Rd. for 0.3 mi., then right (east) onto Deer Run Rd.; this road enters Rudd Pond Farms, a residential develop-ment. Take a left onto Quarry Hill Rd. and follow it about 0.5 mi. as it loops around to the eastern side of the development, where there is a small parking area at the edge of the woods. Look for the Taconic State Park sign about 75 ft. east of the road.

From the parking area at an elevation of 950 ft., the South Taconic Trail travels east along the edge of field, enters the woods, and starts to ascend the western escarpment of the Southern Taconic Highland. A steep, rough section begins at 0.4 mi. where the trail parallels a brook, passing a high waterfall. The grade is eased a little by switchbacks that offer repeated open views to the west over the Harlem Valley. At about 0.75 mi. a red-blazed side trail leads south (right) 0.3 mi. to an overlook. Here the STT turns sharp left (north).

The STT proceeds north along the escarpment, with more views to the west, traversing the flank of South Brace Mtn. and staying west of the summit. The path climbs steeply and reaches an open area with an excellent southerly view into CT of the Riga Plateau and Riga Lake. The trail passes west of the summit of South Brace Mtn. (2304 ft.) and descends moderately to the saddle between South Brace and Brace Mtns., then ascends the attractive open ridge of Brace Mtn. to its summit (2311 ft.) at 1.9 mi. The summit (the STT's highest point) is a grassy bald marked by a loose cairn of stones with wonderful views of Bear Mtn. (CT) to the east and Mt. Frissell (MA) to the northeast.

The trail continues north, descending the mountain on a wide, easy path to the plateau. Here, at 2.2 mi., the trail reaches the junction with a side trail (right) that enters from private land. About 200 yd. farther along the ridge, the trail junction (signed) with the Mt. Frissell Trail is reached. The red-blazed Mt. Frissell Trail leaves right (east) into thick, wind-stunted woods.

The STT proceeds from the Mt. Frissell Trail junction along an open crest with fine views and enters Mt. Washington State Forest (MA) at 2.3 mi. The trail widens into a woods road and at 3.1 mi. a blue-blazed side trail proceeds right (northeast) about 1.0 mi. and connects to the Ashley Hill Trail. The trail proceeds moderately over undulating terrain, reentering NY just before reaching the junction with the Robert Brook Trail at 4.5 mi. (The red-blazed Robert Brook Trail exits left and steeply descends the ravine of Robert Brook in NY. In 1.1 mi. it reaches the Alander Brook Trail near Undermountain Rd. off NY 22.)

The STT continues north, reenters MA, and reaches the Alander Loop Trail at 5.0 mi. The STT curves left while the Alander Loop Trail forks right. (This blue-blazed trail, more than 1 mi. long with fine views, climbs roughly north up to and along the height-of-land to the eastern summit of Alander Mtn., at 2239 ft. It then leads a short distance west over an intervening knob, through a notch, and past the state forest cabin to meet the Alander Mtn. Trail a short distance from the summit. Continue to the summit by turning left onto the Alander Mtn. Trail.) The Alander Loop Trail is a quicker route to Alander Mtn. and the cabin. From the junction with the Alander Loop Trail, the South Taconic Trail descends into NY from MA, crosses a bridge over Alander Brook, and 60 yd. beyond, at 5.2 mi., climbs steeply right. (The blue-blazed 1.5-mi.-long Alander Brook Trail continues straight ahead on a woods road, descending south along the ravine of Alander Brook and making left turns at junctions, crossing Alander Brook, and proceeding on level terrain to Undermountain Rd. in Harlem Valley NY.)

The STT now climbs gradually, then steeply up the southwestern shoulder of Alander Mtn., reaching an open crest at 5.7 mi. The trail then reenters Massachusetts at a boundary marker and goes northeast, ascending along the open shoulder with fine views. The trail reaches the western summit of Alander Mtn.

(2239 ft.) at 6.0 mi., where the foundation of a former fire tower is located. On the summit a nest of signs to the west of the tower footings provides distances to locations along the trail. Just north of the summit the Alander Mtn. Trail enters right (east). The Alander Mtn. Trail descends to a small notch, where it goes straight ahead to the state forest cabin. The Alander Loop Trail goes first east, then south, eventually to rejoin the STT.

The STT goes north, descending gradually along the remainder of Alander's open crest, a splendidly scenic section. To the east is Mt. Everett (2602 ft.), the dominant feature on the eastern escarpment. At 6.4 mi. the trail descends into woods and continues north along the ridge. At 6.8 mi. there is a view of a beautiful secluded valley to the west, with Mt. Washburn beyond. After passing through a beautiful woodland savanna of oaks and grasses the trail reaches a lookout on the northern shoulder of Bash-Bish Mtn. at 7.9 mi. It then makes a quick descent to the junction of the blue-blazed Bash-Bish Gorge Trail, which leaves right from a small, level terrace.

The STT turns left (south) and soon reenters NY, where a short spur trail continues west to a rock outcrop with beautiful views down the valley of Bash-Bish Brook and beyond to the village of Copake Falls NY. The path weaves through rock outcrops and open woods, descending to the unpaved road of Taconic State Park along a brook and shower house on the right. The trail turns left off the road, crosses a bridge over Bash-Bish Brook, and comes out near the lower Bash-Bish parking area on the right. Here the northern section of the South Taconic Trail begins.

South Taconic Trail: Southern Section (Rudd Pond Farms to NY 344)

Distances from Rudd Pond Farms

to summit of South Brace Mtn.: 1.7 mi., 1 hr., 15 min.

to summit of Brace Mtn.: 1.9 mi., 1 hr., 30 min.

to Mt. Frissell Trail: 2.4 mi., 1 hr., 50 min.

to Ashley Hill Trail connector: 3.1 mi., 2 hr., 20 min.

to Robert Brook Trail: 4.5 mi., 3 hr., 15 min.

to Alander Loop Trail: 5 mi., 3 hr., 30 min.

to Alander Brook Trail: 5.3 mi., 3 hr., 45 min.

to western summit of Alander Mtn. and cabin: 6 mi., 4 hr., 30 min.

to Bash-Bish Gorge Trail: 8.2 mi., 6 hr., 15 min.

to lower Bash-Bish parking area: 9.7 mi., 7 hr., 30 min.

Section 2. NY 344 to MA 23 (6.0 mi.)

From the entrance to the lower Bash-Bish parking area on NY 344 (about 1.2 miles east of NY 22), the STT angles west proceeding up the western ridge of Cedar Brook Ravine, while Cedar Brook Trail heads straight ahead generally following the brook. For about the next mile the trail climbs steeply and steadily up Cedar Mountain passing the Blue and Yellow Trails on the left along the way.

After passing the Yellow Trail, the STT coincides with Sunset Rock Trail and the climb relaxes as the path slabs the ridge. At 1.4 mi. the Cedar Brook Trail enters right (south) and the path ascends moderately to an open shelf at 1.8 miles. A short red-blazed spur trail leads from here west to Sunset Rock (1,788 feet) with wonderful views to the west.

The STT continues northeast on a wide path through thick scrub growth. Here it has yellow state-park markers in addition to its white blazes. At 2.1 mi. the trail forks from the STT, turning sharp left off the wide path, soon reaching Sunset Rock Rd. (unpaved, seasonal) just west of the Massachusetts–New York line in New York State. The right fork is a dead-end path that heads a short distance east to Sunset Rock Rd. near the Massachusetts–New York line in Massachusetts. (This unpaved road runs eastward into Mt. Washington MA as part of West St., and westward it descends steeply into North Mountain Rd. in Harlem Valley NY.)

The trail crosses the dirt road and at 2.4 mi. turns right onto a footpath that crosses a brook by an old springhouse. It climbs Prospect Hill northeast through dense scrub oak and mountain laurel and at 2.7 mi. reaches the open summit area (1919 ft.), with good views. It turns left at the Massachusetts–New York boundary monument and reaches an open ledge with outstanding views north, west, and south; the views of Harlem Valley and the town of Hillsdale NY, are especially lovely.

As the trail descends Prospect Hill it reenters Massachusetts and reaches a good northerly view at 3 mi., while it follows the north shoulder. Bending back into New York, it reaches an open area at 3.7 mi. along the edge of an escarpment, with pleasant views of a valley to the southwest. The trail continues to Mt. Fray and parallels its crest, turning right at 4.1 mi. and climbing the short distance to the crest, with a fine view from the open ridge. The trail then goes north along the broad summit area of Mt. Fray (1900 ft.), where open areas in the scrub growth offer distant views, as far as Mt. Greylock about 50 mi. to the northeast. The STT now enters the privately held property of the Catamount Ski Area.

At 4.3 mi. the trail turns right onto Ridge Run, the first ski trail encountered, which descends east along the ridge just below and to the right of the ski lift apparatus on the summit. (A short distance to the left, or west, is an area with splendid views, including the two upper chairlift terminals of the ski area.) The trail follows Ridge Run east (downhill) for 1.0 mi., reentering Massachusetts. Near the end it climbs right a few yards to a pleasant view of Jug End valley and ridge. At the end of Ridge Run, at the top of the ski slope, is a view of the ski area.

The trail then climbs steeply east for a short stretch and continues along a wooded crest, turning north and descending. It enters a driveway at 5.7 mi., follows it downhill, then follows a dirt road coming in from the left, and finally turns left for 65 yd. to reach MA 23, where it crosses the height-of-land and ends. This is the northern terminus of the South Taconic Trail at 6.0 mi. (15.7 mi. from its southern end). (*Note: If the trail is lost at this point, simply follow any ski run down to the base lodge. MA 23 is a short distance away on the ski area access road.*)

A parking area is located on the south side of MA 23; 150 yd. to the left (west) of MA 23 is Hillsdale NY, and to the east is South Egremont MA. Overnight and day parking is allowed in the ski area parking lot. Hikers should ask permission at the ski area office to park. Be advised that the parking lot is locked at dusk and vehicles not removed by then must remain overnight.

South Taconic Trail: Northern Section (NY 344 to MA 23)

Distances from NY 344

  to Cedar Brook Trail: 1.4 mi., 1 hr.

  to Sunset Rock: 1.8 mi., 1 hr., 15 min.

  to Sunset Rock Rd.: 2.1 mi., 1 hr., 25 min.

  to summit of Prospect Hill: 2.7 mi., 1 hr., 45 min.

  to summit of Mt. Fray: 3.7 mi., 2 hr., 30 min.

  to Ridge Run ski trail: 4.3 mi., 2 hr., 45. min.

  to MA 23: 6.0 mi., 3 hr., 45 min.

Yokun Ridge

Yokun Ridge is the name for a section of the central Taconic Range that broadly includes West Stockbridge Mtn. and Lenox Mtn. The ridge is a mix of private and public lands with some excellent public access trails. The primary protective agency for the area is the Berkshires Natural Resources Council (BNRC). The trails constructed and maintained by BNRC have a reputation for being environmentally responsible, well maintained, and logical. The ridge owes its name to a Hudson River Mahican named Jehoiakim Yokun, who owned much of this land around 1740.

Walsh Trail Loop (BNRC)

This short, mostly flat path follows the crest of a portion of Lenox Mtn. high above Stockbridge Bowl. The ridge has many overlooks that peer east, south, and west, depending on where hikers are on the route. It is one of those rare mountaintop hikes that doesn't require climbing the mountain, making this easy hike a nice choice for those not able to manage more difficult trips.

To reach the trailhead from Lenox follow MA 183 south 1.6 mi. to Richmond–Lenox Rd. (just past Tanglewood). Travel up Richmond–Lenox Rd. 1.4 mi. to a gated parking area (Olivia's Overlook) on the left.

From the parking area at Olivia's Overlook the red-blazed Walsh Trail heads through open space to a small bridge. The path then follows the eastern edge of the ridge, passing a knobby overlook before coming to an end at a bench with a fine southerly view of Monument Mtn. The blue-blazed Ridge Trail now begins and traces a path along the western ridge. The Ridge Trail has a number of excellent overlooks as it passes through pine and mountain ash. There are a number of short connector paths that join the Walsh and Ridge Trails, making a hopscotch hike between ridges easy. After the Ridge Trail ends, near the communications tower, follow the red blazes back to the parking area.

Walsh Trail Loop

Distances from Olivia's Overlook

> *to* south end of ridge via Walsh Trail: 0.5 mi., 15 min.
>
> *to* communications tower via Ridge Trail: 0.9 mi., 30 min.
>
> *to* parking area: 1.0 mi., 35 min.

Burbank Trail Loop (BNRC)

This red-blazed easy trail begins directly across the road from the parking area for Olivia's Overlook. The path enters the woods near a sign briefly describing the trail (maps are usually available here) and continues along the rocky footway to a junction at 0.1 mi. The loop trail begins here. Continuing left (north) along the ridge, the path cruises through open woods. The forest is thick enough to allow hints of a view without ever actually providing one. At 0.6 mi. the path swings south and tops a craggy summit (1630 ft.), runs up and over another minor peak (1775 ft.), before heading to a sag and a narrow view through the pines at 1.1 mi. The trail then easily continues to the junction with Old Baldhead Rd. (Old Baldhead Rd. is a woods road that continues north 0.4 mi. to Reservoir Rd. in Lenox. It also runs south, then southeast just south of Shadowbrook Pond to meet Richmond–Lenox Rd. about 0.6 mi. east of Olivia's Overlook.)

Turn right and head downhill on the combined Burbank Trail/Old Baldhead Rd. The ruins of the old John Gorman homestead are on the right. In a shrubby overgrown area the Burbank Trail turns right and traces a narrow path through brambles and wet spots, reaching Shadowbrook Pond at 2.3 mi. A path near the dam leads to Old Baldhead Rd. The Burbank Trail heads easily uphill past a long run of rock cribbing, reaching the parking area at 3.0 mi.

Burbank Trail Loop

Distances from Olivia's Overlook

   to first summit: 0.6 mi., 20 min.

   to overlook: 1.1 mi., 45 min.

   to Shadowbrook Pond: 2.3 mi., 1 hr., 35 min.

Stevens Glen (BRNC)

This short, easy loop trail has its trailhead on Lenox St. on the western side of Yokun Ridge. To reach the parking area from Lenox follow MA 183 south 1.3 mi. to Richmond–Lenox Rd. Turn right and follow Richmond–Lenox Rd. 1.6 mi., then turn left onto Branch Rd. Follow Branch Rd. 0.6 mi. to a pull-off (4 cars) on the right.

The trail descends steps and soon reaches a metal post with trail maps. The loop begins here, heading into a plantation of fragrant fir trees. The trail crosses a power line at 0.4 mi. and then crosses a brook on a bridge at 0.5 mi.

before the loop trails join again high on a forested slope. A single trail descends the hillside and crosses two bridges, the second a one a long span over Lenox Mtn. Brook. The path now scrambles up a steep slope to the steel viewing platform (0.9 mi.) perched over the cascades of Stevens Glen.

Return to where the trails split (1.2 mi.) and take the right branch, which returns to the information area and reaches the roadside parking area at 1.4 mi.

Stevens Glen

Distances from the roadside parking area

  to bridge over Lenox Mtn. Brook: 0.7 mi., 25 min.

  to viewing deck over Stevens Glen: 0.9 mi., 35 min.

  to parking area: 1.4 mi., 50 min.

Mt. Greylock

In the northwest corner of Massachusetts is the state's highest summit, 3491-ft. Mt. Greylock. Running slightly more than 11 mi. in length from north to south, the Greylock Range is bordered on the west by the Taconic Range and on the east by the Hoosac Range. To the north lies the Hoosic River Valley, beyond which lie the Green Mtns. of Vermont. The area encompasses parts of six towns: Adams, North Adams, Williamstown, New Ashford, Lanesborough, and Cheshire.

The principal summits of the main ridge, from south to north, include Rounds Rock (2581 ft.), the three peaks of Saddle Ball Mtn. (3257, 3234, and 3218 ft., respectively), Mt. Greylock, Mt. Fitch (3110 ft.), and Mt. Williams (2951 ft.) On a spur ridge leading east from the summit are the twin peaks of Ragged Mtn. (2528 and 2451 ft.). On the northwest side of the summit is a deep glacial ravine known as the Hopper. Mt. Prospect (2690 ft.) is the high point of the spur ridge on the far side of the Hopper.

An extensive trail network offers a variety of hikes ranging from easy to strenuous. Many of the trails have outstanding viewpoints over the surrounding countryside. The broad, open summit offers panoramic views extending over three states. Principal landmarks at the summit include Bascom Lodge, a radio tower, and a 180-ft.-high granite war memorial.

Efforts to preserve the Mt. Greylock area began during the late 1800s, in a reaction to the devastation caused by logging, mining, and other 19th-century industrial activities. Today more than 12,000 acres are protected as part of the Massachusetts Department of Conservation and Recreation's Mt. Greylock State Reservation.

The summit and several trailheads can be reached via two paved roads extending through the reservation—Rockwell Rd. from the south and Notch Rd. from the north. To reach Rockwell Rd. from Lanesborough center, head north on US 7, bear right onto North Main St., then take the first right at Greylock Rd. (also called Quarry Rd.) and the first left onto Rockwell Rd. Notch Rd. begins on Main St. (MA 2) in North Adams, just east of the middle bridge over the Hoosic River. The two roads meet just below the summit and run together for the last 0.5 mi. as Summit Rd. to the summit. Total distance to the summit via either road is about 9 mi. Neither road is plowed in winter.

The Mt. Greylock Visitor Center, operated by DCR, is located near the lower end of Rockwell Rd. in Lanesborough. Nature's Classroom, Inc., operates Bascom Lodge at the summit, where meals and lodging are available between mid-May and mid-October (reservations required; 413-743-1591). Trail information is available at both the visitor center and Bascom Lodge. Sperry Campground, on the west slope of the mountain at 2400 ft., has facilities for individual and group camping. The campground is located on Sperry Rd. (dirt; passable by car), which leads north off Rockwell Rd. about 3 mi. below the summit. Camping at the Sperry Rd. campground is by reservation (877-422-6762). There are also several shelters and lean-tos on the trails that are available for backpackers on a first-come, first-served basis.

Refer to the North Berkshire map included with this trail guide.

Appalachian Trail

The Appalachian Trail traverses Mt. Greylock, following the crest of the ridge for most of its route. Road access is at Main St. (MA 2) in North Adams, the Greylock summit road, and Outlook Ave. in Cheshire. For a description of the trail route, see Appalachian Trail, Section 9, Cheshire to MA 2 (North Adams).

Roaring Brook Trail (DCR)

This moderate trail is the shortest route to Mt. Greylock from the west. The trailhead is located on Roaring Brook Rd. off US 7 in South Williamstown. Roaring Brook Rd. is 1.5 mi. south of the five-corners (junction of US 7 and MA 43) and 4 mi. north of the Springs Restaurant near Brodie Mtn. Ski Area. Travel down Roaring Brook Rd. about 0.5 mi. to a day-use parking area on the left.

From the road the blue-blazed trail follows Roaring Brook, crossing it several times, and reaches the junction with the Stony Ledge Trail (sign) at 0.5 mi. The trail bears right and ascends steeply through birch and spruce woods. At a footbridge crossing Roaring Brook the trail crosses the Deer Hill Trail and the Circle Trail, both blue-blazed. At 1.9 mi. it bears left over a second bridge and enters Sperry Campground.

Roaring Brook Trail

Distances from Roaring Brook Rd.

   to Stony Ledge Trail: 0.5 mi., 30 min.

   to Sperry Campground: 1.9 mi., 1 hr., 45 min.

   to summit of Mt. Greylock (via Hopper Trail and AT): 3.6 mi., 3 hr., 20 min.

Deer Hill Trail (DCR)

This strenuous blue-blazed loop trail starts from the Roaring Brook Trail a short walk southwest of Sperry Campground. It descends steeply to the cascades on the left, following rock steps in places. After the falls it continues to descend steeply until crossing a bridge over the stream. It then climbs past Deer Hill Shelter at 0.5 mi. and continues upslope to a sharp left turn. A side trail leaves right that reaches Rockwell Rd. in about 0.4 mi., just 0.1 mi. north of a day-use parking area. The Deer Hill Trail continues northeast across the slope, reaching Sperry Rd. at 1.3 mi. and the blue-blazed Hopper Trail at 1.7 mi. To return to the campground follow the Hopper Trail downhill (west), reaching the campground at 2.0 mi.

Deer Hill Trail

Distances from Roaring Brook Trail

   to Deer Hill Shelter: 0.5 mi., 25 min.

   to Sperry Rd.: 1.3 mi., 1 hr., 10 min.

   to Hopper Trail: 1.7 mi., 1 hr., 20 min.

Circle Trail (DCR)

Circle Trail is a strenuous 0.9-mi.-long blue-blazed loop path that makes a circuit through the beautiful Roaring Brook Gorge. From the parking area at Sperry Campground the trail heads south, crossing several small brooks. The path now turns west, following and then crossing a stream. Heading north, the trail traces the steep face of the ravine, crossing more streams before reaching the blue-blazed Roaring Brook Trail near a footbridge. Follow the Roaring Brook Trail 0.1 mi. to Sperry Rd. and Campground.

Stony Ledge Trail (DCR)

This strenuous blue-blazed trail, originally cleared as a ski trail, is now a popular mountain biking path. From the trailhead on the blue-blazed Roaring Brook Trail the path heads north to a ravine carved by a tributary of Roaring Brook. The trail now follows along a spur of the ravine, climbing about 1000 ft. in about 0.6 mi. The path reaches Stony Ledge, with magnificent views, at 1.1 mi. The trail ends here at the north terminus of Sperry Rd.

Stony Ledge Trail

Distances from Roaring Brook trailhead on Roaring Brook Rd.

to Stony Ledge Trail: 0.5 mi., 15 min.

to Stony Ledge: 1.6 mi., 1 hr., 20 min.

Hopper Trail (DCR)

The Hopper Trail is a strenuous, beautiful path passing through the Bacon Ravine portion of this immense glacial gorge and reaching the summit via the AT in 1.7 mi. To reach the trailhead, turn off MA 43 onto Hopper Rd. 2.5 mi. south of Williamstown at a stone gate. Hopper Rd. crosses the Green River and proceeds about 1.5 mi. to a parking area at Haley Farm on the right near a kiosk. Hike the short distance to the end of the road and the trailhead. The blue-blazed trail soon splits, with the blue-blazed Money Brook Trail leaving left and the Hopper Trail continuing right. It passes through fields and then steeply ascends the wooded buttress of Stony Ledge, where many unusual plants can be found. The trail levels off just before reaching Sperry Rd. at 2.4 mi.

The trail bears left and follows Sperry Rd. for about 0.1 mi. before leaving the road to the left just past the contact station and heading steeply uphill. The trail passes the blue-blazed Deer Hill Trail on the right. The Hopper Trail continues uphill, meeting the Overlook Trail (also blue-blazed), then turning sharp right and reaching Rockwell Rd. at the hairpin turn. The trail then ascends steeply to a junction with Rockwell Rd., the Cheshire Harbor Trail (again, marked in blue), and the Appalachian Trail. Turn left (north) and follow the white-blazed AT to the summit.

Hopper Trail

Distances from Haley Farm trailhead

   to Money Brook Trail: 0.2 mi., 5 min.

   to Sperry Campground: 2.4 mi., 2 hr.

   to AT: 3.5 mi., 3 hr.

   to summit of Mt. Greylock (via AT): 4.1 mi., 3 hr., 25 min.

March Cataract Trail (DCR)

This short and moderately easy blue-blazed trail begins at a parking area on Sperry Rd. in Sperry Campground and heads northeast to the scenic March Cataract Falls on Bacon Brook.

March Cataract Trail

Distances from Sperry Rd.

   to March Cataract Falls: 0.8 mi., 45 min.

Overlook Trail (DCR)

The Overlook Trail is a moderate path that runs from the summit area of Mt. Greylock to the Hopper Trail near Rockwell Rd. south of the summit. The path roughly follows the 3000-foot contour for much of its length, passing through beech and spruce forest. The trail begins near the radio tower at the western end of the summit, where this blue-blazed trail enters the forest. The path descends and crosses Notch Rd. at 0.5 mi., then traces the contour of the mountain on the edge of the Hopper Ravine to a short side trail that leads to an overlook at 1.1 mi. The view peers down into the Hopper with Mt. Prospect beyond. The Overlook Trail then crosses Bacon Brook (from this crossing the brook falls about 600 vertical ft. in slightly over 1000 ft. of distance to create the March Cataract waterfall) and ends at the junction with the Hopper Trail, which enters from the right. To continue to the summit, follow the Hopper Trail to the AT, then continue north on the AT to the summit.

Overlook Trail

Distances from summit area

   to Notch Rd.: 0.5 mi., 15 min.

   to overlook: 1.1 mi., 45 min.

   to junction with Hopper Trail: 1.6 mi., 1 hr.

   to summit via Hopper and Appalachian Trails (circuit): 2.2 mi., 1 hr., 15 min.

Robinson's Point Trail (DCR)

Robinson's Point Trail begins on Notch Rd. just north of a day-use parking area. Many people reach the trailhead from the summit area, hiking north on the AT from the eastern end of the parking facility and the ski hut. The white-blazed AT descends a rocky path, crosses Summit Rd., and continues to descend to a blue-blazed side trail on the left at about 0.5 mi. The side path quickly reaches Notch Rd. and a parking area. The blue-blazed Robinson's Point Trail begins a few yards north of the parking area. From Notch Rd. the path descends through a boggy area to a perch at the edge of the Hopper (0.8 mi.) with a view that makes you feel as if you were soaring. The hike back is strenuous.

Robinson's Point Trail

Distances from the summit

   to Notch Rd. via AT: 0.5 mi., 10 min.

   to overlook: 0.8 mi., 30 min.

Money Brook Trail (DCR)

This strenuous blue-blazed trail, in connection with the Appalachian Trail from the north, provides access to Mt. Williams and the Mt. Greylock summit. It is especially attractive in spring because of the number and variety of wildflowers that grow along it as it weaves through the Hopper.

   To reach the trailhead, turn off MA 43 onto Hopper Rd. 2.5 mi. south of Williamstown at a stone gate. Hopper Rd. crosses the Green River and proceeds about 1.5 mi. to a parking area on the right near a kiosk. Hike the short distance to the end of the road and the trailhead. Follow the blue-blazed Hopper Trail 0.2 mi. to where the Money Brook Trail leaves left.

The trail passes a camping area and follows Hopper Brook into the Hopper. The trail now turns to the north, following Money Brook past the blue-blazed Mt. Prospect Trail, which leaves left. The path traces a course deep into the ravine of Money Brook, a favorite haunt of barred owls and once the hideout of counterfeiters whose illegal craftsmanship gave the stream its name.

The trail swings northeast and follows the brook to a dead-end side trail that leads in 0.1 mi. to the base of Money Brook Falls. The main trail ascends steeply, moderating where a connector trail leaves right for Notch Rd. and a day-use parking area. The Money Brook Trail continues north, passing the access trail for Wilbur Clearing Shelter on the left before reaching the AT about 0.2 mi. west of Notch Rd.

Money Brook Trail

Distances from Haley Farm trailhead

   to Mt. Prospect Trail: 1.7 mi., 55 min.

   to side trail to cascades: 2.8 mi., 1 hr., 35 min.

   to Wilbur Clearing Shelter: 3.3 mi., 2 hr., 5 min.

   to AT: 3.5 mi., 2 hr., 15 min.

   to Notch Rd. via AT: 3.7 mi., 2 hr., 30 min.

 * one-way strenuous hike from Notch Rd. to Money Brook Falls: 0.8 mi., 1 hr.

Mt. Prospect Trail (DCR)

Mt. Prospect (2690 ft.) is a steep-sided wooded ridge on the northwest side of the Greylock Range. The blue-blazed Mt. Prospect Trail is a very strenuous 2-mi.-long trail that begins on the Money Brook Trail deep in the Money Brook Ravine and ends at the north end of the mountain where the path meets the AT. The southern trailhead can be reached by following the Hopper and Money Brook Trails from the Haley Farm trailhead 1.7 mi. to the trailhead on the left. The northern trailhead, and a spectacular overlook, can be reached by following the AT 0.3 mi. north from where it crosses Notch Rd. From the AT the trail traces a course atop the attractive wooded ridge of Mt. Prospect, with glimpses of the wide valley to the west. At the south end of the ridge is a rock cairn marking the wooded summit. The trail then descends very steeply, dropping about 1300 ft. in the next mile before reaching the Money Brook Trail.

Mt. Prospect Trail

Distances from AT

to summit of Mt. Prospect: 1.0 mi., 30 min.

to Money Brook Trail: 2.0 mi., 1 hr., 10 min.

Bellows Pipe Trail (DCR)

The blue-blazed Bellows Pipe Trail is open to both hiking and mountain biking. The trail begins as an easy walk and ends as a strenuous climb. The trailhead is on the south side of Notch Rd. where the road takes a sharp turn before it enters the reservation from North Adams. Parking is available at the Notch Rd. gate parking area 500 ft. from the trailhead. From the trailhead the trail heads south along a level dirt access road for Notch Reservoir. Soon the path begins to climb along the flanks of Mt. Williams and Mt. Fitch, with Ragged Mtn. to the east across Notch Brook Ravine. The grade increases, and at 2.0 mi. the blue-blazed Ragged Mtn. Trail leaves left for the top of Ragged Mtn.

Just beyond a grove of red spruce and red pine and after crossing a deep ravine, the trail turns sharp right (northwest) and heads steeply upslope (2.2 mi.). A wide path continues straight ahead and intersects the blue-blazed Thunderbolt Trail before descending toward Greylock Glen.

The Bellows Pipe Trail (so named for the winds that blow between Greylock and Ragged Mtn.) resumes its climb, passing Bellows Pipe Shelter on the right at 2.6 mi. and turning southwest for a level stretch. At 3.2 mi. the trail again turns northwest onto a woods road, ascending the ridge in a series of switchbacks. At the fourth switchback the trail turns northwest off the woods road, which continues south to the Thunderbolt Trail. At 3.7 mi. the Bellows Pipe Trail ends at the white-blazed Appalachian Trail. The summit of Mt. Greylock is about 0.5 mi. south (left).

Bellows Pipe Trail

Distances from Notch Rd.

to Ragged Mtn. Trail: 2.0 mi., 1 hr., 10 min.

to Bellows Pipe Shelter: 2.6 mi., 1 hr., 50 min.

to AT: 3.7 mi., 2 hr., 50 min.

to Mt. Greylock summit (via AT): 4.2 mi., 3 hr., 10 min.

Thunderbolt Trail (DCR)

One of the steepest trails on the mountain, the Thunderbolt was constructed by the Civilian Conservation Corps (CCC) in 1934 as a championship ski trail. From the summit of Mt. Greylock, it drops 2260 vertical ft. on its 2-mi. descent of the mountain. This blue-blazed, very rugged and strenuous trail was named for the roller coaster at Revere Beach near Boston because each trip down the mountain was an unforgettable ride.

The Thunderbolt Trail is accessed via the Appalachian Trail from the summit of Mt. Greylock, 0.4 mi. north of the summit parking area. The trail drops very steeply off the ridge on the wide, overgrown ski trail, crossing numerous woods roads on the lower reaches until reaching Thiel Rd. at Greylock Glen at 1.6 mi.

To reach the Thiel Rd. trailhead in Greylock Glen from the McKinley Monument in Adams, follow Maple St. to West Rd. Turn left and in 0.4 mi. turn right onto Gould Rd. and climb past orchards. At the intersection bear right onto Thiel Rd. and follow it to the day-use parking area on the left. The trailhead is a few yards farther up the road on the left just before Hoxie Brook.

Thunderbolt Trail

Distances from Thiel Rd.

   to summit of Mt. Greylock via AT: 2 mi., 2 hr., 5 min.

Cheshire Harbor Trail

The blue-blazed Cheshire Harbor Trail is open to hiking and mountain biking. To reach the trail, follow MA 8 to the McKinley Monument in Adams center. Maple St. exits right (west) at the monument. Follow Maple St. to West Rd. Turn left (south) onto West Rd., cross Pecks Brook, and take an immediate right onto West Mtn. Rd. Continue 1.5 mi. to the end of the road and the day-use parking area and trailhead.

From West Mtn. Rd. the trail zigzags steeply up the south bluff of Pecks Brook ravine, reaching the junction with Old Adams Rd.—an old stage road—at 1.0 mi. The Cheshire Harbor Trail continues climbing, though less aggressively, reaching the connector path to the Gould Trail at 1.5 mi. Resuming a steep climb, the trail reaches Rockwell Rd. at its junction with the white-blazed Appalachian Trail at 2.5 mi. From Rockwell Rd. follow the AT northbound to the summit, which is reached at 3.1 mi.

Cheshire Harbor Trail

Distances from West Mtn. Rd. (Adams)

to Old Adams Rd.: 1 mi., 40 min.

to Gould Trail connector: 1.5 mi., 1 hr., 10 min.

to Rockwell Rd.: 2.5 mi., 2 hr., 50 min.

to summit of Mt. Greylock (via AT): 3.1 mi., 3 hr., 20 min.

CCC Dynamite Trail

This moderate blue-blazed connector trail runs along a fairly level terrace, roughly tracing the 2500-foot contour of Saddle Ball Mtn. from the blue-blazed Jones Nose Trail to the junction of Rockwell and Sperry Rds. It begins 0.3 mi. from the Jones Nose parking area and heads north 1.3 mi. to its end. On the way it passes the location where CCC crews stored explosives used to build Rockwell Rd. in the 1930s.

CCC Dynamite Trail

Distances from Jones Nose parking area

to CCC Dynamite Trail via Jones Nose Trail: 0.3 mi., 20 min.

to Rockwell Rd. (at Sperry Rd.): 1.3 mi., 45 min.

Jones Nose Trail (DCR)

This strenuous blue-blazed trail scales the steep feature called Jones Nose (named for a local farmer with a nose not quite as large but of similar shape) that marks the south slope of Saddle Ball Mtn. This trail offers numerous fine views as it climbs to the cool boreal forest along the summit ridge. The trail begins at the Jones Nose day-use parking area on Rockwell Rd. about 3.7 mi. north of the visitor center. The trail heads through open areas locally famous for blueberries before entering the woods and beginning a steep ascent. It climbs steeply to a terrace where the blue-blazed CCC Dynamite Trail leaves left at 0.3 mi. The path soon resumes climbing steeply past ledges to a short side trail leading west with fantastic views of the Taconics and Catskills from a rocky ledge. The trail becomes steeper, passing between ledges and conifers to reach the southern summit of Saddle Ball Mtn. (3238 ft.) and the junction with the white-blazed AT at 1.0 mi. To continue on to the summit of Mt. Greylock, hike northbound on the AT 3.6 mi.

Jones Nose Trail

Distances from Jones Nose parking area

　　to CCC Dynamite Trail: 0.3 mi., 20 min.

　　to Saddle Ball Mtn. and AT: 1.0 mi., 45 min.

Rounds Rock Trail (DCR)

This blue-blazed 0.7-mi.-long, easy loop trail leaves the western side of Rockwell Rd. 3.0 mi. north of the visitor center and 0.7 mi. south of the Jones Nose parking area. Park off the road in the designated pull-off. The trail gradually ascends through mature woods to open ledges and blueberry barrens. A short side trail leads to a cliff with outstanding views to the south. At the edge of the barrens a second outlook trail is passed, followed shortly by the Northrup Trail entering from the left. In a beech grove the trail passes a rock cairn and the remains of a twin-engine Cessna aircraft that crashed here August 12, 1948, on a flight from Bendix Field in New Jersey to Albany. The trail continues through mixed hardwoods and curves back northwesterly to the start.

Gould Trail (DCR)

The strenuous blue-blazed Gould Trail can be accessed from the trailhead near the end of Gould Rd. in Greylock Glen and from the day-use parking area about 1 mi. from the West St. intersection. (See the directions to the Cheshire Harbor Trail.) The trail ascends the southeast face of Mt. Greylock, tracing a route along the north side of Pecks Brook ravine, passing a connector trail (1.5 mi.) leading to the Cheshire Harbor Trail and reaching a side trail leading to Pecks Brook Falls at 1.9 mi. At 2.0 mi. Pecks Brook Shelter is passed on the left. The path becomes quite steep as it climbs to the tri-junction with Notch, Rockwell, and Summit Rds. at 3.0 mi. Follow the AT northbound for about 0.4 mi. to the summit.

Gould Trail

Distances from Gould Rd. trailhead

　　to connector trail to Cheshire Harbor Trail: 1.5 mi., 1 hr., 10 min.

　　to Pecks Falls: 1.9 mi., 2 hr.

　　to Pecks Brook Shelter: 2.0 mi., 2 hr., 10 min.

　　to tri-junction: 3.0 mi., 3 hr., 10 min.

　　to summit via AT: 3.4 mi., 3 hr., 25 min.

Ragged Mtn. Trail (DCR)

Ragged Mtn. is a jagged spur forming one wall of Notch Brook ravine on the eastern side of Mt. Greylock. The Ragged Mtn. Trail accesses the rocky peak that stands about 1000 ft. lower than its towering neighbor. The path is lightly used and offers solitude amid the croaks of ravens that nest among the crags.

To reach the blue-blazed Ragged Mtn. Trail follow the Bellows Pipe Trail south 2.0 mi. from the Notch Rd. trailhead. The Ragged Mtn. Trail leaves left and quickly begins a fairly steep ascent of the mountain. The path weaves through outcrops and forest, reaching a rocky clearing marking the summit at 0.4 mi.

Old Summit Rd. (DCR)

From the parking area on Notch Rd. the blue-blazed trail enters the woods and quickly comes to a junction. Continuing straight a few yards leads to the AT; the Old Summit Rd. leaves right, heading easily uphill. The path climbs to the roadbed of the long-abandoned Old Summit Rd. and follows it south. At the burned ruins of an old cabin a connector path leads to Notch Rd. and the blue-blazed Money Brook Trail. Continuing south, the trail swings uphill, passing some ski trails and in part following a streambed to the junction with the white-blazed AT and the blue-blazed Bernard Farm Trail in the saddle between Mt. Williams and Mt. Fitch at 0.8 mi.

To reach the trailhead drive 2.25 mi. up Notch Rd. from the gated entrance of Mt. Greylock Reservation in North Adams. A day-use parking area is on the left 0.1 mi. beyond the point where the AT crosses the road.

Bernard Farm Trail (DCR)

This strenuous blue-blazed trail runs about 3.0 mi. from Notch Rd. at the reservation entrance in North Adams (near the old Bernard Farm) to the AT in the saddle between Mt. Williams and Mt. Fitch. The trail was named for Harry Bernard, who ran a dairy farm on this site in the early 20th century. He also drove children to school with his "school team" before buses, extracted timber used for construction of Bascom Lodge in the 1930s, and operated a small ski area in the 1940s and 1950s (Source: *Most Excellent Majesty* by Lauren Stevens, Berkshire House, 1988).

From the farm and Mt. Greylock Reservation boundary follow an old woods road to the northwest. A series of trails and woods roads link up the mountainside, cross Notch Rd., then traverse the eastern side of Mt. Williams before climbing steeply to the white-blazed AT just south of Mt. Williams.

Bernard Farm Trail

Distance from Notch Rd.

   to AT: 2.3 mi., 2 hr.

Haley Farm Trail (DCR)

This strenuous blue-blazed trail begins at the day-use parking area on Hopper Rd. (see Hopper Trail for directions). The Haley Farm Trail heads south, then southwest to the base of the western spur of Stony Ledge. The path then makes a very steep ascent that moderates briefly before continuing up to the Stony Ledge Trail, also blue-blazed, which it then follows a few hundred feet to Stony Ledge at 2.2 mi.

Stage Trail (DCR)

The Stage Trail is a moderate 0.8-mi.-long blue-blazed connector path that links the Jones Nose parking area on Rockwell Rd. with Greylock Rd.

Northrup Trail (DCR)

The Northrup Trail is a generally easy hiking trail that runs from its trailhead on Rockwell Rd. 2.0 mi. north of the visitor center to the Jones Nose parking area, also on Rockwell Rd. Along the way the Northrup Trail provides a connecting route to the Rounds Rock Trail from the west.

From the visitor center a road walk of 2.0 mi. on Rockwell Rd. is needed to reach the trailhead on the left. From the trailhead the path proceeds easily to the Rounds Rock Trail on the right (3.7 mi.). From Rounds Rock the trail descends and reaches Rockwell Rd. opposite the Jones Nose parking area at 5.0 mi.

Mt. Greylock Visitor Center Trails (DCR)

The Mt. Greylock Visitor Center serves as a base for three easy-to-moderate paths. The Brook and Berry Trail is an easy 1.0-mi. walk through nearby woods and open areas. The Cliff Loop Trail is a moderate 0.8-mi.-long hike through some attractive open woods, and the Bradley Farm Interpretive Trail is an easy 1.8-mi. walk filled with nature and history. Interpretive trail maps and brochures are available at the Mt. Greylock Visitor Center on Rockwell Rd.

Ice Glen Trail System (LHA)

The forested hills and ravines south of Stockbridge are protected in part by the efforts of the Laurel Hill Association (LHA). Founded in 1853, the LHA has the distinction of being the oldest organization of its kind in the country. The acreage around Ice Glen and Laura's Rest contains some of the oldest trees in Massachusetts and is traced by three trails. To reach the trails take US 7 south from the center of Stockbridge and its junction with MA 102. Proceed 0.2 mi. to Park St. on the left. Turn left (Town Park is now on the right) and drive to the end of Park St. Cross over the Housatonic River on the Memorial Foot-bridge to the far bank, where the trails begin.

Mary Flynn Trail (LHA)

The Mary Flynn Trail begins very near Memorial Bridge and heads north between the Housatonic River and the railroad tracks. The path follows the river north along a narrow floodplain for about 0.2 mi., then turns east. At about 0.4 mi. the steep slopes of the hill topped by Laura's Tower crowd the riverbank. The trail now turns south to its end at about 1.0 mi.

Ice Glen & Laura's Tower Trails

The combined Ice Glen and Laura's Tower Trails (blazed with yellow) leave Memorial Bridge and head east, crossing the (active) railroad tracks and entering deep piney woods. The trail has recently been reworked and partially relocated, with the result being a nicer walk on a path that is much less prone to erosion. The trail meanders up the hill, weaving around boulders and through ancient tall pines to a T-intersection (0.4 mi.), where the trails split.

Ice Glen Trail (LHA)

From the trail junction the moderate Ice Glen Trail heads south, reaching the V-cleft entrance to the ravine at 0.5 mi. For the next 0.2 mi. the path weaves through the chilly boulder caves of the glen, where some of the oldest white pines and hemlocks in the state still grow. The path exits the ravine near a 150-ft.-tall, 300-year-old white pine. The path proceeds a short way to a gravel road that leads in about 0.2 mi. to Ice Glen Rd. To return to Park St. via the road follow Ice Glen Rd. 0.6 mi. to US 7. Turn right onto US 7 and walk 0.25 mi. to Park St., then another 0.25 mi. to the parking area.

Ice Glen Trail

Distances from Memorial Bridge

to junction with Laura's Tower Trail: 0.4 mi., 20 min.

to Ice Glen: 0.5 mi., 25 min.

to white pine: 0.7 mi., 40 min.

to Ice Glen Rd.: 0.9 mi., 50 min.

to parking area via US 7 and Park St.: 2.0 mi., 1 hr., 20 min.

Laura's Tower Trail (LHA)

From the junction with the Ice Glen Trail, the moderate yellow-blazed Laura's Tower Trail heads left along the contour of the ridge, crossing a small brook before turning and beginning to seriously climb the hill known as Laura's Rest. The top of the hill is trimmed to keep the trees from interfering with the view from the imposing steel observation tower at its summit (1465 ft.). The radical incline and small steps make climbing the tower a cautious endeavor, but the view is wonderful, reaching to the Catskills in the west, Mt. Greylock in the north, and Monument Mtn. to the south. Laura's Tower and Laura's Rest are named for Laura Belden, the daughter-in-law of David Dudley Field. She came to the hilltop to find refuge from her life's many tragedies.

Laura's Tower Trail

Distances from Memorial Bridge

to Ice Glen Trail junction: 0.4 mi., 15 min.

to Laura's Tower: 0.8 mi., 45 min.

Questing (TTOR)

This 438-acre property of The Trustees of Reservations sits astride the rolling landscape of Leffingwell Hill in New Marlborough. The hilltop was one of the first places settled by Europeans in the early 1700s, and is where twin girls were born, the first non–Native American children born in Berkshire County. The reservation holds old stone foundations and cellar holes, several hundred acres of forest, and a 17-acre upland field that attracts butterflies and birds.

The easy white-blazed trail begins at the parking area and heads uphill on an old woods road to the field. The path then forks, with the left trail entering the woods and passing by stone walls and the settlement ruins before descending through open woods to a field where a mowed path returns to the fork. The loop can also be done in reverse. Up and back from the parking area is about 2 mi. and takes about 1.5 hours.

To reach Questing take MA 23 east from Great Barrington to the junction with MA 57. Follow MA 57 for 5 mi. and turn right onto New Marlborough Hill Rd. Travel 0.6 mi. along the road to the parking area and kiosk on the left.

Dry Hill (TTOR)

Dry Hill is a 206-acre property of The Trustees of Reservations that protects a significant portion of the eponymous New Marlborough landmark, so named for the distinct lack of water on the ridge. Dry Hill is a wild place with bears and bobcats as well as scarlet tanagers and butterflies. The white-blazed trail begins at the information kiosk near the parking area and leads to the craggy cliffs atop the ridge in 1.25 mi. The first mi. is easy, with the last 0.25 mi. a moderate hike over rocks and through mountain laurel tangles. Time up and back is about 1.5 hours.

To reach Dry Hill take MA 23 east from Great Barrington to the junction with MA 57. Follow MA 57 for 5.5 mi. to the New Marlborough town green and turn left onto New Marlborough–Monterey Rd. Continue for 0.7 mi. and turn left onto Harmon Rd. The parking area is on the left about 0.2 mi. down the road.

Bartholomew's Cobble (TTOR)

Bartholomew's Cobble in Ashley Falls is one of the most treasured natural areas in Massachusetts. More than 800 species of vascular plants and over 240 species of birds have been recorded on its 329 acres. Four miles of trails weave through craggy limestone hills, called cobbles, along the banks of the Housatonic River, and through open fields. Bartholomew's Cobble is a National Natural Landmark. A small museum and nature center with restrooms is located off Weatogue Rd. To reach Bartholomew's Cobble follow

US 7 in Sheffield south and turn right onto MA 7A. Continue south on MA 7A for 0.5 mi. and turn right onto Rannapo Rd. Travel 1.5 mi. and turn right onto Weatogue Rd. The nature center is a few yards ahead on the left.

Ledges Interpretive Trail (TTOR)

An interpretive brochure describing the 20 points along this fascinating path is available at the nature center to aid in the enjoyment of the white-blazed Ledges Trail. This easy 0.5-mi. path begins at the nature center and enters the hemlock woods near the kiosk. It descends through cool hemlocks to the riverside at the beginning of the large meander called Corbin's Neck. This area is usually ice-free in winter and attracts hundreds of geese. The path passes limestone outcrops climbing to a bench (0.2 mi.) overlooking the pasture and river. The trail then continues past a rock face before turning west, passing the junction with the Baily Trail (0.25 mi.), cedars, and more ledges. The trail parallels the road briefly then passes a cave on the right before ending at the nature center.

Ledges Interpretive Trail

Distances from nature center

  to bench: 0.2 mi., 10 min.

  to Baily Trail: 0.25 mi., 15 min.

  to nature center: 0.5 mi., 30 min.

Tractor Path (TTOR)

Don't judge a book by its cover. This unappealingly named trail leads from the edge of Ashley Field opposite the nature center and journeys to an overlook atop a 20-acre field with a view that covers most of the southern Berkshires. From the trailhead the path follows a mowed trail parallel to the road before turning right along the fence line. The path passes an apple tree and begins to easily climb into a second field. The Hal Borland Trail leaves right and travels the short distance to the Col. Ashley House, the oldest house in Berkshire County. The path continues to climb, briefly entering the woods before passing through another field. At the top of this field the trail passes through more woods to reach the Tulip Tree Trail on the left. The Tractor Path jogs right and enters an enormous field with tree swallows, bluebirds, and bobolinks. At the top of the field, called Hurlburt's Hill, is a bench that faces north and a view that encompasses the southern Taconics all the way (on a clear day) to Mt. Greylock.

Tractor Path

Distances from trailhead

   to Hal Borland Trail: 0.25 mi., 10 min.

   to Tulip Tree Trail: 0.7 mi., 20 min.

   to hilltop bench and overlook: 0.9 mi., 30 min.

Beartown State Forest

Beartown State Forest in Monterey contains 10,879 acres of largely undeveloped forest, mountains, and wetlands. The AT passes through the preserve, which is crossed by many gravel service roads. The highest point is Mt. Wilcox at 2155 ft. Two shelters serving the AT are found in Beartown State Forest. Wilcox South is southeast of Mt. Wilcox, and Wilcox North is northeast of the mountain. A campground with 12 sites is located on the shore of Benedict Pond just northwest of the dam, and a swimming area (restrooms available) is located a few yards southeast of the dam. Leashed pets are permitted.

Pond Loop Trail (DCR)

This easy blue-blazed 1.5-mi.-long path circles the shore of Benedict Pond in the south portion of Beartown State Forest. From the trailhead at the public boat launch the trail heads southeast through tangles of laurel and azalea that bloom in early June. The path then descends easily to a wet, swampy area where the white-blazed AT enters from the right. The AT and Pond Loop Trail combine briefly, crossing a small stream on bog bridging before crossing a larger stream on a stone bridge. The AT now leaves right; the Pond Loop Trail stays left. (For a nice side trip trek up the AT about 0.4 mi. to the Ledges, an area of open cliffs with great views to the west.) The Pond Loop Trail briefly follows a wide woods road, then descends to the shore, wandering along the edge of the lake and past a marshy area near the north bay. The path then runs through the campground before crossing the dam and swimming area and returning to the parking area by the boat launch.

Pond Loop Trail

Distances from the Benedict Pond boat launch and parking area

to south junction with AT: 0.4 mi., 10 min.

to north junction with AT at stone bridge: 0.55 mi., 15 min.

to campground: 1.1 mi., 30 min.

to boat launch: 1.5 mi., 45 min.

Monument Mtn. Reservation (TTOR)

Monument Mtn. Reservation in Great Barrington is one of the most popular hiking destinations in the Berkshires, drawing about 20,000 visitors annually. The mountain, an isolated hummock of pure white quartzite, was sacred to the Stockbridge Indians, inspired the poetry of William Cullen Bryant, and was the place where Nathaniel Hawthorne gave Herman Melville advice on writing *Moby-Dick*. The depth of history here is equaled by the natural wonders of these stunning cliffs. Wildlife abounds in the forests, and the updrafts that sweep up the cliffs are sought out by many species of raptors that routinely soar close to the rocks.

There are many significant features along this beautiful ridge, including Squaw Peak (1640 ft.), a ragged crest of rock atop the vertical cliffs. Devil's Pulpit is a freestanding pinnacle of rock south of Squaw Peak; it is the "monument of the mountain," a rock cairn with a colorful, mysterious history. *Note: Rock climbing is prohibited throughout the reservation.*

Parking is available at a picnic area located at the base of Squaw Peak on US 7, 3.0 mi. south of Stockbridge and the intersection of US 7 and MA 102. From Great Barrington travel north 3.0 mi. from the north junction with MA 23 in Great Barrington. A trail map and other information is displayed at the kiosk near the trailhead for Hickey Trail.

Indian Monument Trail (TTOR)

This trail begins at the south end of the parking area and parallels US 7 for roughly 0.3 mi. before joining a wide woods road. The trail follows the woods road, swinging sharp right, reaching a stone wall at 0.5 mi. Turning right and following the stone wall about 100 ft. into the woods leads to the Indian Monument, a large stone cairn originally built by the Stockbridge Mahicans centuries ago.

The path continues along the level woods road and gradually becomes steeper in grade, reaching the junction with the Squaw Peak Trail (right) in a woodland clearing at 0.75 mi. The Indian Monument Trail continues easily through the woods, the cliffs and boulders of the mountain ever present on the right. The path swings south as it climbs to the junction with the Hickey Trail at Inscription Rock at 1.5 mi.

Indian Monument Trail

Distances from parking area on US 7

> *to* Indian Monument: 0.5 mi., 20 min.
>
> *to* Squaw Peak Trail: 0.75 mi., 25 min.
>
> *to* Inscription Rock: 1.5 mi., 45 min.
>
> *to* summit (about 0.1 mi. north of Squaw Peak): 1.6 mi., 55 min.

Hickey Trail (TTOR)

This heavily used trail is the quickest way to the summit and leaves the Monument Mtn. Reservation picnic area on US 7 near the kiosk. It proceeds easily east through open woods, with the bouldered slopes of the mountain on the left. It passes a small wet area before beginning a steady, moderate climb, passing a huge boulder on the left. The path now crosses a brook on a log bridge then passes a cave behind a waterfall on the left. Climbing up a gully, the path turns left, crosses the brook on another bridge, and scrambles over a boulder area to reach Inscription Rock and the Indian Monument Trail at 0.75 mi.

Hickey Trail

Distances from Monument Mtn. Reservation picnic area

> *to* Inscription Rock: 0.75 mi., 45 min.
>
> *to* summit (about 0.1 mi. north of Squaw Peak): 0.85 mi., 55 min.

Squaw Peak Trail (TTOR)

Squaw Peak Trail begins at Inscription Rock at the junction of the Hickey and Indian Monument Trails on the far eastern end of the mountain. The trail then runs across the spine of the ridge, crossing the summit of Squaw Peak before angling down the slope to join the Indian Monument Trail 0.75 mi. from the parking area.

From Inscription Rock the trail climbs very steeply up stone steps to the quartzite outcrops that mark the true summit of Monument Mtn. (1642 ft.). The path weaves among the boulders, pines, and azaleas before descending into a small saddle between the two peaks. The path then climbs up to the ragged cliffs of Squaw Peak (1640 ft.), with dizzying sheer cliffs. The path now begins a small loop, with one fork descending along the rocks to Devil's Pulpit. The other loop descends, steeply at first, joins the other loop descending from the Pulpit, then traverses the ridge to end at the Indian Monument Trail.

Squaw Peak Trail

Distances from Inscription Rock

>   *to* true summit: 0.1 mi., 10 min.
>
>   *to* Squaw Peak: 0.25 mi., 15 min.
>
>   *to* Indian Monument Trail: 0.7 mi., 35 min.

Kennedy Park

Kennedy Park in Lenox is home to a complex trail network on the grounds of the old and massive Aspinwall Hotel. The hotel was built in 1902, became very popular with the wealthy of the time, and burned to the ground in 1931. The property was turned into a town park in the 1950s and has been a magnet to hikers, cyclists, skiers, and equestrians ever since. About 30 trails weave through the woods; kiosks complete with maps are placed in various locations throughout the park. There are many entrances to the park, including:

- The Arcadian Sports Shop on US 7 in Lenox about 0.4 mi. north of the merger of US 7 and MA 7A.

- The Lenox Shops on US 7 in Lenox about 0.3 mi. north of the merger of US 7 and MA 7A.

- The DPW parking lot on MA 7A in Lenox about 0.3 mi. south of the merge of US 7 and MA 7A.

Tyringham Cobble (TTOR)

Tyringham Cobble is a prominent hill high above Tyringham village. The storied location once served as pastureland for the livestock of the Tyringham

Shaker community. Today the hillside is traversed by the Appalachian Trail and is covered with forest and pastures that give the "cobble" a unique, inviting feeling. A touch of mystery was added to the place by geologist Daniel Clark, who ascertained that the oldest rocks were at the top of the cobble and the youngest at the bottom, just the reverse of what should be. He concluded that the cobble was dislodged from a nearby mountain and was flipped upside down during a catastrophe of mind-boggling intensity.

To reach the cobble from the Mass Pike (I-90) in Lee (Exit 2) head east on US 20, then turn quickly right onto MA 102, followed in a few yards by a left turn onto Tyringham Main Rd. Travel 4.2 mi. to Tyringham village, take a right onto Jerusalem Rd., and proceed about 0.2 mi. to a parking area on the right. Information and the trailhead are near the big red barn.

Tyringham Cobble Loop Trail

The 1.9-mi.-long white-blazed Tyringham Cobble Loop Trail runs from the red barn near the parking area and follows the fence line to the fork in the loop. Following the trail counterclockwise—as is most popular—the path heads easily uphill through open space and pasture to its union with the AT, also white-blazed. The trail then piggybacks with the AT as it climbs up the shrubby field. The Tyringham Cobble Loop Trail then turns right away from the AT and climbs through patches of field and forest to the overlook atop the cobble. The path next descends past a field with wide views of the village below and enters the woods. The descent of the cobble is easy, passing along old woods roads some of the way. The path now enters a pasture and easily descends to the loop junction and parking area.

Tyringham Cobble Loop Trail

Distance from parking area

   to summit of cobble: 0.9 mi., 45 min.

   to complete loop: 1.9 mi., 1 hr., 10 min.

McClennan Reservation (TTOR)

McClennan Reservation protects 491 acres of wild forest and marsh surrounding Round Mtn. (1517 ft.). The white-blazed foot trail loops around the foot of the mountain visiting ruins, waterfalls, and Hale Meadow along the way. Centuries ago the Mahican Nation had a sugar camp on the banks of Camp Brook where they lived while making maple sugar each spring. Later the land became tended fields, but a few isolated old trees remain to this day. The property is crossed by old road lines, with stone walls and many stone foundations of forgotten homes and barns. It was last part of the Ashintully Estate.

To reach McClennan Reservation from the I-90 (Mass Pike) and US 20 junction (Exit 2) take MA 102 west for a few yards then turn left onto Tyringham Main Rd. Proceed to Tyringham village and continue south 2.0 mi. to Fenn Rd. on the left. Park along the side of the road and walk up the dirt road 0.4 mi. to the trailhead.

Round Mtn. Trail

From the trailhead the easy white-blazed trail soon reaches the foot of Round Mtn. and begins to trace a course along the southern slope. The trail reaches a cluster of foundations and stone walls at 0.6 mi. and enters a dark evergreen forest. At 1.0 mi. the trail splits, the right fork making a straight course to Hale Meadow and the left path following along the cascades of Camp Brook. Bear right to reach Hale Meadow at 1.3 mi. The trail then follows along the edge of the meadow, passing more ruins at 1.5 mi. The trail now joins an old woods road that descends to the trailhead at 2.0 mi.

Round Mtn. Trail

Distances from Fenn Rd.

   to trailhead: 0.4 mi., 20 min.

   to ruins: 0.6 mi., 30 min.

   to trail split: 1.0 mi., 45 min.

   to Hale Meadow: 1.3 mi., 55 min.

   to trailhead: 2.0 mi., 1 hr., 20 min.

   to Fenn Rd.: 2.4 mi., 1 hr., 40 min.

Pittsfield State Forest (DCR)

Pittsfield State Forest contains about 10,000 acres of forests, ponds, and mountains in the central Taconics.

There are numerous peaks, including Berry Mtn. (2182 ft.), Tower Mtn. (2175 ft.), and Pine Mtn. (2221 ft.). Berry Mtn. has 65 acres of wild azaleas, near the Taconic Crest Trail, that bloom in June. Berry Pond, on the flank of Berry Mtn., is either the highest or second highest pond in Massachusetts, depending on what map you look at. There are two camping areas with a combined 31 sites. Berry Pond Campground has 13 sites; Parker Brook has 18. Universal-access restrooms and a universal-access trail are available near the forest headquarters.

Hawthorne Trail (DCR)

This narrow, strenuous trail, steep in places, leads up the eastern slope of Pine Mtn. and serves as a link to the Pine Mtn. Trail. It is open to multiuse, non-motorized activities. From Pittsfield, at the junction of Routes 20 and 7 south of the city center, turn onto Route 20 west (West Housatonic St.). Travel 2.6 miles to Hungerford St., turn right onto Hungerford St., and drive to the intersection with West St. Turn left on West St. and continue 1.2 miles to Churchill St. Take a right onto Churchill St. and drive 1.7 miles to Cascade St. Turn left onto Cascade St. and follow to the State Forest entrance. After crossing the footbridge the Tranquility Trail, a paved universal-access path, is passed on the right. The trail continues straight, passing many side trails, then swings right and ascends the hillside with Hawthorne Brook and its ravine to the left. The ascent is steep at the start, moderates as the path passes through thick laurel, then becomes steeper again. The path crosses the brook, now just a trickle, a few yards before reaching the junction with the Pine Mtn. Trail. It continues past a stone boundary marker on Pine Mtn. and descends to Tilden Pond. At the trail junction, a left leads to Tower Mtn. via a fire road and a right leads to Tilden Pond Dam and to Berry Pond via the same fire road.

Hawthorne Trail

Distances from Pittsfield State Forest ski lodge and parking area

to Pine Mtn. Trail: 0.9 mi., 50 min.

to Pine Mtn. (2220 ft.) via Pine Mtn. Trail.: 1.4 mi., 1 hr., 15 min.

to Tilden Pond via Pine Mtn. Trail: 2 mi., 1 hr., 35 min.

Tranquility Trail (DCR)

This very easy 0.75-mi.-long universal-access trail begins a few yards west of the wooden footbridge opposite the parking area and ski lodge. The smooth paved loop path passes along the bank of Parker Brook then loops back through cool forest to the start. A wheelchair-accessible picnic area and restrooms are near the trail.

Parker Brook Trail (DCR)

This strenuous blue-blazed trail starts in back of the comfort station at the Parker Brook Campground in Pittsfield State Forest. It is open to multiuse, nonmotorized activities. At 500 ft. a cross-country ski trail exits left over a bridge to the blue-blazed Hawthorne Trail (0.3 mi.). The trail then ascends Parker Brook ravine, roughly paralleling the Berry Pond Circuit Rd. that runs along the opposite bank. Small, sparkling cascades are common in the brook along this stretch. At 1.0 mi. the circuit road swings away from the brook, and the path traces a moderate route up the dirt-and-stone trail bed to Tilden Pond, emerging immediately south of the beaver dam at the junction with the Pine Mtn. Trail. To reach Berry Pond turn right, cross the dam, and continue about 0.3 mi. on the Pine Mtn. Trail through beech forest to reach the circuit road. Turn left and ascend about 0.2 mi. to Berry Pond.

Parker Brook Trail

Distance from Parker Brook Campground comfort station

to Tilden Pond: 1.3 mi., 1 hr., 10 min.

Lulu Brook Trail (DCR)

This narrow blue-blazed hiking path parallels the north bank of Lulu Brook just a few yards from the Berry Pond Circuit Rd. that follows the south bank. It starts at the Lulu Cascade picnic area on the right of the circuit road just before the stone bridge. The trail clings to the steep side of the brook and ends at the Taconic Skyline Trail.

Lulu Brook Trail

Distances from Lulu Cascade picnic area

to Taconic Skyline Trail: 1.9 mi., 1 hr., 25 min.

Taconic Skyline Trail

This rutted jeep road runs through Pittsfield State Forest from Potter Mtn. Rd. in Lanesborough to US 20 in Hancock. It crosses the top of the Taconic Ridge and is open to motorized recreational activities. Camping along the Taconic Skyline Trail is prohibited except at Berry Pond Campground (by reservation: 877-422-6762). Historically hikers have used the Taconic Skyline Trail as the primary traverse route for the ridge or to connect to other trails. The Taconic Crest Trail (open exclusively to hiking) now serves this purpose and is the recommended trail for hikers traversing the ridge through Pittsfield State Forest.

Shaker Trail (DCR, BSA)

This very attractive moderate trail combines history and nature into one exciting experience. The 5.0-mi.-long loop trail begins and ends at Hancock Shaker Village on US 20 in Hancock and includes portions of Hancock Shaker Village and Pittsfield State Forest. The trail is maintained by the Boy Scouts of America (Hancock Shaker Village) and DCR (Pittsfield State Forest).

To reach the trailhead, travel 4.2 mi. west along US 20 from its intersection with US 7 in Pittsfield. Park in the Shaker Village parking area and proceed to the visitor center a few yards away. In the visitor center ask to hike the Shaker Trail; a "hiker" sticker will be provided. Once registered, walk to the brick meetinghouse and cross US 20 on the crosswalk. Pass through the gate and hike down the grassy unblazed cart path to the beginning of the path. The trail markers begin near the ruins of the Shaker dam. The path now turns right past more ruins, then heads left and begins to ascend Shaker Mtn. on a wide cart path. At 1.5 mi. the path reaches the top of Shaker Mtn. (1845 ft.), an area used for religious activities in the 1840s. The path then continues north and descends to the junction with the CCC Trail at 2.0 mi. (A shorter loop can be made by turning left and following the CCC Trail to the Shaker Trail and back to Hancock Shaker Village.) The path is level as it passes between Doll Mtn. and Holy Mount. At an abandoned orchard in a marshy area (2.8 mi.) the trail turns left and climbs up to the crest of Holy Mount (1968 ft.), the hilltop used by the Shaker community in New Lebanon NY. The trail crosses the summit (3.0 mi.) and past a stone wall more than a mile long that completely encloses the mountaintop. The Shaker Trail now joins the CCC Trail, following it along a brook. At 4.0 mi. the CCC Trail leaves left and Shaker Trail continues south, passing the overgrown remains of a marble quarry and reaching the ruins of the stone dam at 4.5 mi. From the dam it is a short walk back to the crosswalk at US 20.

Shaker Trail

Distances from Meeting House, Hancock Shaker Village

    to top of Shaker Mtn.: 1.5 mi., 45 min.

    to north junction with CCC Trail: 2.0 mi., 1 hr., 5 min.

    to old orchard: 2.8 mi., 1 hr., 45 min.

    to top of Holy Mount: 3.0 mi., 2 hr.

    to washed-out dam: 4.5 mi., 2 hr., 45 min.

    to Shaker Meeting House: 5.0 mi., 3 hr.

Mtn. Meadow Preserve (TTOR)

Mtn. Meadow Preserve is a 176-acre reservation that protects a wet meadow hillside at the northern edge of Williamstown in the north Berkshires. The property has two main trails. The first and most scenic traces a path around the edge of an impressive open meadow with eye-popping views of the Taconic and Greylock Ranges. The second path leaves from the meadow trail and loops over a wooded hill to a narrow view before returning down to the meadow. The woodland loop trail (0.8 mi. long) is blazed in yellow and is moderately steep. The meadow trail (1.2 mi. long) is unmarked, but the mowed path is easy to follow and to walk.

To reach Mtn. Meadow Reservation and the trailhead from the north junction of US 7 and MA 2 in Williamstown, travel north on US 7 for 1.7 mi. to Mason St. on the right. Follow Mason St. about 0.1 mi. to a parking area and kiosk.

Housatonic River Greenway Trail (HVA)

The easy Housatonic River Greenway Trail runs along the East Branch of the Housatonic River in Hinsdale and Dalton. The path runs about 0.8 mi. from the trailhead off Old Dalton Rd. in Hinsdale to MA 8 in Dalton. The trail follows the river through fields and hemlock forests to historic ruins of the Plunkett mill, including remains of the old dam and penstock. It will open in 2004.

To reach the trailhead, travel about 2.8 mi. south on MA 8 from the intersection of MA 8 and 8A in Dalton. Turn left onto Old Dalton Rd., cross the bridge, then turn left into the parking area. The trail is on land owned by the Crane Paper Company and is maintained by the Housatonic Valley Association (HVA).

October Mtn. State Forest (DCR)

October Mtn. State Forest is the largest state forest in the commonwealth, with more than 16,000 acres of woodlands and lakes. The forest sports five large lakes—Buckley-Dunton Lake, October Mtn. Reservoir, Finerty Pond, Schoolhouse Reservoir, and Felton Lake. Halfway Pond is a wonderful example of a quaking bog, and Washington Mtn. Meadow is a huge fen with many exciting plant and animal communities. Some of the higher points include Walling Mtn. (2220 ft.), Bald Top (2040 ft.), and Beckett Mtn. (2200 ft.). Forty-six campsites are available at the camping area on Woodland St. in Lee; many are universally accessible.

Appalachian Trail

The Appalachian Trail runs through nearly 7 mi. of October Mtn. State Forest from near Greenwater Pond in the south to just east of Sandwash Reservoir in the north. For a complete description see Appalachian Trail, Section 6, US 20 to Pittsfield Rd.

Washington Mtn. Meadow Interpretive Trail System

This little-known trail system is one of the pleasant surprises of the Berkshires, incorporating a 0.2-mi.-long universal-access nature trail and nearly 3.4 mi. of hiking through one of the most unique ecosystems in Massachusetts. The Washington Mtn. Meadow Interpretive Trail is a complex of four trails—the Interpretive Loop Trail (1.5 mi.), Knob Loop Trail (0.4 mi.), Outer Loop Trail (1.4 mi.), and Marsh View Accessible Trail (0.2 mi.). The trail complex thoroughly explores Washington Mtn. Meadow, a huge boggy fen that is the remnant of failed attempts in the 1980s to build a lake on this site. The timber was removed and the dams constructed, but the huge earth-and-stone creations leaked and the lake never came to be. What did come to be was an immense wet meadow that has become a haven for myriad plants and animals.

The Washington Mtn. Meadow Interpretive Trail is in the heart of October Mtn. State Forest, but situated so as to be easily overlooked. To reach the trailhead from Lee and the junction of US 20 and the Mass Pike (Exit 2) follow US 20 east 1.2 mi. and turn left onto Maple St. Continue 2.3 mi. to Mill St. At the stop sign turn right and travel 0.5 mi. to Willow Hill Rd. Turn sharp right onto Willow Hill Rd. (this becomes Woodland Rd.), and drive past the state forest campground on the right, followed by the October Mtn. State Forest Headquarters on the left (maps available). Follow Woodland Rd. to Woods Pond on the left, bear right onto Roaring Brook Rd., and follow the dirt road along the pond's shore for 0.5 mi. to paved but steep Schermerhorn Rd. on the right. Turn right and travel 3.4 mi. over mostly dirt roads to Lenox-Whitney Place. Turn right onto Lenox-Whitney Place and continue 1.3 mi. to a four-way junction. Turn right onto Meadow Trail and drive 0.5 mi. to a parking area on the left. The trailhead is at the north end of the parking area. Trail maps are available at the trailhead.

Marsh View Accessible Trail

This packed-stone-dust trail runs 0.2 mi. from the parking area to a universal-access overlook. The trail passes 19th-century cellar holes and a cemetery, both in the shade of tall Norway spruce planted in the 1930s. The path ends at a northwesterly view overlooking the heart of Washington Mtn. Meadow.

Marsh View Accessible Trail

Distance from parking area
   to overlook: 0.2 mi., 10 min.

Interpretive Loop Trail

From the parking area follow the Marsh View Accessible Trail to the overlook at 0.2 mile, where the blue-blazed Interpretive Loop Trail begins. Turn left from the overlook and descend through shrubby growth to the base of the meadow. The trail crosses the fen on a long run of bog bridging, climbs the far shore, and passes two junctions with the Knob Loop Trail on the left. The path crosses a hemlock swamp on more bridging before reaching the Outer Loop junction at 0.8 mi. Turn right to an overlook with a beautiful view of the marsh and a large beaver pond usually teeming with wildlife. The path skirts the shore and crosses the meadow on a very long run of bog bridging, reaching the far shore and the second junction with the Outer Loop Trail at 1.1 mi. The path now climbs up the ridge and wanders through woods, rejoining the Marsh View Accessible Trail a few yards south of the accessible overlook.

Interpretive Loop Trail

Distances from parking area

to Knob Loop Trail: 0.4 mi., 15 min.

to west junction with Outer Loop Trail: 0.8 mi., 25 min.

to east junction with Outer Loop Trail: 1.1 mi., 40 min.

to junction with Marsh View Accessible Trail: 1.7 mi., 55 min.

Outer Loop Trail

This woodland path begins on a bluff at a signed junction with the Interpretive Loop Trail. From the junction the path descends to the marsh and crosses the outlet of a beaver dam on bog bridging. The path then climbs onto high ground and traces the perimeter of the immense north portion of the meadow. At the far north end of the meadow the trail crosses Washington Mtn. Brook before swinging south and ending at the junction with the Interpretive Loop Trail on the eastern end of the meadow.

Outer Loop Trail

Distances from Interpretive Loop Trail (western trailhead)

to crossing of beaver pond outlet: 0.1 mi., 5 min.

to crossing of Washington Mtn. Brook: 0.75 mi., 20 min.

to junction with Interpretive Loop Trail (eastern trailhead): 1.4 mi., 40 min.

Knob Loop Trail

Knob Loop Trail is a short (0.4 mi.) loop trail that explores the eastern side of Knob Hill, a wooded knoll about 100 ft. higher than the surrounding meadow. The trailhead is located on the western portion of the Interpretive Loop Trail, about 0.4 mi. from the parking area.

Schermerhorn Gorge Trail

To reach the trailhead from Lee and the junction of US 20 and the Mass Pike (Exit 2), follow US 20 east 1.2 mi. and turn left onto Maple St. Continue 2.3 mi. to Mill St. At the stop sign turn right and travel 0.5 mi. to Willow Hill Rd., turn sharp right onto Willow Hill Rd. (which becomes Woodland Rd.), and drive past the state forest campground on the right, followed by the October Mtn. State Forest Headquarters on the left (maps available). Follow Woodland Rd. to Woods Pond on the left, bear right onto Roaring Brook Rd., and follow the dirt road along the pond's shore for 0.5 mi. to paved but steep Schermerhorn Rd. on the right. Turn right and travel up the hill 1.0 mi. to the parking area on the left by the state forest gate. From the gate walk down the woods road about 0.1 mi. and cross the stone bridge below Fenton Lake.

The Schermerhorn Gorge Trail is a moderately difficult loop path that runs along both sides of the brook as it passes through the gorge. On descent, the path following the north bank is best. On ascent, use the south route. The steepest portion is near Roaring Brook Rd., with an overall elevation gain of more than 500 ft. in 0.8 mi.

Schermerhorn Gorge Trail

Distances from trailhead at old stone bridge (Fenton Lake)

to Roaring Brook Rd.: 0.8 mi., 30 min.

to old stone bridge (circuit): 1.6 mi., 1 hr., 15 min.

Pleasant Valley Sanctuary (MAS)

This 1400-acre wildlife sanctuary, maintained by the Massachusetts Audubon Society, is located on the east slope of Lenox Mtn. in the town of Lenox. A large trail network explores beaver ponds, marshes, streams, and forests. All 7 mi. of trails are blazed with blue and yellow marks: the blue blazes lead away from the sanctuary office (primary trailhead), while the yellow blazes lead toward the office. All trail junctions are clearly signed.

From the intersection of US 7 and 20 drive north 3 mi. to West Dugway Rd. on the left. Follow West Dugway Rd. to the intersection at 0.75 mi. Turn left onto West Mtn. Rd. (dirt) and travel 0.8 mi. to the sanctuary entrance and parking. Trail information is available at the office near the parking area.

Pike's Pond Trail (MAS)

A very easy, relaxing walk around the waters and wetlands of Pike's Pond. The trail begins at the office and heads across the lawn to a long boardwalk that negotiates a shrubby swamp. The path then roughly follows the south shore of the pond before crossing a section of Yokun Brook on a wooden bridge at 0.3 mi. The trail swings around the west shore, passing the Trail of the Ledges (left) and Yokun Trail (left) before running very closely along the north shore. The path then leaves the pond and ends at the Bluebird Trail about 400 ft. north of the office.

Pike's Pond Trail

Distances from the sanctuary office

   to bridge over Yokun Brook: 0.3 mi., 15 min.

   to junction with Bluebird Trail: 0.5 mi., 25 min.

   to office (circuit): 0.6 mi., 30 min.

Trail of the Ledges (MAS)

This strenuous, sometimes very steep trail leads from the Pike's Pond Trail to the top of Lenox Mtn. (2126 ft.), an elevation gain of about 800 ft. The summit area is owned by the state of Massachusetts and managed by the Department of Conservation and Recreation (DCR). It offers excellent views to the west and north.

   The trail begins from its junction with the Pike's Pond Trail located 0.3 mi. from the office. The trail initially ascends along a stream and past the junctions of the Waycross and Ravine Trails. The trail then leaves the brook and climbs steeply to the Laurel Trail, where a ledge offers an excellent view. It continues past another lookout on the right at 0.75 mi. and reaches the summit at 1.25 mi. *Note: The Trail of the Ledges is not recommended for descent; use the Overbrook Trail on the return trip*.

Trail of the Ledges

Distances from Pike's Pond Trail

   to Laurel Trail: 0.5 mi., 20 min.

   to lookout: 0.75 mi., 45 min.

   to summit of Lenox Mtn.: 1.25 mi., 1 hr.

Overbrook Trail (MAS)

The recommended route for descent in all weather conditions, this steep and strenuous trail also offers an alternate route to the summit. To reach the trail, follow the Bluebird Trail north from the office to the Ovenbird Trail at 0.3 mi. Turn left onto the Ovenbird Trail, which follows a brook a short distance to the Overbrook Trail. The Overbrook Trail heads northwest up the slope of Lenox Mtn., passing the four-way junction with the Great Hemlock and Laurel Trails at 0.5 mi. The path ascends along a ravine, weaving from bank to bank before leaving the sanctuary and climbing to the summit at 1.3 mi.

Overbrook Trail

Distances from office

> *to* Overbrook Trail: 0.3 mi., 15 min.
>
> *to* Laurel Trail: 0.5 mi., 25 min.
>
> *to* summit of Lenox Mtn.: 1.3 mi., 1 hr.

Field Farm (TTOR)

Field Farm in Willamstown holds more than 300 acres of pasture, fields, wetlands, and woodlands explored by over 4 mi. of trails. The property includes a guest house accommodating up to 14 visitors and landscaped gardens dotted with modern art sculptures. Much of the land surrounding the house has been used for agriculture since at least 1750. The property is shaped like an elongated rectangle 1.5 mi. long astride the foothills of the northern Taconics, offering grand views of Mt. Greylock across the valley to the east. Trails are blazed in white.

To reach Field Farm, from the five-corners junction in South Williamstown (intersection of US 7 and MA 43) turn onto MA 43 west for a few yards, then turn immediately right onto Sloan Rd. Travel 1.1 mi. to the entrance on the right. For hiking follow the right fork of the driveway, which leads to a parking area near the garage. For the guest house continue straight to the parking area on the west side of the house.

South Trail

This trail leaves the Pond Trail at the southeast end of the pond and heads south along a marshy area. It soon crosses Sloan Rd. and continues along the wetland, crossing the outflow at 0.2 mi. The trail then splits. Turning right to begin the loop, the path heads northwest, then west along the border of forest and field, coming to a brook at 0.45 mi. Following the stream for a short distance, the path then wanders downslope, crosses a low ridge, and heads uphill to complete the loop at 1.3 mi., returning to the trailhead at 1.5 mi.

South Trail

Distances from pondside trailhead

    to wetland outlet: 0.2 mi., 10 min.

    to brook: 0.45 mi., 20 min.

    to close of trail loop: 1.3 mi., 50 min.

    to pond trailhead: 1.5 mi., 1 hr.

North Trail

The North Trail begins west of the guest house at a sign in an open field, then runs directly to the fence line at the west end of a cornfield. Turning north, the path reaches a fenced pasture at 0.3 mi. Pass through the stile and into the active pasture. Watch for cows and cow droppings. The trail continues along the fence line, exiting the pasture at 0.5 mi. The path enters the woods, then turns right, descending, swinging right again, and reentering the pasture. This portion of the trail can be difficult to follow, as the trail posts are sometimes knocked over by cows and the animals make their own trails through the bush. At 1.0 mi. the Oak Loop Trail leaves left, and at 1.1 mi. rejoins at its eastern junction. The North Trail follows the fence line, exits the pasture for the last time, then runs south through a cornfield to the southeast corner of the pond. To return to the guest house follow the Pond Trail northwest through the fields to the north side of the house.

North Trail

Distances from the Field Farm guest house

    to first pasture stile: 0.3 mi., 15 min.

    to second pasture stile: 0.5 mi., 25 min.

    to Oak Loop Trail junction: 1.0 mi., 45 min.

    to southeast end of pond: 1.5 mi., 1 hr., 5 min.

Oak Loop Trail

A few years ago the Oak Loop Trail was doubled in length with the addition of the caves loop, a very interesting path that passes by the McMaster cave system. From the eastern junction with the North Trail, the Oak Loop Trail passes through the fence line and into the woods. It crosses a brook and climbs easily through the forest, coming to a short connector path at 0.25 mi. The trail continues up the ridge through open woods and over the height-of-land at about 1090 ft. The path now descends along the ridge line to an intersection in a low, level spot at 0.6 mi. The trail turns left (another dead-end path leaves right) and follows the very level trail bed to the caves at 0.8 mi. The trail is actually on top of the caves, so it is hard to see them. They are a series of three entrances 2–3 ft. wide, at the drainage line of the wetland to the west of the trail. In winter the caves can be clogged with ice, damming the wetland and forming a pond. In spring when everything melts the pond can disappear in minutes as the water floods down the caves.

From the caves the path continues easily past the connector trail to a brook, then back into the pasture to meet the North Trail at 1.1 mi.

Oak Loop Trail

Distance from eastern junction with North Trail

to connector path: 0.25 mi., 10 min.

to north end of loop: 0.6 mi., 20 min.

to caves: 0.8 mi., 30 min.

to western junction with North Trail: 1.1 mi., 45 min.

Taconic Crest Trail (THC, DCR)

The white-blazed Taconic Crest Trail (TCT) runs for 35 mi. in a north–south direction along the ridge of the Taconic Range, passing through Massachusetts, New York, and Vermont. The trail runs from Prosser Hollow in Petersburg NY, to US 20 in Hancock MA. The trail elevation varies from 1000 ft. at Prosser Hollow to 2798 ft. on the summit of Berlin Mtn. The cumulative ascent along the trail in a south–north direction is 6700 ft. The trail's average elevation exceeds 2200 ft. The Taconic Range is densely covered by mixed hardwood forests with red spruce and balsam fir in the highest elevations. Open, grassy balds and meadows dot the mountains, offering many places to sit and enjoy the view of the Green Mtns., the Catskills, Greylock and the Hoosac Range, and even the far-off Adirondacks.

The trail was established and is mostly maintained by the Taconic Hiking Club (THC) of Troy, NY. The Massachusetts Department of Conservation and Recreation maintains the trail within Pittsfield State Forest. The TCT is marked at intersections with blue squares with white-diamond inserts that say Taconic Crest Trail, and within the trail corridor with white diamonds. Access trails are designated by similar blue markers. Because this is a ridge trail, water sources close to the trail are infrequent. The following descriptions run from north to south and are divided into sections, each a day's hike apart. Several side trails and access trails that connect with the Taconic Crest Trail are described later in the book, under North Taconic Trails.

Section 1. Prosser Hollow NY to Petersburg Pass (NY 2) (7.4 mi.)

Note: This section of the trail is closed to mountain bikes and motorized vehicles. The northern terminus of the TCT is located on Prosser Hollow Rd., which is off NY 22 about 2.4 mi. north of NY 2 in Petersburg. The trail rises steeply to the ridge and turns south, reaching a sharp dropoff to the east. Continuing south, at 4.5 mi. a side trail (marked S.H.) enters from the left (east). Following it downhill a short distance leads to the fabled Snow Hole. The side trail approaches the cliff from the crest, then swings around to the narrow mouth of the crevice. The rock is similar to soapstone, and there are initials with dates as far back as the middle 1800s here. In the Snow Hole it's cold all the time, with snow frequently lasting until June.

From the Snow Hole the trail continues south through hardwoods, emerging into a number of clearings—some brushy, some grassy—on the western side of the ridge that look out over the valley. Visible below is NY 2 to Petersburg NY, the old abandoned ski area at Petersburg Pass, and Mt. Greylock to the southeast. About 1 mi. after the clearings the red-blazed Birch Brook Trail descends left to Hopkins Memorial Forest. In another 0.75 mi. the blue-blazed Shepherd's Well Trail exits left. The TCT now eventually emerges in a clearing near a sign prohibiting mountain bikes and motorized vehicles from this section of trail, and descends to meet NY 2 at Petersburg Pass at 7.4 mi. Parking is available on the south side of NY 2.

Taconic Crest Trail: Prosser Hollow NY to Petersburg Pass (NY 2)

Distances from Prosser Hollow Rd.

to top of ridge: 1.8 mi., 1 hr.

to side trail to Snow Hole: 4.5 mi., 2 hr., 50 min.

to Birch Brook Trail: 5.5 mi., 3 hr., 30 min.

to Shepherd's Well Trail: 6.9 mi., 4 hr., 30 min.

to Petersburg Pass (NY 2): 7.4 mi., 4 hr., 50 min.

Section 2. Petersburg Pass (NY 2) to Southeast Hollow and Mills Hollow Trails (5.2 mi.)

Note: This section is heavily used by mountain bikes, ATVs, and dirt bikes. The trail from the south side of Mt. Raimer to the top of Berlin Mtn. is a mess of mudholes, erosion, and bootleg bypass trails. The parking lot is located 4.0 mi. west from the intersection of MA 2 and US 7 in Williamstown. The parking area has a kiosk at the south end near bootleg trails that dirt bikes and mountain bikes have created up the north slope of Mt. Raimer. The white-blazed TCT exits the parking area at the southwest corner, past placed boulders and a small view west. It soon reaches a side trail that descends right while the TCT keeps left, briefly dips, then rises steeply on a badly eroded old woods roads with sections of loose rock. The path ascends to a junction with a red-blazed trail that leaves left to climb to the top of Mt. Raimer. Stay to the right, following white markers on a heavily rutted woods road that winds along the wooded ridge. The trail turns right and descends to an open clearing high above Berlin Pass, with extensive views over the back of Berlin Mtn.

Descending to the pass on a path of loose stone and ruts, the trail intersects the old Albany–Boston Post Rd. (also known as the Greene Hollow Access Trail and the Berlin Pass Trail; description under North Taconic Trails). To the west it is 1.4 mi. to Greene Hollow and 4.5 mi. to Berlin, NY. To the east it is 0.8 mi. to Berlin Rd., in Williamstown MA. There is water down the Berlin Pass Trail to the east. Bottle gentians are common here in late summer.

Crossing Post Rd. and ascending the woods road south, the trail winds up the woods road toward Berlin Mtn. Near the top is a badly eroded section of staircase ledge and a long bootleg bypass on the left used by ATVs and mountain bikes. The summit is a grassy meadow dotted with hardwoods and evergreens. The concrete footings of the fire tower mark the summit (2798 ft.) at 2.67 mi. To the east the Class of '33 Trail descends into the woods toward the old Williams College ski area. From the summit, the highest point on the trail, there are fine views in all directions. Especially prominent is Mt. Greylock to the east.

From Berlin Mtn. the TCT descends southeast through a dense spruce grove then open, predominantly hardwood, forest, crossing the crest of an unnamed peak (2721 ft.) 0.35 mi. southeast of Berlin Mtn. The trail now makes a long descent along the ridge, reaching a saddle at 3.7 mi. It then climbs steeply for 0.25 mi. and moderates as it crests the next summit (2542 ft.), overlooking South Williamstown. The trail now descends to a col where the Phelps Trail (Williamstown Rural Lands Foundation) enters left at 4.2 mi. This steep 1.5-mi.-long blue-blazed trail follows the ravine of a brook down to Oblong Rd. in South Williamstown.

From the Phelps Trail the path cruises over a pretty section of ridge, crossing two low peaks before dropping down to the saddle at the head of Southeast Hollow. Here it intersects the Southeast Hollow Trail at 5.2 mi.; this trail leads 1.7 mi. to Southeast Hollow Rd., then on to Berlin NY. To the left is Mills Hollow Trail, which leads to Oblong Rd. in Williamstown MA.

Wild ginger is found near the junction with the Southeast Hollow Trail. Water is found about 0.7 mi. down this access trail. A few yards south of the junction is a stone monument marking the New York–Massachusetts border.

Taconic Crest Trail: Petersburg Pass (NY 2) to Southeast Hollow and Mills Hollow Trails

Distance from Petersburg Pass (NY 2)

   to Albany–Boston Post Rd. (Berlin Pass Trail): 1.9 mi., 1 hr., 15 min.

   to summit of Berlin Mtn.: 2.7 mi., 1 hr., 50 min.

   to Phelps Trail: 4.2 mi., 3 hr.

   to Southeast Hollow and Mills Hollow Trails: 5.2 mi., 3 hr., 30 min.

Section 3. Southeast Hollow and Mills Hollow Trails to Mattison Hollow Trail (2.5 mi.)

The TCT proceeds south from the junction with the Southeast Hollow Trail and in a few yards turns sharp left at the stone monument marking the New York–Massachusetts border. After a short distance it climbs steeply to a nearly level terrace, runs its length, then climbs to an open peak (2646 ft.) that straddles the state line at 0.7 mi. From the peak the trail makes an easy descent over a really nice stretch to a trail passing over three small knobby summits before bending right (southwest) and dropping to the junction of the Mattison Hollow Trail in a col at 2.5 mi.

Taconic Crest Trail: Southeast Hollow and Mills Hollow Trails to Mattison Hollow Trail

Distances from Southeast Hollow and Mills Hollow Trails

  to open peak: 0.7 mi., 30 min.

  to Mattison Hollow Trail: 2.5 mi., 1 hr., 15 min.

Section 4. Mattison Hollow Trail to Potter Mtn. Rd. Trailhead (9.8 mi.)

The TCT proceeds south from the junction with the Mattison Hollow Trail, climbing moderately for about 0.4 mi., then leveling out as it crosses the wide shoulder of a peak. At 0.5 mi. is a metal state-line marker; farther on is a stone state-line monument. Water is available in the next low place, where the TCT joins a snowmobile trail.

The trail now wanders over Misery Mtn., a ridge with steep slopes creased with deep ravines on the east and west. The ridge crest is broad and generally level, with undulations typical of mountainous terrain. The wide nature of the ridge and the wooded knolls along the way can make following the path more challenging here than elsewhere on the range. After crossing the main peak (2611 ft.) of Misery Mtn. at 2.2 mi. the trail veers south through hardwoods and across several knobs. It exits off the jeep trail that was the old TCT (watch for blazes) and comes out on the last summit in an open meadow. From the last summit the trail descends steeply about 0.4 mi. to the crest of Rathburn Hollow at 3.2 mi.

The trail crosses a small stream immediately south of Rathburn Hollow, then easily ascends along the ridge through hardwoods to the top of an open meadow known as Bill's Lunch. Here there is a small grove of evergreens and good views of the Taconic Valley.

For the next 0.75 mi. the trail descends steeply through the meadow, enters the woods, and follows a small stream. It then turns westward downhill through mixed hardwoods and evergreens. After crossing a stream, it crosses a snowmobile trail and begins a long ascent to the open summit of Rounds Mtn. (2257 ft.) at 2.5 mi.

At Rounds Mtn. the trail turns left for about 100 yd. on a well-used dirt road, then turns sharp left into the woods. The unmarked Rounds Mtn. Trail continues straight ahead. (*Caution*: *Due to an absence of trees, neither of the two trail junctions with this dirt road is well marked.*)

The trail now descends steadily, steeply in spots, finally meeting a well-used woods road at about 3.2 mi. Crossing the road, the trail makes a gradual ascent through a birch grove, turns sharp right, and descends steeply to the village of Hancock MA. From here the trail follows roads a short distance through the village to MA 43 and Potter Mtn. Rd., then continues on Potter Mtn. Rd. about 1.2 mi. to a trailhead at 5.9 mi.

Taconic Crest Trail: Mattison Hollow Trail to Potter Mtn. Rd. Trailhead

Distances from Mattison Hollow Trail

  to main peak of Misery Mtn.: 2.2 mi., 1 hr., 15 min.

  to meadow on last summit: 2.8 mi., 2 hr., 15 min.

  to Rathburn Hollow: 3.2 mi., 2 hr., 35 min.

  to summit of Rounds Mtn.: 6.4 mi., 3 hr., 45 min.

  to woods road: 7.1 mi., 4 hr., 10 min.

  to Potter Mtn. Rd. trailhead: 9.8 mi., 5 hr., 30 min.

Section 5. Hancock (Potter Mtn. Rd.) to US 20 (8.9 mi.)

The TCT has been relocated through Pittsfield State Forest so that it no longer intersects the Taconic Skyline Trail at any point between Potter Mtn. Rd. and the trail's southern terminus at US 20 in Hancock. The TCT is open only as a footpath and is closed to ATVs, ORVs, and mountain bikes in the forest. Due to the heavy use of ATVs, ORVs, and mountain bikes, the Taconic Skyline Trail is not recommended for hiking.

From the trailhead on Potter Mtn. Rd. located about 0.25 mi. west for the trailhead of the Taconic Skyline Trail and about 1.2 mi. east of MA 43 in Hancock, the trail heads south, downhill. It then turns left (east) for a short distance, then regains its southerly course. As it nears the Taconic Skyline Trail the TCT begins a long slab of Pease Ridge, hugging the extreme western edge of the mountain. The trail reaches the far northwestern loop of Berry Pond Circuit Rd. (paved) at 2.5 mi., emerging to a great view west amid the azalea fields.

The trail then follows the road for a short distance, passing more azaleas (bloom time is late May to June) and Berry Pond (campground here)—the highest or second highest pond in the state, depending on whom you talk to. The trail now leaves Berry Pond Circuit Rd. for the last time at 3.0 mi. and heads southwest, descends to a low point, and then climbs to the top of Tower Mtn. and the junction with the Pine Mtn. Trail at 3.7 mi. From Tower Mtn. the path descends to Brickhouse Mtn. Rd., crosses this woods road at 4.0 mi. a few yards west of the Taconic Skyline Trail, then very closely parallels the Taconic Skyline Trail to Lebanon Springs Rd. at 5.7 mi. The trail along this section is most often thickly wooded with oak and other hardwoods, with some narrow glimpses of the valley to the west through the trees.

The trail continues to closely parallel the Taconic Skyline Trail, staying just to its west and crossing a woods road at 6.7 mi. The TCT continues south, skirting the Taconic Skyline Trail near the dam of Twin Ponds at 7.3 mi. Twin Ponds were built generations ago by the Shakers of New Lebanon as a water source, and the stonework of the dam is an example of their precise craftsmanship. From Twin Ponds the TCT continues south, coming close to the Taconic Skyline Trail near Cranberry Pond, then tracing a path down the slope to end at the west end of the parking area on the north side of US 20 at 8.9 mi.

Taconic Crest Trail: Hancock (Potter Mtn. Rd.) to US 20

Distances from Potter Mtn. Rd.

  to Berry Pond Circuit Rd.: 2.5 mi., 1 hr., 20 min.

  to Lebanon Springs Rd.: 5.7 mi., 3 hr.

  to woods road: 6.7 mi., 3 hr., 50 min.

  to Twin Ponds: 7.3 mi., 4 hr., 40 min.

  to southern terminus at US 20: 8.9 mi., 5 hr., 35 min.

North Taconic Trails
Birch Brook Trail (WOC)

This access trail to the Taconic Crest Trail begins in the Hopkins Memorial Forest of Williams College in Williamstown MA. To get to the forest, go west on Main St. in Williamstown to US 7 north, turn right, and proceed north for 0.3 mi. Bear left onto Bulkley St., continue 1 mi. to Northwest Hill Rd., and turn right. The Birch Brook Trail is 1.4 mi. along Northwest Hill Rd.

On the left side of the road are two circular turnouts. From the first turnout the trail ascends gently and then descends, making a sharp bend to the left. It continues to the north branch of Birch Brook at 0.9 mi., bearing right along the north side of the brook. The trail climbs to the west, parallel to the brook. The Hopkins Forest Loop Trail exits left at 1 mi. The trail gradually moves away from the brook, and the loop trail reenters from the left at 1.3 mi. The trail then turns left and ascends to the last stream crossing at 1.4 mi. A mile-long steep climb through deciduous forest (crossing the Massachusetts–New York line at 2 mi.), interspersed with several beautiful patches of ferns along the trail, ends at the junction with the white-blazed Taconic Crest Trail.

Birch Brook Trail

Distances from Northwest Hill Rd.

to Birch Brook: 0.9 mi., 35 min.

to Taconic Crest Trail: 2.7 mi., 1 hr., 50 min.

Berlin Pass Trail (WOC)

To reach this blue-blazed trail, start 3 mi. southwest of Williamstown at the junction of US 7 and MA 2. Take MA 2 uphill (west) for 0.5 mi. and turn left onto Torrey Woods Rd., which meets Berlin Rd.; continue west on Berlin Rd. to the abandoned Williams College ski area parking lot. Park on the right (north) side of the lot and take the path to the dirt road just ahead. (Do not take the trail blocked by a vandalized gate.)

This strenuous trail, once a section of the Boston–Albany Post Rd., leads uphill through a forest that gradually transitions from ash, sugar maple, poplar, and red oak to a beech and paper birch mix with oak, hop hornbeam, and red maple. At 0.8 mi. the trail reaches the Taconic Ridge at Berlin Pass (2220 ft.), where it intersects the white-blazed Taconic Crest Trail. Following the TCT to the left (south), it is 1.2 mi. to the summit of Berlin Mtn. (The remains of an old charcoal kiln are located off the trail 100 ft. to the right, 0.5 mi. beyond the pass.) For a loop back to the parking lot climb Berlin Mtn. and then descend via the Class of '33 Trail (4.5 mi.) or the steep and unmaintained paths of the old Williams College ski area (3.0 mi.). The old Post Rd. crosses the pass and descends the west slope of the Taconic Range to Berlin NY. Following the TCT to the right (north) from the junction leads across scenic open meadows to an abandoned ski area and NY 2 in Petersburg Pass.

Berlin Pass Trail

Distances from Williams College ski area parking lot

to Berlin Pass (Taconic Crest Trail): 0.8 mi., 1 hr.

to summit of Berlin Mtn. (via TCT south): 2 mi., 1 hr., 30 min.

to NY 2 in Petersburg Pass (via TCT north): 2.7 mi., 2 hr., 15 min.

Class of '33 Trail (WOC)

This blue-blazed trail, once known as the Berlin Mtn. Trail, was originally constructed in 1933 by members of the Williams Outing Club. It was relocated around its original trailhead at Haskin Farm in 1980. To reach the trailhead by car, follow the instructions under the Berlin Pass Trail. The trail begins on Berlin Rd., 1.1 mi. from the junction with Torrey Woods Rd. The parking lot, located on the left side of the road a short distance past some residences and the Haskin Farm, can accommodate 2–3 cars.

From the parking area, the blue-blazed trail enters the woods, quickly turning left along a woods road. Follow blazes through left and right turns to Haley Brook and the first interpretive sign of the WRLF Loop Trail (0.2 mi.). Cross the brook and climb the far bank to a well-signed junction. Bear left (east) to stay on the Class of '33 Trail; the WRLF Loop Trail continues to the right. After crossing the brook, it joins another woods road, turning left along it and then right up a steep gully. The trail levels off and then descends to the site of the old Williams Outing Club Berlin Cabin, marked by the remains of an outhouse, at 0.7 mi. Here the trail turns sharp right, crosses a stream, and turns right again onto another woods road. At 1.0 mi. the trail leaves the woods road and begins a steep ascent to a ridge at 1.2 mi. Recent logging (1995–98) has widened old tracks into a confusing network. Large blue blazes mark a boundary line, not the trail that follows the ridge-line logging road. Stay high on the ridge—if you start to head downhill, you are going the wrong way.

At 1.5 mi. is a fantastic view of Broad Brook and the Dome to the northeast. At 1.8 mi. continue straight on the ridge through a confusing nexus of roads toward the summit. One last turn left up the top of the old Williams College ski area leads to the clear summit of Berlin Mtn. at 2.0 mi.

Four small cement piers mark the site of an old fire tower. A panoramic view includes the rolling hills of Southeast Hollow to the southwest, with the Catskills rising in the distance. Albany and Troy are visible to the west, and on a clear day the southern Adirondacks to the northwest may be in view.

There are three options for the return to the parking lot. The Class of '33 Trail can be retraced for a 4.0-mi. round trip. Alternatively, instead of taking the first right onto the '33 Trail, continue straight (northeast) down the abandoned ski slope (3.5 mi. total). This route is unmaintained and extremely steep, so use caution. Finally, you can follow the Taconic Crest Trail (white markers) and off-road vehicle tracks north to the Berlin Pass Trail and back to the lot at 4.3 mi.

Class of '33 Trail

Distances from Berlin Rd.

   to Hemlock Brook: 0.3 mi., 15 min.

   to ridge: 1.2 mi., 1 hr.

   to summit of Berlin Mtn.: 2.0 mi., 1 hr., 50 min.

R.R.R. Brooks Trail (WOC)

Paralleling MA 2, this blue-blazed trail is a direct route from Williamstown toward Petersburg Pass through 930-acre Taconic Trail State Forest. One of the highlights is Flora Glen, a beautiful wooded area that is believed to have been the inspiration for William Cullen Bryant's poem "Thanatopsis." From the junction of MA 2 and US 7 at the Williams Inn in Williamstown, go south on US 7 for 0.8 mi. to graveled Bee Hill Rd. on the right. Ascend to a small reservoir and dam.

The moderate trail starts on the left end of the dam, turns right into the woods, clings to the side of Flora Glen, and gradually meets a stream. Vegetation along the valley side above the stream alternates between northern hardwood (mostly maple, beech, and birch) and evergreen (spruce and hemlock). The trail descends to the level of the stream (0.5 mi.), then makes an abrupt left (0.6 mi.) to climb steeply up a series of steps out of the streambed. Just below the remains of an old Boy Scout shelter (0.8 mi.), the Fitch Trail enters from the left.

At 1.4 mi. the trail comes out on the southeast end of a field and continues across the field on a barely noticeable footpath until the narrow field opens up on both sides. The trail is often wet and waist-high with weeds. It goes diagonally left across the field and toward the treeline straight ahead. (When MA 2 becomes visible, keep it in sight but do not hike toward it, heading instead for the opposite treeline.) The trail bears left along a dirt road after entering the treeline and becomes more visible just before the dirt road meets the highway. The trail follows the woods road that parallels the highway for 0.5 mi., reaching the junction with the Shepherd's Well Trail at 2.4 mi. The Shepherd's Well Trail eventually ascends the ridge past a scenic clearing, enters the woods, and soon meets the white-blazed Taconic Crest Trail at Petersburg Pass.

R.R.R. Brooks Trail

Distances from dam on Bee Hill Rd.

   to Fitch Trail: 0.8 mi., 40 min.

   to Shepherd's Well Trail: 2.4 mi., 2 hr., 10 min.

   to Taconic Crest Trail (at Petersburg Pass) via the Shepherd's Well Trail: 3.3
      mi., 2 hr., 30 min.

Pine Cobble Trail (WOC)

Pine Cobble (1894 ft.), to the northeast of Williamstown, offers one of the finest panoramic views of the Hoosic River Valley. Within easy walking distance of the Williams College campus, this blue-blazed trail is a favorite with many Williams College students. The word cobble refers to the exposed outcropping of quartzite bedrock that is the destination of most of those who use the trail. On a clear day, the outcrop is easily visible from the valley floor, several miles away.

To reach the Pine Cobble trailhead by car, take MA 2 east from its intersection with US 7 at the Williams Inn in Williamstown. After 0.6 mi. turn left onto Cole Ave. at the first stoplight. Cross a bridge over the Hoosic River and railroad tracks just before North Hoosac Rd. Turn right onto North Hoosac Rd. (1.4 mi from the Williams Inn), then left onto Pine Cobble Rd. (1.8 mi.). Park in the parking area on the left 0.2 mi. up the hill. The trailhead is across the road.

To reach the trailhead on foot from the Williams College campus, walk down Stetson Rd. past the tennis courts to Cole Field. Follow the road around Eph's Pond, east through a gate to Cole Ave. Turn left and cross the Hoosic River to the intersection with North Hoosac Rd. Head diagonally right across North Hoosac Rd. to Cole's Grove Rd., around a gate, and into the Pine Cobble Development. At the mailboxes, turn right. The trailhead is 300 yd. down the road on the left.

From the Pine Cobble Trail sign hike parallel to the road for 200 yd. before turning left and ascending gradually into the woods. At 0.5 mi. the trail levels out on a plateau that was once the shore of glacial Lake Bascom, which once filled the entire Hoosic Valley to a depth of about 500 ft.!

At 0.8 mi. a side trail to the right marks the halfway point. It leads 350 ft. downhill to Bear Spring, a slight upwelling at the base of a steep cliff topped with hemlocks. Since the spring is the only open water on the south side of Pine Cobble, it attracts many species of wildlife, including chipmunks, rabbits, and deer. About 200 ft. above the Bear Spring trail, the blue-diamond-blazed Class of '98 Trail diverges to the left. Currently, there is no sign announcing the beginning of the '98 Trail, but there is a sign at this intersection labeling the Pine Cobble Trail.

Continue at a moderately steep grade to a more level area at 1.0 mi., where the trail turns to the southeast. Yellow diamond-shaped blazes mark the entrance to the Williamstown Rural Lands Foundation Pine Cobble Summit Natural Area of Clarksburg State Forest. Cross two small jumbled rock outcroppings and follow a sharp left turn at the intersection with an old trail (1.1 mi.).

Watch for an unusual triplet oak tree with a water-filled basin at its center at 1.4 mi. After the original tree was cut down, three shoots sprouted around the edges of the old stump while the center rotted away. This flat section of the trail is also an excellent place to see trailing arbutus, the Massachusetts state flower, which usually blooms in early April.

A steep stretch completes the climb (1.5 mi.). From the trail sign at the crest of the hill, several short (0.1 mi.) trails to the right lead out onto the quartzite outcrops of Pine Cobble. Enjoy an excellent view of the Greylock Range across the valley to the south, with the summit of Mt. Greylock clearly distinguished by the War Memorial and communications towers. The Taconic Range forms the western horizon, while the top of the Dome is visible to the north. Looking down into the Hoosic River Valley, North Adams is to the east and Williamstown is to the south.

North of the trail sign, pass an anchor point for an old fire tower and emerge onto a boulder field. A short climb leads to the summit of East Mtn., where the Pine Cobble Trail joins the white-blazed Appalachian Trail at 2.1 mi. The site of an old forest fire, now covered with blueberry bushes, it provides additional views of the Taconic and Greylock Ranges.

Pine Cobble Trail

Distances from Pine Cobble Rd.

to Class of '98 Trail: 0.9 mi., 30 min.

to Pine Cobble summit: 1.6 mi., 1 hr.

to AT: 2.1 mi., 1 hr., 20 min.

Class of '98 Trail (WOC)

The Class of '98 Trail was conceived by Chris Elkinton (Williams College class of 1998) as a gift from his class to the Williams College and Williamstown communities. Following the tradition of the Class of '33 Trail, the Class of '98 Trail was constructed by members of the Williams Outing Club between 1998 and 2000. Together with the Pine Cobble Trail and the Appalachian Trail, the Class of '98 Trail forms a pleasant 5-mi. lollipop-shaped loop on the side of Pine Cobble. A similar loop can be formed by substituting the Chestnut Hill Trail for the lower section of the Pine Cobble Trail. The '98 Trail can only be reached via the Pine Cobble, Chestnut Hill, or Appalachian Trails.

The '98 Trail begins on the northwest side of the blue-blazed Pine Cobble Trail approximately halfway between the trailhead and the Pine Cobble summit. Currently there is no sign announcing the beginning of the '98 Trail, but there is a sign at this intersection labeling the Pine Cobble Trail. At first the blue-diamond-blazed trail meanders through forest at easy grades. After 0.3 mi. sheer granite cliffs become visible through the trees on the right and a significant logging road diverges to the left. At this point the trail becomes noticeably wider. Granite cliffs and boulders of varying size continue to be visible on the right side of the trail. At 0.6 mi. the blue-blazed Chestnut Trail, which is marked by a sign about 30 ft. below the '98 Trail, enters from the left. The '98 Trail makes a slight right at this intersection.

After the Chestnut Trail the '98 Trail narrows and the forest surrounding it gradually becomes denser. At 0.7 mi. the trail makes a sharp right, marked by a double blaze, then begins to climb somewhat steeply over progressively larger rocks. After 100 yd. a sign warns hikers to watch their step because of loose rock. At 0.9 mi. the trail emerges from the rocky ascent and reenters a relatively dense forest. After several gradual ascents the trail begins a steeper climb at 1.5 mi. At the top of this final ascent the trail winds through dense underbrush until it terminates at the white-blazed Appalachian Trail at 1.7 mi. The upper terminus of the Pine Cobble Trail is 0.2 mi. to the right.

Class of '98 Trail

Distances from Pine Cobble Trail

  to Chestnut Trail: 0.6 mi., 20 min.

  to AT: 1.7 mi., 1 hr.

Chestnut Trail

To reach the Chestnut trailhead by car, take MA 2 east from its intersection with US 7 at the Williams Inn in Williamstown. After 0.6 mi. turn left onto Cole Ave. at the first stoplight. Cross a bridge over the Hoosic River and railroad tracks just before North Hoosac Rd. Turn left onto North Hoosac Rd. (1.4 mi from the Williams Inn), then right onto Chestnut St. Follow Chestnut St. up a hill and around a sharp left turn. The Chestnut Trail begins as a gated logging road on the right side of Chestnut St. 0.25 mi. from North Hoosac Rd. A sign to the left of the logging road labels the trail, and a sign on the gate prohibits vehicles.

The trail climbs moderately through forest on a wide logging road. Follow the blue blazes carefully—streambeds and other logging roads branch off from the trail at various locations. The trail is likely to be wet in places. At 0.2 mi. the trail makes a slight right at a double blaze and a streambed continues straight ahead. At 0.6 mi. the trail makes a sharp right, marked by double blazes, while other logging roads continue straight and left. The trail levels off shortly after the right turn, then terminates at the Class of '98 Trail at 0.7 mi.

Chestnut Trail

Distance from Chestnut St.

   to Class of '98 Trail: 0.7 mi., 20 min.

Hopkins Forest Loop (Williams College Center for Environmental Studies)

Hopkins Memorial Forest is a 2425-acre research site operated by the Williams College Center for Environmental Studies (CES). There is a wide variety of forest types, ranging from recently overgrown farmland to old woodlot stands from the 19th century. Old farm roads, stone walls, and partially visible cellar holes reflect the complex human history of the property. Much of this information is recorded in *Farms to Forest*, a naturalist's guide published by the Center for Environmental Studies and available in local bookstores. This book also features a "guided" tour of the ecology of the lower loop trail. Research projects are in progress throughout the forest. To avoid disturbing them, please stay on trails and do not remove stakes or other markers.

The Hopkins Memorial Forest Loop Trail is actually a figure-eight composed of a 1.5-mi. Lower Loop and a 2.6-mi. Upper Loop. Information at the Rosenburg Center describes more trails within the forest. To reach the trailhead, follow US 7 north from its intersection with MA 2 at the Williams Inn in Williamstown. After 0.3 mi. turn left onto Bulkley St., cross a bridge over Hemlock Brook (0.4 mi.), and ascend a long, gradual rise. At the T-junction with Northwest Hill Rd. at 1.1 mi., turn right. The entrance to Hopkins Memorial Forest is on the left. Please park in the first parking area to the left. A few hundred feet beyond is the Rosenburg Center, which contains a small historical museum; and the Moon Barn, a historic structure that once stood on the farm belonging to Albert Moon.

The Lower Loop starts at the Moon Barn along a carriage road improved by the Civilian Conservation Corps during the 1930s. Walk to the right past the Williams Outing Club Cabin (0.1 mi.) and an experimental weather station in a vestigial field. The trail winds through forest of various composition and age before reaching a four-way intersection at 0.8 mi.

To return to the Moon Barn via the Lower Loop, turn left, away from the Upper Loop. This section of the trail may be a little swampy in spring, but please resist the temptation to trample the vegetation to either side. After a level section the trail descends steeply back to the Rosenburg Center, which it reaches at 1.5 mi.

For a longer hike, venture on to the Upper Loop Trail. If in search of the Birch Brook Trail, follow the north (right) leg of the Upper Loop for a more direct approach. Otherwise, choose either at whim. The wide path was once a carriage road from which Amos Lawrence Hopkins would view his estate. The trail crosses the middle and north branches of Birch Brook while passing through beautiful forest. This route is a fantastic ski or snowshoe jaunt with enough snow. Upon returning to the four-way intersection, return along the Lower Loop for a 4.1-mi. total trip.

Hopkins Forest Loop

Distances from Moon Barn

   to Moon Barn via Lower Loop (circuit): 1.5 mi., 45 min.

   to Moon Barn via Lower and Upper Loops (circuit): 4.1 mi., 2 hr.

Fitch Trail (WRLF)

For a short hike ascend Bee Hill through the Edward H. Fitch Memorial Woodlands, protected by the Williamstown Rural Lands Foundation. For a pleasant loop link up with the R.R.R. Brooks Trail and return to Bee Hill Rd.

To reach the trailhead by car, follow US 7 south from its intersection with MA 2 at the Williams Inn in Williamstown. Turn right onto Bee Hill Rd. at 0.6 mi. and drive up the hill, over a bridge, and up a steeper hill. At 1.3 mi. a wooden sign on the right marks the Fitch Trail. Several small pull-outs along the left side of the road provide space for 2–3 cars here. Within 0.1 mi. are three more, larger pull-outs for additional parking.

From Bee Hill Rd. follow the well-marked path on gentle grades through young forest. At 0.7 mi. reach the rounded top of Bee Hill, where only a few decades ago a clear view of the Greylock Range and valley below was visible.

For a 2.4-mi. loop, continue over the west side of the hill to meet up with the blue-blazed R.R.R. Brooks Trail at 1.1 mi. near an old Boy Scout shelter. Turn right to reach Bee Hill Rd. at 1.9 mi. through Flora Glen. To return to your car, turn right and walk 0.5 mi. uphill to the Fitch Trail parking.

Fitch Trail

Distances from Bee Hill Rd.

to Bee Hill: 0.7 mi., 30 min.

to R.R.R. Brooks Trail: 1.1 mi., 45 min.

Shepherd's Well Trail (WOC)

The Shepherd's Well Trail can be reached either from the R.R.R. Brooks Trail or the Taconic Crest Trail. From the R.R.R. Brooks Trail junction, the Shepherd's Well Trail branches to the right and climbs gently through a forest of maple, beech, and oak trees.

At 0.4 mi. a white sign indicates the boundary of Hopkins Memorial Forest. Notice the red and yellow bands painted on the trees. These are part of a permanent grid system for vegetation surveys established by the USFS in 1936 and still maintained by Williams College professors and students.

Just beyond a double blaze signaling an abrupt left turn, the trail enters an open area filled with huckleberries and blueberries. The spectacular view encompasses the Greylock Range to the east and the Taconic Range, the old Williams ski area, and Petersburg Pass to the south.

Across the clearing, the trail levels off, passing through a stand of birch and reentering the hardwood forest at 0.6 mi. Descend gradually and turn right at 0.9 mi. to skirt the ridge. To the right was once a well belonging to a farmer named Shepherd, but all traces of it have now disappeared. Follow the contours around the rise in the ridge to meet the Taconic Crest Trail at a trail sign at 1.0 mi.

Shepherd's Well Trail

Distance from R.R.R. Brooks Trail

   to Taconic Crest Trail: 1.0 mi., 40 min.

WRLF Loop Trail (WRLF)

During the summer of 1998 the Williamstown Rural Lands Foundation designed and installed this short interpretive loop trail. Small signs along the trail offer natural history information to hikers. The trail begins at the same parking area as the Class of '33 Trail.

From the parking area you can begin directly on the Haley Brook Cut-Off Trail for a shorter loop; or walk 400 ft. down the entrance road to the trailhead for the Loop Trail and the blue-blazed Class of '33 Trail. Both trails are well blazed and cross Haley Brook to reach a relatively level logging grade. On the road, walk west, passing four old pits on the left that were once used to make charcoal from trees on this land. The trail ends at the old Williams College ski area. Retrace the hike or return via Berlin Rd.

WRLF Loop Trail

Distance from Berlin Rd.

   to Berlin Rd. (circuit): 1.4 mi., 1 hr.

Stone Hill

Early settlers of the Williamstown area named Stone Hill for the outcroppings of white, garnet, and amethyst quartzite that were visible along the ridge when all trees had been cleared from the hill in the 18th century. Geologists speculate that these rocks, now obscured by vegetation, are the solidified and metamorphosed remains of submarine landslides that occurred 550–600 million years ago, when the majority of this region was underwater and in the tropical latitudes. Settlers often used the intensely fractured rock for building.

Stone Hill is one of the most popular places to walk and hike in the Williamstown area. A number of trails may be combined to form loops of various lengths and difficulty. Described here are the Pasture Loop, Stone Bench Loop, Stone Hill Loop, Stone Hill Rd., and Gale Rd. Cut-Off, in that order. The town of Williamstown, the Clark Art Institute, and several private landholders own and manage the land here. While Stone Hill has long been open to public wandering, please respect postings and private property.

Pasture Loop (WOC and Clark Art Institute)

This is a wonderful walk to and through the pasture above the Clark Art Institute. Students and townspeople alike return again and again to enjoy the spectacular view of Williamstown, Pine Cobble, and the Dome to the north.

From the intersection of MA 2 and US 7 at the Williams Inn in Williamstown, go south on South St. (opposite US 7 north). After 0.5 mi. turn right into the Clark Art Institute. Those on foot may continue around the building through the grassy area on the left. In a car, go under the overhead walkway, turn left, and park in the rear of the parking lot. A sign and two small gravestones mark the trailhead.

The two small gravestones mark the burial place of dogs that belonged to an earlier property owner, Dr. Vanderpool Adriance. The lower portion of this trail, and the footbridge that leads to it, were constructed in 1985 to help celebrate the 30th anniversary of the Clark Art Institute.

Crossing the footbridge at 0.1 mi., the trail winds uphill past birch, beech, and maple, as well as some hemlock and pine. At 0.3 mi. a signed trail junction marks the turnoff for the pasture loop to the right. Straight ahead the trail leads to the Stone Bench Loop, Stone Hill Loop, Stone Hill Rd., and Gale Rd. Cut-Off.

To continue the Pasture Loop, turn right and continue to a gate. Pass through the gate, being sure to close it behind you. A worn path leads west across the pasture to a grove of trees with excellent views. Grazing cows may glance at you, but pose no threat to your safety. To return to the Clark Art Institute below, follow a worn grassy double-track downhill on the far side of the field, through a hedgerow, and either right or straight to gates in the fence (0.7 mi.). Again, please close the gates behind you.

Pasture Loop

Distance from Clark Art Institute parking lot

    to Clark Art Institute parking lot (circuit): 0.7 mi., 30 min.

Stone Bench Loop (WOC and Clark Art Institute)

For a slightly longer walk than the Pasture Loop, try a trip to the Stone Bench. The bench is dedicated to George Moritz Wahl, a former professor of German at Williams College who climbed to this spot every evening to watch the sunset. During World War I he was subjected to substantial abuse because of his ethnic background, but when he died shortly after the war his students and fellow townspeople erected the bench as a memorial and symbol of their regret. Although trees now obscure the view, the bench is a pleasant place for a quiet moment of reflection.

To reach the trailhead, refer to directions for the Pasture Loop. Begin at the trail sign and gravestones as for the Pasture Loop. At the first junction (0.3 mi.) continue straight to a gravel road that services Williamstown's buried water tank (0.4 mi.). The road links up to Stone Hill Rd. and the Stone Bench. For a more pleasant walk, cross the road and reenter the woods on a wide trail that ascends more steeply.

During fall and early winter a thick carpet of leaves covers the trail and adds wonderful crinkle to your steps (but also slippery footing, so beware). At 0.6 mi. the trail forks with a double orange blaze. Straight ahead is the Stone Hill Loop; bear right to find the Stone Bench over a small rise at 0.7 mi., a bit tilted after 80 years.

Return by crossing a small clearing to the west and then following a path north to a gate. Alternatively, turn right (north) along Stone Hill Rd. to the gravel road and clearing. Ahead and to the left is another gate to enter the pasture. Either way, please close the gate behind you. Walk across the pasture to the grove of trees and follow the directions in the Pasture Loop section to return to the Clark Art Institute below.

Stone Bench Loop

Distance from Clark Art Institute parking lot

    to Clark Art Institute parking lot (circuit): 1.5 mi., 1 hr.

Stone Hill Loop (WOC)

As its name suggests, this trail winds up and around Stone Hill before looping back to its starting point. It shares trails with the Pasture Loop and Stone Bench Loop.

To reach the trailhead, refer to directions for the Pasture Loop. Start at the sign and gravestones, continue past the Pasture Loop turnoff to the right (0.3 mi.), across the gravel road (0.4 mi.), and uphill to a junction at 0.6 mi., marked with a double orange blaze. Approximately 100 yd. to the right is the Stone Bench; the Stone Hill Loop continues straight ahead.

Here is perhaps the most pleasant path on Stone Hill: wide, smooth, sinuous, and rolling, with hemlock groves and intermittent phyllite outcrops. In fall the bare trees afford a fantastic view east and south of the Taconic Range. At 0.9 mi. a lone hemlock marks a spot to sit, reflect, and enjoy the view.

At 1.0 mi. a stone wall marks the former boundary between two fields, and a junction offers a spur trail right to the Gale Rd. Cut-Off. Bear left instead and follow the wide track down a couple of switchbacks, ignoring the logging roads that cross the trail. At 1.7 mi. small yellow diamonds on trees to the left mark Williamstown land; a hedgerow of large red oak and sugar maple dominates the boundary. At a small creek follow the sign straight ahead across a footbridge, avoiding the roped-off road to the right. The trail continues on town land to the gravel water tank road at 2.0 mi.

To return to the Clark Art Institute, turn right and descend to Gale Rd. Proceed straight and enter the delivery or main entrance on the left at 2.3 mi.

Stone Hill Loop

Distance from Clark Art Institute parking lot

　to Clark Art Institute parking lot (circuit): 2.3 mi., 1 hr., 30 min.

Stone Hill Rd. (WOC)

"This, after all, was the prime North–South road in New England. Over this road went soldiers to Bennington in 1777; President Washington, riding over the hill in 1790, paused at this spot to take in what was then an open view of the fledgling town, with its new Free School; and every day townsfolk trafficked the road between North and South villages. To the struggling college this was the slender umbilicus of an indifferent world."—Arthur Latham Perry

To reach the trailhead, refer to directions for the Pasture Loop. From the Clark Art Institute there are a number of ways to join Stone Hill Rd. If on foot, follow the first 0.7 mi. of the Stone Bench Loop.

Another option takes a wider road grade the entire way. From the trailhead return to South St. using the main or delivery entrance. Turn right and follow the gated gravel road that ascends steeply as South St. bears left and becomes Gale Rd. At the top of the steep rise the Stone Hill Loop returns from the left; continue uphill. The Stone Bench Loop crosses the road before reaching a field under which the Williamstown water tank lies buried.

Gravel gives way to mulch and dirt as the road leads to the Stone Bench on the left. The Stone Bench Loop joins at this point. From here Stone Hill Rd. continues to the south, just below and to the west of Stone Hill, and passes a number of quartzite outcrops on the left. At approximately 1.3 mi. the Gale Rd. Cut-Off heads east while Stone Hill Rd. continues south. A number of fields border the road and offer fine views east and west.

At about 2.0 mi. Stone Hill Rd. becomes a maintained town road and continues to Scott Hill Rd. at 2.6 mi. Return along the same route or be picked up; the alternative is a long return trip on US 7 or MA 43.

Stone Hill Rd.

Distance from South St. just south of Clark Art Institute

  to Scott Hill Rd.: 2.6 mi., 1 hr., 15 min.

Gale Rd. Cut-Off (WOC)

In 1994 the Williams Outing Club and townspeople cut this trail to connect Stone Hill Rd. to the Pine Cobble School and Gale Rd. A spur trail also connects it to the main Stone Hill Loop Trail.

To reach the trailhead follow the description for Stone Hill Rd. This trail begins on the east side of Stone Hill Rd., 0.5 mi. beyond the Stone Bench. A white sign stating Trail West to Gale Rd. marks the turnoff. Alternatively, hike the Stone Hill Loop to the spur trail at 1.0 mi. and turn right (south). Walk 0.2 mi. to reach the yellow blazes of the Gale Rd. Cut-Off.

From Stone Hill Rd. the trail ascends gently into the woods, passing through the remains of an old stone wall. At 0.1 mi., after covering some rolling terrain, reach the orange-blazed spur trail that connects to the Stone Hill Loop Trail. From here the Gale Rd. Cut-Off makes a gradual descent through a mixed deciduous forest.

At 0.3 mi., just beyond a small clearing, watch for a sharp right turn down the hill, while an old woods road continues straight ahead. Be aware of unstable footing and several crisscrossing skidder trails. Cross a stream on a small log bridge at 0.5 mi. and ascend to a level open wood. Notice the old rusted gate left open one last time by a farmer years ago. Across another small stream the trail empties into a wide-open cornfield at 0.7 mi. To reach Gale Rd. follow the treeline left (north) to the foot of the hill at 1.1 mi. Please respect the lands of the Pine Cobble School. Turn left (northwest) on Gale Rd. to return to the Clark Art Institute.

Gale Rd. Cut-Off

Distance from Stone Hill Rd.

   to Gale Rd.: 1.1 mi., 40 min.

Monroe State Forest (DCR)

Monroe State Forest in the towns of Florida and Monroe covers some 4321 acres in the northern part of the Hoosac Range. A 9-mi. trail system explores the ravines and overlooks throughout the forest. The trails are blue-blazed, and elevations range from almost 1000 ft. to 2730 ft. on Spruce Mtn. Trail information is available at the Bear Swamp Visitor Center on River Rd.

To reach the visitor center and eastern trailhead from MA 2, turn north at the Mohawk Bridge (1.7 mi. west of Charlemont) onto Zoar–Rowe Rd. Continue 2.4 mi. to a T-intersection. Turn left onto River Rd., crossing the Florida Bridge 1.0 mi. from the junction, and continue on River Rd. through the village of Hoosac Tunnel. Pass the railroad tunnel on the left at 4.5 mi. The Bear Swamp Visitor Center is on the right at 7.6 mi. The trail parking area is on the left at 8.5 mi., just before the Monroe–Florida line.

Raycroft Lookout Trail

To reach the Raycroft Lookout Trail from MA 2 and Monroe Rd. (about 0.5 mi. south of the Whitcomb Summit lookout on MA 2), travel along Monroe Rd. 2.3 mi. to Hunt Hill. A dirt road travels southeast 0.2 mi. along Hunt Hill to where transmission lines cross overhead. Parking is available here. From the transmission lines the Raycroft Lookout Trail follows the ridge downhill 0.3 mi. to Raycroft Lookout (1826 ft.), a stone "balcony" built by the CCC that stands 1000 ft. above the Deerfield River and dam, affording an outstanding view of the Deerfield River Gorge.

Raycroft Lookout Trail

Distance from parking area

   to lookout on Hunt Hill: 0.3 mi., 15 min.

Dunbar Brook Trail (DCR)

This trail follows Dunbar Brook through a rocky, rugged landscape where clear waters fall over mossy boulders, creating endless cascades. From the parking area on River Rd. just north of the Bear Swamp Visitor Center the trail traces a route along the south bank of Dunbar Brook. At 0.7 mi. the path turns right (north), crosses the stream on a bridge, then goes up the north bank about 0.1 mi., passing three small camping areas. The trail then climbs moderately northwest, crossing two brooks on bridges and reaching the Dunbar Shelter at 1.2 mi. at the confluence of Haley and Dunbar Brooks. The trail continues to trace the streambank, passing under transmission lines at 1.5 mi. and crossing Parsonage Brook at 1.8 mi.

   A short distance past the brook the path turns right, climbing uphill steeply, and zigzags among large boulders. After passing almost under one of the largest, it turns sharp left (an obscure turn on the descent) and soon reaches the top of the hill, continuing nearly level on an old woods road. About 0.3 mi. from the boulder field the trail branches left and continues downhill. (The right fork leads shortly to paved Main Rd. 100 ft. east of its junction with Raycroft Rd.) After descending some worn wooden steps, the trail bears right, paralleling the brook, crosses a small stream, passes an old foundation on the right, and ends just north of the bridge on Raycroft Rd.

   To reach the blue-blazed Spruce Mtn. Trail, turn left onto Raycroft Rd. and continue 0.2 mi. across a bridge and past a small parking area on the left. The Spruce Mtn. Trail is on the right.

Dunbar Brook Trail

Distances from parking area on River Rd.

   to Dunbar Shelter: 1.2 mi., 30 min.

   to transmission lines: 1.5 mi., 45 min.

   to Raycroft Rd.: 2.8 mi., 1 hr., 30 min.

Spruce Mtn. Trail (DCR)

Spruce Mtn. (2730 ft.), the highest point in Monroe State Forest, is reached by a clearly defined, blue-blazed trail that begins and ends on Raycroft Rd. 0.2 mi. south of the intersection of Raycroft and Main Rds. From the trailhead the trail climbs moderately southwest, reaching a ledge outcrop with views east at 0.5 mi. The path continues climbing, becoming relatively level as it swings more westerly. Turning south at 1.0 mi., the path continues gradually uphill, reaching the summit in 1.3 mi. The summit itself is wooded, but a rocky clearing reached by a short path on the right offers good views to the west and south.

From the summit the path heads east, reaching Spruce Mtn.'s second summit (2592 ft.) at 1.6 mi. with a nice view to the south. The trail then descends southeast along the crest of the ridge through open hardwoods. At 2.5 mi. the trail passes under transmission lines, then ends on Raycroft Rd. at 3.1 mi.

Spruce Mtn. Trail

Distances from Raycroft Rd. (northern trailhead)

> *to* overlook: 0.5 mi., 20 min.
>
> *to* summit of Spruce Mtn.: 1.3 mi., 50 min.
>
> *to* second summit, Spruce Mtn.: 1.6 mi., 1 hr., 5 min.
>
> *to* transmission lines: 2.5 mi., 1 hr., 30 min.
>
> *to* Raycroft Rd. (southern terminus): 3.1 mi., 1 hr., 50 min.

Savoy Mtn. State Forest (DCR)

This 11,118-acre state forest is located in the Hoosac Range, a highland region that is an extension of the Green Mtns. in Vermont. Savoy Mtn. State Forest is known for its population of bears that like to loiter around campgrounds. Listen to the advice of the rangers and follow it exactly. Most of the forest roads are passable by car, but some are not, and advice from the rangers is often better than the current maps. There are 45 camping sites available, as well as four rustic log cabins on the edge of South Pond. There are about 60 mi. of multiuse trails and roads but few hiking trails.

The forest headquarters can be reached from North Adams by traveling east 5.3 mi. from the intersection of MA 2 and 8 to Central Shaft Rd. on the right. Follow the signs to the headquarters.

Busby Trail (DCR)

This blue-blazed trail provides access to Spruce Hill (2566 ft.) and Hawk Lookout, a rocky crag atop the mountain. Spruce Hill is on the western edge of the Hoosac Range, with a splendid view across the Hoosic River Valley to Mt. Greylock and the southern end of the Green Mtns. In fall the mountain-top perch is used by hawk watchers to view the annual raptor migrations.

The trail begins on Old Florida Rd. about 0.2 mi. southwest of the forest headquarters on Central Shaft Rd. Parking is available on a wide turnout. From the parking area hike about 30 yd. down Old Florida Rd. to where the Busby Trail begins on the right (north). The trail ascends easily, crossing beneath two transmission lines (0.1 and 0.4 mi.). It then traces a path along a small brook, passing spruce plantations planted by the CCC in the 1930s. At 1.0 mi. the ruins of the Sherman farm, built in the 1830s, are reached. The trail becomes steep as it climbs toward the top of the mountain. Beneath the summit the path splits into a loop trail; both paths climb to the top at 1.3 mi. The north route (right) passes through more picturesque landscape.

Busby Trail

Distances from trailhead on Old Florida Rd.

  to second transmission line: 0.4 mi., 15 min.

  to Sherman farm ruins: 1.0 mi., 40 min.

  to summit of Spruce Hill (Hawk Lookout): 1.3 mi., 1 hr.

Tyler Swamp Loop Trail (DCR)

To reach the trailhead from the forest headquarters travel south 1.7 mi. along paved Central Shaft Rd. and then unpaved Florida Rd. to a small pull-off on the right. From the pull-off the trail splits into the swamp loop. Turning left, the path follows the edge of a marsh, though the treadway stays in the woods. The trail then becomes a wide cart path that leads to rocky talus slopes. The trail swings north through beds of ferns before coming to a swamp of tall standing driftwood-gray trees where great blue herons nest. The path continues north to the junction with the South Pond Loop, which leads (0.3 mi.) to the campground on South Pond. The trail now swings south through open woods to return to the trailhead at 2.0 mi.

Tyler Swamp Loop Trail

Distances from trailhead on Florida Rd.

to junction with South Pond Loop Trail: 1.25 mi., 45 min.

to trailhead (circuit): 2.0 mi., 1 hr., 30 min.

Notchview Reservation (TTOR)

Notchview consists of 3108 acres of forests, hills, and open fields traversed by 23 mi. of trails. The reservation is astride the Hoosac Range, with much of the property above 2000 ft. in elevation. The highest point is Judges Hill at 2297 ft. Some of the fields are still used for agriculture, but the majority of the property is cloaked in hardwood forest interspersed with plantations of spruce and pine. Notchview is famous for its cross-country ski trails, which double as comfortable hiking paths in the warmer months.

Information (and year-round restrooms) can be obtained at the Arthur D. Budd Visitor Center located near the parking lot (30 cars) off MA 9 in Windsor. Notchview is located on MA 9 about 1 mi. east of the junction of MA 9 and 8A in Windsor or 8.4 mi. west of the intersection of MA 112 and 9 in Cummington.

The extensive trail system is blazed in a variety of colors. Most trails range in difficulty from easy to moderate.

Judges Hill Trail

This 1.1-mi.-long path to the crest of wooded Judges Hill begins on the north portion of the Circuit Trail. To reach the Judges Hill Trail from the parking area follow the Circuit Trail north to the Ant Hill Trail, which leaves right soon after entering the woods. Follow the Ant Hill Trail to its end, where it rejoins the Circuit Trail near the Judges Hill trailhead.

The path now heads north through wet woods, reaching and crossing Shaw Rd. Pass some cellar holes and descend to cross Shaw Brook on a bridge. The path then climbs up the slopes of Judges Hill, where the woods are a sea of trout lily in spring, and passes the Windsor Trail on the right. The summit hosts Judges Fort, a stonework "patio" where a social group, some of whom were judges, used to meet to cook lunch in the fireplace and eat at the stone table. From the summit the trail descends easily through open hardwoods to end at Bates Rd.

Judges Hill Trail

Distances from Budd Visitor Center

   to Judges Hill trailhead: 0.4 mi., 20 min.

   to Shaw Brook: 0.8 mi., 40 min.

   to Judges Fort and summit of Judges Hill: 1.1 mi., 1 hr.

   to Bates Rd.: 1.5 mi., 1 hr., 15 min.

Circuit Trail

The Circuit Trail is an easy 1.8-mi.-long loop path that passes through a wide array of forests and fields. From the Budd Visitor Center follow the mowed path southeast through a field and between two farm buildings. The trail then comes to an overgrown landscape of rhododendrons and conifers at 0.3 mi. In a grove of red spruce the Spruce Hill Trail leaves left just before passing a maintenance garage on the right. The Circuit Trail then passes the Quill Tree Trail, crosses over a small brook, and then passes junctions for the Mixed Woods Trail, Elbow Tucker Trail, and Mushroom Trail in quick succession.

At a sharp left (0.7 mi.) the trail heads north on a wide woods road, then shortly turns left as the Minor Trail continues straight (there is a weatherproof map on a post here). The trail now heads northwest through a spruce plantation, passing a slew of trail junctions and a glacial boulder at 1.3 mi. The Ant Hill and Judges Hill Trails are passed before the path begins a comfortable stretch ending at a bench under a beech tree at 1.6 mi. The path now makes an easy descent back to the visitor center.

Circuit Trail

Distances from Budd Visitor Center

   to weatherproof map at Minor Trail: 0.8 mi., 30 min.

   to glacial boulder: 1.3 mi., 50 min.

   to bench under beech tree: 1.6 mi., 1 hr., 15 min.

   to Budd Visitor Center (circuit): 1.8 mi., 1 hr., 30 min.

SUGGESTED HIKES

Easy Hikes
Bartholomew's Cobble

Hurlburt's Hill via the Tractor Path [rt: 1.8 mi., 0:50]. A pleasant walk through woods and wide fields to the grand views atop Hurlburt's Hill.
Ledges Interpretive Trail [lp: 0.5 mi., 0:30]. A winding interpretive path that skirts the Housatonic River and weaves through limestone cobbles.

Mtn. Meadow Preserve

Meadow Trail [rt: 1.2 mi., 0:45]. A wide mowed path around a high meadow with stunning views of the northern Taconics and Mt. Greylock.

Mt. Greylock

Rounds Rock Trail [lp: 0.7 mi., 0:25]. An easy walk through forest and blueberry barrens, punctuated with long southerly views.

Moderate Hikes
Tyringham Cobble

Tyringham Cobble Loop Trail [lp: 1.9 mi., 1:10]. A climb to the top of Tyringham Cobble that briefly follows the Appalachian Trail and affords fine views of the village below.

Notchview Reservation

Circuit Trail, Ant Hill Trail, and Judges Hill Trail [rt: 2.2 mi., 1: 20]. A hike through the cool Berkshire woods to stone ruins atop Judges Hill.

Pine Cobble (North Taconic Trails)

Pine Cobble Trail [rt: 3.2 mi., 1:45]. This attractive hike travels along a wooded path to reach the summit of Pine Cobble and its views of the Hoosic River Valley.

Strenuous Hikes

Mt. Everett State Reservation

Race Brook Trail, Appalachian Trail [rt: 7.2 mi., 6:00]. This sometimes demanding route ascends past a number of waterfalls before climbing the south flank of Mt. Everett. Excellent views scattered throughout.

Monument Mtn. Reservation

Hickey Trail, Squaw Peak Trail, and Indian Monument Trail [lp: 2.4 mi., 2:30]. One of the most popular hikes in the Berkshires, this loop crosses the spine of the mountain and visits overlooks with great views and gliding raptors.

Mt. Greylock

Jones Nose Trail, Appalachian Trail [rt: 5.1 mi., 4:00]. This route scales Jones Nose and then runs along the balsam ridge of Saddleball Mtn. to reach the summit of Mt. Greylock.

Part II

Pioneer Valley and Vicinity

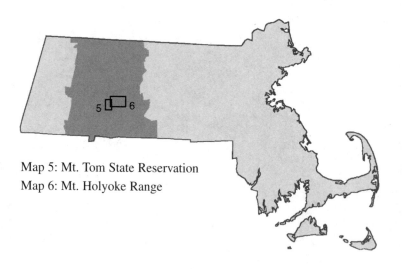

Map 5: Mt. Tom State Reservation
Map 6: Mt. Holyoke Range

LIST OF TRAILS

LIST OF TRAILS

The Pioneer Valley and Vicinity includes the part of the state between Worcester County on the east and Berkshire County on the west. It is composed of Hampden, Hampshire, and Franklin Counties, generally forming the Massachusetts watershed of the Connecticut River and its principal tributaries, the Millers, Deerfield, Chicopee, and Westfield Rivers.

This is an area of natural beauty and historic interest. From the fertile valley of the Connecticut River rise sturdy hills, mostly wooded but many with rocky summits or open ledges, the sources of clear, tumbling brooks. Heavily traveled Indian trails once crisscrossed the region, and some of the bloodiest battles of the Indian wars were fought here. At one time or another elegant summit houses or hotels, accessible by carriage roads or inclined railways, graced the tops of Mt. Tom, Mt. Nonotuck, Mt. Holyoke, Mt. Toby, and Mt. Sugarloaf.

Metacomet–Monadnock Trail

The Metacomet–Monadnock Trail (M–M Trail) in Massachusetts, 98 mi. long, is a continuation of the Metacomet Trail in Connecticut and begins near the Connecticut–Massachusetts state line at Rising Corner CT. From Rising Corner the trail passes through marshy areas, then climbs to the north crest of a traprock ridge. It passes through private land before reaching the crossing of MA 57 near the Southwick–Agawam town line at 2.4 mi. From MA 57 the trail heads north along the traprock ridge that borders the Connecticut River Valley on the west, passing over Provin Mtn. and the Mt. Tom Range. Leaping the Connecticut River at Mt. Tom Junction, the trail proceeds east over the Mt. Holyoke Range, including Mt. Norwottuck and Long Mtn., then north along the hills that line the eastern edge of the Connecticut River Valley. Turning east in the Bald Hills of Northfield to the summit of Mt. Grace in the town of Warwick, it continues to the Massachusetts–New Hampshire state line. An additional 20-mi. section of trail brings the hiker to the summit of Mt. Monadnock in New Hampshire. There it joins with the 51-mi. Monadnock–Sunapee Greenway Trail to the summit of Mt. Sunapee.

The trail has shelters and other established campsites along its route. At suitable intervals it crosses paved highways and other roads passable by car and can be easily traversed in successive one-day or half-day trips. The description below is divided into sections that each take about one day to hike. White rectangular blazes mark the route. Double blazes (one above the other) indicate abrupt changes in direction or turns in the trail. White plastic triangles are often used at road crossings and trail junctions.

The M–M Trail was originally laid out by Prof. Walter M. Banfield of the University of Massachusetts. It is maintained by the AMC's Berkshire Chapter (BCAMC) with the aid of other local groups and individuals belonging to the Metacomet–Monadnock Trail Conference. The trail's existence is a tribute to the cooperation of numerous state forest and park organizations, town conservation and water departments, nonprofit organizations, wildlife sanctuaries, and the many private landowners whose generosity allows hikers to use this special resource. The following descriptions emphasize the Massachusesetts portion of the trail.

A published guidebook for the M-M Trail with maps is available. For more information, write to: BCAMC Trails Committee, P.O. Box 369, Amherst, MA 01004.

Section 1. Massachusetts–Connecticut Line (Rising Corner CT) to MA 57 (2.4 mi.)

From the intersection of Stone St. and Barry St. in Rising Corner CT, the trail runs left up South Longyard Rd. After 0.2 mi. the trail leaves the road sharp to the right and enters an open field, following a fence. Walk along the edge of the field in a counterclockwise direction, staying to the right. After circumnavigating the field the trail drops down right (east) to a wet, marshy area with bog bridges. New bridging was installed in fall 2002 by the Pioneer Valley Hiking Club. After crossing the bridge over a stream, a logging road leaves left. The trail then proceeds steeply up the side of the Provin Mtn. ridge.

At 0.8 mi. the trail reaches the ridge top, bears left into the woods, and continues north to cross a gas pipeline at 1.4 mi. There are limited views here to the west. Just beyond and about 150 ft. left of the trail is a spring. The trail continues north on an old logging road, turns east, crosses a small brook, and after some sharp turns reaches a crossroad at 1.8 mi. It then turns left, passing through land owned by the Agawam Bowman Archery Club, and eventually enters a private driveway just before reaching the MA 57 crossing at 2.4 mi. *Note: The crossing of MA 57 may change if a planned extension into Southwick is funded. Watch for construction and a change in route if this happens.*

Metacomet–Monadnock Trail: Massachusetts–Connecticut Line (Rising Corner CT) to MA 57

Distance from intersection of Stone & Barry Sts. (Rising Corner)

to MA 57: 2.4 mi., 1 hr., 35 min.

Section 2. MA 57 to US 20 (4.3 mi.)

This section of the trail follows the ridge of Provin Mtn., mostly along the western rim. The trail begins on MA 57, entering a wide driveway on the right leading to a locked iron gate. The Lane Quarry sign reads, No Trespassing, but permission has been granted to use this right of way. Do not block the gate or the private driveway on the right with cars. The trail goes straight ahead and soon bears right, then left, with the quarry excavation on the right. (*Caution: The excavation area is dangerous due to loose stone.*) The trail now enters the woods (watch for the turn, as this area can become overgrown) and turns sharp right, then climbs moderately along the base of a talus slope to reach the top of the ridge at 0.6 mi.

Turning left at an intersection, the trail passes a stone town-line marker at 1.5 mi. At 1.9 mi. it passes an observation tower and WWLP-TV (visitors and picnickers are welcome). Just beyond the television station the trail turns left off the paved road and goes downhill. It bears right, now proceeding north, and descends along the ridge.

With little ups and downs the trail continues along this ridge, passing near and just above the hairpin turn on the access road for the city of Springfield's underground reservoir. The trail now descends the western slope of the ridge side and crosses a large, open field on a grassy trail at 3.3 mi. Follow along the right edge of the field at the base of the rock slope for about 300 yd. Enter the woods and proceed to a chain-link fence at 3.6 mi., following it steeply uphill through a stand of hemlocks to the ridge. From the ridge the path descends on a wide path to a town-line boundary marker. It then turns left and descends steeply, reaching a power line at 3.9 mi. At the power-line access road turn left, following beneath the transmission lines for a few yards, then turn right and enter Robinson State Park. The trail now reaches MA 187 near a utility shed just above the Westfield River at 4.3 mi.

Note: Because the river cannot be forded safely, thru-hikers must make a long detour to the left (west) on MA 187 to the US 20 bridge that is reached at 5 mi. From the bridge follow US 20 back east to the traffic light across from the Big Y Shopping Center (6.7 mi.), where the trail resumes.

Metacomet–Monadnock Trail: MA 57 to US 20

Distances from MA 57

> *to* observation tower and WWLP-TV: 1.9 mi., 1 hr., 20 min.
>
> *to* Westfield River: 4.3 mi., 1 hr., 50 min.
>
> *to* bridge on US 20: 5 mi., 3 hr., 15 min.
>
> *to* resumption of trail on US 20: 6.7 mi., 4 hr.

Section 3. US 20 to Bush Notch (4.9 mi.)

From the traffic light at the shopping center on US 20, turn left at the light under the railroad overpass and left again onto Sykes Ave. Proceed 0.2 mi. to a gravel road with a Pioneer Valley Sportsman's Club sign on the left. Here the trail turns sharp left, past a large rock barrier onto an ORV trail leading uphill. After passing a sand-and-gravel pit on the left, turn sharp right at an intersection and proceed on level footing through a reclamation area of young red pines. Proceeding along the rim of this sandy plateau and bearing left, the trail shortly reaches the gravel road to the Pioneer Valley Sportsman's Club. The trail crosses this road and descends to a small ravine. It winds along the edge of a swamp and crosses several small bridges east of the sportsman's club to emerge at a power line. Turn right on this line and after about 100 ft. enter woods on the left. Follow ATV trails and another power line to the west.

Turning right and left, the trail then ascends, crossing a power line and continuing to the top of the ridge. It soon enters a hemlock grove with the Lane Quarry on the western horizon. (*Caution*: *This is a blasting area; trespassing is prohibited.*) The trail passes through another hemlock grove and descends, crossing a brook at 2.5 mi. It continues north, ascending the ridge once again, and at 2.7 mi. descends into a forest of stately hemlock trees and oaks with many fallen chestnut trees, relics of the chestnut blight that swept across New England in the early 1900s.

The trail now turns northeast under a power line at 3 mi. and slowly descends, passing through a long stretch of hemlock mixed forest. It crosses an east–west tote road diagonally, a small brook, and another east–west woods road. The trail now bears left uphill, continues along a little ridge, and descends. After turning left it continues up a shallow gully, climbing steeply.

It then bears right a bit to the top of the ridge's shoulder and winds along, always on about the same contour, reaching a logging road and then descending. It soon leaves the road, bearing left and climbing but remaining parallel to the top of the main ridge.

At 4.3 mi. the trail turns left and proceeds up and along the side of a small ridge. It continues up and over the main ridge and descends toward the Massachusetts Turnpike (I-90). A relocation here turns left away from the highway fence. Follow the quarry access road or use the railroad underpass, then turn left onto Old Holyoke Rd. at Bush Notch.

Metacomet–Monadnock Trail: US 20 to Bush Notch

Distances from Riverbend Shopping Center (US 20)

   to Pioneer Valley Sportsman's Club parking lot: 1 mi., 40 min.

   to Bush Notch: 4.9 mi., 2 hr., 50 min.

Section 4. Bush Notch to US 202 (Hugh McLean Reservoir) (4.0 mi.)

Note: Parts of the trail in this section are heavily used by ATVs. From Bush Notch northward, the trail climbs to the crest of East Mtn. and follows its ridge. It proceeds entirely in the solitude of seemingly remote woodlands and passes a spectacular viewpoint from the western edge of the escarpment. An alternate route to the main trail meanders along old mossy woods roads to the lovely shores of the Hugh McLean Reservoir, joining the main trail south of US 202.

The trail goes right and down Old Holyoke Rd. in Bush Notch, continues about 50 yd., and exits left opposite a small, swampy pond. It climbs very steeply up the end of the ridge and bears right uphill, with the ridge crest above on the left. It passes a fine outlook on the edge of the traprock cliff, then ascends sharp to the ridge top just beyond an iron pipe town-line post. The trail now descends gradually to the left. At 0.3 mi. it crosses a tote road and climbs the eastern side of the East Mtn. ridge. The trail turns right near the top and follows several jeep roads north, continuing past an abandoned beacon tower at 0.5 mi. and another beacon at 1.0 mi. There are excellent views south and west. Soon the trail turns left, follows briefly along the ledges on the western end of the ridge, and turns right to proceed down the center of the descending north slope.

At 2.0 mi. the trail ascends the southern end of Snake Pond Mtn., reaches its bare ledge crest, continues along the narrow rocky ridge, and descends to join an old woods road at 2.7 mi. It proceeds east down the well-worn road, descending left for 100 yd., and leaves the woods road to the right on steep, loose footing. The trail ascends to a summit (some views) at 2.9 mi. Descending from the summit, the trail comes out at a woods road at 3.2 mi., crossing the road to the right and leaving it abruptly to the left. The trail now follows a narrower footpath on the ridge, crossing a buried telephone cable and then descending gradually to a woods road. Follow the road left and soon bear right and descend to US 202, where limited parking is available.

Metacomet–Monadnock Trail: Bush Notch to US 202 (Hugh McLean Reservoir)

Distances from Bush Notch

to Snake Pond Mtn.: 2 mi., 1 hr., 30 min.

to US 202: 4.0 mi., 3 hr.

Section 5. US 202 to MA 141 (Easthampton Rd.) (6.0 mi.)

This very scenic section of the trail runs along the wooded crest of the northern spur of East Mtn., from whose abrupt traprock ledges a succession of fine views of the valley unfolds. It follows old logging roads up the south slope of the mountain and similar woods roads north of East Mtn. to Mt. Tom. A portion of this section follows the eastern segment of the old Westfield–Holyoke streetcar route.

From US 202 the trail enters the woods to the right of a water line and fence and turns right, paralleling the highway to a shallow draw. At the old reservoir access road turn left, noticing an interesting rock wall on the right that separates the trail from the isolated northern tip of the McLean Reservoir. Proceed to paved Apremont Way and cross it directly into the woods. Soon veer right, uphill and away from a wetland on the left. The trail has been recently relocated to climb gradually to the ridge through a logging operation, now overgrown. It now follows a narrow, flat ridge north with occasional views west.

At 0.8 mi. cross a steep, eroded ORV trail that goes left. Continue up a knob on the ridge; at 0.9 mi. watch for a sudden turn left and descend steeply on a talus slope of uncertain footing. Turning right through some laurel, cross the old Westfield–Holyoke streetcar right of way. The trail then ascends a talus slope. Turning right and picking up the old route, it continues north along the ridge about 100 yd., then turns abruptly west away from the steep eastern face. It crosses the top of the ridge and at 1.6 mi. crosses a bare rocky ledge on the southern end of the ridge, with views of the Hugh McLean Reservoir and Hampden Ponds.

The trail now runs north along the western rim of this ridge through hardwoods and some hemlock. The trail crosses a little steep-sided hillock, turns away from the western edge of this ridge, and at 2.1 mi. crosses a narrow rock ledge with views south, west, and north. From here the top of the East Mtn. beacon tower appears above the treetops to the north. After crossing this ledge and descending into the woods, the trail winds around north and east to a junction at 2.4 mi. with a service road that goes up the mountain to an abandoned beacon. It passes under the tower of the beacon at 2.5 mi., continues north, and passes a huge rock at 2.6 mi.

The trail turns abruptly left and continues southwest down a draw with many fallen chestnut poles. At the end of the descent the trail turns right and climbs to the top of a rock escarpment. There are splendid views westward all along the rim of these cliffs to 3.2 mi., at which point the trail leaves the rim. It descends a steep talus slope to the north and turns right (east) at 3.4 mi. onto the Cherry St. extension, a paved town road.

The trail exits left off Cherry St. at about 3.7 mi. at the edge of a swamp on the boundary of the Holyoke Revolver Club. Please stay to the right of the stone wall in this area. The trail proceeds north, crossing a stone wall, then turns abruptly right (east) across a small spring and climbs steeply to the crest of a small ridge, which it follows along the rim of cliffs overlooking the western countryside. Following this ridge on new trail, it crosses a buried pipeline and passes several vernal pools. The trail now turns left (west), descends to a woods road, follows it to paved Southampton Rd., and then makes a left.

The trail soon makes a 160-degree right turn off the paved road onto a sandy lane running north into the woods. It bears right at the intersection with another woods road that was once the route of an old stagecoach line to Northampton. The trail continues north on this road, then turns right at a fork. After descending, the trail bears left at another fork, then passes under a row of huge sugar maples on the site of an abandoned farm. The trail emerges onto a road pull-off (commonly used by hikers to park cars) beside MA 141 (Easthampton Rd.) at 6.0 mi.

Metacomet–Monadnock Trail: US 202 to MA 141 (Easthampton Rd.)

Distances from US 202

to Holyoke Revolver Club: 3.7 mi., 2 hr.

to Southampton Rd.: 4.8 mi., 3 hr.

to MA 141: 6.0 mi., 4 hr., 15 min.

Section 6. MA 141 to MA 47 (6.6 mi.)

This is one of the more spectacular sections of the Metacomet–Monadnock Trail, cruising the skyline near the rim of steep talus slides and cliffs of Mt. Tom (1202 ft.) and Whiting Peak (1014 ft.). It then passes through the hemlock glens of the Mt. Tom Reservation on its way over Goat Peak and Mt. Nonotuck. From there the path descends on an old carriage road that lead to the "Eyrie House," the remains of which can be seen via a short spur trail from a small parking area.

Leaving MA 141 (Easthampton Rd.), the trail turns east onto a mossy woods road, which it then follows north. At 0.3 mi. the trail leaves this road and climbs steeply to the top of Mt. Tom and the site of the old Mt. Tom Hotel, now occupied by a radio and television transmission station, at 0.7 mi. The trail continues north along the edge of the cliffs to the west, offering a succession of panoramic views of the countryside to the south, west, and north.

At about 2 mi. the trail meets and coincides for a few feet with the orange-blazed D. O. C. Trail. (The upper branch of this trail leads right 0.2 mi. to the tote road of the Mt. Tom ski area; the lower branch leads right 1.1 mi. to the Quarry Trail.) At 2.7 mi., after a steep descent from Whiting Peak, partly on stone steps, the trail passes the woodsheds and shop area of the Mt. Tom State Reservation. The northern terminus of the Quarry Trail (orange blazes) is at this point. (It leads to the old Mt. Tom ski area at 1.1 mi.) The Metacomet–Monadnock Trail continues north through hemlock groves and a picnic area, reaching paved Smiths Ferry Rd. at 3.0 mi. It exits right onto the road for 70 yd., then turns left into the woods opposite the Mt. Tom Reservation Museum. There is now a water sprinkler and new pavilion about 100 ft. to the left. The trail continues north, soon leading up a low ridge clad with hemlocks. At 3.2 mi. the trail turns right and goes steeply uphill, then bears left, following the northern edge of the escarpment.

Widening views herald the summit clearing of Goat Peak (830 ft.) at 3.4 mi. The trail crosses the clearing, with the summit observation tower on the right, then reenters the woods, following a zigzag course downhill through mountain laurel and mixed hardwoods. It crosses paved Goat Peak Rd. at 3.6 mi. and continues through the woods to the blue-blazed Beau Bridge Trail at 3.8 mi., which exits right and leads to Hampden Field in 0.7 mi. Within a few yards the orange-blazed Teabag Trail also branches right and leads to lower Lake Bray and Smiths Ferry Rd. in 0.9 mi. The Metacomet–Monadnock Trail continues north, reaching Dry Knoll at 4.2 mi., which overlooks the oxbow and floodplain of the Connecticut River.

Descending and proceeding northeast, the trail intersects a paved road at 4.4 mi. To reach the summit of Mt. Nonotuck (827 ft.), whose northern ledges provide wide views of the countryside, turn right onto the road and continue to a parking lot. From there follow a well-worn path to the ledges and the ruins of the old Eyrie House hotel. The Metacomet–Monadnock Trail turns left onto the paved road, then right in about 50 yd. down the bank onto an old carriage road that also leads to the summit of Mt. Nonotuck.

The trail descends on the carriage road under a continuous arch of giant hemlocks, past a woods road entering left at 4.8 mi. On a sweeping curve at 4.9 mi. the trail, still descending, turns left onto another carriage road, which descends the mountain on a long, gentle grade. The trail follows the carriage road past two side roads coming down off the hill on the left and turns right at a fork in the carriage road, reaching a clearing and a power line at 5 mi. It turns right onto a path under the power line and continues to Underwood St. The trail turns left onto Underwood St. and follows it a short distance to East St. It turns right onto East St. and soon passes under the I-91 overpass to reach US 5 at the Mt. Tom Junction at 5.6 mi. The trail follows blazed telephone poles on a grassy section next to an electric-transformer yard adjacent to US 5. The trail leads to the state boat ramp on the Connecticut River oxbow.

(*Note: There is no public service by which hikers can cross the river here, but a free boat ride from this heavily used ramp usually can be obtained. Hikers should ask to be let off on the sandy beach between the two power-line crossings just upstream from a private camping area referred to as tent city.*)

From the opposite bank, the white blazes lead a short distance to a large open field, where the trail follows the blazed power-line right of way to MA 47 on the Hadley–South Hadley line. The old Hockanum Cemetery is located at the intersection of MA 47 and the dirt entrance road into Skinner State Park (Mt. Holyoke) on the town line.

Metacomet–Monadnock Trail: MA 141 to MA 47

Distances from MA 141

   to summit of Mt. Tom: 0.7 mi., 45 min.

   to D. O. C. Trail: est. 2 mi., 1 hr., 15 min.

   to Mt. Tom Reservation woodsheds and shop: 2.7 mi., 2 hr.

   to Quarry Trail: 2.7 mi., 2 hr.

   to Smiths Ferry Rd.: 3 mi., 2 hr., 10 min.

   to Goat Peak: 3.4 mi., 2 hr., 25 min.

   to Beau Bridge Trail and Teabag Trail: 3.8 mi., 2 hr., 35 min.

   to Dry Knoll: 4.2 mi., 2 hr., 50 min.

   to paved road to Eyrie House: 4.4 mi., 3 hr.

   to carriage road: 4.9 mi., 3 hr., 30 min.

   to US 5: 5.9 mi., 4 hr.

   to Connecticut River boat ramp: 6.0 mi., 4 hr., 10 min.

   to MA 47 (Hockanum Cemetery) across Connecticut River: 6.6 mi., 4 hr.,
      40 min.

Section 7. MA 47 (Hockanum Cemetery) to MA 116 (6.3 mi.)

The first 2-mi. portion of this trail (from Hockanum Cemetery to Taylor
Notch) contains some of the nicest views along the Metacomet–Monadnock
Trail, with a succession of sweeping vistas of the Connecticut River and
patchwork farm fields. At the center of this section in the western Mt.
Holyoke Range is the restored Mt. Holyoke Summit House (accessible by
car), with its beautiful picnic grounds. East of the Summit House is Taylor
Notch; from here to Granby Notch (MA 116) there are fewer overlooks. This
section of the range is composed of a series of minor hills that result in what
seems an endless succession of ascents and descents. The area is forested,
wild, and quite unspoiled.

   From MA 47 the trail turns left onto the entrance road to Skinner State
Park across from the Hockanum Cemetery. It proceeds about 100 ft., then
turns right up a driveway (no cars allowed). About 80 ft. east on this driveway
the trail turns left (north) and ascends a traprock ledge. At 0.15 mi. it turns
right, then descends east along the retaining bank of a pond. At the eastern end
of the pond the trail turns left (north) uphill through hemlocks and passes

under high-tension lines. It proceeds briefly along the ledge, then turns northeast into the woods.

After descending into a hemlock dell the trail turns right (east) and continues south through a narrow defile. It turns east again and goes uphill, reaching a bare ledge at 0.6 mi. with good views of the Connecticut River to the south. The trail continues north up a bare rock slope, descends into another hemlock dell, bears north up a grade on rock ledges, and reaches the top of a narrow rock ridge at 0.9 mi. It then descends a talus slope to the western rim of traprock cliffs overlooking the river and valley.

Turning east and then north, the trail climbs a ledge farther back in the woods, reaching a junction with a blue-blazed trail entering from the west at 1.1 mi. The merged trails climb higher on the rising ridge, heading east and then north. The trail crosses a rock wall and bears left, descending on an old road northward. At 1.5 mi. it intersects the blue-blazed Halfway House Trail, which descends left to the tollgate in the park. The Metacomet–Monadnock Trail follows this broad trail right, ascending to the Mt. Holyoke Summit House at 1.6 mi.

The Summit House affords superb views of surrounding country. The trail passes around the rear of the house and continues east through the picnic area. At 1.7 mi. it descends abruptly east from the end of the picnic area along broad switchbacks and reaches Taylor Notch Rd. at 1.9 mi. (This road leads back 1.5 mi. to Hockanum Cemetery at the southern entrance to the park.) After crossing the road to the Mtn. House, the trail climbs steeply east to a rocky ledge at 2.1 mi. along the eastern rim of Taylor Notch. It continues to the top of one hill (858 ft.) at 3.1 mi., with good views north, and to the top of a second hill (919 ft.) at 3.5 mi. At 4.5 mi. the trail passes an abandoned beacon on the crest of Mt. Hitchcock (1005 ft.). (Mt. Monadnock in New Hampshire is visible from this tower on a clear day.) At 5.4 mi. it reaches the crest of Bare Mtn. (1010 ft.), with superb views of the countryside north, east, south, and west. The trail bears right and descends by easy gradients and many stone steps on a switchback route to MA 116 opposite the Mt. Holyoke State Park Notch Visitor Center at 6.3 mi.

Metacomet–Monadnock Trail: MA 47 (Hockanum Cemetery) to MA 116

Distances from MA 47 (Hockanum Cemetery)

   to Halfway House Trail: 1.5 mi., 1 hr., 15 min.

   to Mt. Holyoke Summit House: 1.6 mi., 1 hr., 20 min.

   to Taylor Notch Rd.: 1.9 mi., 1 hr., 45 min.

to beacon tower on Mt. Hitchcock: 4.5 mi., 3 hr., 30 min.

to Bare Mtn.: 5.4 mi., 4 hr., 15 min.

to MA 116: 6.3 mi., 5 hr.

Section 8. MA 116 to Harris Mtn. Rd. (5.4 mi.)

The commanding heights of Mt. Norwottuck (1106 ft.) and Long Mtn. (920 ft.) and the historic overhanging ledges of Mt. Norwottuck (the so-called horse caves of Revolutionary War days) make this is a very popular section of the trail. It runs along the ridge top through a naturalist's delight of unbroken hardwood forests and hemlock coves.

From MA 116 the trail proceeds across the Holyoke State Park Notch Visitor Center parking area and up the driveway to the right of the building. It enters the woods, turns right, and descends to an old streetcar right of way. The trail turns right onto the right of way for 100 ft., then turns left onto a gravel road and left again, skirting the quarry on the right. The trail soon crosses a high-tension line and bears right (south) at 0.6 mi. to ascend the ridge. (The orange-blazed Robert Frost Trail goes straight ahead from this intersection.) At 1.3 mi. it reaches the summit of Mt. Norwottuck and an abandoned beacon. The trail continues southeast above the high cliff on the eastern edge of the ridge, then descends steeply to the left. At 1.5 mi. it reaches the horse caves, a series of overhanging ledges, climbs through a crevice descending to the bottom of the ledge (caves on the right), and proceeds gradually downhill to the saddle of Mt. Norwottuck and Rattlesnake Knob, where the Robert Frost Trail reenters from the left and the red-blazed Swamp Trail leaves to the right. (From here to Harris Rd. in Amherst, the Robert Frost Trail and M–M Trail coincide.) The trail continues east along the ridge, passing the yellow-blazed Ken Cuddebank Trail on the left, then turns sharp right (just before a scenic viewpoint) onto a steep descent on an old woods road. At 2 mi. the road goes right and the trail merges with another woods road, bears left, and soon enters a hemlock stand.

At 3.1 mi. the trail turns right, leaving the woods road at the Amherst–Granby line. It reaches a ridge crest (775 ft.) at 3.3 mi., with a good view of Mt. Norwottuck. The trail continues east-northeast along the ridge and descends into a little dell. It continues uphill, swinging to the right and reaching the ledge top at 3.6 mi., with a good view southeast. The trail proceeds east, then north, on this ridge, reaching at 3.7 mi. a steep descent to a small flat. At 3.8 mi. the trail turns right onto a woods road and follows it southeast, ascending. It leaves the road at 3.9 mi., bearing left, and ascends a steep, smooth-floored gully up Long Mtn. to reach cliff ledges with superb 180-degree views west.

The trail turns left at an abandoned beacon at 4.1 mi., descending briefly, then continues along the ridge to another open ledge. It now bears right, descending into a hardwood forest, and then goes east on an old tote road. At 5.1 mi. the trail turns abruptly left (northeast) off the tote road, ascends a gentle slope through hardwood cover, crosses the top of a knob, then drops steeply. At 5.3 mi. it turns abruptly right (east), continuing through a hardwood forest to Harris Mtn. Rd. at 5.4 mi.

Metacomet–Monadnock Trail: MA 116 to Harris Mtn. Rd.

Distances from MA 116

to summit of Mt. Norwottuck: 1.3 mi., 1 hr.

to horse caves: 1.5 mi., 1 hr., 20 min.

to Robert Frost Trail: 1.7 mi., 1 hr., 30 min.

to Ken Cuddebank Trail: 1.9 mi., 1 hr., 40 min.

to Harris Mtn. Rd.: 5.4 mi., 4 hr., 15 min.

Section 9. Harris Mtn. Rd. to MA 9 (Holland Glen) (4.2 mi.)

This is a very pleasant walk over a succession of low, forested hills with occasional glimpses of the Holyoke Range to the west and the Belchertown ponds to the east. Lots of woods and solitude.

From Harris Mtn. Rd. the trail continues east on a sandy woods road. At 0.2 mi. the trail leaves the road to the right (while the Robert Frost Trail continues straight ahead) and continues east, ascending a gentle slope through a hardwood forest and briefly following an old tote road northeast. At 0.3 mi. turn abruptly southeast, ascend a steep hillside, and continue along the hilltops through a hardwood forest on rolling ground. At 0.5 mi. ascend a short, steep slope to the crest of the ridge, then turn abruptly left (northeast) and continue along the ridge, crossing a power line. There is a new loop trail to the right just before the power line that descends to a new conservation area. At the eastern end of the ridge the trail bears right down a steep bank, crosses a little flat, and climbs eastward to a grassy knoll at the southern end of an apple orchard, with a good view of Mt. Toby to the north. It then descends steeply to Bay Rd. at 1.1 mi. and turns right onto the road.

At 1.2 mi. the trail continues on Bay Rd. past its intersection with Wright St., then turns sharp left at 1.2 mi. onto an old woods road, ascending into a hemlock mixed forest. This area was recently purchased with the help of the Kestrel Trust and other groups. At 1.5 mi. the trail reaches the top of a hill (517 ft.) then bears right, descending steeply. It merges with a sandy lane at 1.7 mi., follows the lane briefly north, then bears right at a fork.

The trail ascends, traverses a low hill, and descends into a tall pine stand on a flat, crossing a stone wall and then a ditch at 1.9 mi. Soon ascending, it traverses a second low hill covered with mixed forest and descends through tall pines to a tote road that crosses a tiny stream at 2.2 mi. The trail follows the tote road east through a hardwood sapling stand with clumps of hemlocks, crosses the plateau at 2.6 mi., and abruptly turns south through a semimature hardwood forest. At 2.7 mi. it abruptly turns left at the southern edge of this plateau overlooking Metacomet Lake.

The trail turns sharp left at right angles to and away from the edge of the plateau and continues north to a junction with a woods road coming up from Federal St. just north of Arcadia Lake in Belchertown. After bearing right at the top of the ridge, the trail reaches a side trail to a ledge overlooking Holland Lake. It then turns left downhill through hardwoods. At 3.6 mi. it bears right onto a skid road, then turns right onto a path and descends about 100 ft. to Federal St. Turn left just before a private home, proceed on a level contour through a recently cutover area, and descend steeply to Orchard St. Care should be taken here.

Turn right just before the road. Cross it, then Federal St., and then follow Cheryl Circle for about 200 yds., making a left just after the steep-banked streambed. The trail continues over a brush knoll and descends to the Central Vermont RR tracks at 4.0 mi. It crosses the tracks, continues east briefly on the shoulder of the railroad bed, then turns left (north) into the woods. After crossing the stream, it ascends the bank of MA 9 across from the entrance to Holland Glen at 4.2 mi.

Metacomet–Monadnock Trail: Harris Mtn. Rd. to MA 9 (Holland Glen)

Distances from Harris Mtn. Rd.

    to apple orchard: 1 mi., 45 min.

    to Bay Rd.: 1.1 mi., 55 min.

    to side trail to ledge overlooking Holland Lake: 3.3 mi., 2 hr., 15 min.

    to MA 9 (Holland Glen): 4.2 mi., 3 hr.

Section 10. MA 9 (Holland Glen) to Mt. Lincoln (5.0 mi.)

An interesting walk over ridges and along streams on footpaths and old town roads, this section of the trail is bordered on the west by sturdy stone walls and old cellar holes that mark the site of an old agrarian community, now overgrown by mixed forest. Holland Glen is a steep-sided ravine with a clear stream shaded by a mature hemlock stand, which has been preserved by the Belchertown Historical Society.

From MA 9 the trail continues east through the woods into Holland Glen. At 0.15 mi. it crosses a brook and follows its right bank into the ravine. The trail climbs the steep side of the ravine, exiting right from the stream, continuing amid mature hemlocks, and passing a waterfall at 0.4 mi. at the top of the glen. The trail continues upstream on the right bank, crossing a tributary stream. At 0.5 mi. it turns abruptly left across a brook (good water) onto a woods road, which is overgrown by hemlocks west of here. Ascend a moderate slope covered with hardwoods and at 0.8 mi. cross a bare rock ledge, which affords a good view southwest in winter toward Long Mtn.

The trail reaches the top of the ridge at 1.4 mi., then descends to a left turn onto a woods road. It passes an old farm clearing, now in Johnson grass, at 1.6 mi. on the top of the plateau. At 2.6 mi. the trail turns left onto a woods road, soon crossing a brook and continuing north through a cutover hardwood stand. At 3.1 mi. it crosses a stone wall on West Hill into young pine growth and proceeds north through stone wall pasture fences, with cellar holes on the left. At 3.4 mi. the trail follows a woods road to the right for about 150 yd. to a trail junction. Turn left here, then quickly bear left at another junction and continue downhill to a driveway and cabin at unpaved Gulf Rd. at 3.6 mi.

Continuing straight across the road into the woods, the trail proceeds north, then west, paralleling Gulf Rd. At 3.9 mi. it turns left, crosses a wet, grassy trail, and heads north up a sandy bank through a white pine forest. The trail passes near an open field on the right with abandoned cars on the left. This route is followed west along the woodline, bearing left at 4.3 mi. Turning right, the trail passes through young scrub oak, and at 4.5 mi. crosses Enfield Rd. and proceeds north through the Cadwell Memorial Forest (University of Massachusetts). The trail leaves the road at 4.8 mi. and bears right uphill through a scrub oak hardwood stand. At 5.0 mi. it passes the observation and fire tower atop Mt. Lincoln (360-degree view), passing to the left of the maintenance shed.

Metacomet–Monadnock Trail: MA 9 (Holland Glen) to Mt. Lincoln

Distances from Holland Glen

  to Gulf Rd.: 3.6 mi., 2 hr., 45 min.

  to Enfield Rd.: 4.5 mi., 3 hr., 20 min.

  to summit of Mt. Lincoln: 5.0 mi., 3 hr., 50 min.

Section 11. Mt. Lincoln to N. Valley Rd. (3.3 mi.)

A delightful walk in any season, this section of the trail descends the northwest slope of Mt. Lincoln beside a fast-falling brook in a narrow hemlock glen, passes through a pine-hemlock mixed forest to Amherst's Hill Reservoir, and continues downstream beside Harris Brook. From the confluence of Harris and Buffum Brooks the trail continues upstream under a canopy of hemlocks and pines along a series of waterfalls to a footbridge over Buffum Brook beside N. Valley Rd. in Pelham.

From the summit of Mt. Lincoln the trail continues west down the service road. At 0.2 mi. it exits right into the woods and descends across a woods road at 0.4 mi. It continues downhill to the northwest, crossing the brook at 0.85 mi. The trail bears left onto a woods road, then almost immediately turns left to follow the north bank of the brook downhill. At 1.35 mi. it turns right onto a woods road at the base of a rocky glen, crosses the brook, and descends left. At 1.45 mi. it turns right onto another woods road, which soon crosses the brook. The trail then emerges in a brushy field beside Pelham–Amherst Rd. and continues north to this road at 1.6 mi.

After crossing Pelham–Amherst Rd. the trail bears left up a steep sand bank into pines on a plateau. It continues through a dense seedling pine grove, then slowly descends to the west through beautiful pines to an intersection with an old, grassy road at 1.9 mi. The trail turns right on the grassy road and then quickly left onto a trail leading west through mixed woods and then hemlocks. It descends gradually, then steeply, to a gravel road at 2.2 mi. This next section of trail has been recently relocated and veers away from Buffam Brook, reaching N. Valley Rd. via a new route and new blazing. Parking is available on a road shoulder under power lines to the left.

Metacomet–Monadnock Trail: Mt. Lincoln to N. Valley Rd.

Distances from summit of Mt. Lincoln

to Pelham–Amherst Rd.: 1.6 mi., 1 hr., 10 min.

to Hill Reservoir spillway: 2.6 mi., 1 hr., 55 min.

to Buffum Brook: 3.1 mi., 2 hr., 20 min.

to N. Valley Rd.: 3.3 mi., 2 hr., 30 min.

Section 12. N. Valley Rd. to Market Hill Rd. (4.6 mi.)

This 4.6-mi. section has been designated the Walter Banfield Memorial portion of the M–M Trail in honor of the trail's founder. The trail ascends the bare ledges of Mt. Orient, then runs the length of this ridge through oak and white birch woods, descending on a gravel road to Big Hearthstone Brook. The path then swings south, crossing the shoulder of Poverty Mtn. and following a pleasant old woods road down the western slope and through cool evergreen woods. The trail reaches the old Adams homestead, recently the home of Walter Banfield, on Pratt Corner Rd.

Turning south (left) onto N. Valley Rd., the trail initially follows the road for 0.2 mi. to a power line that heads to the junction with the Robert Frost Trail. (The M–M Trail and the Robert Frost Trail coincide from here to Atkins Reservoir.) At 0.6 mi. the road crosses a little stream; here the trail turns right and proceeds north along the stream, leaving it at 0.8 mi. The trail bears right uphill, soon crosses a woods road, and climbs in a slow right swing up the southwest slope of Mt. Orient. At 1.3 mi. it makes a hand-and-foot climb up the steep slope of the mountain and at 1.5 mi. reaches the southern end of the ridge.

From the ridge crest, the trail swings west and descends through hemlock woods to the western edge of the ridge, then leaves the ledges and bends back east and then north along the crest. After traversing the ridge the trail descends gradually, crosses a stone wall, and continues downhill to cross Little Hearthstone Brook at 2.4 mi. It continues north over this tableland, then descends steeply on erosion-control water bars to an old gravel road.

Turning right onto the road, the trail crosses Big Hearthstone Brook on a culvert, then turns quickly left into the woods. Continuing west, it slowly veers away from the brook on the left and descends to a low point between

Mt. Orient and Poverty Mtn. The trail soon crosses a bog bridge over a swampy area, proceeding southwest amid mature white pines. At 3.2 mi. the trail bears left onto a woods road that ascends up and over a shoulder of Poverty Mtn. Follow the woods road downhill through tall pines and a hardwood forest, descend more steeply, then bear right (north) onto another tote road.

From here the trail turns left, descending through a mature mixed forest. It then turns right, descending through hemlock woods. After crossing a streamlet, the trail turns left at 4.2 mi. onto Pratt Corner Rd. (A swimming hole is located upstream from the bridge on the left of Pratt Corner Rd.) Pass over the bridge and immediately turn right onto a woods road. Follow this road north to Atkins Reservoir and unpaved Market Hill Rd. at 4.6 mi.

Metacomet–Monadnock Trail: N. Valley Rd. to Market Hill Rd.

Distances from N. Valley Rd.

   to Little Hearthstone Brook: 2.4 mi., 2 hr.

   to Market Hill Rd.: 4.6 mi., 3 hr., 15 min.

Section 13. Market Hill Rd. to Shutesbury–Leverett Rd. (3.5 mi.)

In forested country, mostly on old woods roads, the trail climbs over the January Hills through forests of oak, white birch, and white pine saplings, reaching Roaring Brook on the Shutesbury–Leverett Rd. This section repeatedly intersects and runs along power lines and underground cables, affording panoramic views from the hilltops.

Turn right onto unpaved Market Hill Rd. and then left at a cabled gate after 75 yd. Follow a wooded lane under a pine forest, skirting the eastern shore of the reservoir on the left. Several unmarked side trails lead to the water's edge. Crossing a small streamlet at 0.4 mi., the trail turns right onto a woods road at 0.5 mi. Ascending gently, the trail bears right at a junction, crosses a small stream, and bears left uphill as the road becomes a grassy lane. At 1 mi. it passes under two power lines in quick succession. Turn left under the second power line and continue uphill on its maintenance road to the height-of-land, then downhill to an underground cable right of way at 1.7 mi. Turn left onto the cable line and proceed to the woodline, where there is a narrow trail on the right. Follow this downhill, joining with another woods road, and at 2.8 mi. turn left onto a narrow path and descend gradually to the steep bank of Roaring Brook at 3.2 mi. Cross the brook on a bridge (now within the Roaring Brook Conservation Area) and turn right, following the brook upstream. Here the trail turns left, ascending steeply to the paved Shutesbury–Leverett Rd. at 3.5 mi.

Metacomet–Monadnock Trail: Market Hill Rd. to Shutesbury–Leverett Rd.

Distances from Market Hill Rd.

to Roaring Brook: 3.2 mi., 2 hr.

to Shutesbury–Leverett Rd.: 3.5 mi., 2 hr., 15 min.

Section 14. Shutesbury–Leverett Rd. to N. Leverett–Lake Wyola Rd. (4.7 mi.)

This section is interesting from two perspectives: (1) the wilderness character of the terrain along the winding trail (actually an old town road, as its enduring stone culverts make clear) through hardwood forests, white birches, and pure stands of hemlocks beside pleasant streams; and (2) the historic character of the area, indicated by the miles of sturdy stone walls and many cellar holes that echo an early pastoral community from centuries ago.

Cross paved Shutesbury–Leverett Rd. to an abandoned town road on the right and go north for some 300 yd., ascending. Pass near the clearing of a power line on the right in 0.3 mi. at a log landing, then go left on a woods road that crosses a stream and soon turns right toward Brushy Mtn. At 0.8 mi. cross Mtn. Brook, then turn right at a fork and begin the ascent. At 1.9 mi. the woods road begins climbing the shoulder of a mountain, passing through dense laurel. At 2 mi. the trail crosses a small stream in a delightful hemlock dell at the height-of-land west of Brushy Mtn. At 2.6 mi. begin a gradual descent to a woods road on the right at 2.9 mi., passing an old mill site on the left. Continuing to descend moderately and passing over two small streams, the trail joins a power line on an eroded, wide lumber access road, where it bears left (north-northwest) and continues descending through a recently harvested area.

At 3.9 mi. the trail turns right at the junction with Rattlesnake Gutter Rd. Descending, it exits left onto a woods road through a mixed pine-hemlock forest. At 4.3 mi. the trail turns left onto a gravel road, passing charcoal beehive kilns. At 4.3 mi. it turns right and crosses the bridge over the Saw Mill River. At 4.7 mi. it turns left onto paved N. Leverett–Lake Wyola Rd.

Metacomet–Monadnock Trail: Shutesbury–Leverett Rd. to N. Leverett–Lake Wyola Rd.

Distances from Shutesbury–Leverett Rd.

   to Rattlesnake Gutter Rd.: 3.9 mi., 2 hr., 35 min.

   to Saw Mill River: 4.5 mi., 3 hr., 15 min.

   to N. Leverett–Lake Wyola Rd.: 4.7 mi., 3 hr., 25 min.

Section 15. N. Leverett–Lake Wyola Rd. to Farley (9.8 mi.)

This section begins by following a power line over Diamond Match Ridge where the path is framed with laurel and blueberries. It then brushes past the eastern side of Catamount Swamp, follows old roads to Hemmingway Rd., and crosses Montague Rd. From Montague Rd. the trail turns left in the direction of Ruggles Pond and intersects the Ruggles Pond Trail. The trail descends Lyons Brook and Mormon Hollow Brook before reaching the village of Farley.

The trail turns right off N. Leverett–Lake Wyola Rd. onto gravel Richardson Rd. just after crossing Williams Brook. At 0.4 mi. it passes farm buildings on the left and continues uphill on a gravel road. At 0.9 mi. it passes the fields of an abandoned farm at the top of the slope, then turns west at 1.5 mi. at the dead-end intersection with an east–west gravel road. It crosses a bridge at 1.9 mi. and turns right at the crossroads. At 2.1 mi. it turns left onto a power-line service road at the bridge on the west side of the brook. The trail crosses the power-line clearing, bears left past a private camp, then bears right at a fork in the road. At 2.6 mi. it bears right at a second fork in the road, then passes a Forest Service water hole and continues straight onto Burkhart Rd., a Forest Service road. This road rises high on the east slope of Dry Hill, then descends to the north. The trail turns left onto a gravel road at 4 mi. and continues to the intersection of Montague Rd. at 4.7 mi. It crosses Montague Rd., entering Wendell State Forest, and continues northeast on Ruggles Rd. to reach Ruggles Pond.

The foundation and clearing at 4.9 mi. mark the site of a CCC camp, now maintained by the Forest Service. Picnic tables, fireplaces, and swimming are available. (A parking fee is charged in season.) The trail turns left across the parking lot, then proceeds downhill about 200 yd. to an Adirondack shelter suitable for 8–10 persons. A fireplace, wood, and outhouse are available. A fine-walled spring is located a few yards farther down the trail. The trail continues downhill on an old tote road east of Lyons Brook. At 5.3 mi. it turns left to the east bank of the brook, then proceeds downstream and crosses the brook at 5.7 mi. The trail soon turns right, away from the brook and up the steep bank through laurel scrub, before crossing the brook at 5.9 mi. The trail then heads north along the base of a ridge, before turning right and ascending south on a Forest Service road to Jerusalem Rd.

At the junction with unpaved Jerusalem Rd. the trail takes a sharp right turn, going uphill on Jerusalem Rd. for 150 yd. to a junction with a side trail next to a small parking area. The trail turns left up this side trail to the ridge and then turns right (north) to follow the ridge line, where there are some nice views. The narrow track trail continues over several wooded hills for about 1 mi. to the junction of two woods roads.

Following woods roads, the trail drops down at the end of the ridge to an unpaved camp road and turns left. Follow the camp road a short distance to Davis Rd., then descend steeply to the right on Davis Rd. toward Mormon Hollow Brook.

The trail continues right and downhill on a washed-out section of Davis Rd. and crosses Mormon Hollow Brook on a rustic bridge. After crossing the bridge, take a sharp left and follow the scenic brook. The trail passes some old dam structures and cellar holes to emerge on Mormon Hollow Rd. Go left on the road, then sharp right under the power lines down to a meadow used for parking by local anglers. The trail leaves Wendell State Forest near Mormon Hollow Rd. and continues along Mormon Hollow Brook, with its attractive cascades, pools, and glades of mature hemlock. Crossing the brook three times (use caution), it finally picks up an old skid road on the north side and proceeds to the Millers River, passing just below the railroad bridge. Climb the steep railroad bank, cross the bridge, and descend to the river. (*Note: During low water it may be possible to ford the river on a gravel bar under the bridge.*)

At the river the trail heads east along the densely vegetated floodplain. At the end of the floodplain it rises steeply up onto the railroad embankment and follows the tracks for several hundred yards before descending again into the woods and the riverbank. (*Caution*: *The railroad tracks are active.*) The trail continues through woods parallel to the river before passing the foundations of a 19th-century knitting factory and piano works. The trail emerges on Farley Rd. next to the Farley Bridge at 9.8 mi.

Metacomet–Monadnock Trail: N. Leverett–Lake Wyola Rd. to Farley

Distances from N. Leverett–Lake Wyola Rd.

> *to* recreation area and Adirondack shelter at Ruggles Pond: 4.9 mi., 3 hr., 10 min.
>
> *to* Lyons Brook: 5.5 mi., 3 hr., 35 min.
>
> *to* Farley: 9.8 mi., 5 hr., 15 min.

Section 16. MA 2 (Farley) to Gulf Rd. (7.9 mi.)

This section of the trail climbs steeply from Farley in the shadow of the high cliffs of Rattlesnake Mtn., then along the hemlock-shaded ravine of Briggs Brook. From here it proceeds northeast on the ridge and ledges of Hermit Mtn., passing the blue-blazed trail that leads to Hermit Castle high above the Millers River. The trail then abruptly turns north through Irving State Forest to the bare ledges of Crag Mtn. in Northfield.

Cross MA 2 to the right of the old Erving Cycle Shop (parking available here) and continue to Holmes St. Turn left onto Wells St. and continue to the end. Enter the woods on a wide woods road, ascending gradually to a right turn across Briggs Brook on a primitive footbridge. Turn left, climbing on the right side of the brook. At 0.6 mi. the trail crosses Briggs Brook a short distance above the lip of some high falls, then turns upstream into a hemlock ravine. At 0.8 mi. it passes a side trail to Rose Ledge. (This Rose Ledge trail runs upstream beside Briggs Brook, then west and south to the southern rim of Northfield Mtn., known as the Rose Ledge. There are spectacular views of the Connecticut River Valley to the south and west from this ledge. This trail intersects several hiking, snowshoe, and ski trails maintained by Northeast Utilities Co. as the Northfield Mtn. Recreational Area. For maps and information, write to Recreation Supervisor, RR 1, Box 377, Northfield, MA 01360.)

At this junction the M–M Trail turns right (northeast) and crosses the brook. In a few yards it turns right again and climbs out on a rocky ledge. At 0.9 mi. it crosses a woods road, continuing north and rising slightly while staying close to the rim of the ridge, which falls away steeply from the trail to the river. The Northeast Utilities pumped-storage reservoir is on the left. At 1.4 mi. the trail turns right and proceeds east downhill on a woods road to Packard Brook. At 1.7 mi. it intersects a tote road coming up from Farley and turns left onto this road. The trail leaves the road among hemlocks at 1.9 mi., bears right beyond a big hemlock, then climbs upward on a ridge. At 1.8 mi. it traverses ledges overlooking the Millers River and continues eastward from ledge to ledge. The trail turns east 0.25 mi. east of the last ledge and descends the ridge, crossing a dry brook bed at 2.9 mi.

The trail now turns sharp left (north) and continues ascending moderately for 0.3 mi. on a north-northwest bearing through hardwood forest. The terrain levels off, and hemlocks soon become the principal forest component. At 3.4 mi. the trail turns right (east) onto a tote road; then, as this road changes its bearing from east to southeast, the trail turns left (north) at 3.2 mi. It turns east once more at 4.0 mi. onto a second, much broader tote road but soon jogs south from this broad road onto a narrower road, and within 80 ft. the trail leaves the road, turning east. It climbs slightly, reaching a high ledge at 4.2 mi., and shortly descends the ledges, bearing north to more level terrain. It proceeds northeast through hardwoods with some pines to the junction with Mtn. Rd. at 4.3 mi., just south of the padlocked gate on the west side of the road. This gate leads to Northfield Mtn. Reservoir, which is off-limits to hikers.

The trail continues north on Mtn. Rd. to the Northfield–Erving line at 4.5 mi., where it turns right (east) onto an abandoned town road. After crossing a tiny streamlet it continues east. At 4.7 mi., opposite a meadow, the trail turns left (north) into a gray birch–pine forest and soon crosses a small swampy stream. It continues north through pole stands of birch, maple, and pine, then begins climbing gently. It jogs left through pines, turns north, then descends slightly and crosses a little dell, turning west as it skirts the base of a rock outcrop. It soon turns north again through a break in the ledge and within 150 ft. turns right onto S. Mtn. Rd. At the crest of the ridge (5.2 mi.) the trail turns left (north) onto a long gravel private driveway. Turn right before reaching the house and begin a short but steep climb to the summit of Crag Mtn., which offers views east to Mt. Grace, east-northeast to Mt. Monadnock in New Hampshire, and south. At 6.3 mi. another ledge looks to the north and west. The trail continues north, turning right to leave the woods road at 7.0 mi. At 7.1 mi. there are more ledges with open views of Mt. Grace and Mt. Monadnock. At 7.5 mi., on a northerly descending rock ledge, the trail leaves the ledge. Bearing right and then left, the trail descends on a woods road that soon turns east next to a power line and reaches Gulf Rd. in Northfield at 7.9 mi.

Metacomet–Monadnock Trail: MA 2 (Farley) to Gulf Rd.

Distances from MA 2

   to Rose Ledge side trail: 0.8 mi., 30 min.

   to ledges overlooking Millers River: 2.2 mi., 1 hr., 15 min.

   to Mtn. Rd.: 4.3 mi., 2 hr., 15 min.

   to southern summit of Crag Mtn.: 6.2 mi., 3 hr., 45 min.

   to Gulf Rd.: 7.9 mi., 4 hr., 30 min.

Section 17. Gulf Rd. to Mt. Grace (6.8 mi.)

Passing across the forested tops of Northfield's Bald Hills, the trail descends to a woods road extension of Warwick's White Rd. before continuing east (bypassing the old trail route of White Rd.) to the southern end of Mt. Grace. From there it climbs on the old Snowshoe Trail to the fire tower at the summit of Mt. Grace (1617 ft.).

At 0.2 mi. the trail turns right off Gulf Rd. under a power line, then left onto a woods road before reaching the first pylon, proceeding northeast. At 0.5 mi. it turns left onto an old tote road, proceeding on the same contour north to a brook at 0.8 mi. The trail crosses the brook, proceeds on its north bank upstream for 100 ft., then turns left and goes another 100 yd. northeast. It bears left, climbing hills and soon reaching some rock outcrops. At 1.1 mi. it turns right from the ledge and continues through an open pine forest, soon ascending sharply through hardwoods to cross a power line near the top of the Bald Hills. The trail continues east on bare rock, following several cairns to the eastern rim of the hill (1345 ft.). Mt. Grace looms ahead through the trees.

Here the trail turns left, descending through pine forests, then ascending. At 1.8 mi. it emerges on the eastern rim of a hardwood-covered ridge and proceeds north, soon descending. It crosses a boulder-strewn, fast-falling streamlet (mostly dry in summer) at 2.1 mi., then ascends through a mixed forest of hemlock. Skirting the east slope of the hill (1285 ft.), the trail drops rapidly to the junction with the woods road extension of Warwick's White Rd. at 2.4 mi. As you descend for 0.3 mi. from the Bald Hills on White Rd., look for a sign marking a sharp left into the woods. From here the trail winds through open hardwoods of a recently harvested area to join a snowmobile trail, where it turns left (northwest) to join a major woods road at 2.9 mi. The trail proceeds right on this road (the historic Fifth Massachusetts Turnpike, dating from

1775), crossing a junction with unpaved White Rd. at 3.4 mi., and continues east to a small clearing.

The trail crosses a brook on a culvert, then narrows to a woods road, ascending and crossing another woods road at 3.6 mi. after detouring around a new house. The trail continues east on snowmobile trails to connect with paved Northfield Rd. The trail parallels the highway and emerges near the junction of White Rd. and Northfield Rd. The trail crosses the road, passes over a brook on a rustic bridge, and then climbs up to join the Round the Mountain Trail in Mt. Grace State Forest at 5.1 mi.

Here hikers can either turn right at once (an unmarked shortcut) or, for a more leisurely walk, continue left on the Round the Mountain Trail for about 0.2 mi., then turn right off the trail, ascending steeply to the old Snowshoe Trail and turning sharp right onto this. The trail proceeds to a cluster of seven oaks at 5.7 mi., turns sharp left, and begins a steady ascent of a knife-edge ridge. Beneath the hemlocks at the crest of the ridge are lookouts to the west.

The trail descends through the forest to a draw in a tall pine grove at 6.1 mi., then climbs again amid pines and hemlocks past more westward lookouts and a northward glimpse of the Mt. Grace summit and fire tower. With a gradual descent the trail joins the fire tower service road from Warwick village at 6.4 mi. and follows this steep road for 0.2 mi., where it leaves the road to follow a telephone line. It soon rejoins the road and follows it to the summit of Mt. Grace at 6.8 mi.

Metacomet–Monadnock Trail: Gulf Rd. to Mt. Grace

Distances from Crag Mtn.

to White Rd.: 2.4 mi., 2 hr.

to Northfield Rd.: 5 mi., 3 hr., 30 min.

to summit of Mt. Grace: 6.8 mi., 4 hr., 50 min.

Section 18. Mt. Grace to MA 32 (8.5 mi.)

From the summit of Mt. Grace the trail descends to MA 78 along Old Winchester Rd. After another 1 mi. eastward, the trail passes above attractive Highland Falls, enters a stretch of unbroken woodland, and, climbing up and down over an interesting series of steplike ridges, reaches a high point just south of the Massachusetts–New Hampshire line. From here the trail proceeds roughly parallel to the state line to the end of this section.

The trail runs along the summit of Mt. Grace, past the fire tower on the left and a boulder with a plaque on the right, to begin its northerly descent via a ski trail. It bears left onto the trail away from the service road and on its steep descent affords a glimpse of the ultimate goal, Mt. Monadnock. At 0.3 mi. the trail turns abruptly left off the ski trail to descend steeply past a spring (right) at 0.5. mi. Then it winds down more gently, on and off through old woods, to a junction with a tote road just below a large sawdust pile. This road descends through hemlocks to a level stretch at 1 mi., where it crosses a brook and passes an Adirondack shelter built in 1970 by DCR.

The trail continues down the road to a beautiful pool, then descends along the edge of the ravine. It bears right around a white pine grove, still on the road, then crosses Mirey Brook below a broken dam to reach MA 78 at 1.6 mi. (Turning right onto MA 78 leads to Mt. Grace State Forest picnic area in 0.5 mi.) The trail crosses MA 78, climbs a steep bank, and at the top of a grassy knoll turns right through a corridor cut in thick pines. Emerging onto a faint path, it turns abruptly left at 1.7 mi., angles down to cross a brook, and 40 ft. east of the brook meets a woods road. The trail turns left onto the road, proceeds north 0.1 mi., bears right, and travels continuously through a white pine forest, gradually ascending on an easterly bearing. The trail enters a pole stand of Scotch pine, turns sharp left (north), and presently emerges on Old Winchester Rd. (gravel). It crosses the road and in another 70 ft. bears right, ascending. At 1.9 mi. it turns left onto a woods road and soon descends to cross another woods road. Continuing northeast, it crosses Kidder Brook under a power line at 2.1 mi. and bears left at a fork in the road beyond the bridge, ascending. There is a good lunch spot at 2.5 mi., with views west from the ledges a few yards from the trail under a power line.

In a small clearing at 2.8 mi. the trail turns left, then right, and descends briefly. It then ascends again, past an interesting pothole swamp to the right, and leaves the road at 3.1 mi. to climb straight up the ridge. After a dip through a little dell, the trail climbs steeply to a second ridge at 3.4 mi., descends, and climbs again to the top of the ledges at 3.6 mi. Here the trail turns sharp left, descending along a boundary line, then climbs once more through many fallen hemlocks to an important right turn at 3.8 mi. The trail makes a steep descent into a gully and an equally sharp ascent over a rocky knoll, repeating this pattern twice within 0.5 mi., until at 4.3 mi. it emerges onto and turns left down an abandoned farm road. At 4.5 mi. the trail leaves this road to go straight uphill, and at 4.7 mi. it reaches Richmond Rd. (graded gravel) within sight of the Massachusetts–New Hampshire state-line marker on the left, on the south slope of Whipple Hill.

The trail proceeds right (south) onto Richmond Rd. and turns left at 5.0 mi. onto a maintained gravel road. The maintenance ceases at the entrance to the last house. As the road and trail wind steeply down, there are winter views of Ball Hill ahead. The trail crosses the headwaters of Tully Brook at 5.1 mi. and continues past a cellar hole, then turns left onto another abandoned road at 5.3 mi. The trail goes up and over the shoulder of Ball Hill through hemlock woods, then descends past another cellar hole to a road entering right at 6.3 mi. Shortly, the road turns sharp left onto Parker Rd. and the trail goes straight up, down, and up again to reach the southern end of a rocky ridge. Ball Hill is visible to the west and White Hill is visible to the east across the valley. After crossing and then following the ridge to its northern end (where a glimpse of Mt. Monadnock is possible), the path descends in steep zigzags.

At 6.8 mi. the trail enters a clearcut, proceeds to the brook, goes downstream briefly, then crosses and soon proceeds right along a logging road. Near a small open area at 6.9 mi. the trail turns left and proceeds up a steep slope on a logging road, which soon shrinks to a narrow footpath, still climbing southeast to a tote road. The trail turns right onto the road and follows it up and over the summit of White Hill (1361 ft.). At the summit the trail goes left into an old timber cut, descends steeply, passes a slight rise at the foot of the hill, continues through a small clearing, and joins Bliss Rd. (graded gravel) at 7.6 mi. (limited parking available).

The trail crosses Bliss Rd. and its stone wall fence and proceeds generally east through interesting forest terrain. It soon crosses another stone wall, then another at 7.9 mi., at a blue-stake boundary of a former pasture. With still another stone wall on the left and descending slightly through hemlock hardwoods, the trail soon enters a red pine pole plantation, bearing left over the needle carpet. It leaves the plantation at 8.1 mi., crosses a small hill, continues over a flat area, then ascends a hardwood slope with a tiny streamlet on the right (south) side. At 8.3 mi., now on a plateau, the trail enters a stand of large hemlocks with great boulders scattered over the undulating terrain. At 8.5 mi. it crosses an east–west stone wall about 80 ft. west of MA 32.

Those not wishing to end this hike at MA 32 can take a side trip to Falls Brook, which is less than 1 mi. farther along the trail. Follow the trail right onto MA 32. The trail crosses the highway in about 50 ft., then follows along the more northerly of two dirt roads. The trail soon passes the entrance to

Newton Cemetery, bearing right (east), then at 8.6 mi. bears right (south) at a fork onto a skid road. It continues south-southeast past a tote road that descends a steep slope. At 8.8 mi., with two great, declining beech trees on the right, the trail descends into a brushy area. It enters a closed canopy of hardwoods, now steeply descending, and crosses a tiny stream, continuing parallel to the stream on its north bank. At 9.0 mi. the trail recrosses the stream and continues south. In about 100 ft. Falls Brook is visible to the east at the base of the glen. Still bearing south, the trail now descends to Falls Brook and continues along its bank.

The trail crosses the brook at 9.1 mi. on a boulder ford that is only 250 ft. from the lip of the falls. (*Caution*: *This can be a dangerous place for children.*) In the interest of safety, follow a more interesting route and a spectacular approach to the falls by continuing uphill due east from the brook, bearing right as you crest the slope. You will soon enter the well-used but unmarked trail to the falls. (This path leads from Falls Rd. about 0.3 mi. to the east. Falls Rd. south to this path is passable only by four-wheel-drive vehicles.) The path leads 0.1 mi. to a high ledge overlooking the falls. It proceeds along the edge of the gorge, guarded by a steel-cable fence, to the M–M Trail beside the brook.

Metacomet–Monadnock Trail: Mt. Grace to MA 32

Distances from summit of Mt. Grace

   to brook crossing and Adirondack shelter: 1 mi., 30 min.

   to MA 78: 1.6 mi., 45 min.

   to Kidder Brook: 2.1 mi., 1 hr.

   to Richmond Rd.: 4.7 mi., 2 hr., 20 min.

   to Tully Brook: 5.1 mi., 2 hr., 45 min.

   to Bliss Rd.: 7.6 mi., 3 hr., 50 min.

   to MA 32: 8.5 mi., 4 hr., 15 min.

   to Falls Brook: 9.1 mi., 4 hr., 30 min.

Section 19. MA 32 to NH 119 (4.8 mi.)

From MA 32 the trail follows Fall Brook and enters New Hampshire south of Greenswoods Rd. The trail now runs east of Wheeler Pond for about 1 mi. before connecting with an abandoned town road. The old road leads to a maintained road that in turn reaches NH 119 in 0.5 mi. Turn right onto NH 119 and hike back to a dirt road that leaves the road diagonally to the left. The blazes can be picked up a short way down the dirt road.

Section 20. NH 119 to NH 12 (7.5 mi.)

From NH 119 the trail enters a fairly remote, forested section that passes over undulating terrain. Initially heading north, the path swings east to cross the shallow slopes and marshy floor of the Tully Brook valley. From Tully Brook the trail again gains high ground and long views, including Grand Monadnock from the north portion of Little Monadnock.

Section 21. NH 12 to NH 124 (4.7 mi.)

From the village of Troy the trail follows NH 12 before turning onto Quarry Rd. The path ascends Fern Hill, then descends, crossing a tributary of Quarry Brook. From the brook it climbs Gap Mtn., which provide more views of Grand Monadnock. The section ends at the foot of the mountain at NH 124.

Section 22. Grand Monadnock (2.3 mi.)

From NH 124 the climb up Grand Monadnock follows the Royce and White Arrow Trails southeast of Fassett Brook to an old picnic area. From here the route follows the White Arrow Trail to reach the summit of Grand Monadnock and the northern end of the Metacomet–Monadnock Trail.

Robert Frost Trail

The Robert Frost Trail (RFT) was begun in 1982 as a way to link Amherst conservation properties, but has since grown into a major hiking trail that travels some of the most attractive areas of the Connecticut River Valley. The trail covers more than 40 mi., beginning at Mt. Holyoke Range State Park in Granby and ending at Wendell State Forest in Wendell. It traverses a number of attractive ridges and hills with views across the Connecticut River Valley, passes through 1000-acre Lawrence Swamp, and visits assorted other interesting and scenic places including Mt. Toby and the cascades of Cushman Brook. The Kestrel Trust and the Amherst Trails

Committee (413-256-4045) produce detailed, up-to-date maps as well as the very detailed *Guide to the Robert Frost Trail.* Maps and guides are available from the Amherst Conservation Committee's website and local outlets, including stores in downtown Amherst and outfitter shops. Maps of Mt. Holyoke Range State Park and Mt. Toby State Reservation are available at their headquarters.

Motorized vehicles, open fires, and camping are prohibited on the trail. Equestrians and mountain bikers should only use the trail when the trail bed is dry and firm, which helps reduce the erosion and soil compaction that can damage the trail and nearby plant communities. Much of the trail is on private property; please stay on the trail and respect property rights.

The RFT is marked with rectangular orange blazes. It coincides with numerous other trails along its route, especially the white-blazed Metacomet–Monadnock Trail (M–M Trail). The following description traces the trail from south to north, the direction of frequent blazes.

Section 1. Notch Visitor Center (Mt. Holyoke Range West) to Harris Mtn. Rd. (5.1 mi.)

Parking is available at the Notch Visitor Center on MA 116. The well-blazed trail leaves from behind the visitor center, in concert with the M–M Trail. At 0.6 mi. the M–M Trail leaves to the right while the RFT continues east along the wooded slopes of the Holyoke Range. At 1.7 mi. the RFT turns right to rejoin the M–M Trail in the Mt. Norwottuck–Rattlesnake Knob col. A short steep section of the joined trails reaches Rattlesnake Knob (787 ft.), which provides views. The trails continue together for the next 4 mi., crossing the wooded summit of Long Mtn. (no tower) and descending to Harris Mtn. Rd. Parking is available on Harris Mtn. Rd.

Robert Frost Trail: Notch Visitor Center (Mt. Holyoke Range West) to Harris Mtn. Rd.

Distances from Notch Visitor Center

to M–M Trail: 1.7 mi., 1 hr., 10 min.

to summit of Long Mtn.: 3.9 mi., 2 hr., 5 min.

to Harris Mtn. Rd.: 5.1 mi., 3 hr.

Section 2. Harris Mtn. Rd. to Goodell St. (1.5 mi.)

Starting from the eastern side of Harris Mtn. Rd. (parking) the RFT and M–M Trail continue together briefly through the woods of the eastern Mt. Holyoke Range until the M–M Trail branches right and the RFT turns north (left) then northeast. The RFT reaches the power lines at 0.5 mi. and swings left (north) following the power lines right-of-way to Bay Rd. at 0.6 mi. The trail then crosses Bay Rd. and continues under the power lines north to Hulst Rd. (Orchard Street on some maps) at 0.9 mi. The RFT now turns right (east) on Hulst Rd. to the intersection with Warren Wright Rd. at 1.2 mi. The trail turns left (north) following Warren Wright Rd. through a swamp reaching Goodell St. at 1.5 mi.

Robert Frost Trail: Harris Mtn. Rd. to Goodell St.

Distances from Harris Mtn. Rd.

   to Bay Rd.: 1.0 mi., 30 min.

   to Goodell St.: 1.9 mi., 1 hr.

Section 3. Goodell St. to Station Rd. (3.7 mi.)

The RFT turns left (west) off Wright Rd. and follows the edge of a field. Reaching a second field, it turns north, crosses a small stream, and makes a left turn into the woods. The RFT follows a series of woods roads through Lawrence Swamp, heading generally northwest past Town Well No. 4, a cinder-block building approx. 1.5 mi. from Goodell St. From the building the trail follows a gravel road west that merges with the Baby Carriage Brook Trail at 2.4 mi. Just before the gravel road leaves the woods, the RFT turns sharp right (north) while the Baby Carriage Brook Trail continues west to S. East St. The RFT now passes the east end of farm fields, turns left into the woods, and emerges onto Station Rd., where there is a white sign for Lawrence Swamp and parking to the east on the roadside.

Robert Frost Trail: Goodell St. to Station Rd.

Distances from Goodell St.

   to Town Well No. 4: 1.4 mi., 40 min.

   to Baby Carriage Trail: 2.4 mi., 1hr., 10 min.

   to Station Rd.: 3.7 mi., 2 hr.

Section 4. Station Rd. to Pelham Rd. (4.2 mi.)

The trail turns right (east) onto Station Rd. (parking) and continues across the Norwottuck Rail Trail at Norwottuck Depot, then turns left (north) onto an old road at 0.5 mi. The trail turns right (east) to follow the southern edge of the last small field, then picks up a woods road and turns left into the Amherst Woods subdivision. Zigzag north through the development, following easements and short sections of road to Wildflower Dr. Turn left onto Wildflower Dr. and in 0.1 mi. reenter the woods on the right. The trail continues north to Old Belchertown Rd. at 1.8 mi., where it turns left for 0.2 mi. to reach MA 9, 0.5 mi. west of the Amherst–Belchertown line. Following MA 9 west for 200 ft., the trail then turns right (northeast) near a chain-link fence and continues north past the Amherst landfill and into the Harkness Brook Conservation Area. At 2.7 mi. the trail turns left (east) onto Stony Hill Rd., continues past Gatehouse Rd., and turns left onto a woods path. At 4.2 mi. it reaches Ward St., heads north 200 yd., and crosses Pelham Rd. to the Amethyst Brook Conservation Area parking lot.

Robert Frost Trail: Station Rd. to Pelham Rd.

Distances from Station Rd.

   to Old Belchertown Rd.: 1.8 mi., 45 min.

   to Stony Hill Rd.: 2.7 mi., 1 hr., 15 min.

   to Pelham Rd. and Amethyst Brook Conservation Area: 4.2 mi., 2 hr.

Section 5. Pelham Rd. to Pratts Corner Rd. (4.4 mi.)

The RFT heads north from the parking lot, then east along garden plots and into the woods. It crosses a bridge over Amethyst Brook, then turns left across a second bridge to the north side of the brook. The trail now follows Amethyst Brook to a third bridge. After crossing, the path turns left (northeast) away from the brook and toward Mt. Orient. The trail ascends a woods road (passing a very old car) and rejoins the M–M Trail. There is a short steep section, but the route is generally moderate to the wooded summit of Mt. Orient (957 ft.) at 1.9 mi. There are excellent views from the ledges, with vistas to the west and south. From the summit the RFT continues around the side of Poverty Mtn. through some wooded tracts with active logging operations, journeys through the remainder of the Pelham woods, and reaches Pratts Corner Rd. at 4.4 mi.

Robert Frost Trail: Pelham Rd. to Pratts Corner Rd.

Distances from Pelham Rd. and Amethyst Brook Conservation Area

to Mt. Orient: 1.9 mi., 1 hr., 10 min.

to Pratts Corner Rd.: 4.4 mi., 2 hr., 20 min.

Section 6. Pratts Corner Rd. to Juggler Meadow Rd. (4.9 mi.)

The RFT continues from Pratts Corner Rd. (a.k.a. Shutesbury Rd.) generally northward through the woods to Market Hill Rd. and Atkins Reservoir, a good place to view waterfowl, especially in fall. There the trail turns left (west) along the reservoir before turning left (southwest) away from the water and into the woods. It ascends wooded Mt. Boreas at 1.6 mi. before reaching Flat Hills Rd. (parking). The trail then descends, following Cushman Brook's southern bank in deep woods. Crossing Market Hill Rd., it then stays left of the power lines and ascends a steep bank.

The trail continues north to Bridge St., crosses the brook south of the bridge, passes numerous cascades and pools, and eventually reaches the RR tracks at the south end of the Cushman Brook trestle. Crossing the tracks, the path descends to the Kevin R. Flood Universal Access Trail on the left. The RFT continues to the Robert Francis footbridge, crossing the 70-ft.-long steel span over Cushman Brook and reaching State St. at 2.8 mi. It crosses State St. and goes to the right of Puffer's Pond at 3.2 mi. What looks like an asphalt spillway is all that is left of a gravel road of the Ruxton Gravel Co. The RFT turns right up this "road," then turns left onto a dirt trail and continues to Pulpit Hill Rd. 0.6 mi. east of MA 63. After passing Pulpit Hill Rd., the path proceeds generally north through maple woods and enters the fields of the Eastman Brook Conservation Area. It proceeds west for a short distance, then turns north again, staying on the left side of the fields until it reaches a junction with a loop trail (marked with a white sign) going into the woods. The RFT turns right (east) and heads toward the RR tracks, tracing a course along the side of a field. At the RR tracks (white signs and a brown conservation sign) the trail turns north parallel to the tracks, reaching Juggler Meadow Rd. at 4.9 mi.

Robert Frost Trail: Pratts Corner Rd. to Juggler Meadow Rd.

Distance from Pratts Corner Rd.

   to Mt. Boreas: 1.6 mi., 40 min.

   to State St.: 2.8 mi., 1 hr.

   to Puffer's Pond: 3.2 mi., 1 hr., 25 min.

   to Juggler Meadow Rd. (parking): 4.9 mi., 2 hr., 10 min.

Section 7. Juggler Meadow Rd. to Reservation Rd. (9.4 mi.)

The trail continues north through wooded country west of the tracks, turns east and crosses the tracks, and follows a series of rocky knolls to Depot Rd. at 0.9 mi. It turns left (west) onto Depot Rd. and follows it to MA 63. The trail turns left onto MA 63 and then right onto Bull Hill Rd. Just past the bridge over Long Plain Brook (2.5 mi.), a short distance before reaching the Leverett–Sunderland line, the trail turns right into the woods along the west bank of the brook.

There are maps specifically for Mt. Toby and its numerous interwoven trails. The well-blazed RFT leaves from the Bull Hill parking lot to ascend on a woods road, then bears right at a saddle. It continues east, and ascends a steep ridge, which it follows northwest to the wooded summit of Bull Hill at 3.0 mi. The trail continues on the ridge to blue-blazed South Mtn. Rd., an abandoned woods road. It turns right (east) onto the road and descends, crossing a stream and a north–south woods road. Continuing northeast, the trail crosses several more streams before ascending steeply to a power-line crossing and a left turn onto yet another woods road. As the ascent becomes steeper, the Frost Bypass Trail leaves on the left. The main trail continues to a saddle, where it turns left (north) to cross a broad plateau and descend to an old cabin. A side trail leading east from the cabin ascends Roaring Mtn.

The RFT descends northwest to Roaring Brook, then turns left and follows a well-hiked old road south. Finally winding back around to the north and passing the other end of the Frost Bypass Trail, the trail reaches the Mt. Toby fire tower at 7.4 mi. The descent follows a cleared power line that strikes off to the northeast. A left at a saddle and another left off the power line leads to a woods road near Cranberry Pond. The trail turns left here and continues to a gate on Reservation Rd. in Sunderland at 9.4 mi.

Robert Frost Trail: Juggler Meadow Rd. to Reservation Rd.

Distance from Juggler Meadow Rd.

   to Bull Hill: 3.0 mi., 1 hr., 10 min.

   to Mt. Toby fire tower: 7.4 mi., 2 hr., 45 min.

   to Reservation Rd.: 9.4 mi., 3 hr., 30 min.

Section 8. Reservation Rd. to Ruggles Pond (Wendell State Forest) (7.0 mi.)

From the gate on Reservation Rd. (parking), the RFT turns right, follows Reservation Rd. downhill and then turns left into the woods. Weaving through the Montague WMA, the trail next emerges onto Chestnut Hill Rd. It follows Chestnut Hill Rd. roughly northeast to the intersection with Montague Rd. (white sign) opposite the Wendell State Forest headquarters. The trail continues a short distance into the state forest and ends near the day-use area of Ruggles Pond (parking) and the junction with the M–M Trail.

Robert Frost Trail: Reservation Rd. to Ruggles Pond (Wendell State Forest)

Distance from Reservation Rd.

   to Ruggles Pond: 7.0 mi., 3 hr., 15 min.

Pocumtuck Ridge Trail (BCAMC)

The Pocumtuck Ridge Trail (PRT) is a newly created 15-mi. hiking path that runs from South Sugarloaf Mtn. in Mt. Sugarloaf State Reservation, South Deerfield MA, to the Poet's Seat Tower in the town of Greenfield. Completed by the BCAMC in 2001 with the assistance of AmeriCorps and trail crews from nearby Deerfield Academy, it traces a ridge-top route high above the Connecticut and Deerfield River Valleys. The trail connects public and quasi-public lands including DCR tracts, town conservation lands, land trusts, and Deerfield Academy properties. To date approximately 70 percent of the trail corridor lies on these protected lands. The trail is marked with blue paint blazes and supplemental blue metal diamonds at road crossings and trail intersections.

Section 1. Base of Mt. Sugarloaf Reservation to Pine Nook Rd. (7.9 mi.)

Trailhead parking is available on Sugarloaf Ave. at its junction with MA 116 in South Deerfield. The PRT enters the reservation on a sandy lane and quickly turns right to cross the paved summit access road leading to the summit of South Sugarloaf Mtn. From here the trail climbs steeply on a switchback route to the summit at 0.5 mi. An observation platform offers extensive panoramic views of the Pioneer Valley and beyond. Water and restrooms are available May–October. Descend a paved walkway to a parking area and follow alongside a chain-link fence a short distance to another, larger parking area.

The PRT enters the woods and descends easily along the forested eastern edge of the mountain's steep escarpment. Turning left, descend steeply on a narrow switchback route to a hairpin turn on the paved summit access road. Descend on wooden stairs and follow a wide footpath to the col separating the summits of South and North Sugarloaf Mtns. at 0.8 mi. Bear right, then left, and finally right again, ascending below the cliffs of North Sugarloaf Mtn. The route descends an old ATV trail and leaves it to the left after 100 yd. Follow this narrow footpath along the steep eastern base of the mountain, passing an abandoned field visible through the trees on the right.

The trail now ascends steadily along the base of a talus slope and swings left to gain the forested eastern ridge of the mountain. Turn left at a trail intersection for a pleasant, gradual climb on narrow foot trail. Along the way are limited views of South Sugarloaf Mtn. to the south. Continue along to a viewpoint on the summit of North Sugarloaf Mtn. at 1.5 mi. Extensive views west of the Deerfield River Valley, the Berkshire Hills, and the southern Green Mtns. are available from this cliffside vantage point.

From the view, proceed downhill on a wider trail passing a yellow-blazed side trail on the right. Continue downhill on the western ridge of North Sugarloaf, passing over a narrow drainage stream of a red maple swamp visible on the right. At 2.0 mi. come to an intersection with the red-blazed Hillside Trail and turn right onto it. The PRT and Hillside Trail run together from this point to Hillside Rd.—follow the dual red-and-blue blazes. The trail swings around the north side of the red maple swamp and then begins descending moderately, crossing a small stream. Descend along the north bank of the stream to an intersection with a yellow-blazed trail that goes off to the right. Go left at this intersection on level footing northbound. Come to a brief switchback and descend to the gated parking area on Hillside Rd. at

3.1 mi. There is parking here for 4 vehicles. Turn left onto paved Hillside Rd. for 30 yd. and enter the woods to the right on UMass property, following a fence line downhill to a footbridge over a brook. Climb steeply 50 ft. to the top of a rise above a second brook and descend to cross it over another footbridge.

The trail climbs to the left of a small hill then levels out, passing through a shaded hemlock forest and following close to and above a stream. Heading due north, come to an old wire fence and turn left, descending to cross the brook (no bridge). After the crossing, bear right onto Deerfield conservation land and climb briefly to the remains of an old cinder-block slaughterhouse. From here the trail follows a wider, forested track on a trail easement close to and behind a private residence. Come out to paved Pocumtuck Ave. and turn right, following the road for 300 yd. to a small parking area on the left at 4.0 mi. Enter the woods through a small grassy clearing onto protected land trust property. Come to a trail intersection in 100 yd. and bear left, climbing easily to the top of the Pocumtuck Range at 4.3 mi. From here to Pine Nook Rd. the PRT utilizes the ridge line of this mountain range. *Note: This section is not yet well blazed but is easy to follow, as the trail never leaves the ridge.*

Proceeding due north along the ridge on gentle terrain, pass under power lines at 5.3 mi. Scenic views west and east are available here. Continuing north over several minor ups and downs, the PRT comes out to the summit area of Pocumtuck Rock at 6.1 mi., marked with a communications tower and utility shed. Turn left from the tower onto a narrow trail to the scenic viewpoint over- looking the Deerfield River Valley, Berkshire Hills, and southern Green Mtns.

From here the trail follows a wide, gravel service road. Swing to the right on this road, descending to the first switchback turn. The PRT leaves the service road directly into the woods. Descend moderately to a woods road, crossing it directly and passing over some exposed bedrock to the base of a talus slope and a small, abandoned, concrete service building on the left. Climb briefly on steep footing to the top of some cliffs. Follow along the top of the cliffs for 50 yd. and leave the ledge to the right into a small dell. Climb briefly again to the summit area of the abandoned Deerfield Academy Ski Area at 6.9 mi., following a grassy ski trail past the remains of some towrope equipment near the summit. Limited views are available just off the trail to the left at the top of some cliffs.

From the summit enter a thick hemlock grove, descending to a narrow woods road and turning left onto it. After 200 yd. turn abruptly right and follow a narrower trail as it swings around to join the gravel summit access road. Turn right onto this road and descend to the gated entrance off unpaved Pine Nook Rd. at 7.9 mi. There is parking on the road shoulder for a few vehicles.

Pocumtuck Ridge Trail: Base of Mt. Sugarloaf Reservation to Pine Nook Rd.

Distances from base of Mt. Sugarloaf

   to South Sugarloaf summit: 0.5 mi., 30 min.

   to North Sugarloaf summit: 1.5 mi., 1 hr., 15 min.

   to Pocumtuck Rock: 6.1 mi., 2 hr., 55 min.

   to Pine Nook Rd.: 7.9 mi., 3 hr., 45 min.

Section 2. Pine Nook Rd. to Canada Hill via Poet's Seat Tower (6.9 mi.)

Turn left onto Pine Nook Rd., following it for 300 yd. The PRT leaves the road, turning right to follow a level contour to dirt Rices Ferry Rd., an abandoned town road, at 0.8 mi. Turn right onto this road, descending past a small swamp on the right. After the swamp turn left onto a narrow trail, heading north onto land owned by the Woolman Hill Conference Center. Turn left, uphill, through a red pine plantation onto traprock ledges.

The PRT goes along the top of this small ridge, passing two separate viewpoints looking west. After the second viewpoint begin a steeper descent over several narrow switchbacks, coming out onto paved Keets Rd. at 1.8 mi. Turn left onto this road and, at the bottom of its sharp turn, go right onto a powerline service road. Follow this a short distance and reenter the forest. The trail parallels the power lines out of sight inside the woods. Approach the railroad tracks (*Caution: These are in use*) and cross them directly into a narrow draw, descending a paved road above the Deerfield River. Turn left then right onto MA 5, crossing the river safely on the bridge's sidewalk at 2.8 mi. Turn right onto Cheapside St., following it a short distance to Hope St. on the left. Pass under a small railroad bridge and then immediately leave Hope St., to enter the woods on the right. This section of trail from Hope St. to the Poet's Seat Tower lies entirely on conservation land owned by the town of Greenfield.

The PRT first follows an old RR grade, then leaves it left to join the trail system of Rocky Mtn. Park. Turn right then left and come to a five-way intersection of trails. The PRT swings left briefly, then turns right and climbs a small, unnamed rocky summit. Passing under a power line, it descends to gravel Bears Den Rd. The Bears Den, an open fissure in the cliff face, is 50 yd. to the left on this road. The PRT turns right a short distance then goes left up a short, steep track to the summit of Sachem Head, where the remains of an old wooden viewing platform can be found. Caution is needed here, as a steep cliff is close by. Continue north along this ridge line on a narrow footpath to paved Mtn. Rd. at 4.2 mi. Use caution crossing this busy road. The PRT proceeds close to a paved access road that leads to the Poet's Seat Tower and then follows the road for 200 yd. to the tower at 4.5 mi. The tower offers commanding views of Greenfield and the surrounding countryside.

Proceed north from the tower over a bare rock ledge with more views and enter the woods, descending along the ridge top. Come to an intersection with a red-blazed trail—part of the extensive trail system of Greenfield's Rocky Mt. Park/Temple Woods Conservation Area—and turn right, following dual blue-and-red blazes. The PRT soon turns left, descending steeply from the ridge to the banks of the Connecticut River. Proceed left, following the river upstream to an ascending left turn. Climb from here to paved Turners Falls Rd. at 5.5 mi. Use caution crossing this busy road. Enter the woods, pass under a power line with views east, and continue along the ridge of Canada Hill. The PRT ends at a small residential neighborhood at 6.9 mi. A trail extension is planned that will end the PRT on MA 2A.

Pocumtuck Ridge Trail: Pine Nook Rd. to Canada Hill via Poet's Seat Tower

Distances from Pine Nook Rd.

to Keet's Rd.: 1.8 mi., 45 min.

to Poet's Seat Tower: 4.5 mi., 2 hr., 5 min.

to Turners Falls Rd.: 5.5 mi., 2 hr., 35 min.

to end of PRT: 6.9 mi., 3 hr., 20 min.

Mt. Tom State Reservation

Mt. Tom State Reservation preserves an area of 1800 acres, including that section of the traprock cliffs that lie between Easthampton and Holyoke just west of the Connecticut River commonly known as the Mt. Tom Range. It sports some of the best views in all the Connecticut River Valley, from the Berkshires in the west to the Pelham Hills to the east and long vistas north and south. In fall Mt. Tom is one of the premier raptor-watching sites in the valley, with thousands of hawks and other birds of prey soaring past the mountain. Within its present boundaries are Mt. Nonotuck (827 ft.), Goat Peak (822 ft.), Whiting Peak (1014 ft.), and Dry Knoll (835 ft.). The Mt. Tom Range hosts one of the largest tracts of unbroken forest in the Connecticut River Valley and is an oasis of biodiversity in the area.

Picnic areas, two observation towers, five scenic vistas, canoeing and fishing on Lake Bray, and ice skating (in season) are some of the additional attractions. Mt. Tom Reservation also offers a universal-access (UA) fishing pier on Lake Bray, a UA hiking trail on the shores of the lake, and nearby UA restrooms.

The Mt. Tom Reservation trail system consists of 20 mi. of blazed and maintained trails. Trail signs at roadheads are usually posted a short distance in from the road. (*Note: On trail signs the Metacomet–Monadnock Trail and Smiths Ferry Rd. are identified as M–M Tr. and Bray Rd., respectively.*) About half the trails are suitable for cross-country skiing, of easy-to-moderate difficulty. Mountain bikes and motorized vehicles are not permitted on the trails.

Recently some important changes have taken place on the mountain. The former Mt. Tom ski area was recently purchased for conservation, recreation, and environmental education by a group of partners that includes the United States Fish and Wildlife Service (USFWS), the Massachusetts Department of Conservation and Recreation (DCR), The Trustees of Reservations (TTOR), and the Holyoke Boys and Girls Club (HBGC). DCR owns the northern portion of the area, adjacent to the existing Mt. Tom reservation. USFWS owns the southern part of the property, including the former ski trails and a small pond; it is managed as part of the Silvio O. Conte National Fish and Wildlife Refuge. TTOR owns the northern portion of Little Tom Mtn., and HBGC owns the former base lodge and surrounding area.

The partners are cooperating in inventorying and planning for passive recreation. As activities are allowed, information will be available on signs and kiosks at the property, or by contacting any of the partners. The road accessing the base lodge is currently gated; only authorized vehicles are allowed beyond it. Caution should be used in this area since there is an active quarry on site and large, heavy trucks frequently use the roads.

To reach the Easthampton/MA 141 entrance from the south, take I-91 Exit 17-B to MA 141 west. Travel west about 4 mi. on MA 141 to the entrance on the right. From the north, take I-91 Exit 18 to US 5. Travel US 5 south about 1.5 mi. and turn right onto East St. Follow this road for 3 mi., turn left onto MA 141, and continue to the entrance on the left. To reach the main Holyoke entrance from the south, take Exit 17-A off I-91 to US 5 north. Follow US 5 north for 4 mi. to the entrance on the left. From the north, take Exit 18 off I-91 to US 5 south. Follow US 5 about 4 mi. to the entrance on the right.

Information on trails and regulations can be obtained at the visitor center near the junction of Christopher Clark Rd. and Smiths Ferry Rd., and at park headquarters near Lake Bray at the south end of Smiths Ferry Rd. See maps 5 and 6 included with this book.

Metacomet–Monadnock Trail

This is perhaps the most scenic section of this long-distance hiking trail. For a complete description of this section, see Metacomet–Monadnock Trail, Section 6, MA 141 to MA 47.

Beau Bridge Trail (DCR)

This blue-blazed trail begins on a short dead-end road off Smiths Ferry Rd. From the visitor center follow Smiths Ferry Rd. about 0.4 mi. northwest to the dead-end road on the left. There is a parking area a short distance down the road; the trailhead is on the western bank of Cascade Brook.

The trail proceeds northwest for about 100 yd. through open woods, then turns sharp right (the obvious path straight ahead is an unmarked route that leads to Goat Peak in 0.3 mi.) and descends to Cascade Creek. For the next 0.3 mi. the trail follows the creek downstream, repeatedly crossing and recrossing it on the bridges for which the trail was named. After the ninth bridge the trail leaves the stream and heads north. The path makes a beeline up the hill, merging with and following an old woods road for 0.3 mi. to its junction with the white-blazed Metacomet–Monadnock Trail. To reach the observation tower on Goat Peak turn left onto the M–M Trail and proceed along the top of the ridge for about 0.25 mi.

Beau Bridge Trail

Distances from trailhead on Cascade Brook

to final crossing of Cascade Creek: 0.4 mi., 20 min.

to Metacomet–Monadnock Trail: 0.7 mi., 35 min.

to Goat Peak observation tower via M–M Trail: 1.0 mi., 50 min.

Lake Bray Universal Access Trail (DCR)

This 0.5-mi.-long trail begins near the north shore of Lake Bray near restrooms and a picnic area. From the trailhead the path follows the shore of Lake Bray, passing a universal-access fishing pier along the way. At the junction with the Bray Loop Trail (which continues straight) the UA trail turns right, cruises gently uphill, and reaches the Kay Bee trailhead. The UA trail turns right and proceeds on a slight downhill grade back to the starting point.

Link, Bee Line, & Lost Boulder Trails (DCR)

These trails serve as a link between Smiths Ferry Rd. and some of the major interior trails of the reservation, including the Keystone Trail, Kay Bee Trail, and Bray Loop Trail. Marked with white blazes, the trail begins at a barway on the south side of Smiths Ferry Rd., a short distance above the Cascade Creek bridge. The path ascends the moderately steep hillside to reach the Kay Bee Trail at 0.2 mi. The grade moderates and at 0.3 mi. crosses the Keystone Trail. The path crosses a small stream, then steeply climbs a loose rock embankment before proceeding through hemlock, then open hardwoods, reaching a large glacial erratic (the Lost Boulder) at 0.8 mi. From the boulder the trail descends, steeply at times, on a straight southeasterly course to end at the junction with the Bray Loop Trail.

Link, Bee Line, & Lost Boulder Trails

Distances from Smiths Ferry Rd.

> *to* Kay Bee Trail: 0.2 mi., 10 min.
>
> *to* Keystone Trail: 0.3 mi., 15 min.
>
> *to* Lost Boulder: 0.5 mi., 30 min.
>
> *to* Bray Loop Trail: 0.7 mi., 50 min.

Bray Inner Loop Trail (DCR)

The Bray Inner Loop Trail is a short, easy walk around much of the shore of Lake Bray. At the north shore the blue-blazed path joins the universal-access path for the short walk back to the trailhead at the northern end of Bray Lake. The loop ends on Smiths Ferry Rd. near the picnic area about 0.25 mi. north of the trailhead.

Bray Inner Loop Trail

Distances from Smiths Ferry Rd.

   to lower loop Bray Loop Trail: 0.2 mi., 10 min.

   to upper loop of Bray Loop Trail: 0.3 mi., 15 min.

   to Smiths Ferry Rd. via UA trail: 0.5 mi., 25 min.

Bray Loop Trail (DCR)

This sometimes steep trail begins at the western end of Lake Bray at the junction of the Keystone Trail and the Bray Inner Loop Trail. It can be combined with the UA trail and Inner Loop Trail to provide a moderate-to-strenuous woodland hike through the Bray Brook ravine that encircles much of Lake Bray. From the junction of the Keystone and Bray Inner Loop Trails the Bray Loop Trail swings northwest and ascends, sometimes steeply, before turning southwest. The grade moderates as the path crosses several seasonal streams, and, shortly before it reaches its highest point, the white-blazed Lost Boulder Trail branches right.

    The trail now descends at a moderate rate and crosses Bray Brook on a bridge at 0.9 mi. The Bray Valley Trail is passed on the right as the path begins to cross a level, frequently wet area, passing the Knox Trail at 1.1 mi. The trail then makes an easy descent to the junction with the Inner Loop Trail at 1.4 mi., and then gradually descends toward the lake. It reaches the Inner Bridge Link at 1.4 mi. and continues almost at water level along the southeastern shore of the lake. This section is frequently very muddy. The trail ends on Smiths Ferry Rd., about 0.2 mi. below the Lake Bray parking area.

Bray Loop Trail

Distances from Keystone and Bray Inner Loop Trail junction

   to Lost Boulder Trail: 0.5 mi., 15 min.

   to Bray Valley Trail: 0.8 mi., 30 min.

   to Knox Trail: 1.0 mi., 45 min.

   to lower end of Inner Loop Trail: 1.3 mi., 1 hr.

   to Smiths Ferry Rd. via Inner Loop Trail: 1.7 mi., 1 hr., 15 min.

Kay Bee Trail (DCR)

This blue-blazed woods road connects the Lake Bray area with the central part of the reservation and is an alternative to the longer and somewhat steeper

Keystone Trail. It begins at the west end of the loop on the UA trail about 0.1 mi. from the Lake Bray parking area. The trail immediately begins a steady climb westward, away from the lake. At 0.2 mi., just before a small rocky knoll on the right, the junction of the white-blazed Bee Line/Link Trail is reached and the grade soon eases. The final 0.3 mi. is almost level, and the trail ends at Keystone Junction, where it meets the Keystone Trail and the Keystone Extension.

Kay Bee Trail

Distances from Lake Bray parking area

  to Bee Line/Link Trail: 0.3 mi., 15 min.

  to Keystone Junction: 0.6 mi., 25 min.

Keystone Trail (DCR)

This was one of the original ski trails cleared in the reservation long before the advent of private ski areas. The trail follows a woods road for much of its length; it is unblazed but sparsely marked with red wooden Keystone signs. It begins as a path on the south side of Smiths Ferry Rd., opposite the second of the two upper parking areas, about 0.3 mi. from the visitor center and a short distance before the dead-end road to Hamden Field. At 0.1 mi. a blue-blazed trail linking the Nature Trails is reached. The Keystone Trail veers southeast, ascending slightly and reaching Keystone Junction in a clearing at 0.3 mi. Here the Kay Bee Trail branches left, the Keystone Extension branches right, and the Keystone Trail continues along a woods road straight ahead, descending in wide-sweeping curves through hemlock and hardwood forests. It crosses the Bee Line/Link Trail at 0.7 mi., and descends, steeply at times, to the foot of the hill where the trail reaches its lowest point. It then ascends easily and ends at the junction of the Bray Loop Trail and Bray Inner Loop Trail. The Lake Bray parking areas are about 0.2 mi. to the left.

Keystone Trail

Distances from Smiths Ferry Rd.

  to Keystone Junction: 0.3 mi., 15 min.

  to Bee Line/Link Trail: 0.7 mi., 20 min.

  to Bray Loop Trail: 1 mi., 30 min.

Keystone Extension (DCR)

The red-blazed Keystone Extension links the Keystone Trail with the Quarry Trail and can then be used to access the M–M Trail by following either the orange-blazed D. O. C. Trail west or the Quarry Trail northwest. The path begins at Keystone Junction, 0.3 mi. from the Keystone Trail trailhead on Smiths Ferry Rd. Proceeding west, the trail crosses several ledgey areas and at 0.3 mi. descends from a rise to cross a swampy section on a series of bog bridges. At 0.4 mi., near the top of a second rise, a blue-blazed link trail branches right and leads in 0.1 mi. to the Nature Trails. Just over the rise, the trail makes a sharp left and circles a swamp. The trail now descends and reaches the valley floor at 0.7 mi. The path swings left as it runs over level ground, crossing a stream on a bridge before ending at the Quarry Trail, opposite the junction with the D. O. C. Trail.

Keystone Extension

Distance from Keystone Junction (Keystone Trail)

   to Quarry Trail: 0.8 mi., 30 min.

Nature Trails (DCR)

The Nature Trails are a group of loop paths and connector trails, with the trailhead located near the museum about 0.2 mi. southeast of the visitor center on Smiths Ferry Rd. A printed guide to the flora and geology of the area is available at the museum and at the visitor center. An updated, colorful trail map is sold there as well.

Quarry Trail (DCR)

This yellow-blazed woods road is the shortest and most convenient route across the range from the visitor center and provides access to several other trails, thus permitting circuits of varying length and difficulty. From the visitor center on Smiths Ferry Rd., go southwest 0.1 mi. along Christopher Clark Rd., then turn left uphill onto a paved road, passing the maintenance buildings and a small parking area. Continue through a metal gate and follow an old road about 100 yd. to the beginning of the Quarry Trail, where it crosses the Metacomet–Monadnock Trail.

Initially almost level, the trail soon circles a small pond on the left, gradually bears south, and begins a gentle climb. At 0.3 mi. the orange-blazed D. O. C. Trail and the red-blazed Keystone Extension diverge right and left, respectively. At 0.7 mi., shortly before reaching the height-of-land, the Middle Loop Trail branches right. The descent to the south is noticeably rougher and steeper. At 1.0 mi. the trail crosses a stream and, just beyond the Knox Extension, branches left. Presently the trail ends, but it may be extended into recently acquired lands or be connected to other trails in the system shortly.

Quarry Trail

Distances from Metacomet–Monadnock Trail

   to D. O. C. Trail and Keystone Extension: 0.3 mi., 20 min.

   to Middle Loop Trail: 0.7 mi., 30 min.

   to Knox Extension: 1 mi., 40 min.

Knox Extension

The Knox Extension swings south from the Quarry Trail near the reservation's western boundary, roughly following that boundary for about 0.25 mi. to its end north and west of the Bray Valley Trail.

Bray Valley Trail

The Bray Valley Trail runs from the southwestern end of the Bray Loop Trail generally west to near the southern end of the Knox Extension. The trail begins along the south bank of Bray Brook and follows the stream southwest for less than 0.25 mi. It then begins to climb and ends at about 0.4 mi., close to the Knox Extension at the end of the DCR reservation property. This trail may soon connect to nearby trails.

Teabag Trail (DCR)

The Teabag Trail links the southern portion of Smiths Ferry Rd. and the M–M Trail on the ridge line about 0.2 mi. east of Goat Peak. The trailhead is on the north side of the road, about 0.25 mi. north of the Smiths Ferry Rd. gate near Lake Bray. The red-blazed strenuous path climbs, very steeply at times, gaining about 500 ft. of elevation over its 1.0-mi. length. It proceeds at an easy grade through mature hemlock woods, then crosses and descends a rocky out-crop at 0.5 mi. The trail now resumes its climb, with numerous changes of direction, and soon enters a more open hardwood forest with luxuriant mountain laurel thickets. Crossing a small divide at 0.9 mi., it bears slightly west and follows another woods road to the trail's end at the M–M Trail, a few yards east of the Beau Bridge Trail.

Teabag Trail

Distance from Smiths Ferry Rd.

   to Metacomet–Monadnock Trail: 1 mi., 50 min.

Knox Trail

The Knox Trail begins on the southern portion of the Bray Loop Trail about 0.5 mi. from the western end of Lake Bray. The trail begins on a fairly flat portion of the Bray Loop Trail and heads south, climbing easily. The path levels out and veers more southwest for nearly 0.25 mi. Beginning an easy-to-moderate climb, the trail now turns west and ends near the point that the Knox Extension and Bray Valley Trail end. This trail, too, could soon connect to other nearby trails.

Mt. Holyoke Range: West

Named for Elizur Holyoke, one of three men appointed by the General Court of the Massachusetts Bay Colony in 1653 to divide lands in this region into plantations for the first settlers, this traprock range extends from the Connecti-cut River east about 7 mi. in the towns of Hadley, South Hadley, Granby, and Amherst. It includes Mt. Holyoke (940 ft.); Mt. Hitchcock (1002 ft.), named in honor of Edward Hitchcock, a president of Amherst College who did much geological research in the area; Bare Mtn. (1014 ft.); Mt. Norwottuck (1106 ft.), which takes its name from the Norwottuck Indians who lived in the area; and Long Mtn. (920 ft.). The range contains two passes, or notches: Taylor Notch east of Mt. Holyoke, through which runs the automobile road to the summit of Mt. Holyoke (closed in winter), and Amherst Notch (or simply "the Notch") between Bare Mtn. and Mt. Norwottuck, through which runs MA 116. The state-run Notch Visitor Center is located here.

With its open ledges providing extensive views, its lush deciduous, hemlock, and pine forests, and the Metacomet–Monadnock Trail along its entire length, the Holyoke Range is attractive to hikers, skiers, geologists, and naturalists. Much of the land is protected as part of the Skinner State Park, the Holyoke Range State Park, and adjoining town conservation lands. Refer to maps 5 and 6 included with this book, and also the USGS Mt. Holyoke and Belchertown quadrangles.

The western part of the range, between MA 47 and MA 116, has three principal summits: Mt. Holyoke, Mt. Hitchcock, and Bare Mtn. Mt. Holyoke is the farthest west and provides impressive views of the Connecticut River Valley and of the Mt. Tom Range extending southwest on the opposite side of the river. An automobile road (closed in winter) leads to the summit, where the Summit House is a popular picnic spot.

J. A. Skinner State Park (390 acres) off MA 47 in Hadley includes the summit area of Mt. Holyoke. It offers universally accessible restrooms, 20 picnic sites (many with great views) and the Summit House atop the mountain.

Tramway Trail

This yellow-blazed trail begins on MA 47 about 0.3 mi. north of the main entrance. The trail heads directly and strenuously up the western side of the mountain, jogging back and forth on switchbacks as it gains elevation. The trail crosses the summit road below the Summit House, then makes a final steep climb to the Summit House at the mountaintop.

Tramway Trail

Distance from MA 47

   to Summit House: 0.8 mi., 40 min.

Dry Brook Trail

This red-blazed trail on the south side of Mt. Holyoke makes a good snowshoe and ski route in winter and a pleasant hiking route in spring because of the profusion of wildflowers. The trail leaves the summit road (not open to cars in winter) at Taylor Notch, where the Metacomet–Monadnock Trail crosses the road heading east and west. Leaving the south side of the summit road, the trail descends gradually along the western edge (right) of a broad, wooded hollow. Bearing more right at the head of a ravine with a small brook, the trail soon becomes a cleared path on the hillside and continues down the ridge line to join a well-defined woods road. The yellow-blazed Lithia Springs Trail exits left (south) here.

The Dry Brook Trail turns right (southwest) down the road and continues through a splendid forested glen. Beyond a power-line crossing the trail bears right onto a road just above a deep, rocky ravine and follows it to a small pond on the left. The trail soon turns right onto the cleared strip of an underground telephone line (marked with posts). It continues several yards to its junction with the Metacomet–Monadnock Trail. Continuing straight, the trail ends at a gravel one-way road that connects MA 47 to the summit road.

Dry Brook Trail

Distances from summit road

  to Lithia Springs Trail: 0.4 mi., 20 min.

  to Metacomet–Monadnock Trail: 1.7 mi., 1 hr., 15 min.

Taylors Notch Trail

Starting from the dirt parking area on MA 47 in Hadley, this yellow-blazed trail follows the same route as the blue-blazed Halfway House Trail for 0.2 mi., where the Halfway House Trail turns right. The Taylors Notch Trail goes left a short distance, then turns right and begins a gradual ascent. Soon the trail follows a gully and begins a steeper ascent, terminating at the elbow of the paved summit road. The white-blazed Metacomet–Monadnock Trail crosses the summit road just ahead, and the red-blazed Dry Brook Trail descends from Taylors Notch on the south side of the road.

Taylors Notch Trail

Distance from MA 47 parking area

  to summit road: 0.9 mi., 40 min.

Metacomet–Monadnock Trail

This white-blazed long-distance hiking trail passes through the Mt. Holyoke Range and Skinner State Parks for about 9 mi. of its total length. It is a scenic hike that never leaves the ridge of the Mt. Holyoke Range. For a more complete description, see Metacomet–Monadnock Trail, Section 7, MA 47 to MA 116.

Halfway House Trail

This blue-blazed trail starts from the same parking area as the Taylors Notch Trail. It follows the yellow-blazed Taylors Notch Trail for 0.2 mi., then turns right (west) where the two trails split. It immediately crosses a wooden footbridge and follows a well-worn woods road across another stream, where the trail begins to climb after turning left. After a series of gentle switchbacks and moderate climbing, the trail terminates at the paved summit road. (Parking is available here.)

Halfway House Trail

Distance from MA 47 parking area

   to summit road: 0.8 mi., 35 min.

Mt. Holyoke Range: East

The eastern portion of the Mt. Holyoke Range is roughly bounded by MA 116 on the west and Harris Mtn. Rd. to the east, a distance of about 3 mi. In between are the two principal peaks of the range, Mt. Norwottuck (1106 ft.) and Long Mtn. (920 ft.), the summits connected by a broad traprock ridge covered with hardwoods, hemlock stands, and laurel. The overhanging ledges on Mt. Norwottuck are the so-called horse caves of Revolutionary War days, supposed to have been used to shelter the horses of Daniel Shays and his men at the time of Shays' Rebellion. There are several cliffs and open ledges accessed by trails that afford excellent views. The eastern Mt. Holyoke Range is traversed by both the Metacomet–Monadnock and Robert Frost Trails. Information and maps are available in the state park's Notch Visitor Center on MA 116 in Amherst.

Laurel Loop Trail

This short loop trail starts and ends at the Notch Visitor Center. It is marked by blue triangles. After descending a hill shaded by large evergreen trees, it takes a sharp left and follows the old trolley bed together with the Trolley Bed Trail (blazed yellow) for 0.3 mi. The trail then exits left from the trolley bed and ascends gradually back to the Notch Visitor Center.

Laurel Loop Trail

Distance from Notch Visitor Center

   to visitor center (circuit): 0.75 mi., 30 min.

Brookbank Trail

To reach the trailhead follow Laurel Loop Trail to the Trolley Bed Trail, turn left (north) onto the Trolley Bed Trail, and travel to the trail junction where the Brookbank Trail leaves right. The trail is marked with yellow blazes and descends along the ravine of Sweet Alice Brook. It follows the brook for a while, roughly parallel to the Trolley Bed Trail to the west. At the junction with the combined Northside Trail and Sweet Alice Trail on the right the Brookbank Trail swings left (west) and meets the Trolley Bed Trail about 0.25 mi. south of Bay Rd. To return to the visitor center turn left (south) onto the Trolley Bed Trail.

Brookbank Trail

Distances from Trolley Bed Trail

   to Sweet Alice Brook: 0.4 mi., 20 min.

   to Notch Visitor Center via Laurel Loop Trail and Trolley Bed Trail: 2.4 mi., 1 hr., 20 min.

Northside Trail

The Northside Trail is marked by blue triangles and is used primarily as a cross-country ski trail. It connects with the Brookbank Trail near Sweet Alice Brook and winds eastward along a series of old logging roads. The trail exits right (east) from the Brookbank Trail and in 0.1 mi. turns sharp left, then sharp right. After crossing a small brook it immediately goes left and ascends across a side slope to a large white pine stand. It turns left onto a logging road and in 100 yd. comes to the corner of an orchard, where it turns right, ascending gradually to a power-line right of way. The trail bears right, following the power line a short distance, then bears left under the line and into the woods.

    After crossing a brook, the trail turns right onto a logging road and ascends, eventually turning right onto another logging road. It follows this road north for 0.3 mi., then turns sharp left into a hemlock grove. After descending a hill, the trail bears right and then turns sharp right onto a logging road. In 25 yd. it exits left, ascending a steep hill and then turning left onto yet another logging road. The trail leaves this road on the right and continues through the woods until it ends at a yellow-blazed trail in the town of Amherst's Holyoke Range Conservation Area.

Northside Trail

Distance from Brookbank Trail

   to Holyoke Range Conservation Area: 1.6 mi., 1 hr., 10 min.

Metacomet–Monadnock Trail & Robert Frost Trail

These two long-distance trails coincide for much of the traverse of the range except near Mt. Norwottuck, where the M–M Trail goes over the mountain, passing near the horse caves, and the RFT circles the base of the mountain.

   See Metacomet–Monadnock Trail, Section 8, MA 116 to Harris Rd., or Robert Frost Trail, Section 1, Notch Visitor Center to Harris Rd.

Amherst Conservation Commission Trails

A significant portion of the land in this part of the range belongs to the town of Amherst's Conservation Commission, acquired by purchase or gift. A trail guide prepared by the Conservation Commission is available in local bookstores. Conservation area trailheads and access points can be found as follows (all areas have trails unless otherwise noted):

   Eastman Brook: Entrance at a gate on the west side of Leverett Rd. in North Amherst, 0.1 mi. south of the Leverett–Amherst line.

   Podick Sanctuary and Katharine Cole Sanctuary: Entrance and parking area on the west side of MA 116, 0.4 mi. south of the Amherst–Sunderland line.

   Mill River: Entrance from Pine St., State St., Mill St., or MA 63 in North Amherst; handicapped-accessible trail parking is on the south side of State St., 100 yd. east of the main gate and entrance to Puffer's (Factory Hollow) Pond.

   Wildwood: Entrance from the back (east) end of the Village Park Apartments off E. Pleasant St., 1.3 mi. north of Amherst center.

   Amethyst Brook: Entrance and parking on the north side of Pelham Rd., 0.5 mi. west of the Amherst–Pelham line.

   Skillings Path: Trailhead just south of the junior high school on the corner of Chestnut and High Sts.

Larch Hill: Parking and environmental education headquarters building (Hitchcock Center for the Environment) on the west side of MA 116 (S. Pleasant St.), 1.1 mi. south of Amherst center.

Larch Hill North: Entrance from Larch Hill (see previous entry) or from the end of Hillcrest Place (west off S. Pleasant St., 1 mi. south of Amherst center).

Upper Fort River: Entrance and parking on S. East St., just north of the bridge over the Fort River, 1.1 mi. south of MA 9.

Lower Fort River: Trailhead on the west side of MA 116, across from the entrance to Crocker Farm School, 2 mi. south of MA 9.

Harkness Brook: Entrance on the west side of Harkness Rd. on the Amherst–Pelham line, 0.6 mi. north of MA 9.

Mt. Castor: Entrance at the end of Valley View Dr., off S. East St., 1.6 mi. south of MA 9.

Hop Brook: Entrance on the east side of S. East St., 2.1 mi. south of MA 9.

Plum Brook: Entrance on the south side of Potwine Lane, 0.5 mi. east of MA 116 in South Amherst and on the north and south sides of Pomeroy Lane, 0.5 mi. east of MA 116.

Mt. Pollux: Entrance at 1403 S. East St. (Take the gravel road uphill through the gate to the parking area.) There is no trail, but it's possible to walk through the orchard to the summit, which affords fine 360-degree views.

Lawrence Swamp: Entrance and parking on Station Rd. at the Central Vermont Railroad crossing, 0.9 mi. east of the South Amherst common; other entrances at 1290 S. East St. (Baby Carriage Trail) and Station Rd., just west of the Hop Brook road crossing.

Elf Meadow: Entrances on Hulst Rd., off Bay Rd., in South Amherst.

Mt. Holyoke Range: Take Bay Rd. from MA 116. Entrance and parking via a paved drive off the south side of Bay Rd., just west of the junction of Chapel Rd. and Bay Rd.

Kenneth Cuddebank Trail (7 mi. from Rattlesnake Knob on the Holyoke Range north to MA 9 via the Plum Springs, Plum Brook, and Mt. Castor trails.

Hop Brook Conservation Areas: Access points on Chapel Rd., 200 ft. north of Bay Rd.; Middle St., 0.25 mi. north of Bay Rd.; Shays St., 0.6 mi. east of MA 116; S. East St., 1.5 mi. south of MA 9; and Old Belchertown Rd., 0.1 mi. south of MA 9.

Arcadia Nature Center and Wildlife Sanctuary (MAS)

Managed by the Massachusetts Audubon Society, the sanctuary is located in Easthampton and Northampton. It comprises approximately 698 acres of floodplain forest, marsh, meadow, and upland forest on an ancient oxbow of the Connecticut River that borders the present famous oxbow. The sanctuary offers 5 mi. of trails (one designed especially for children) and a nature center with a solar greenhouse. It is noted for its exhibitions of food and cover plantings for wildlife and the observation tower that overlooks Arcadia Marsh. A modest admission fee is charged. For a pleasant walk along river and marsh follow the Old Coach Rd. to the River Trail, which then hugs the shore to the Trolley Line. The Fern Trail continues along the marsh, coming to the observation tower. From the tower continue along the shore and follow the Cedar Trail and Tulip Tree Trail, respectively, back to the nature center and parking area.

To reach the sanctuary take I-91 to Exit 18 (US 5, Northampton). Turn right onto US 5 south and travel 1.4 mi. Turn right onto East St. at the sign for Easthampton Center (Oxbow Sports is on the corner); follow East St. for 1.2 mi. and turn right onto Fort Hill Rd. at the Massachusetts Audubon sign. Travel 0.9 mi. and bear right at the next Massachusetts Audubon sign, then turn left into the sanctuary entrance.

Holland Glen (BHS)

The Belchertown Historical Society (BHS) preserves this steep-sided ravine and its sparkling stream shaded by a majestic stand of mature hemlock. From the intersection of US 202 and MA 9 in Belchertown follow MA 9 west for 2.8 mi. to parking on the right. The glen and the white-blazed Meta-comet–Monadnock Trail are about 0.25 mi. north of the parking area.

Mt. Lincoln

Mt. Lincoln (1240 ft.), located in the town of Pelham, has a flat summit and offers extensive views in all directions from the fire tower. The University of Massachusetts Department of Forestry and Wildlife Management owns and manages 1195 acres as Cadwell Memorial Forest. Several miles of unmarked woods roads are open to the public. There is presently a debate whether the area should support hiking and mountain biking—an issue that is still unresolved. A section of the white-blazed Metacomet–Monadnock Trail passes through the forest and over the summit. The summit also has transmission facilities for the five-college radio station. Refer to the USGS Belchertown and Shutesbury quadrangles.

Metacomet–Monadnock Trail (BCAMC)

Several miles of the 98-mi. Metacomet–Monadnock Trail pass through Cadwell Memorial Forest and over the summit of Mt. Lincoln. For a complete description, see Metacomet–Monadnock Trail, Section 10, MA 9 (Holland Glen) to Mt. Lincoln.

Northfield Mtn. Recreation Center (NU)

Northfield Mtn. Recreation Center is a multisport facility operated by North-east Utilities (NU) that sits atop a huge electrical generating station carved from the mountain's bedrock. Best known as a center for winter sports, including cross-country skiing and snowshoeing, the 26 mi. of mountaintop trails offer excellent hiking in the warmer months (hiking is not allowed once the ski season begins).

Most of the trails are wide woods roads; some have been set aside just for hikers and generally travel north to south through the center of the property. One of the nicest is the Rose Ledge Trail, which begins just south of the visitor center and proceeds south roughly parallel to the 10th Mtn. Ski Trail. Along the way are overlooks with long views over the Connecticut River Valley. To reach the crest of Northfield Mtn. and the overlook turn right onto the Hill 'n Dale Trail, which leads to the 10th Mtn. Trail. Turn left onto the 10th Mtn. Trail and walk about 0.2 mi. to a short trail on the right that leads to the overlook at about 1100 ft. in elevation.

In addition to hiking, Northfield Mtn. offers diverse educational programs, including fly fishing, bird watching, studying old-growth forests, and carving your own canoe paddle.

The visitor center is located off MA 63 about 2.1 mi. north of the junction of MA 2 and MA 63 in Millers Falls.

Mt. Grace State Forest (DCR)

Mt. Grace (1625 ft.) is the second tallest peak in Massachusetts east of the Connecticut River. During King Philip's War in 1676 warriors of the Wampanoag Nation captured Mary Rowlandson and her infant daughter Grace. As they were being taken west, the baby died and was buried by her mother at the mountain that has since borne her child's name. Situated in the town of Warwick, this 1458-acre state forest includes a wooded summit and a steel fire tower that provides a 360-degree view, including Mt. Monadnock in New Hampshire and the Quabbin Reservoir in Massachusetts. The summit is reached via the white-blazed Metacomet–Monadnock Trail (M-M Trail) or by Fire Tower Rd. For a description of the trail, see Metacomet–Monadnock Trail, Sections 17 and 18, Gulf Rd. to Mt. Grace, and Mt. Grace to MA 32.

To reach Mt. Grace, take MA 2 to MA 2A, travel east to MA 78, then continue north to Warwick. The park entrance is on the left.

Fire Tower Rd.

The trail begins on MA 78 opposite the fountain on the common of Warwick village. The trail follows a road that is one house north of the village store (a sign reads, Northfield 8). It turns right in 100 yd. onto a dead-end lane beside a barn (where parking is available in summer), passes through a gate leaving a new house on the right, continues past a barn on the left, and goes through a second gate into the woods. Water is available on the right, just inside this gate. The trail ascends along the road, with a telephone line close by. The M–M Trail enters on the left at the foot of the final steep climb to the summit.

Fire Tower Rd.

Distances from Warwick village (MA 78)

   to Metacomet–Monadnock Trail: 0.9 mi., 30 min.

   to summit of Mt. Grace: 1.3 mi., 40 min.

Mt. Toby State Demonstration Forest (UMASS)

Mt. Toby (1269 ft.) lies partly in Sunderland and partly in Leverett on the east bank of the Connecticut River roughly across the river from Mt. Sugarloaf. Its rugged sides are well forested and have numerous brooks. There is a fire tower on the summit affording excellent views. Mt. Toby State Demonstration

Forest, operated by the University of Massachusetts, comprises 755 acres. The trails described here are the usual routes used to climb the mountain, but numerous woods roads also invite exploration. Refer to the USGS Mt. Toby quadrangle.

Woodbury Trail (Middle Mtn. Rd.)

This trail is for the most part a logging or jeep road. To reach the trailhead follow MA 116 for 1.0 mi. south of Sunderland (6.0 mi. north of Amherst) to N. Silver Lane. Turn left (north) onto N. Silver Lane, continue 0.4 mi., then turn right onto Reservoir Rd. Follow this 0.2 mi. to Nebo Rd., turn left, and continue for a short distance to a place where cars can be parked on the left.

The trail enters the woods and climbs gradually in a generally northeast direction, following white blazes at each of several junctions. It passes a deep, forested brook ravine on the right and at 1.5 mi. passes the blue-blazed Link Trail on the left. At about 1.8 mi. the trail passes under a power line (where a side path leads left to a view from the height-of-land) and becomes less traveled. A short distance beyond, after a moderate climb, the trail emerges in a clearing. (In the 1800s this area was farmed by Irish immigrants and was referred to as the Paddy Farms area.) The trail leads right onto a level grade, following the white blazes over an eroded streambed. In a short distance the trail joins the orange-blazed Robert Frost Trail, which eventually leads over the summits of Roaring Mtn. and Mt. Toby.

Woodbury Trail (Middle Mtn. Rd.)

Distances from Nebo Rd.

to Link Trail: 1.5 mi., 35 min.

to clearing: 2 mi., 50 min.

to Robert Frost Trail: 2.2 mi., 1 hr.

North Mtn. Rd.

This red-blazed trail follows a jeep road from MA 116 to near the summit and from there follows a cleared and blazed path. To reach the trailhead follow MA 47 north from the center of Sunderland (at the junction of MA 116 and MA 47) for 0.5 mi. to N. Silver Lane. Turn right onto N. Silver Lane and continue 0.2 mi. to Park St. Turn left onto Park St. and continue to the end.

Parking is available near the entrance to Sunderland Town Park or at the small pond a short distance down gravel North Mtn. Rd. on the right.

The trail continues straight ahead on the gravel road, which goes uphill past a house on the left and bears left into the woods. The trail passes puddingstone ledges on the right and soon a small clearing on the left. (Avoid the gravel road that comes in on the left. This road leads to Sunderland–Montague Rd. 1 mi. north of Sunderland.)

The trail follows the red blazes through a red pine plantation and gradually ascends to blue-blazed Gunn Mtn. Rd. on the left. Eventually the trail crosses under power lines and bears left. The blue-blazed Link Trail bears right here to cross a small stream and eventually connect with the white-blazed Middle Mtn. Rd. After passing under the power lines, North Mtn. Rd. soon passes the blue-blazed Sugar Farms Trail on the left. It continues uphill past an abandoned sugar shack on the left (last water) and soon leaves the woods road on the right. The trail ascends steeply 0.3 mi. to the summit of Mt. Toby and its junction with the orange-blazed Robert Frost Trail.

North Mtn. Rd.

Distances from Park St.

to Gunn Mtn. Rd.: 1 mi., 35 min.

to Link Trail: 1.3 mi., 50 min.

to Sugar Farms Trail: 1.4 mi., 55 min.

to summit of Mt. Toby: 2.1 mi., 1 hr., 25 min.

Summit Rd.

This white-blazed service road is passable for trucks and jeeps but is not ordinarily open to the public as an automobile road. It provides an easy descent after dark, and unless it is icy, it is suitable for travel on snowshoes and skis in winter. The road was used to reach the summit with mountain wagons in the late 1800s. At that time there was a passenger stop and picnic area at a railroad station at the foot of the mountain in Leverett. To reach the trail, follow Reservation Rd. to the gate into Mt. Toby State Demonstration Forest, where parking is available. (Reservation Rd. runs south of the Sunderland–Montague line between MA 47 and MA 63.) The gate is just west of the white forest headquarters building and shed. The Central Vermont

Railroad tracks are a short distance east at Cranberry Pond, and both the tracks and the pond are just off MA 63.

The road, which is well maintained, leads south through conifer plantations, leaving the orange-blazed Robert Frost Trail, which it follows for a short distance in the beginning on the right. At 0.2 mi. leave the Robert Frost Trail and follow the white blazes. Soon after the road passes a clearing on the left, the red-blazed Telephone Line Trail exits right from the road. The road continues straight ahead and ascends into the glen of Roaring Brook, passes the blue-blazed Roaring Brook Trail on the left, and swings right and close to the brook. After several brook crossings, the road climbs gently, joins again with the Robert Frost Trail, and continues straight ahead. (Do not turn left onto the Robert Frost Trail, which climbs past the Metawampe Cabin.) The road soon passes the red-blazed Upper Link Trail on the right, then bears left to reach the junction with the yellow-blazed Robert Frost Bypass Trail. Summit Rd. turns sharp right at the junction with the Robert Frost Bypass Trail and follows the Robert Frost Trail to the summit.

Summit Rd.

Distances from gate to Mt. Toby State Demonstration Forest

to Telephone Line Trail: 0.5 mi., 20 min.

to Roaring Brook Trail: 0.8 mi., 30 min.

to Robert Frost Trail: 1 mi., 40 min.

to Upper Link Trail: 1.2 mi., 50 min.

to Robert Frost Bypass Trail: 1.6 mi., 1 hr., 15 min.

to summit of Mt. Toby: 3 mi., 1 hr., 45 min.

Telephone Line Trail

Many hikers use this trail to descend the mountain because it is somewhat steep just below the summit. Combined with Summit Rd., it provides an alternate route on the eastern side of the mountain.

Follow the white-blazed Summit Rd. 0.8 mi. south to the red-blazed Telephone Line Trail, which exits right. The trail soon merges with the orange-blazed Robert Frost Trail, but stays left under the lines as the Robert Frost Trail exits right. The trail continues uphill past the red-blazed Hemlock Hill Loop Trail on the right. At a notch well up on the mountain, it turns right at the junction with the red-blazed Upper Link Trail, which goes left. The trail continues under the telephone lines as it steeply ascends to the summit. (*Note: When descending, it is important to turn left at the foot of the steep section below the summit and again left at the junction with white-blazed Summit Rd.*) Most of this trail is part of the long-distance Robert Frost Trail and is marked with its orange blazes.

Telephone Line Trail

Distances from Summit Rd.

   to Hemlock Hill Loop Trail: 0.5 mi., 25 min.

   to Upper Link Trail: 0.9 mi., 45 min.

   to summit of Mt. Toby: 1.7 mi., 1 hr., 10 min.

Mt. Sugarloaf Reservation

Mt. Sugarloaf Reservation (532 acres) includes South Sugarloaf Mtn. (652 ft.) and North Sugarloaf Mtn. (791 ft.). South Sugarloaf, commonly called Mt. Sugarloaf, offers an unsurpassed view of the Connecticut River and its fertile valley. A narrow, paved automobile road (not open in winter) winds up to the summit, where it terminates at an ample paved parking area. The original summit house, built in 1864, burned years ago, but a modern pavilion has been built and a caretaker is on the premises during summer. The steep Pocumtuck Ridge Trail at the southern end of the mountain ascends via many switchbacks to the summit directly from the parking area off Sugarloaf St. near the junction of MA 116 and the summit road. Several picnic tables and restrooms are located on the summit. The summit road leaves MA 116 about 1 mi. west of its intersection with MA 47 in Sunderland and 1 mi. east of South Deerfield and US 5. Refer to the USGS Mt. Toby quadrangle.

West Side Trail

This trail begins at the dirt parking area at the junction of MA 116 and the paved summit road. The trail skirts a ball field on the left and follows along a telephone line a short distance into the woods. From here it follows a level grade, then ascends gently to its junction with the blue-blazed Pocumtuck Ridge Trail in the saddle between South Sugarloaf Mtn. and North Sugarloaf Mtn. The Pocumtuck Ridge Trail leads to the summit of South Sugarloaf Mtn.

West Side Trail

Distances from parking area at beginning of summit road

> *to* Pocumtuck Ridge Trail: 0.6 mi., 35 min.
>
> *to* summit of South Sugarloaf Mtn. (via Pocumtuck Ridge Trail): 1.1 mi., 1 hr., 15 min.

Hillside Trail

This trail is a good access path to the summit on the northern side of North Sugarloaf Mtn. from the gate on paved Hillside Rd. in Deerfield. To reach the trailhead, take River Rd. north from its junction with MA 116 next to the Sunderland Bridge over the Connecticut River. Follow River Rd. several miles, past the open fields of the University of Massachusetts experimental farm, to its junction with Hillside Rd. on the left. Proceed up Hillside Rd. a short distance to the gated trail entrance on the left.

The trail goes south on a level grade, then turns right to follow a small stream gully, rather steeply at times, to a lovely swamp on the left. There it joins the blue-blazed Pocumtuck Ridge Trail, which continues to the summit of North Sugarloaf Mtn.

Hillside Trail

Distances from Hillside Rd.

> *to* Pocumtuck Ridge Trail: 1.1 mi., 1 hr.
>
> *to* summit of North Sugarloaf Mtn. (via Pocumtuck Ridge Trail): 1.3 mi., 1 hr., 15 min.

DAR State Forest (DCR)

The fire tower on Moore's Hill (1697 ft.) in Daughters of the American Revolution (DAR) State Forest affords a panoramic view of the area and is well worth visiting. This 1517-acre state forest has two lakes (Upper and Lower Highland Lakes), more than 15 mi. of hiking, skiing, and snowmobile trails, two camping areas with 50 campsites, and a swimming beach. DAR State Forest has been a leader in providing universally accessible (UA) facilities; it now offers UA restrooms, swimming, fishing, nature trails, boating, camping, and picnicking. Hiking trails are marked with blue triangles, and multiuse trails have orange markers. Bridle paths are marked with red triangles and are suitable for hiking, skiing, and snowmobile use. Refer to the USGS Goshen quadrangle.

To reach the DAR State Forest Headquarters and campground, take Goshen–Ashfield Rd. (Cape St.) north from MA 9 in Goshen. Turn right onto a side road to the headquarters and campground. Parking is available here.

Universal Access Nature Trail (DCR)

This short trail—about 0.4 mi. long—runs along the south shore of Upper Highland Lake. Starting from the south boat launch area just east of the grassy earthen dam, it leads to the parking area on the east bay just south of the camping area and the Long Trail trailhead. An information kiosk by the south boat launch has maps as well as additional information in Braille. There is a UA fishing area and UA gazebo perched on a promontory along the way. The trail, wooded and cool, passes through hardwoods and hemlocks. There are many relaxing views of the lake and a scattering of benches as well.

Long Trail (DCR)

The trail starts just north of the southeastern boat launch on Upper Highland Lake and just south of the campground. The trail closely follows the upper shore of the lake, starting out as a narrow footpath and gradually widening. At about 0.5 mi. the blue-marked Darling Trail enters on the right. The Long Trail continues cruising along the lakeshore, reaching the northern end of the lake at 0.75 mi. The trail now briefly follows a feeder brook northeast before swinging southeast to a trail junction at 1.0 mi. From the junction a connector path leads south about 0.25 mi. to the northern end of the main forest campground. The Long Trail continues northeast, climbing steadily. At 1.5 mi. the Twinning Brook Trail (left) leads in 0.3 mi. to the campground near Twinning Pond. The Long Trail continues the short way to Moore Hill Rd.

Long Trail

Distances from trailhead

to north end of lake: 0.75 mi., 25 min.

to Moore Hill Rd.: 1.6 mi., 45 min.

Darling Trail (DCR)

Marked with blue triangles, this trail climbs east from its junction with the Long Trail on the eastern shore of Upper Highland Lake. It passes through the campground, then climbs steadily through the forest, crossing power lines twice along the way. It reaches Moore Hill Rd. at 0.75 mi., with the fire tower about 0.1 mi. farther on.

Darling Trail

Distance from Long Trail

   to summit of Moore's Hill: 0.8 mi., 30 min.

Sunset Trail (DCR)

Marked with blue blazes (other colors may also be evident), the trail leaves from near the boat launch on Lower Highland Lake. The one-lane access road is nearly opposite the information booth at the MA 112 forest entrance on the right upon entering). It climbs gradually to the fire tower on Moore Hill.

Sunset Trail

Distance from boat launch

   to summit of Moore Hill: 2.3 mi., 1 hr., 15 min.

Balancing Rock Trail (DCR)

Marked with orange and blue triangles, this trail connects Headquarters Rd. to Balancing Rock (a glacial erratic). The trail then loops back to Headquarters Rd.

Balancing Rock Trail

Distance from Headquarters Rd.

   to Balancing Rock: 0.4 mi., 15 min.

Twinning Brook Trail (DCR)

This trail is marked with blue triangles and connects the Long Trail to the Twinning Brook group-camping area.

Twinning Brook Trail

Distance from Long Trail

  to Twinning Brook camping area: 0.3 mi., 15 min.

Dubuque Memorial State Forest (DCR)

This 7822-acre forest, situated principally in the town of Hawley but also extending south into the town of Plainfield, is adjacent to Savoy State Forest and Mohawk Trail State Forest. It comprises rugged terrain, much of it above 1500 ft. with some points as high as 1800 ft., and includes several ponds and brooks. Many grassy woods roads and old town roads bordered by stone walls crisscross the forest. To follow these roads, refer the USGS Plainfield quadrangle.

The DCR has constructed a trail system in the central part of the forest and has erected four large Adirondack shelters, three of which are accessible by Forest Service roads and hiking trails, and the fourth by trail only. The shelters are available on a first-come, first-served basis. Each shelter site has a stone fireplace, a picnic table, a good source of drinking water, and an outhouse. The trails are not uniformly blazed (although there are some paint blazes), but the footway is clear except when obscured by forest litter. There are signs at some intersections.

The trail system is accessible from the south via Central St., which exits north from MA 116 about 9 mi. west of Ashfield center. The Shaw-Hudson House is located on the northwest corner of MA 116 and Central St. At the junction of Central St. and Union St. (0.5 mi.), continue northeast on Union St. until it makes an abrupt right (east) turn and becomes North St. at 1.3 mi. Proceed straight ahead, approx. north, on gravel Middle Rd. (not plowed in winter) to the Hawley–Plainfield line at 2.3 mi. Continue past a path on the right (east) of the road at 3.6 mi. (The path leads into a grove and to a small pond.) At 3.8 mi. turn left (west) onto Moody Spring Rd. (there might not be a sign). (*Note: When traveling in the reverse direction, be sure to turn right at this intersection. The corner is somewhat confusing because the roads form a small triangle.*) Continue on Moody Spring Rd. past a small cemetery on the right at 4.3 mi. At 4.5 mi. look for a parking area on the right (north). This is Gould Meadow (no sign) and probably the best place to begin a circuit walk on the trails.

Gould Meadow also is accessible from the west via a Forest Service road (Hallockville Rd.) that exits east from MA 8A (Hawley Rd.) at a point about

1 mi. north of its intersection with MA 116 in Plainfield. Going northeast on the Forest Service road, avoid a road on the left at 0.9 mi. (King Corner Rd.) and a road on the right at 1.3 mi. Pass the Basin Brook Trail on the left at 1.4 mi., the Gould Meadow Trail on the right at 1.5 mi., and Moody Spring Rd. on the left at 1.8 mi. At 1.9 mi. note a parking area on the left (north) and the beginning of the Basin Brook Trail on the right (south). This is Gould Meadow (no sign).

A 5.1-mi. continuous walk that begins and ends at Gould Meadow can be made via the Moody Spring Trail, the Hitchcock Meadow Trail, and the Basin Brook Trail (with or without the Ridge Trail as an alternative for part of the Hitchcock Meadow Trail). See the following trail descriptions.

Moody Spring Rd. (DCR)

This Forest Service road begins near the junction of Middle Rd. and Hunt Rd. and runs west-northwest to Gould Meadow, then southwest to a corner where it turns sharp right (northwest). (The road that goes straight ahead at the corner is the Forest Service road to MA 8A.) Moody Spring Rd. continues to Moody Spring and the Moody Spring Shelter, built of stone with a dirt floor. Beyond Moody Spring, the road continues northwest to Hitchcock Meadow.

Moody Spring Trail (DCR)

This trail begins at a sign at the northwest corner of the Gould Meadow parking area and runs north. Gould Meadow Shelter, facing an open field with good views east and north, is on the right of the trail a short distance from the parking area. Drinking water is available at a spring about 100 yd. down a little grade to the left (west) of the trail and shelter. The trail runs northwest, bearing left (west), and continuing past a good view south at 0.5 mi. It then starts steeply downhill, crosses a lovely brook at 0.6 mi., and climbs, bearing right and then left, to Moody Spring and Moody Spring Shelter. Here it joins the Hitchcock Meadow Trail and Moody Spring Rd.

Moody Spring Trail

Distances from Gould Meadow

    to brook: 0.6 mi., 25 min.

    to Moody Spring: 0.9 mi., 35 min.

Hitchcock Meadow Trail (DCR)

This trail begins at the dead end of Moody Springs Rd. about 0.25 mi. northwest of Moody Spring. It heads northwest over level ground then climbs to the southern shoulder of a low ridge at 0.5 mi. The trail then follows the contour of the hill, swinging south before tracing a course along the ridge, heading again northwest. When the trail reaches a second shoulder, this one reaching west, it descends the slope in a generally westerly direction, reaching Basin Brook and the junction with the Basin Brook Trail at 1.2 mi. The trail then continues west to reach MA 8A at 1.5 mi.

Hitchcock Meadow Trail

Distances from trailhead (0.25 mi. from Moody Spring)

  to south shoulder of hill: 0.5 mi., 20 min.

  to Basin Brook Trail: 1.2 mi., 50 min.

  to MA 8A: 1.5 mi., 1 hr., 5 min.

Basin Brook Trail

This trail begins on Hallockville Rd., an unpaved Forest Service road that bisects the forest from west to east. To reach the trailhead from the parking area at the northeast end of Hallockville Pond (just off MA 8A) travel 1.4 mi. east along Hallockville Rd. The trail begins on the left and heads north. At a trail junction the path turns left (west) and descends the short distance to Basin Brook, which it follows for the remainder of the trek. At 1.25 mi. a tributary enters left at the junction of the Hawley Pass Trail. The Basin Brook Trail continues to descend the ravine, reaching the Hitchcock Meadow Trail at 1.6 mi. and MA 8A at 2.0 mi.

Basin Brook Trail

Distances from trailhead on Hallockville Rd.

  to Hawley Pass Trail: 1.25 mi., 45 min.

  to Hitchcock Meadow Trail: 1.6 mi., 1 hr.

  to MA 8A: 2.0 mi., 1 hr., 20 min.

Pond Trail (DCR)

This attractive trail loops around the shore of Hallockville Pond on the west side of MA 8A about 1 mi. north of its junction with MA 116. The parking area and trailhead are at the north end of the pond, north of the stone dam. Some of the buildings here are now used as a camp for AmeriCorps volunteers.

From the trailhead on the northwest shore the trail passes a picnic area (with tables) and a primitive camping area (with a stone fireplace) on the left, then continues amid large white pines and some signs of former beaver activity. It crosses two brooks at the southwestern end of the pond, one on a rock causeway. Nearby on the higher land are the stone foundations of an old dam, spillway, and mill.

After crossing another brook on a plank bridge laid close to the water, the trail turns left and continues northeast on the eastern side of the pond. There are several huge boulders in this area and considerable evidence of former beaver activity. Side trails on the right lead to pumphouses and a dwelling. Shortly beyond on the right is a spring with water flowing from a pipe. MA 8A appears through the trees on the right, and a short trail leads to the highway. The Pond Trail remains close to the water until it ends at the eastern side of the concrete dam on the northern end of the pond. A short trail leads right (east) to MA 8A. To the left (west) of the dam are the buildings and parking area where the trail begins.

Pond Trail

Distance from sign at Hallockville Pond

to eastern side of dam (circuit): 1.0 mi., 40 min.

Hawley Pass Trail

The Hawley Pass Trail has two trailheads, but the one near Hallockville Pond is close to parking. From the parking area at Hallockville Pond head up Kingholt Rd. (dirt) the few yards to the trailhead on the right. The trail heads north and soon crosses King Brook and MA 8A. The trail then slowly swings from north to east, reaching a fork at 0.2 mi. The path heads north, reaching King Corner Rd. at 0.7 mi. Crossing the road, the trail jogs east and descends to the brook, following the ravine, to reach the junction with the Basin Brook Trail at 1.5 mi. To reach MA 8A follow the Basin Brook Trail west for 0.7 mi.

Hawley Pass Trail

Distances from trailhead

to King Corner Rd.: 0.7 mi., 25 min.

to Basin Brook Trail: 1.5 mi., 45 min.

to MA 8A via Basin Brook Trail: 2.2 mi., 1 hr., 5 min.

Mohawk Trail State Forest (DCR)

This forest lies in the towns of Charlemont, Florida, Savoy, and Hawley and is accessible from MA 2. It includes 6457 acres of mountain ridges, deep gorges, and 18 mi. of cold rivers and streams with excellent trout fishing. Champion trees are scattered throughout the forest, including a 130-ft.-tall red oak that is the tallest in New England. The forest has 56 campsites and four cabins that can be reserved year-round. There is also a swimming area and day-use picnic area.

The trails within Mohawk Trail State Forest explore some of the most beautiful wilderness left in Massachusetts, with old-growth stands towering 100 ft. tall. Some of the hiking trails, including the Mahican–Mohawk Trail, are the very same paths used by Native Americans centuries ago. Good views are available from Clark Mtn. (1920 ft.) and Todd Mtn. (1697 ft.).

Mahican–Mohawk Trail

A 1.5-mi.-long segment of this historic trail traces a path over Clark and Todd Mtns. It is blazed with round golden markers with a green maple leaf in the center. The trailhead is located off MA 2. From the main entrance on MA 2 cross over the Cold River, reaching the forest headquarters at 0.1 mi. Continue on the road, bear right, and follow it to the gate. Just beyond the gate is the trailhead for a short loop path called the Nature Trail. Head north on the Nature Trail about 0.25 mi. to the junction with the Mahican–Mohawk Trail. The Mahican–Mohawk Trail continues north (the Nature Trail loops south to follow along the Deerfield River) along the edge of the Deerfield River flood-plain and just to the east of Todd Mtn. The trail then follows the contour of the mountain and swings roughly west around the north buttress. It slabs the north slope, reaching the saddle between Todd Mtn. and Clark Mtn. at 1.3 mi. and the junction with the Indian Trail.

The Mahican–Mohawk Trail continues west, climbing the narrow ridge in a nearly straight line to the summit of Clark Mtn. (1919 ft.) and excellent views at 2.1 mi.

Mahican–Mohawk Trail

Distances from the north end of the Nature Trail loop

   to saddle between Todd and Clark Mtns.: 1.3 mi., 50 min.

   to summit of Clark Mtn.: 2.1 mi., 1 hr., 40 min.

Indian Trail

The Indian Trail begins at the north end of the campground about 0.7 mi. from the forest entrance. The trail heads northwest and strikes a steep, strenuous course up the flank of the Cold River ravine. It reaches the saddle between Todd and Clark Mtns. and the junction with the Mahican–Mohawk Trail at 0.3 mi. after gaining about 700 ft. in elevation. From the junction the Indian Trail heads east and ascends the double peaks of Todd Mtn. The climb begins moderately, then becomes steep as it crests the first summit (1580 ft.). The path now descends before scrambling up to the true summit (1697 ft.) at 0.75 mi.

Indian Trail

Distances from Mohawk Trail State Forest camping area

   to saddle: 0.3 mi., 35 min.

   to summit of Clark Mtn.: 0.75 mi., 1 hr., 10 min.

Totem Lookout Trail (DCR)

This trail leaves the south side of MA 2 opposite the state forest picnic area, about 1 mi. west of the main entrance. (A sign that says Leaving Pioneer Valley is located a short distance west on MA 2.) The trail enters the woods near a brook, follows a short woods road leading to a small Forest Service building, and almost immediately turns left (east). It then starts to ascend the side of the hill, climbing southeast through the woods. The grade moderates near the crest of the hill, then the trail turns a sharp left (east) and emerges on a rocky ledge (1627 ft.), which affords good views to the east and northeast.

Totem Lookout Trail

Distance from Mohawk Trail

   to lookout on ledge: 1.1 mi., 50 min.

Fannie Stebbins Memorial Wildlife Refuge

This 338-acre wildlife refuge is maintained by The Fannie Stebbins Memorial Wildlife Refuge, Inc., whose officers and trustees are members of the Allen Bird Club of Springfield, the founding organization. The refuge is located in Longmeadow, just above the Connecticut state border on the floodplain of the Connecticut River known as the Longmeadow Flats. The tract is set between the Connecticut River and I-91.

To reach the refuge, follow US 5 (Longmeadow St.) 2.4 mi. south of the Springfield–Longmeadow line to Bark Haul Rd. Turn right (west) onto Bark Haul Rd., continue 0.4 mi. to the intersection of Pondside Rd., and park there. A large map of the refuge and adjacent town conservation lands, including the main walking roads and trails, is at the parking area. The Stebbins Refuge is very popular with birders. The trails are concentrated at the southern end of the property, where the Fern Trail, Knoll Trail, Perimeter Trail, Elm Trail, and Meadow Trail go through the swamps and floodplain forest. An interesting path is the Penninsula Trail, which explores a narrow spit of land extending south into the river. A small map of the area is available by writing to the refuge in care of the Allen Bird Club, P.O. Box 1084, Springfield, MA 01101.

Laughing Brook Wildlife Sanctuary (MAS)

This property of the Massachusetts Audubon Society is located at 789 Main St. in Hampden. The sanctuary has 356 acres of woodland, fields, and streams, and offers miles of well-maintained and blazed trails. The area includes pleasant woods with wildflowers in season, Laughing Brook, and the Scantic River. Native animal and bird exhibits are located near the sanctuary's headquarters building, which was built in 1742 and is the former home of the late writer Thornton Burgess. An environmental center houses an auditorium, classrooms, a library, and a gift shop.

The many trails that course through the property can be divided into short, high-interest walks and longer hikes. Short walks include Smiling Pond Path that wraps around the pond, and Big River Loop that explores the Scantic River. Longer trails include the Storyteller's Trail, Green Forest Trail, and Neff Trail.

To reach the sanctuary from I-91 in Springfield, take either Exit 2 (northbound) or Exit 4 (southbound) to MA 83. Follow MA 83 (which becomes Summer Ave., then Allen St.) for 8.1 mi.; it swings right near a McDonald's restaurant. At the end of Allen St. (by the Mobil station) take a left onto Main St. The sanctuary entrance is 2 mi. down Main St. on the left.

From Boston and Worcester, take the Mass Pike (I-90) to Exit 8 in Palmer. Take a right to reach Palmer Center and US 20. Proceed west on US 20 for 5.3 mi., and turn left on to Main St. (opposite the Wilbraham Fire Department). Travel 6.6 mi. on Main St. (which turns into Wilbraham Rd. in Hampden) to a stop sign and turn left onto Allen St. After 0.2 mi. on Allen St. take a left onto Main St. The sanctuary entrance is 2 mi. down Main St. on the left.

Ridge Trail

This pleasant forest trail, involving some mild climbing, extends roughly north and south along a ridge forming the eastern boundary of the Connecticut River Valley. The trail runs through the towns of Hampden and Wilbraham and is marked by orange and red blazes. It is maintained by Boy Scout Troops 171 and 172. The southern terminus of the trail is located on Main St. in Hampden, opposite the VFW building, which is about 0.4 mi. east of Wilbraham and about 0.8 mi. west of the Hampden Post Office. The northern terminus lies at the eastern end of the American Foreign Legion building parking lot, located on US 20 just west of the railroad overpass in North Wilbraham. The intention is eventually to connect this trail with the Shenipsit Trail in Connecticut.

Beginning at the VFW in Hampden, the trail is marked by an orange blaze on a tree high on the hillside above the paved road. It heads north along the edge of the woods and through a clearing atop the first rise, then turns uphill onto a logging road. In 0.1 mi. Goat Rock is located on the left, with fine views to the south and east. The trail follows the logging road on and off for 0.4 mi. and bears right uphill after a grove of hemlocks. It then levels off for 0.2 mi. before it turns sharp left at a spot overlooking Hampden center.

The trail soon rejoins the logging road and heads downhill to the northeast. (*Note: Watch carefully for blazes, as other trails intersect.*) In 0.2 mi. the trail turns left (north) at an intersection, and in 0.4 mi. it comes out in an extensively logged area. It continues north and then east on the logging road, crosses a small brook, and bears right off the road at the next rise. It soon passes a small pond on the left and in 0.1 mi. turns north onto another logging road. In 100 ft. it bears right into a wet, logged-over area. It continues 0.1 mi., then turns west to parallel some power lines.

At 2.1 mi. the trail turns left onto Mtn. Rd. and then turns right, following the power lines uphill. At the top of the hill the trail heads north through a young forest. After crossing a stone wall and a small brook, the trail begins to ascend forested Mt. Vision. It bears right and shortly reaches the summit. In 0.2 mi. the trail joins a private drive to Burleigh Rd. It turns right onto Burleigh Rd., passes the Hampden–Wilbraham town-line marker, and shortly turns northeast onto a logging road. In 0.6 mi. the trail passes a small hill on the right with fine views west. In another 0.6 mi. the logging road becomes paved and intersects Monson Rd. at 4.6 mi. From here to the American Foreign Legion in North Wilbraham (at 9.0 mi.) the trail is hard to follow and is in the process of being blazed and relocated.

Ridge Trail

Distances from VFW in Hampden

to Goat Rock: 0.1 mi., 5 min.

to Mtn. Rd.: 2.1 mi., 1 hr., 20 min.

to summit of Mt. Vision: 2.6 mi., 1 hr., 45 min.

to Burleigh Rd.: 3.3 mi., 2 hr., 10 min.

to Monson Rd.: 4.6 mi., 3 hr., 30 min.

to American Foreign Legion: 9.0 mi., 6 hr., 10 min.

Chester–Blandford State Forest

Chester–Blandford State Forest has several outstanding natural attractions but just one signature feature—Sanderson Brook Falls, one of the most striking waterfalls in the region. Like many other state forests, Chester–Blandford is a mix of gravel forest roads and narrow hiking trails. The roads are closed to motor vehicles, making them good walking routes. The trails explore the steep hills and brooks, often passing by holes dug into the mountain years ago by miners of mica, emery, and corundum. The forest headquarters are off US 20. About 0.5 mi. east of the headquarters is the parking area for the Boulder Park Accessible Trail.

To reach the forest from the Massachusetts Turnpike (I-90), take Exit 3. Turn onto MA 10/US 202 south and continue to US 20. Proceed on US 20 west of Huntington and follow signs.

Sanderson Brook Falls

To reach the falls from the parking area off US 20 (4 mi. west of Huntington near a concrete bridge over Sanderson Brook) hike south on the gravel road along the brook. The grade is easy, and the footing is good. Over the next mi. the road crosses over three bridges before coming to the side trail on the right (west) side of Sanderson Brook Rd. The unmarked but easy-to-follow path descends from the road to the foot of the falls in about 5 min.

Boulder Park Accessible Trail (DCR)

The Boulder Park Accessible Trail is a short universally-accessible path off US 20 about 0.5 mi. east of the forest headquarters. Parking is available here. The trail runs roughly parallel to the highway over the Westfield River valley.

Mica Mine Trail

This steep 1.5-mi.-long trail begins at the forest headquarters on US 20 in Chester. From the trailhead the path ascends straight up the slope for about 0.1 mi. before slabbing to the side of Gold Mine Brook. The trail now hugs the stream, reaching the junction of the Bad Weather Bypass at about 0.6 mi. The bypass takes a route over higher ground with better footing and is used mostly in winter and during periods of high water in Gold Mine Brook. The main trail continues along the stream, reaching the junction with the Bad Weather Bypass and Mica Mine Rd. at 0.9 mi. Mica Mine Rd. and the Mica Mine Trail both lead to Observation Hill and the H. Newman Marsh Memorial Trail.

From Mica Mine Rd. the trail crosses undulating, mostly level ground fairly close to the ridge overlooking the Westfield River valley. At about 1.2 mi. the path swings northwest and climbs to the junction with the H. Newman Marsh Memorial Trail at 1.5 mi. Turn right onto the H. Newman Marsh Memorial Trail and proceed 0.1 mi. to a scenic vista on the right.

Mica Mine Trail

Distances from Chester–Blandford State Forest Headquarters

  to first Bad Weather Bypass junction: 0.6 mi., 35 min.

  to Mica Mine Rd. and second Bad Weather Bypass junction: 0.9 mi., 55 min.

  to H. Newman Marsh Memorial Trail: 1.5 mi., 1 hr., 15 min.

  to scenic vista via H. Newman Marsh Memorial Trail: 1.6 mi., 1 hr., 25 min.

Dynamite Box Trail

This 1.1-mi.-long path begins and ends at different points along Beulah Land Rd. From a parking area near a wetland at about 1400 ft. elevation the trail ends just 0.1 mi. from the junction of Beulah Land Rd. and Sanderson Brook Rd. The path leaves the road at the trailhead and descends the slope fairly steeply for nearly 0.5 mi. It then jogs right and begins to run nearly due north, roughly parallel to Sanderson Brook about 100 ft. below. At 0.75 mi. the path crosses a tributary stream of Sanderson Brook to end at Beulah Land Rd. at 1.1 mi.

Dynamite Box Trail

Distances from parking area on Beulah Land Rd.

  to tributary stream: 0.75 mi., 40 min.

  to lower trailhead on Beulah Land Rd.: 1.1 mi., 1 hr.

H. Newman Marsh Memorial Trail

The H. Newman Marsh Memorial Trail begins on Sanderson Brook Rd. and aggressively climbs up the hillside. The path reaches a ravine and follows the valley upslope, cresting the plateau at about 0.5 mi. The trail splits into a loop path. Continuing straight, the trail jogs along the base of Observation Hill, reaching a fork in the path at 0.7 mi. Mica Mine Rd. is a short walk to the right, while the loop trail continues left. The trail turns left (north) and passes the Mica Mine Trail on the right at 0.8 mi., then quickly reaches an overlook of the valley at 0.9 mi. The trail continues to wander along the edge of the long shoulder of Observation Hill to an overlook at the tip of the shoulder. The trail then turns south and closes the loop at 1.2 mi. Retracing its path down the slope, the path reaches Sanderson Brook Rd. at 1.7 mi.

H. Newman Marsh Memorial Trail

Distances from trailhead on Sanderson Brook Rd.

   to loop junction: 0.5 mi., 35 min.

   to Mica Mine Rd. link: 0.7 mi., 50 min.

   to Mica Mine Trail junction: 0.8 mi., 55 min.

   to first observation area: 0.9 mi., 1 hr.

   to end of loop: 1.2 mi., 1 hr., 15 min.

   to Sanderson Brook Rd. trailhead: 1.7 mi., 1 hr., 35 min.

Bear Swamp (TTOR)

Bear Swamp is a 285-acre preserve owned and managed by The Trustees of Reservations in Ashfield. The property has about 3 mi. of trails that explore the forests, beaver pond, and ridges. Pastoral views over orchards and on to the Green Mtns. are found at the Apple Valley Overlook and the vista on the Lookout Trail. The path to Apple Valley Overlook begins opposite the entrance on Hawley Rd. The Beaver Brook Trail traces a path along an old beaver dam that sits astride a long-abandoned stone mill dam.

   To reach Bear Swamp from the junction of MA 116, MA 112, and Hawley Rd. in Ashfield, turn onto Hawley Rd. and proceed west for 1.7 mi. The entrance and parking are on the left.

William Cullen Bryant Homestead (TTOR)

In the 1800s William Cullen Bryant was as much a part of western Massachusetts as any landmark. His family home in Cummington is now part of a 195-acre reservation owned and managed by The Trustees of Reservations. In addition to the house and other buildings is a loop path called the Rivulet Trail that explores the banks and environs of this feisty stream, which inspired a number of Bryant's writings. The trail also passes through acres of old-growth forest that was ancient when Bryant tramped the woods.

To reach the William Cullen Bryant Homestead from the MA 9 and MA 112 junction in Cummington, turn onto MA 112 south and travel 1.5 mi. to a five-way junction (Bryant five-corners). Continue straight through the intersection onto Bryant Rd. and proceed 0.2 mi. to the parking area behind the red barn on the right.

Rivulet Trail (TTOR)

Near the parking area behind the big red barn is a kiosk with information and a large map. Walk down the long gravel driveway, which offers a pleasant view to the left over the fields and woods. Continue walking beneath the alley of sugar maples, some more than 200 years old, to the intersection called Bryant five-corners. Turn right and walk less than 0.1 mi. to the trailhead on the right.

The yellow-blazed path goes easily downhill, gradually entering an area of old-growth timber along the banks of the brook. The trail splits at the beginning of the loop. Follow the brook to where the path veers away from the stream. Here a plaque etched with some verses of Bryant's poem "Rivulet" adds a nice touch to the hike. The trail continues through the woods, crosses a brook on a bridge, and comes to a fork. The left trail is a short connector path to the main loop, while the trail straight ahead curves through tall pines before rejoining the connector trail. The path swings right and soon closes the loop at Rivulet Brook. Turn right and follow the path to the trailhead by the road.

Rivulet Trail

Distance from parking area

to parking area (circuit): 1.8 mi., 1 hr.

SUGGESTED HIKES

Easy Hikes
William Cullen Bryant Homestead

Rivulet Trail [lp: 1.8 mi., 1:00]. A relaxing walk through woods and rare old-growth forest. The poet William Cullen Bryant played here as a child.

Mt. Holyoke Range: East

Laurel Loop Trail [lp: 0.75 mi., 0:30]. Beginning and ending at the Notch Visitor Center, this path passes through attractive evergreens and along an old trolley bed.

DAR State Forest

Universal Access Nature Trail [rt: 0.8 mi., 0:30]. An easy walk that meanders along the shore of attractive Upper Highland Lake.

Dubuque Memorial State Forest

Pond Trail [lp: 1.0 mi., 0:40]. This trail traces a path around elliptic Hallockville Pond. It can be wet in spots and caution is advised when crossing the brooks.

Moderate Hikes
Mt. Tom State Reservation

Beau Bridge Trail, M-M Trail [rt: 2.0 mi., 1:40]. A hike to the observation tower and wide views atop Goat Peak.

Mt. Sugarloaf Reservation

West Side Trail, Pocumtuck Ridge Trail [rt: 2.2 miles, 2:30]. This sometimes challenging hike leads to the top of South Sugarloaf Mountain and its clear views of the Connecticut River below.

Mohawk Trail State Forest

Totem Lookout Trail [rt: 2.2 miles, 1:40]. Leaving from the Mohawk Trail (MA 2) this hike climbs to ledges and rocky outcrops with beautiful views.

Strenuous Hikes

Mt. Holyoke Range: West

Metacomet–Monadnock Trail [rt: 9.0 mi., 7:00]. This portion of the M–M Trail includes parts of Sections 7 and 8 and runs the ridge of the Mt. Holyoke Range, affording numerous, splendid views.

Metacomet–Mondanock Trail to Mt. Lincoln

Metacomet–Monadnock Trail, Section 10 [rt: 10 mi., 7:40]. From beautiful Holland Glen the trail climbs to the summit of Mount Lincoln and its 360-degree view.

Pocumtuck Ridge Trail to Poet's Seat Tower

Pocumtuck Ridge Trail, Section 2 [rt: 9.0 mi., 4:10]. A long hike on a newly created trail, this section passes many viewpoints. The long views of Greenfield from the Poet's Seat Tower are some of the best.

Part III

Central Massachusetts

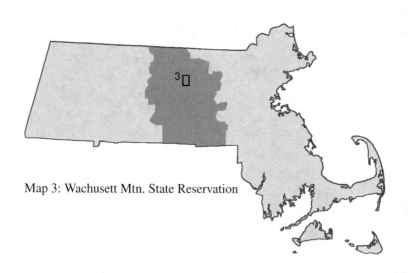

Map 3: Wachusett Mtn. State Reservation

LIST OF TRAILS

Worcester County is an area of small hills dominated by woodlands, despite the fact that it includes 60 cities and towns. Reaching from Connecticut to New Hampshire in the heart of Massachusetts, Worcester County averages about 800 ft. above sea level, with its highest point at the summit of Wachusett Mtn. (2006 ft.) in the town of Princeton. Except for the Midstate Trail and the new Tully Trail, the hiking trails in the county are scattered rather than being part of one continuous trail system. A small portion of the Bay Circuit Trail crosses through Southborough, the easternmost town of Worcester County. This section of the Bay Circuit Trail is covered in parts 4 and 6 of this book.

Tully Trail

The Tully Trail is an 18-mi. loop trail maintained by The Trustees of Reservations. Completed in 2001, it connects three TTOR properties (Doane's Falls, Jacob's Hill, and Royalston Falls) as well as Tully Lake Campground and the Tully Dam. It travels through both the Tully Mtn. and the Fish Brook Wildlife Management Areas, managed by MassWildlife. Also, it passes through three state forests—Orange, Royalston, and Warwick—and climbs Tully Mtn. (1163 ft.) with its extensive views from open ledges. Much of the eastern section passes through the Tully Lake Flood Control Area. Some of this section can be flooded in wet weather; call the Tully Lake Park Office (978-249-9150) for current conditions.

The trail is well marked with yellow rectangular blazes, as well as an occasional white-and-purple Tully Trail sign. Because this is a new trail and not yet well worn, the footway in some sections is indistinct. In these areas, please pay careful attention to the blazes; they are abundant and usually highly visible. Maps can be downloaded from www.thetrustees.org. and are available at the Tully Lake Campground and Royalston Falls trailheads.

To reach the trailhead at Tully Lake Campground in Royalston from MA 2, take Exit 18, Athol. Turn left onto MA 2A toward Athol. From Main St. (MA 2A) in Athol follow MA 32 north about 4 mi., crossing Tully Dam and passing the Tully Recreation Area on the right. Continue for another 0.5 mi., then turn right onto Doane Hill Rd. Proceed 1.0 mi to the Tully Lake Campground entrance on the right.

Section 1. Tully Lake Campground to Athol–Richmond Rd. (6.5 mi.)

This section begins at the entrance to the Tully Lake Campground. From the campground head right (east) on Doane Hill Rd., crossing the Tully River on a bridge. Just beyond the bridge the trail turns left (north) and follows a wide, flat woods road that borders the Tully Lake Flood Control Area. At 0.7 mi. the trail turns right (east) and begins a steep ascent of the escarpment using switchbacks. At the top of the ridge the trail levels off and bears left (north) to run the edge of the ridge. At 1.0 mi. the scenic overlook called the Ledges is reached, with a view across the Tully Valley.

The trail continues on easy grades along the forested ridge, enters Jacob's Hill (TTOR), then descends and crosses the brook on the rocks above Spirit Falls at 1.5 mi. (use caution on crossing, especially at high water). At the north bank of the brook the trail crosses a side trail that (right) leads to a parking area for Jacob's Hill or (left) descends along the falls to the woods road at the base of the valley.

At 2.0 mi. the trail reaches a rocky overlook providing extensive views of the Tully Flood Control Area as well as Tully Mtn., Mt. Grace, and the Berkshire Hills. From here the trail descends slightly to a woods road and follows it north out to a large power line. At 2.2 mi. it crosses the power line and turns left (yellow arrow on tree), descending the power line on a rough, indistinct footpath.

Near the bottom of the hill it merges with an orange-blazed trail coming from the left (south), bears right into the woods, and at 2.5 mi. crosses a marshy area on a boardwalk with a beaver dam on the right. (*Caution: Can be flooded in wet weather.*) The trail emerges back to the power-line clearing, follows it briefly, then merges with a wide woods road (orange blazes) coming from the left. The trail turns right (north) away from the power line at 3.0 mi., heading through the woods to a clearing near a house. It turns left (northwest) down a grassy right of way, crossing the Tully River on a footbridge at 3.5 mi. At 3.7 mi. it reenters the woods; the orange-blazed path leaves left (south) as it heads to Tully Lake Campground.

The Tully Trail continues straight ahead with the steep slope of Davis Hill on the left, crossing through a yellow gate onto Warwick Rd. (MA 68) at 4.0 mi. The trail turns left (northwest) uphill on Warwick Rd., then bears right into the woods and enters Royalston State Forest at 4.2 mi. on a wide woods road. The trail follows this road northwest through pine and mixed forest on an almost level grade. At 5.4 mi. the trail crosses Falls Brook on a footbridge and enters Royalston Falls Reservation (TTOR). On a rough pathway it ascends partway up the steep hillside on the northeast side of the brook, then slabs along the hillside with many small ups and downs, finally climbing to the top of Royalston Falls at 5.8 mi. A railing prevents viewers from getting too close to the falls. After the falls the trail joins the white-blazed Metacomet–Monadnock Trail and at 6.0 mi. turns left (west), crossing Falls Brook on rocks. (*Caution: This can be difficult in high water.*) It climbs the hillside on moderate grades, reaching Athol-Richmond Rd. and the parking area for Royalston Falls at 6.5 mi.

Tully Trail: Tully Lake Campground to Athol–Richmond Rd.

Distances from Tully Lake Campground

> *to* the Ledges: 1.0 mi., 45 min.
>
> *to* Spirit Falls Brook: 1.5 mi., 1 hr.
>
> *to* Royalston Falls: 5.8 mi., 3 hr.
>
> *to* Royalston Falls parking area: 6.5 mi., 3 hr., 50 min.

Section 2. Athol–Richmond Rd. to Tully–Warwick Rd. (6.7 mi.)

From the intersection of MA 68 and 32 in West Royalston, proceed on Rt. 32 N about 1.7 mi. to a parking area on the right side of a road for Royalston Falls, marked with a Trustees of Reservations sign.

This portion of the trail begins at the parking area for the Royalston Falls property. There is a small information board where maps for the Tully Trail can sometimes be obtained. The beginning of the section also coincides with the white-blazed Metacomet–Monadnock Trail. From the parking lot cross Athol–Richmond Rd. (MA 32), heading west across the broad crest of Wyman Hill and descending through a red pine grove at 0.4 mi. to gravel Bliss Hill Rd. at 0.8 mi. Here the Metacomet–Monadnock Trail crosses Bliss Hill Rd. and the Tully Trail turns left (south), following the road for 0.4 mi. At 1.2 mi., the trail turns right (west) into a private driveway. *Note: For the next 2 mi. the trail exists through the courtesy of private landowners. Please stay on the trail.*

At 1.6 mi. the path runs straight ahead, heading slightly uphill at a fork. The road climbs slightly, curves left, and then descends gently downhill, crossing a power line at 2.2 mi. At 2.4 mi. the trail joins a private drive coming from Warwick Rd., turning left (southwest) downhill on this road. At

2.5 mi. the trail turns abruptly left on a woods road, ascending in pleasant grades up the slope of Bliss Hill. The trail narrows to a footpath, coming to a ledgey outlook at 3.3 mi. with views to the west across the valley to Mt. Grace. The trail turns left (east) away from the outlook, ascending to the wooded summit of Bliss Hill at 3.5 mi. Steeply descend the south slope of Bliss Hill on a rough path; watch blazes with care here.

The grade soon becomes easier, and the trail descends gradually through mixed woods to (paved) Bliss Hill Rd. at 4.2 mi. The trail crosses the road and ascends to the top of a low ridge at 4.5 mi. It then descends steadily to Fish Brook, entering the Fish Brook WMA. The trail curves left (north), following this lively brook, then bears slightly away from it on an abandoned cart road. At 4.9 mi. the trail crosses Fish Brook on a bridge and bears sharp right (southeast), ascending Butterworth Ridge on easy grades. It crosses the wooded ridge, enters Orange State Forest, then descends on moderate grades through hemlock mixed forest to unpaved Butterworth Rd. at 6.2 mi. The trail turns right (southwest) onto Butterworth Rd., following it on mostly level grades to its intersection with Tully–Warwick Rd. at 6.7 mi.

Tully Trail: Athol–Richmond Rd. to Tully–Warwick Rd.

Distances from Athol–Richmond Rd.

   to Bliss Hill Rd.: 0.8 mi., 25 min.

   to summit of Bliss Hill: 3.5 mi., 1 hr., 40 min.

   to Fish Brook Bridge: 4.9 mi., 2 hr., 35 min.

   to Tully–Warwick Rd.: 6.7 mi., 3 hr., 25 min.

Section 3. Tully–Warwick Rd. to Tully Lake Campground (5.2 mi.)

This section begins at the intersection of Tully–Warwick Rd. and Butterworth Rd., about 2 mi. northwest of the village of North Orange. The trail begins with a road walk generally southeast on Tully–Warwick Rd. *Caution: The road has very narrow shoulders.*

At 1.5 mi. cross a road bridge over the Tully River, then turn abruptly left onto a wide logging road. The trail proceeds north through pine forest on flat grades, passing a clearing at 1.7 mi. At 1.8 mi., in a logged area, the trail turns right (east), ascending the fairly steep west side of Tully Mtn. on moderate grades through forest that is being actively logged. Pay close attention to the yellow blazes here, ignoring other blazes and flagging. At 2.1 mi., just north of the Tully Mtn. summit, the path comes to a T-intersection. The Tully Trail now forks into a loop path at 2.5 mi. The right (south) fork passes over the summit of Tully Mtn. (1163') at 0.1 mi. from the T-junction before making a steep descent of the mountain's south flank. Just downslope of the summit is a long rock ledge providing extensive views east of Tully Lake with Mt. Monadnock visible to the north (left) and the Wapack Range in the distance. At 0.5 mi. from the junction the loop trail turns left (north) while the access trail continues to the Mountain Rd. parking area (0.6 mi.). The left fork heads north on easy grades down a woods road through mixed forest. The trail makes a long curve right eventually turning south, meeting the south loop trail at about 0.3 mi. from the T-junction (the parking area on Mountain Rd. is about 0.5 mi. down the south loop). From the loop junction the Tully Trail heads east descending easily into a pine forest, crossing a brook on logs and reaching a grassy driveway at 3.1 mi. The trail continues straight ahead (east) through the Tully Mtn. WMA, following the edge of a bouldery hillside through hemlock woods. Crossing a wet area, the trail reaches an old woods road and turns right (south). It follows the road gently downhill, passing through a marshy area and reaching unpaved Royalston Rd. at 3.7 mi. It turns left (east) onto Royalston Rd., climbing slightly, then descends a short hill to paved Athol–Richmond Rd. (MA 32) at 3.9 mi.

The trail turns right (south) onto MA 32, crosses the busy road, and turns left into the parking lot for the Tully Lake Recreation Area at 4.0 mi. Continue straight (east) toward the lake at a sign for the Tully Trail. Turn left at the lakeshore, to pass through beautiful pine forest on easy grades. The Interpretive Trail leaves left, then rejoins the trail at 4.3 mi. At the northern end of Tully Lake the trail approaches Doane Hill Rd. and turns right, briefly parallel to the road. At 4.7 mi. turn abruptly right (southwest) away from the road to travel on a lovely point of land extending along one arm of the lake. The trail soon heads left (east) along the lake, finally leaving the lakeshore and passing through thick woods to reach the Tully Lake Campground at 5.2 mi.

Tully Trail: Tully–Warwick Rd. to Tully Lake Campground

Distances from Tully–Warwick Rd.

   to Tully River Bridge: 1.5 mi., 40 min.

   to trail junction on Tully Mtn.: 2.5 mi., 1 hr., 20 min.

   to parking area for Tully Lake Recreation Area: 4.0 mi., 2 hr., 35 min.

   to Tully Lake Campground: 5.2 mi., 3 hr., 20 min.

Midstate Trail (WCAMC)

The yellow-triangle-blazed Midstate Trail runs north-south through Worcester County from the Rhode Island to the New Hampshire border. It provides hikers with access to most of the significant summits and many of the scenic areas of central Massachusetts. Its 92-mi. length provides numerous opportunities for overnight treks, and its connection in the north with the Wapack Trail extending into New Hampshire makes it part of one of the longest trail networks in the region.

The Midstate Trail was originally developed in the 1920s, when it ran from Mt. Watatic to Wachusett Mtn. In 1972 plans for the trail's extension to the Rhode Island line were formulated, and the complete trail was dedicated on September 7, 1985. The AMC Worcester Chapter's Midstate Trail Committee produces the 55-page *Massachusetts Midstate Trail Guide* containing topographical maps, trail descriptions, and community highlights covering the entire length of the trail. For more information call 508-797-9744 or visit www.midstatetrail.org for trail updates.

Section 1. NH State Line to MA 12 (7.7 mi.)

The Midstate Trail begins east of the state boundary marker on the Massachusetts–New Hampshire line. Heading south on the combined Midstate and Wapack Trails (blazed with yellow triangles), the path follows old cart roads, climbs Nutting Hill (1615 ft.), and descends to a saddle before ascending Mt. Watatic (1813 ft.) via switchbacks. From the summit the trail proceeds west down the mountain on what was once the Blueberry Ridge Trail (signs for this trail have been removed) and reaches the state parking area on MA 119 at about 1.1 mi. The parking area is 1.6 mi. west of the intersection with MA 101. This is the closest car access to the northern end of the trail.

From the parking area the Midstate Trail crosses MA 119 and goes south on paved Pierce Rd., turning left off the road at 1.7 mi. to ascend Fisher Hill (1548 ft.) at 2.4 mi. From here the trail descends to a saddle then climbs to the crest of Blueberry Hill (1473 ft.) before descending through the Camp Winnekeag parking lot to MA 101 at 3.8 mi.

From the junction of MA 101 and Holt Rd. (look for a sign on a tree) the trail follows Holt Rd. then turns right off it onto a woods trail at 4.1 mi. The trail now climbs steeply up the ridge, passing views to Stodge Pond and reaching the flat crest of Mt. Hunger (1450 ft.) at 5.5 mi. The trail descends and crosses Russell Hill Rd. (6.3 mi.). From the road the trail has been relocated and is marked with yellow tape flags to MA 12, which it reaches at 7.7 mi.

Midstate Trail: NH State Line to MA 12

Distances from NH state line

   to Camp Winnekeag parking lot: 3.8 mi., 1 hr., 45 min.

   to Mt. Hunger: 5.5 mi., 3 hr.

   to MA 12: 7.7 mi., 3 hr., 35 min.

Section 2. MA 12 to Wyman Brook (10.6 mi.)

The trail crosses Phillips Brook on a footbridge, then bears left uphill. It crosses Whitney Hill Rd., continues along a low ridge, and enters an isolated section of state forest where a blue-blazed connector trail leaves right to a parking area in less than 0.2 mi. The path reaches Muddy Pond Shelter (Westminster Conservation Commission) at 2.3 mi. on the shore of Muddy Pond.

After following a circuitous route around Muddy Pond on an old roadway, the trail turns right into the woods, continues about 1 mi., and comes to a junction with Bragg Hill Rd. and S. Ashburnham Rd. Cross S. Ashburnham Rd. and follow Whitmanville Rd. (paved) to an intersection with a dirt road. Follow the paved road onto Oakmont Ave. to a woods road (posted, but open to hikers) that continues over bridges and boardwalk to a gravel road crossing, then reach the intersection with North St. and Town Farm Rd. in Westminster (7.2 mi.).

Reentering the woods just a short distance south and on the same side of Town Farm Rd., the trail heads in a generally south-southeast direction, passing many trail intersections. The trail crosses Bathrick Rd., MA 2A, and then MA 2 at 17.3 mi. Crossing MA 2 on the Wyman Rd. overpass, the trail follows Wyman Rd. and then Narrows Rd. before joining a path along Wyman Brook at 10.1 mi. This path crosses Wyman Brook before reaching the junction of Narrows Rd. and Stone Hill Rd. at 10.6 mi.

Midstate Trail: MA 12 to Wyman Brook

Distances from MA 12

   to Muddy Pond Shelter: 2.3 mi., 55 min.

   to Town Farm Rd.: 7.2 mi., 3 hr., 5 min.

   to Wyman Brook: 10.1 mi., 4 hr., 50 min.

   to Stone Hill Rd.: 10.6 mi., 5 hr., 10 min.

Section 3. Wyman Brook to Redemption Rock (MA 140) (3.4 mi.)

From Wyman Brook at the junction of Narrows Rd. and Stone Hill Rd. (cumulative mile mark 18.3) the trail follows Stone Hill Rd. about 400 ft., then turns left into the woods. After 600 ft. it descends along a stone wall, then turns right. After passing through a boulder-strewn area, the trail turns right at an unmarked trail junction. Continuing south, it reaches a stone stairway built by the CCC in the 1930s that leads to a fine view at Crow Hills, from which Boston is visible in the distance. (Rock climbers use the cliffs here.) The trail descends very steeply as it reaches a rocky outlook with a view of Wachusett Mtn., passes a large glacial boulder, then crosses MA 140 about 200 ft. from Redemption Rock, a historic site, at 3.4 mi.

Midstate Trail: Wyman Brook to Redemption Rock (MA 140)

Distance from Stone Hill Rd.

   to MA 140 (Redemption Rock): 3.4 mi., 1 hr., 50 min.

Section 4. Redemption Rock (MA 140) to Wachusett Meadows (5.2 mi.)

The trail leaves Redemption Rock (cumulative mile mark 21.8) in a southwesterly direction and soon crosses a brook. For the next 1.0 mi. the trail traverses a city of Fitchburg watershed area. After 0.75 mi. the trail crosses Mtn. Rd. (paved) and proceeds into the Wachusett Mtn. Ski Area and Wachusett Mtn. State Reservation parking area. Information, water, and toilet facilities are available at the state park visitor center, about 1 mi. south on Mtn. Rd. The trail continues uphill behind the buildings on a woods road, bearing right, and passes a glacial boulder called Balance Rock at 1.6 mi. It proceeds up the slope to a junction with the Old Indian Trail and Semuhenna Trail. At 2.2 mi. the trail crosses paved Up Summit Rd. then proceeds through old-growth forest as it ascends Wachusett Mtn., reaching the top (2006 ft.) with its stone lookouts at 3.2 mi.

   Descend the mountain on a number of trails, including Mtn. House and Link Trails, to a bridge where the Midstate Trail follows the Harrington Trail west past the Princeton Wind Electric Generator Farm and enters the Massachusetts Audubon Society's Wachusett Meadows Wildlife Sanctuary at 5.2 mi. The trail follows well-marked trails (yellow Midstate blazes) on relatively level ground through the sanctuary to Goodnow Rd., where the sanctuary's offices are located.

Midstate Trail: Redemption Rock (MA 140) to Wachusett Meadows

Distances from MA 140 (Redemption Rock)

to Balance Rock: 1.6 mi., 40 min.

to Wachusett Mtn.: 3.2 mi., 2 hr., 25 min.

to Wachusett Meadows Wildlife Sanctuary: 5.2 mi., 3 hr., 50 min.

Section 5. Wachusett Meadows to Barre Falls Dam (10.8 mi.)

From Goodnow Rd. the Midstate Trail continues atop a low ridge through woodlands and open fields with wetlands below to the east to its intersection with MA 62 in Princeton opposite Ball Hill Rd. at 2.25 mi. (cumulative mile mark 29.25). The trail here follows several paved roads (Ball Hill Rd., Wheeler Rd., and Bigelow Rd.), the last of which turns into unpaved Bushy Lane. The trail follows Bushy Lane across MA 68 at 5.5 mi., and less than 0.25 mi. farther on crosses MA 56. *Caution*: *The highways are busy.* After crossing MA 56 the trail briefly follows a jeep road before joining Davis St. heading into North Rutland. Davis St. ends at MA 68. Cross the Ware River on a highway bridge (6.4 mi.). On the far side of the river the Midstate Trail picks up a woods path on the west bank.

The path follows the river, then turns away from it and crosses Intervale Rd. at 7.0 mi. Follow woods paths and roads around a small hill, reaching an old foundation at 9.6 mi. Cross the west branch of the Ware River on a plank bridge at Brigham Rd. (9.8 mi.), then enter land mananged by Mass Wildlife and cross the Barre Falls flood-control dam, operated by the Corps of Engineers, at 10.8 mi.

Midstate Trail: Wachusett Meadows to Barre Falls Dam

Distances from Wachusett Meadows (MAS)

to MA 62: 2.25 mi., 1 hr., 10 min.

to Ware River: 6.4 mi., 2 hr., 25 min.

to Intervale Rd.: 7.0 mi., 2 hr., 50 min.

to Barre Falls Dam: 10.8 mi., 4 hr., 10 min.

Section 6. Barre Falls Dam to MA 122 (5.7 mi.)

The Midstate Trail at Barre Falls Dam is accessible from the junction of MA 62 and MA 68 by following MA 68 west about 2.2 mi. The road to the dam exits left (marked by a sign). Continue down the road 1.5 mi. to a parking area.

From the parking area the trail follows the road east 0.1 mi. There it turns left into the woods and continues to Harding Hill (1031 ft.), where there is no view. After descending 0.5 mi., the trail crosses a dirt road near a small pond. It traverses a field, continues through pines, and skirts Stevens Brook before following alongside Blood Swamp for a considerable distance. Just before coming to a dike, the trail turns left onto an old road and continues as far as the Rutland–Oakham town-line marker, where it turns left toward another dike. After ascending the dike, it goes straight ahead (south) on a ramp road, then at 3.5 mi. passes under a power line onto a gravel road (closed to vehicles). It continues on this road 1.6 mi. to a junction of roads, where it enters the woods. After 0.6 mi. it comes out on MA 122 (busy) in Rutland at 5.7 mi.

Midstate Trail: Barre Falls Dam to MA 122

Distances from Barre Falls Dam

to gravel road: 3.5 mi., 1 hr., 15 min.

to MA 122: 5.7 mi., 1 hr., 55 min.

Section 7. MA 122 to MA 31 (6.9 mi.)

From MA 122 the Midstate Trail climbs around a hill, first southeast and then south through several stone walls, and continues to Crawford St. at 0.6 mi. It crosses Crawford St. and a small brook, then climbs gradually to a woods road and enters Rutland State Park. A pipe spring is passed at 1.9 mi., just 0.1 mi. from the shore of Long Pond. The trail turns left (south) onto this road and continues through open woods to an access trail on the right. A shelter that can house 4–5 persons (no water) is located here. The trail proceeds downhill (south) on the woods road past the Midstate Trail halfway marker to reach the Treasure Valley Boy Scout Reservation. After passing under high-tension lines, it crosses diagonally to the right and continues through a deciduous forest. After crossing a stream, it passes an old cottage on the right. In 0.5 mi. the trail crosses a cutover area 50 yd. south of East Hill Rd.

The trail continues south through mixed woods to a large glacial erratic called Samson's Pebble at 4.7 mi. (cumulative mile mark 48.1). After descending southeast and skirting the edge of a swamp on the left, the trail passes over several stone walls. After a long downgrade it reaches the southern shore of Browning Pond. Browning Pond Rd. is just 100 yd. south. The trail turns left onto Browning Pond Rd. and passes several houses, then turns left onto Boy Scout land. After continuing 0.7 mi. through the woods, the trail again intersects Browning Pond Rd. It turns left onto the road and in 0.2 mi. reaches MA 31 (paved) in North Spencer, across from a sign for Camp Marshall 4-H camp at 6.9 mi.

Midstate Trail: MA 122 to MA 31

Distances from MA 122

   to spring: 1.9 mi., 45 min.

   to MA 31: 6.9 mi., 2 hr., 50 min.

Section 8. MA 31 to MA 9 (7.2 mi.)

Reach the parking area for this section from MA 9 by traveling north on Paxton Rd. for 1.4 mi., turning left onto Gold Nugget Rd., and traveling 0.6 mi. to McCormack Rd. Take a right onto McCormack Rd. and continue north 1.9 mi. to the 4-H Club and parking area on the left.

   From MA 31 the trail enters Spencer State Forest and follows a path marked Wildflower Trail. At the end of this nature walk the Midstate Trail ascends Buck Hill (1014 ft.), where there are no views. It then descends steeply southeast past Buck Hill Shelter on the right. The trail reaches Paxton Rd. at 3.3 mi., turns right onto Paxton Rd., proceeds 100 ft., then turns left through open woods bordering the Spencer Airport.

   The trail now ascends to the top of Moose Hill (1099 ft.), with excellent views at 5.1 mi. Sugden Reservoir can be seen just below the hill. At the bottom of the hill parking is available off Cross Rd. at the gate to the dam (5.6 mi.). From here the trail proceeds south through Spencer on paths and roads, finally reaching its intersection with MA 9 at 7.2 mi.

Midstate Trail: MA 31 to MA 9

Distances from MA 31

   to Paxton Rd.: 3.3 mi., 1 hr., 25 min.

   to Moose Hill: 5.1 mi., 2 hr., 40 min.

   to MA 9: 7.2 mi., 3 hr., 40 min.

Section 9. MA 9 to Railroad Bridge (Charlton) (8.4 mi.)

Parking for this section is in the lot of the abandoned courthouse on MA 9 across from the Spencer Country Inn and about 100 yd. east of the trail crossing.

From MA 9 the trail enters a driveway and continues along the town line. When the driveway bends right the trail goes straight along the edge of a field for 0.4 mi. to reach the Sibley memorial stone at 0.8 mi. Sibley Audubon Reservation is entered at 1.5 mi. The trail turns left onto the road and in 0.1 mi. comes to Greenville St. (paved). It follows a stone wall for about 500 ft., passes by a woodland for the same distance, then cruises atop a stone wall and beneath a power line, soon reaching Jones Rd. at 3.5 mi. It turns right onto Jones Rd., then continues 0.8 mi. to Wilson Rd. (paved), turns right onto Wilson Rd., then turns left onto Charlton Rd. It follows Charlton Rd. 0.8 mi., then turns left onto Clark Rd.

In 0.1 mi. the trail turns onto Borkum Rd., follows Borkum Rd. across the Four Chimneys Wildlife Management Area (parking available). At 7.5 mi. the trail takes a cart road over the pipeline and reaches the intersection of the pipeline and Gould Rd. at 7.9 mi. The trail turns right onto Gould Rd. and arrives at the railroad bridge at Charlton at 8.4 mi.

Midstate Trail: MA 9 to Railroad Bridge (Charlton)

Distances from MA 9

   to Sibley Audubon Reservation: 1.5 mi., 40 min.

   to Jones Rd.: 3.5 mi., 1 hr., 20 min.

   to Gould Rd.: 7.9 mi., 3 hr., 45 min.

   to Railroad bridge (Charlton): 8.4 mi., 4 hr., 5 min.

Section 10. Railroad Bridge (Charlton) to Cascade Brook (6.1 mi.)

After crossing the railroad bridge onto a blacktop road, the trail continues south, passing a campground on the left (east) and Wee Laddie Pond on the right (west). At a road junction the path continues on Cemetery Rd. to Fay Mtn. Orchard—a white colonial homestead that was the home of Dr. William T. Morton, the first doctor to use ether as an anesthetic. (See the historical marker there.) The trail turns left onto a paved road, then right onto Northside Rd. to the historic Ryder Tavern on the corner. The trail follows Northside Rd. over a bridge spanning the Massachusetts Turnpike (I-90) at 1.4 mi., then turns left over wire fences into the woods. In 0.4 mi. it turns right onto a gas pipeline and follows this 0.3 mi. to a dirt road. The trail turns left onto the road toward some abandoned buildings and continues 0.3 mi. to paved Carroll Hill Rd., where it turns right and passes beneath US 20 using a cow tunnel at 3.1 mi.

Bearing left at the crossing, the trail enters the woods, turns right onto a blacktop road, then turns left onto a woods road. At a horse pasture it crosses a barbed-wire fence on a stile, then crosses a dam and passes a small pond on the right to emerge from the woods at a power line at 4.1 mi. The trail follows the power line 0.3 mi. to paved Putnam Hill Rd. It turns right onto Putnam Hill Rd., left onto paved Turner Rd., and reaches Cascade Brook as it is piped beneath Old Charlton Rd. at 6.1 mi.

Midstate Trail: Railroad Bridge (Charlton) to Cascade Brook

Distances from railroad bridge

to Mass Pike: 1.4 mi., 35 min.

to cow tunnel (US 20): 3.1 mi., 1 hr., 20 min.

to power lines: 4.1 mi., 1 hr., 55 min.

to Old Charlton Rd.: 6.1 mi., 2 hr., 50 min.

Section 11. Cascade Brook to MA 16 (Douglas) (14.9 mi.)

The trail leaves Old Charlton Rd. in Oxford at the Cascade Brook crossing, bearing right. It follows the left side of this attractive brook, which might be dry in fall. The trail passes a large pile of rocks along the brook and in less than 0.5 mi. crosses the French River on a pedestrian bridge, coming to a dirt road that ends on paved Rocky Hill Rd. at 2.8 mi. The trail turns right (east) and continues through a residential area to MA 12 at a traffic light, then proceeds past the Oxford Police Station to reach paved Dana Rd. and head beneath I-395 through the underpass. From Dana Rd. the trail travels on Brown Rd. for about 1.25 mi., then turns left onto Lovett Rd. The trail heads east to the end of Lovett Rd. and a cable gate with views of Sacarrappa Pond.

From the gate the road becomes rutted and steep at 6.9 mi., then evens out and crosses a brook on a plank bridge before turning right onto Town Farm Rd. at 7.8 mi. The path runs up Whittier Hill, with long pastoral views including Wachusett Mtn. to the north. At Central Turnpike in West Sutton the trail turns left and proceeds 1 block, then bears right to continue south on Douglas Rd. (paved) past the Whittier dairy farm. The path crosses the town line, where the road changes its name to Northwest Main St. and after another 0.3 mi. turns right onto an old woods road at 10.6 mi.

The trail now follows paths and old woods roads on a winding, 4.2-mi. route through Douglas State Forest, generally skirting rather than climbing the hills. It emerges from the forest just north of its intersection with MA 16 at 14.9 mi.

Midstate Trail: Cascade Brook to MA 16 (Douglas)

Distances from Cascade Brook

    to Rocky Hill Rd.: 2.8 mi., 1 hr., 10 min.

    to Town Farm Rd.: 7.8 mi., 2 hr., 35 min.

    to MA 16: 14.9 mi., 5 hr., 10 min.

Section 12. MA 16 (Douglas) to Rhode Island Line (5.5 mi.)

To reach the parking area for the Midstate Trail from Exit 2 off I-395, drive east on MA 16 for 4.3 mi. to the trailhead and small parking area located just east of the trail. The final section of the Midstate Trail is in many respects the most remote. The trail meanders for slightly more than 5 mi. through the southern section of Douglas State Forest, following paths and woods roads and crossing several old railroad grades and jeep roads. At 2.0 mi. it crosses Southwest Main St. An open shelter with a table and fireplace near an old cellar hole is reached at 5.0 mi. The trail ends 0.5 mi. beyond, at the Rhode Island state line at 5.5 mi.

Midstate Trail: MA 16 (Douglas) to Rhode Island Line

Distances from MA 16

    to Southwest Main St.: 2.0 mi., 50 min.

    to southern terminus of Midstate Trail: 5.5 mi., 2 hr., 35 min.

Wapack Trail (FOW) (Massachusetts portion only)

The Wapack Trail, marked with the same yellow triangles used by the Midstate Trail, begins at the small parking lot on MA 119, 1.4 mi. west of MA 101. This section of trail coincides with the Midstate Trail, heading north through a marshy area to reach a trail junction at 0.3 mi. The State Line Trail (blazed blue) now follows the old route of the Midstate Trail and continues north about 1 mi. to the NH border. Signs are present at this junction. The combined Midstate/Wapack Trail turns right and begin to ascend the south face of Mt. Watatic. Slabbing the steep south face of the mountain, with moderate grades alternating with steep pitches, the Wapack/Midstate Trail reaches the summit at 1.2 mi.

From the summit the Wapack/Midstate Trail heads northwest (aim for Monadnock's summit and keep a few feet to the right of the fire tower), following a grassy path downhill about 30 ft. to the trees. Passing abandoned ski lifts and slopes from the Mt. Watatic Ski Area, the trail descends moderately through a state wildlife conservation area before ascending an open ledgy area known as Nutting Hill at 1.9 mi. Descending from Nutting Hill, the trail widens into an old cart track, passes through an unmarked junction at 2.1 mi., and at 2.4 mi. reaches a stone wall marking the New Hampshire state line. The State Line Trail ends nearby at the original terminus of the Midstate Trail.

Wapack Trail

Distances from MA 119 parking area

  to summit of Mt. Watatic: 1.2 mi., 1 hr.

  to Massachusetts–New Hampshire line: 2.4 mi., 1 hr., 35 min.

State Line Trail

This blue-blazed trail runs generally north–south from near MA 119 in Ashburnham to the original terminus of the Midstate Trail on the New Hampshire border. From the Wapack Trail parking area follow the Wapack/Midstate Trail (yellow triangles) north 0.3 mi. to the start of the State Line Trail. Here the Wapack/Midstate Trail turns right (east), while the State Line Trail heads north along the old route of the Midstate Trail. The path edges over Nutting Hill before ending at the NH state line at 1.1 mi.

Wachusett Mtn. State Reservation (DCR)

Wachusett Mtn. (2006 ft.) is the highest point east of the Connecticut River and south of New Hampshire. It is the outstanding feature of Wachusett Mtn. State Reservation, which now comprises 3000 acres in the towns of Princeton and Westminster. Panoramic views from its summit stretch to the Boston skyline on a clear day.

The area offers 17 mi. of hiking trails, including 3.9 mi. of the Midstate Trail. The reservation harbors the largest tract of old-growth timber east of the Connecticut River, with trees up to 350 years old. The park headquarters and visitor center is located on Mtn. Rd. in Princeton, which is also the starting point for several of the hiking trails. A paved automobile road to the summit is open to vehicular traffic from late spring to early fall. Other roads on the reservation are generally closed to cars at all times. A major ski area operates on the north slope of the mountain during winter. Hikers are not permitted on the alpine ski slopes and trails except at crossings. Universal-access restrooms and picnic areas are available.

Hiking trails are generally marked with blue triangles. Those trails that are part of the Midstate Trail system also have yellow blazes.

To reach the Wachusett Mtn. State Reservation headquarters and visitor center from MA 2, take MA 140 south 2 mi. and turn right onto to Mile Hill Rd. Pass the ski area and continue uphill to the reservation entrance on Mtn. Rd. Approaching from the south, take Mtn. Rd. about 3.0 mi. north of the MA 31 and MA 62 junction in Princeton center.

Midstate Trail

The long-distance Midstate Trail, marked by yellow triangular blazes, traverses Wachusett Mtn. See Midstate Trail, Section 4, Redemption Rock (MA 140) to Wachusett Meadows.

Jack Frost Trail (DCR)

This trail was named for the late Dr. Harold P. Frost, who scouted and cleared most of its length. Located on the south side of the mountain, it climbs the peak's southern shoulder. To reach the trailhead, take Mtn. Rd. 1.2 mi. north from Princeton center. Turn left (uphill) at a Y-intersection onto Westminster Rd. Parking is available at the intersection with Administration Rd., which is closed to motor vehicles. An attractive picnic site is located at the right of this intersection, beside Machias Pool. The water is not potable, and swimming is prohibited. Proceed on foot up Administration Rd. for 0.4 mi., where the trail begins on a woods road on the right.

The trail crosses a brook and an intersection with the Lower Link Trail, then turns right and continues east until it crosses a power line at 0.3 mi. Here it begins to ascend more steeply through hemlocks, gaining the lower ridge and passing High Meadow Trail on the right. The trail then turns north along the brow of the ridge before climbing to the Mtn. House Trail about 0.4 mi. below the summit.

Jack Frost Trail

Distances from Administration Rd.

    to Mtn. House Trail: 1.5 mi., 45 min.

    to summit of Wachusett Mtn. (via Mtn. House Trail): 1.9 mi., 1 hr.

Pine Hill Trail (DCR)

The shortest route to the top of Wachusett Mtn. is via this very steep old ski trail on the eastern side of the mountain. From the visitor center parking take Bicentennial Trail south to the Pine Hill Trail junction. Turn right onto Pine Hill Trail, which strenuously scales the buttress to emerge at the top at a break in the stone wall about 200 ft. from the end of the "up" road.

Pine Hill Trail

Distance from Mtn. Rd.

    to stone wall: 0.5 mi., 40 min.

Mtn. House Trail (DCR)

This trail ascends Wachusett Mtn. from the south. Parking is available at the trailhead near the junction of Gregory Rd. and Mtn. Rd., 2.4 mi. north of Princeton center. The trail takes its name from the famous Mtn. House, which was formerly located nearby. (The stone walls and cellar holes are still visible.) There are no trail markings, but the trail is broad and easy to follow.

    The trail climbs rather steeply up an eroded path through hardwood forest, passing junctions with the Bicentennial Trail, the Loop Trail, the Jack Frost Trail, and the Link Trail. It then turns more to the north, crossing a stone wall and the summit road. From here the trail levels off and parallels the summit road, reaching the summit at 1.0 mi.

Mtn. House Trail

Distance from Mtn. Rd.

    to summit of Wachusett Mtn.: 1.0 mi., 45 min.

Harrington Trail (DCR)

This trail begins on Westminster Rd., 0.5 mi. west of its junction with Administration Rd. It leaves on the north side of the road opposite the Dickens Trail. Parking is available at the trailhead.

The trail begins by heading uphill through a field, switching to the northeast, and following a stone wall on the left as it enters the woods. Shortly the trail turns left onto a woods road and continues until it meets the Stage Coach Trail at 0.4 mi. The Harrington Trail soon crosses a stone wall, then passes through a stand of large hemlocks. Shortly the trail bears left (north) and crosses a streambed. It then bears right (northeast) to cross West Rd.

As the trail starts climbing again, painted white blazes are visible, and at 1.0 mi. the trail crosses Administration Rd. (This point is about 0.8 mi. north of the lower end of Administration Rd.) After passing the Lower Link Trail and crossing three streams (dry in summer), the trail climbs more steeply, levels off, and resumes climbing among rocks. The Semuhenna Trail enters left; the path slabs to the right and climbs onto ledges, then turns sharp left, paralleling the ledges for a short distance, then turns right and climbs steeply over rocks. The Link Trail enters on the right, and the Harrington Trail continues climbing steeply over rocks.

Shortly the trail goes over a stone wall along the side of the summit road, crosses the road, then climbs northeast over less difficult rocks and ledges. The open summit is soon visible, and the trail terminates on the flat rocks southwest of the fire tower.

Harrington Trail

Distances from Westminster Rd.

to Administration Rd.: 1 mi., 40 min.

to summit of Wachusett Mtn.: 1.5 mi., 1 hr., 15 min.

West Side Trail (DCR)

This trail ascends Wachusett Mtn. from its western side and begins on W. Princeton Rd. (gravel) in Westminster, 1 mi. north of its junction with Westminster Rd. and 200 yd. north of the intersection of West Rd. A parking area is near the trailhead. The trail terminates at the Old Indian Trail, about 0.6 mi. below the summit. It is difficult to follow in places.

The trail enters the woods on the eastern side of W. Princeton Rd., passing through a fairly large hemlock stand and over rocks, then swings south to slab up a hillside. The trail crosses more rocks and climbs steeply straight ahead over a cliff.

Above the cliff the trail levels off into hardwoods, mostly small beeches, and then climbs gradually. It swings left and right and climbs steeply before leveling off again. A short distance along, the trail crosses the Up Summit Rd. and continues southeast to an open spot with large, flat rocks surrounded by scrub oak. Nearby, a cairn marks the Princeton–Westminster line.

The trail veers northeast and briefly runs parallel to the road. Here the trail crosses the Semuhenna Trail and passes near a picnic table within sight of the road, then heads back into the woods. It climbs gradually to a junction with the Old Indian Trail.

West Side Trail

Distances from W. Princeton Rd.

to Old Indian Trail: 1.5 mi., 1 hr., 15 min.

to summit of Wachusett Mtn. (via Old Indian Trail): 2.1 mi., 1 hr., 45 min.

Semuhenna Trail (DCR)

This trail, constructed in 1971 and named for longtime trail volunteer Anne Humes, proceeds essentially north from the ledges on the Harrington Trail southwest of the summit to the Old Indian Trail near Balance Rock on the north slope. It crosses the West Side Trail once and Up Summit Rd. twice. Through the Link Trail, it also has access to the Jack Frost Trail and the Mtn. House Trail, providing opportunities for a variety of loops.

The upper end of this trail starts at the Harrington Trail 0.2 mi. east of Administration Rd., just below the ledges, and about 40 yd. below the western end of the Link Trail. Descending from the Harrington Trail, it follows a low ridge, crosses a small intermittent stream, rises slightly over two open ledges, and crosses Up Summit Rd. at a picnic site. Almost immediately it crosses the West Side Trail and enters a stand of large hemlocks. It passes the top of the west T-bar ski lift (right) and continues gently descending through the hemlocks to the second crossing of Up Summit Rd., 60 yd. east of its intersection with North Rd. Beyond this crossing the trail passes through another old hemlock grove, swings gently left to cross another intermittent stream, then ascends slightly on approach to a stone wall. Beyond the wall the trail soon intersects the Old Indian Trail 0.2 mi. from Balance Rock.

Semuhenna Trail

Distance from Harrington Trail

  to Old Indian Trail: 1.2 mi., 45 min.

Old Indian Trail (DCR)

This steep, rocky trail ascends the north slope of Wachusett Mtn. It begins on Balance Rock Rd. (closed to vehicular traffic), opposite the end of the Balance Rock Trail. To reach the trailhead begin at the parking area for the Balance Rock Trail, located to the north of the ski lodge off Mile Hill Rd. Alternatively, park on Bolton Rd. and climb to the trailhead on the Bolton Pond Trail.

    The Old Indian Trail leaves the road on the south side and proceeds through mixed hardwoods and pines. The Semuhenna Trail enters right at 0.2 mi. At 0.4 mi. the trail diagonally crosses a ski trail, reenters the woods, and passes under the ski lift at pole 12. The trail crosses Up Summit Rd. and then begins to climb gradually. After crossing an intermittent stream the trail climbs steeply to a junction with the West Side Trail. It continues steeply upward over stone steps and zigzags over rocks, crossing a ledge where there is an excellent view of Mt. Monadnock and Mt. Greylock on a clear day. A few hundred feet above this point the trail levels off and climbs gradually to the summit. It ends at the beacon tower on the north side of the summit.

Old Indian Trail

Distances from Balance Rock Rd.

  to West Side Trail: 0.6 mi., 30 min.

  to summit of Wachusett Mtn.: 1.3 mi., 1 hr.

Balance Rock Trail

This trail begins at the far end of the ski area parking lot on Mtn. Rd., about 1.2 mi. north of the park visitor center. Follow the jeep path for about 0.3 mi. before turning onto a woods path, which soon reaches Balance Rock, a glacial erratic. The path continues a few hundred feet farther to Balance Rock Rd. (closed to vehicles). Across the road, the Old Indian Trail continues toward the summit.

Balance Rock Trail

Distances from ski area parking lot

    to Balance Rock: 0.4 mi., 20 min.

    to Balance Rock Rd: 0.4 mi., 20 min.

Connecting Trails

The following trails, although relatively short, provide useful connections among the major trails described above, permitting a number of interesting loops and circuits.

    Link Trail (0.2 mi.) connects the Mtn. House Trail (just above the upper end of the Jack Frost Trail) with the Harrington Trail.

    Lower Link Trail (0.5 mi.) parallels the Administration Rd., connecting the lower end of the Jack Frost Trail with the Harrington Trail.

    Loop Trail (0.4 mi.) provides a cutoff between the Bicentennial Trail and the middle part of the Mtn. House Trail.

    Bicentennial Trail (0.6 mi.) begins at the visitor center and runs south parallel to Mtn. Rd., passing the Pine Hill Trail, the Loop Trail, and the Mtn. House Trail before turning steeply upward to end at the High Meadow Trail.

    Stage Coach Trail (0.5 mi.), previously called Old Logging Rd., runs between the Harrington Trail and Westminster Rd. (near the locked gates at the beginning of Administration Rd.).

Wachusett Meadows Wildlife Sanctuary (MAS)

This 1024-acre bird and wildlife sanctuary is located 1.5 mi. west of Princeton center, and is owned and maintained by the Massachusetts Audubon Society. An 11-mi. trail network explores the sanctuary, including a 200-acre beaver pond. Located near Wachusett Mtn., one of the best hawk-watching sites in New England, the sanctuary often treats visitors in fall to the sight of many raptors soaring overhead.

    To reach the sanctuary, follow MA 62 west from Princeton center for 0.5 mi., then turn right onto Goodnow Rd. (blacktop) at a Wachusett Meadows Sanctuary sign. In 1.1 mi. there is a parking area on the left. Three suggested walks are described below. (The long-distance Midstate Trail also passes through the Wachusett Meadows; see Midstate Trail, Section 5, Wachusett Meadows to Barre Falls Dam.)

Pasture Trail

Pasture Trail is a pleasant woodland-and-field walk—sometimes called Fifth Pasture Loop—that passes through five picturesque pastures. To reach the Pasture Trail trailhead follow Beaver Bend Trail south beginning about 500 ft. west of the parking area on Goodnow Rd. The path passes through a pasture where Pasture Trail begins near the pasture's south stonewall. The trail continues through another pasture, called the third pasture, where a rain shelter is located. Continuing south it passes the Rock Fire Pond before crossing fourth pasture. At a junction with Fern Forest Trail the Pasture Trail turns right (northwest) and continues to a second junction with the Fern Forest Trail on the left. Pasture Trail soon bends right, crosses a rock wall, then turns left (west) as the Hemlock Seep Trail leaves straight (north). Pasture Trail meanders through the woods to Goodnow Rd., which it follows back to the junction with Beaver Bend Trail.

Pasture Trail

Distance from Goodnow Rd.

    to Goodnow Rd. (circuit): 2 mi., 1 hr.

Chapman Trail

This trail is named for the late Lawrence B. Chapman, a former MIT professor, amateur ornithologist, and chairman of the Wachusett Meadows Advisory Committee. The trail extends from the glacial boulder to Thompson Rd., where it meets the southern end of the Dickens Trail.

From the sactuary headquarters, the trailhead is accessible by one of two routes along the North Meadow Trail. The first route, on the western side of the big meadow, passes the Crocker Maple and a hickory grove; the other, on the eastern side of the big meadow, continues on the east side of a stone wall up a gentle grade through the woods. From the North Meadow Trail, follow the Glacial Boulder Trail to its namesake rock.

The Chapman Trail begins 50 yd. north of and below the glacial boulder, where the West Border Trail enters from the left. The trail veers slightly right and proceeds northeast through white pine woods. At 180 yd. it passes a walled springhole (dry in summer). It crosses a small brook 160 yd. from the spring and another brook 110 yd. farther along; both brooks are dry in summer. Shortly after the second brook the trail swings gently right through a brushy area, then turns left again to join the West Border Trail 250 yd. from the second brook. Beyond this junction the trail turns 90 degrees left, and crosses a stone wall to follow another stone wall, which marks a sanctuary boundary line. About 30 yd. from this turn the trail veers slightly right and drops gently down to Thompson Rd.

Chapman Trail

Distance from glacial boulder

   to Thompson Rd.: 0.6 mi., 30 min.

Dickens Trail

This trail connects the trails of Audubon Wachusett Meadows Wildlife Sanctuary with the Wachusett Mtn. State Reservation trail system. It starts from Thompson Rd., 2.5 mi. west of Mtn. Rd., and continues north to Westminster Rd. opposite the Harrington Trail.

   The trail leaves the north side of Thompson Rd. at the western end of a small pond opposite the Chapman Trail. It starts uphill and continues to a logging road, where it turns left onto a road for a short distance and then turns right, leaving the road. It passes a communications tower on the right and then crosses the boundary line of the Wachusett Meadows Wildlife Sanctuary at a break in a stone wall. The trail joins a woods road and continues, crossing the right of way for the AT&T continental underground lines just before it terminates on Westminster Rd.

Dickens Trail

Distance from Thompson Rd.

   to Westminster Rd.: 0.8 mi., 30 min.

Leominster State Forest (DCR)

This forest of 4300 acres is known for its beautiful stands of mountain laurel. It is easily reached from Worcester and Boston, with many parking areas located off MA 31. The main parking area from which most trails lead is on MA 31 at the Princeton–Westminster line, about 2 mi. south of the junction of MA 31 and MA 2. A wooden sign in the parking area shows most of the marked trails. The Midstate Trail traverses the property (see Midstate Trail, Section 3, Wyman Brook to Redemption Rock), and there are many miles of hiking trails. There also are many mountain biking trails in the forest, but the hiking trails are closed to cyclists. There is a swimming beach at Crow Hill Pond (off MA 31) with lifeguards on duty in season; restrooms are available.

The twin summits of Crow Hills (1234 ft.) are located in Leominster State Forest. The shortest way to the top of Crow Hills—also the usual approach to the cliff by rock climbers—is from MA 31, starting at a point 100 ft. north of the Princeton–Westminster line. After proceeding about 200 yd. through the woods, come to a junction of two trails, both of which lead to the Midstate Trail. The trail on the left follows the base of the cliff, and the trail on the right ascends steeply to the northern ridge. Total distance to the top of the ridge by either trail is 0.3 mi. (20 min.).

Purgatory Chasm (DCR)

Located west of MA 146 in Sutton, Purgatory Chasm State Reservation includes 900 acres of scenic land and odd rock formations. The reservation has picnic facilities that include fireplaces, tables, and springwater. Universal-access restrooms are available. The chasm is a great fissure in solid granite approximately 0.5 mi. long with sheer walls rising 70 ft. The Chasm Loop Trail courses through the gorge and follows a well-marked route. Beginning at the chasm entrance near the pavilion on Purgatory Rd., the trail heads generally west through the length of the chasm. It turns left and gains the top of the cliffs, skirts a long rock ledge, then passes by side trails that lead to some of the colorfully named rock formations the chasm is famous for. The Chasm Loop Trail then ends at the starting point. The origin of the gorge is believed to trace back to the massive erosion caused by the immense floods at the end of the last ice age.

Blackstone River and Canal State Park (DCR)

This state park occupies slightly more than 1000 acres in the towns of Northbridge and Uxbridge. Included within the park are 6 mi. of the Blackstone River and some of the best-preserved sections of the historic Blackstone Canal, built 1826–1828.

The main hiking route is a 3.75-mi. patchwork of trails that runs roughly north–south along a wide, grassy path with gentle grades. Parking is available at both ends of the route: in the north at Plummer's Landing on Church St. in

Northbridge, just east of MA 122; in the south at the Stanley Woolen Mill on Cross St., just off MA 16 in Uxbridge. Parking is also available at the Stone Arch Bridge off Hartford Ave. in Uxbridge, which bisects the trail about 2.4 mi. from its northern end.

Parts of the trail follow the original canal towpath. Along its route the trail passes locks, dams, bridge abutments, and other remnants of the early industrial era, as well as scenic outlooks over Rice City Pond and the Blackstone River valley.

From the north the route begins on Church St. at Plummer's Landing. The Plummer's Trail (a.k.a., the Tow Path Trail) heads south from here following the river, but continues straight as the river bends left. It reaches the river again in a wetland area roughly opposite Lookout Rock. Soon the Goat Hill lock is reached and the Goat Hill Loop branches into two paths, one that runs the high ground to Goat Hill, and another loop that continues south along the river. There are fine views from the top of Goat Hill in fall, winter, and spring. The southern end of the Goat Hill Trail Loop ends at Stone Arch Bridge. From the bridge the Tow Path Trail crosses the river and follows the eastern bank to the Cross St. parking area near the Stanley Woolen Mill. The distance for the hike (one way) is about 3.5 mi.

Bearsden Forest (ACC)

Bearsden Forest is an area totaling about 1000 acres under the supervision of the Athol Conservation Commission, and is located off Bearsden Rd., which formerly connected Athol with South Royalston. The bridge over the Millers River was swept away by a flood many years ago and was never replaced. The farms along the northern end of the road have long been abandoned, and the fields and pastures are now forest and open space. About 20 mi. of trail now explore the hills, brooks, ponds, and scenic vistas. A descriptive map flyer is available on request from the Athol Conservation Commission, Town Hall, Athol, MA 01331. Also refer to the USGS Athol quadrangle.

To reach Bearsden Forest, take MA 2A (Main St.) in Athol east to Athol Memorial Hospital. Bearsden Rd. is located approximately opposite the hospital and is marked by an Athol Conservation Area sign. Follow Bearsden Rd. to the end of the tar surface, then continue straight ahead on a one-lane gravel road (rough) for 0.4 mi. to a 4-car parking area. A posted map nearby shows the trails and roads in the forest.

One suggested walk is as follows: Follow the trail marked with yellow paint blazes through pines to Big Round Top (0.5 mi., 15 min.). At the summit (1278 ft.) there is a picnic table and a 360-degree view of three states, including Mt. Grace, Wachusett Mtn., and Mt. Monadnock. Head northeast along a meandering trail, continuing past another picnic table at Warren Vista, left of the main trail. A short distance beyond, a cairn marks an alternate trail that goes about 100 yd. Bear left at the next signpost, in the direction of the Lawton Barway, leaving the yellow paint blazes here. Turn sharp right at the next signpost, toward Old Stage Rd. Proceed downhill and cross Buckman Brook. Bear right along the 1799 Old Stage Rd. and continue 1.1 mi. to Newton Reservoir, a small, attractive woodland pond that serves as a water supply for Athol.

Return via Old Stage Rd. to the trail to the Lawton Barway. Upon reaching the Lawton Barway intersection, turn right onto Old Bearsden Rd. for a 15-min. walk to Sheep Rock, bearing left at By-Pass Rd. and then passing through the rock cut. Bear left at the signpost for Sheep Rock. At Sheep Rock a 12-ft. viewing tower overlooks the Millers River, B&M Railroad, and adjacent wooded hills. Return via this road and Old Bearsden Rd. to the parking area.

Brooks Woodland Preserve (TTOR)

This 558-acre tract on Quaker Dr. in Petersham was once the home of the Nipmuck Nation before being cleared for farms and pastures. Today the land is forest and hillside traced by stone walls and accented with scenic views. More than 13 mi. of trails course through the woods, which are drained by the Swift River, and Roaring and Mocassin Brooks. Swamps and ponds have formed behind the beaver dams that cross the streams, and bedrock ledges provide habitat for many animals, including porcupines.

The reservation is divided into three tracts—Roaring Brook, Swift River, and Connor's Pond. To reach the Roaring Brook tract from Petersham center, follow East St. for 0.8 mi. to the entrance on the left. To reach the Swift River and Connor's Pond tracts from the junction of MA 122 and MA 32 south of Petersham, drive south on combined MA 122/32 for 1.5 mi. Turn left onto Quaker Dr. and follow it for 0.5 mi. to roadside parking, located immediately after the bridge on both sides near the dual entrances.

Rutland Brook (MAS)

This wildlife sanctuary in Petersham and Barre consists of 1480 acres and is maintained by the Massachusetts Audubon Society. It is operated in conjunction with the nearby Cook's Canyon Sanctuary, and some of the latter's summer camp programs are conducted here. To reach the sanctuary, take MA 122 for 5 mi. north of Barre Common. Just before reaching the bridge near Connor's Pond, proceed east on the hardtop for about 100 ft. Bear left at the sanctuary sign, then continue 0.3 mi. to a parking area on the left.

One suggested walk is as follows: After parking, continue on the road past a cottage on the right. About 150 ft. along, turn left onto a trail that leads to a dam and House Pond. Cross the dam and go straight ahead about 200 ft. Turn right onto a path to Beaver Meadow. Turn left onto a path beside Rutland Brook and continue through a forest of big hemlocks. Then turn left onto the road to return to the main gate and parking area. The circuit is 1.0 mi. long and takes about 30 min. A trail map of this area is available from the Massachusetts Audubon Society.

Harvard Forest

Harvard Forest is a 3000-acre research and experimental forest in Petersham maintained by Harvard University and open to the public, with many miles of trails and roads available for hiking. The headquarters and museum are on the east side of MA 32, approximately 3 mi. north of Petersham center. The museum contains many informative and entertaining exhibits, including spectacular models portraying the history of the central New England forests. Trail maps and guides are available at the information kiosk at the museum.

John Sanderson's Farm Nature Trail (HF)

This 0.25-mi.-long interpretive trail begins at the museum and is marked with red disks. In summer 2003 new interpretive signs were erected along the trail. It wanders through what was once John Sanderson's farm some 160 years ago. Along the way it explains the dynamics of the landscape as it exists today and compares it with what it was generations ago.

The 21-station trail begins by following wide roads edged with stone walls and hardwoods. The trail passes a plantation of white pine planted in the 1920s, then turns right onto another wide road. It descends into a swale and through red pine plantations, some of which have been clearcut in recent years. The trail then leaves the road and traces a path through white spruce, over stone walls, and meanders through a broad hardwood forest that has grown here since the 1920s. The trail finally slips through a stone wall and returns to the museum.

Black Gum Trail (HF)

This 1.5-mi.-long interpretive trail begins at the museum and heads east on a wide old farm road. It passes through a stone wall and beneath plantations to another old road that leaves right. Continuing east, the path turns sharp left (north), passing through a woodlot with a wetland to the left. The trail now swings west, where a road leaves right and passes along the edge of a swamp. To the right is a recently burned tract. Near the end of the swamp the main trail continues straight (west) and a side trail leaves left. This side trail is a loop path that rides above the swamp on a boardwalk pathway and reconnects to the Black Gum Trail just beyond the swamp. At a road junction the trail turns left (south) again along a road lined on both sides by stone walls and joins the route of the red-marked John Sanderson Nature Trail. The path turns left down a wide road near a stand of white pines and ambles the short way back to the museum.

Slab City Loop (HF)

This short trail through a portion of Harvard Forest leaves MA 122 (Barre–Petersham Rd.) 4.5 mi. north of Barre Common. Parking is available on the east side of MA 122 at the Harvard Forest Boundary sign. The trail enters the woods on the west side of MA 122, at first following an old black-top road, then turning left after about 350 ft. to follow white paint blazes. The trail turns right at a cairn near the east branch of the Swift River. (A side trail on the left leads to a lookout over the river.) The trail proceeds along and above the river, passes through mature pines, and crosses a small bridge before returning to MA 122. The parking area is about 800 ft. to the right.

Slab City Loop

Distance from MA 122 (Barre–Petersham Rd.)

   to MA 122 (circuit): 1.3 mi., 35 min.

Swift River Reservation (TTOR)

This 438-acre preserve is a combination of three separate properties—the Nichewaug tract, the Slab City tract, and the Davis tract. Each tract has its own unique character and hiking opportunities. About 7 mi. of generally moderate trails cross the property. The Nichewaug tract is known for a number of attractions, including rocky ledges offering long views, a beaver dam and associated wetlands, open sunny fields, riverside habitat, and, in spring, vernal pools sought out by salamanders and frogs.

To reach the Nichewaug tract from the intersection of MA 122 and MA 32 south of Petersham center, follow South St. 0.9 mi. to Nichewaug Rd. Turn right onto Nichewaug Rd. and continue 0.6 mi. to the entrance and parking area (6 cars) on the left.

Avery Williams ran a farm on what is now the Slab City tract back in the late 1800s. When the farm was abandoned it grew into a young succession forest that was nearly destroyed by the hurricane of 1938. Since then the land has grown back to a mature forest of white pine and hardwood, and some laboriously reclaimed fields offer refreshing open spaces that are reminders of what the land must have looked like more than a century ago.

To reach the Slab City tract from intersection of MA 122 and MA 32 south of Petersham center, follow combined MA 122/32 south for 2 mi. to Connor's Pond. The entrance and parking area (6 cars) are on the right across from the dam.

To reach the Davis tract from the intersection of MA 122 and MA 32 south of Petersham center, travel south on combined MA 122/32 for 3.3 mi. Turn right onto Nichewaug Rd. in Barre (this becomes Glen Valley Rd. in Petersham) next to Penn Valley Country Store. Travel 0.4 mi. on Glen Valley Rd. to the entrance and parking area in an old gravel pit excavation.

Rock House Reservation (TTOR)

This 193-acre reservation in West Brookfield was named for the ledge and boulder cave aptly called the Rock House. The shelter is formed by a large overhanging ledge, with the entrance protected by large blocky boulders. Native Americans once used this spot as a meeting place and winter camp, and the cave is located near two trails frequented by Native Americans centuries ago. Some of the destinations reached by the 3 mi. of trails include the Rock

House, Balance Rock, and Carter Pond. There are also plantations of spruce and pine planted in the 1930s and an overlook taking in the fields and woods.

To reach Rock House Reservation from the Massachusetts Turnpike, take Exit 8 and pick up MA 32 north toward Ware. MA 32 joins MA 9 in Ware. Stay on combined MA 32/9 and, when the routes separate, follow MA 9 east for 1.1 mi. to a parking area (12 cars) and entrance on the left.

Norcross Wildlife Sanctuary (Norcross Wildlife Foundation)

Located in Monson, this approximately 4000-acre preserve protects woods, hill, lakes, and streams as well as the varied flora and fauna that live here. The mission of the sanctuary is the conservation of biodiversity through the collection and propagation of plants and preservation of bird and other animal species. About 3 mi. of marked trails explore a variety of habitats as well as tended gardens. There are two natural history museums and a picnic area. Some of the areas visited by the trails include a cedar swamp, postglacial kettle pond, pine barrens, and hickory grove. Gardens include a rose, herb, and rock garden.

To reach the sanctuary from the west, take the Mass Pike (I-90) to Exit 8 (Palmer). Follow MA 32 south through Monson Center and turn left onto Wales Rd. Continue on Wales Rd., bearing right at the fork, for about 3 mi. to Wales. Once in Wales continue about 0.5 mi. to Peck Rd. Turn right onto Peck Rd. and drive the short way to the entrance on the left.

From the east take Mass Pike (I-90) west to Exit 9 (Sturbridge). Take US 20 west to Brimfield, then turn left onto MA 19. Travel south on MA 19 to Wales and turn right onto Monson Rd. Drive about 2 mi. (bearing left at the fork) to Peck Rd. Take a left onto Peck Rd.; the entrance is a short distance down this road.

Suggested Hikes

Easy Hikes

Wachusett Meadows Wildlife Sanctuary

Pasture Trail [lp: 2.0 mi., 1:00]. A lovely and relaxing walk through fields and forest.

Harvard Forest

Black Gum Trail [lp: 1.5 mi., 0:40]. This hike wanders through fragrant plantations of pines and passes through wetlands and swamps on boardwalks.

Wachusett Mtn. State Reservation

Balance Rock Trail [rt: 0.8 mi., 0:40]. A walk to a large glacial boulder.

Moderate Hikes

Royalston Falls

Tully Trail, Section 1 [rt: 1.4 mi., 1:45]. This short hike traverses difficult terrain, including a brook crossing and the rough topography around the falls.

Mt. Watatic

Wapack Trail, Midstate Trail, Section 1 [rt: 2.4 mi., 2:00]. An energizing hike that alternates between steep areas and moderate stretches as it ascends the south side of the mountain.

Wachusett Mtn. State Reservation

Mtn. House Trail [rt: 2.0 mi., 1:35]. One of the shorter paths up the mountain, this trail is steep in spots with rough footing, but leads to great mountaintop views.

Strenuous Hikes

Wachusett Mtn. State Reservation

Midstate Trail, Section 4 [rt: 6.4 mi., 4:50]. Beginning and ending at Redemption Rock, this hike leads to the beautiful views atop Wachusett Mtn.

Blackstone River and Canal State Park

Many trails [rt: 7.0 mi., 4:10]. This long hike explores the shore of the Blackstone River and the historic Blackstone Canal via a series of trails.

Jacob's Hill

Tully Trail, Section 1 [rt: 4.0 mi., 3:00]. An exciting hike that passes Spirit Falls on its way to views atop ledges. The terrain can be challenging.

Part IV

North and West of Boston

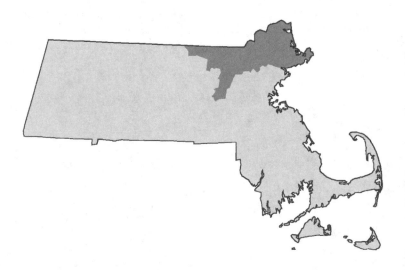

LIST OF TRAILS

LIST OF TRAILS

This chapter covers most of Essex and Middlesex Counties in Massachusetts, stretching from the Atlantic coast north of Boston to the gently rolling terrain northwest and west of the metropolitan area. (Part V, Boston and Vicinity, includes those parts of Middlesex County closest to Boston.) There are no summits of any significance in this area, but it does include parts of the Merrimack River and Charles River watersheds. Much of the region is still covered with woodlands or farmland, but development pressures have been intense as suburbanization extends outward.

Bay Circuit Trail

Though the Bay Circuit Trail (BCT) is not yet completed, substantial portions have been opened and offer wonderfully varied hiking experiences close to Boston. The original concept was proposed by Henry M. Channing and by urban planner Charles Eliot II, both of The Trustees of Reservations, in 1929 as an outer "emerald necklace" (to complement Boston's urban "emerald necklace" of parks and open spaces, laid out by Frederick Law Olmsted in the 19th century). The BCT would link parks, open spaces, and greenways in a grand arc around the Boston metropolitan area from Plum Island in the north to Kingston Bay in the south. The Massachusetts legislature enacted legislation creating the Bay Circuit Program in 1956. In 1985 the Massachusetts Department of Environmental Management (now the Department of Conservation and Recreation) was directed to provide planning and acquisition funds to designated cities and towns in the Bay Circuit corridor. Interested citizens, town officials, and representatives of private land-protection organizations attended regional meetings and raised public awareness of the Bay Circuit Program. Land acquistion, funded by a bond issue in 1985, included Bay Farm in Kingston and Duxbury, the southern terminus of the Bay Circuit Trail.

The Bay Circuit Alliance (BCA) was founded in 1990 with the assistance of the National Park Service Conservation Assistance Program. The goal of the BCA is to establish a trail, for passive recreation, connecting green space from the south of Boston in Duxbury and Kingston to the north of Boston in Newburyport. The trail will traverse up to 50 communities in the broad corridor between MA 128 and I-495 and is estimated to be between 170 and 200 mi. long when completed.

The BCA is best described as a partnership of organizations and individuals, public and private. BCA's membership consists of local, regional, and statewide member organizations and individuals. The BCA helps local communities establish their portions of the Bay Circuit Trail through planning and technical assistance on route identification, land-protection issues, and trail management and construction.

The development of the Bay Circuit Trail is the largest trail project presently underway in Massachusetts, and volunteers are needed in all of the Bay Circuit communities. Volunteer activities include trail mapping and description (including history and natural history), trail location, trail clearing, cleanup and maintenance, bridge building, contacting landowners for permission, identifying and aiding in the protection of green space, leading walks, and more. In 1995, 90 mi. of trail in 16 communities had been dedicated and opened to the public. By 2003, 150 mi. of trail in 21 communities connecting 79 parcels of protected land were open.

If you are interested in joining this effort, contact the Bay Circuit Alliance at 3 Railroad St., Andover, MA 01810 (508-470-1982).

Two detailed trail guides have been published that cover a 35-mi. stretch of the Bay Circuit from the Ipswich River in Willowdale State Forest, through Boxford, North Andover, and Andover, to the Merrimack River. These are *The Bay Circuit and AVIS Guide to Walks in Andover*, published by the Andover Trails Committee and the Andover Village Improvement Society; and *The Bay Circuit Guide to Walks In and Around Boxford*, published by the Boxford Bay Circuit Program Committee. They can be purchased at the AMC headquarters in Boston and at other retail outlets. As the trail develops, more detailed trail descriptions will be prepared for other areas and will also be included in future editions of this guidebook.

Some of the trail's more popular sections also are described in greater detail in conjunction with the parks and reservations through which the trail passes.

The standard trail marking adopted for the Bay Circuit is a white, vertical blaze the size of a dollar bill. Offset double stacked blazes indicate a turn, with the turn in the direction of the upper blaze. Four-inch-square Bay Circuit emblems will be placed at road crossings and trailheads. Where the trail is well trod and obvious, there are fewer blazes. Hikers should expect to find sections that have not yet been blazed to this standard.

Section 1. Plum Island (Newburyport) to MA 1A (Rowley) (9.6 mi.)

The northern trailhead of the Bay Circuit Trail is found in Newburyport at the end of the Plum Island Turnpike. To reach the trailhead travel to the large parking lot at the northern end of Plum Island. From the lot walk east along the Merrimack River to the unsigned beginning of the Merrimack River Trail (blazed in white). Continue south along the beach to the start of the BCT.

The trail now leads away from the beach, following along the Plum Island Turnpike, across the bridge over the Plum Island River. Continue past the Plum Island Airport (there is a kiosk with information on the Newbury section of the BCT here) following the Eliza Little Trail. The path skirts the end of the airport runway before traversing the fields of the Spencer-Pierce-Little Farm (Society for the Preservation of New England Antiquities). At 2.6 mi. the trail passes the Spencer-Pierce-Little House before wandering down Littles Lane to High Rd.

At High Rd. (MA 1A) turn left (southeast) and follow the road past Tendercrop Farm, then turn right onto Hay St. at 3.5 mi. After 0.5 mi. take a right (north) onto Green St., continue 0.2 mi., then turn left (southwest) onto Boston Rd. The road leads past the Fuller Dome House and enters Old Town Reservation at a gate. The BCT quickly bears left from the path and follows cart paths over boardwalks to Hay Rd. Cross the Little River at 5.3 mi. and turn left (south) onto Newman Rd. Causeway. There are excellent views of the salt marshes here.

From the end of the marsh continue about 0.2 mi. to a trail on the left that ascends knobby Old Town Hill. The crest is about 150 ft. above sea level and offers long views. From the hilltop the trail descends and again reaches Newman Rd. at 6.5 mi. Turn left onto Newman Rd. and hike to historic Newbury Lower Green. Follow a dirt road past the west side of the green before crossing MA 1A (High Rd.), then follow a sidewalk over the Parker River at 6.9 mi. Once over the river bear left onto Newbury Neck Rd. Follow the road as it swings over high ground, crosses MA 1A again, and then follow Old Rowley Rd. to the Newbury–Rowley town line about 0.75 mi. from MA 1A. Head left (west) on Redgate Rd., but do not cross the RR tracks. Follow along MA 1A for 0.75 mi. and cross over the RR tracks on the MA 1A bridge at 9.6 mi.

Note: The BCT does not presently continue through Rowley. To reach the next section of trail follow MA 1A about 1.8 mi. to Summer St. Turn right onto Summer St. and go 0.4 mi. to its end. Turn left onto Bradford, travel

0.2 mi., and turn right onto MA 133. The trailhead parking area is about 0.2 mi. farther, on the left (south) side of the road.

Bay Circuit Trail: Plum Island (Newburyport) to MA 1A (Rowley)

Distances from Plum Island

> *to* Hay St.: 3.5 mi., 1 hr., 10 min.
>
> *to* Parker River: 6.9 mi., 2 hr., 30 min.
>
> *to* MA 1A bridge: 9.6 mi., 3 hr., 50 min.

Section 2. Prospect Hill (Rowley) to Middleton Rd. (Boxford) (19.5 mi.)

From the parking area off MA 133 follow the dirt road past the summit road on the right. Continue straight through a field and ascend Prospect Hill (267 ft.) along a white-blazed trail, reaching the summit at 0.3 mi. Descend Prospect Hill and cross Dow Brook on a bridge. Pass beneath power lines, then cross the far west end of Bull Brook Reservoir on a bridge at 2.0 mi. From the reservoir the trail passes along the edge of an athletic field to reach Mile Lane at 2.3 mi. Turn right (southwest) onto Mile Lane and in 0.2 mi. turn right (west) onto Linebrook Rd. *Note:This road portion of the BCT will likely be relocated in the future. Be alert for blazes.*

At 2.5 mi. turn left (southwest) onto a dirt road with Doyon Memorial School on the right. At Jersey barrier turn right onto a trail (Willowdale State Forest). The trail junctions are numbered in the state forest, with junctions 1–12 following the BCT route. At a T-junction (3.6 mi.) turn left, followed in 0.2 mi. by a sharp right at junction 3. At junction 4 turn left; at junction 5 pass a woods road on the left. Junction 6 is reached at 5.0 mi. and can be confusing, as white blazes of the Discover Hamilton Trail enter from the left. Many side trails enter over the next 0.7 mi.; follow blazes carefully. At junctions 7–9 continue straight. At 5.7 mi. turn left at junction 10, then right at junction 11, leaving the woods road and crossing a wetland area. At 6.2 mi. reach a bridge that spans Howlett Brook.

Reach West St., following to, and crossing over, US 1. (*Caution*: *Heavy traffic*.) At 7.6 mi. cross Old Right Rd., then turn right onto a side trail and descend a hill to a footbridge. Reach Rowley Rd. and turn right to continue toward Linebrook Rd., but before reaching the road turn left into the woods. After a short woods walk cross Linebrook Rd. The trail now passes through an area of eskers—long, flowing hills—before reaching Boxford Rd. (Rowley) at 9.7 mi. Turn right and briefly follow Boxford Rd., then leave the road left and ascend into the woods. Descend an esker and cross a bridge before passing through an eroded area. Turn left, paralleling I-95. In Georgetown turn right (11.2 mi.) before the I-95 fence, then cross I-95 on the Pingree Farm Rd. bridge at 11.5 mi.

Bear left (west) at a fork in the road, then right at a T-junction. Pass onto a private driveway, then onto King George Dr., which leads to MA 97 at 14.9 mi. Cross MA 97 onto Kelsey Rd., follow this road about 0.2 mi., and turn left (south) onto an old railroad bed. The trail now heads up an embankment to run parallel to Kelsey Rd. Turn left onto Hemlock Rd., right onto Ipswich Rd., and left onto Round Top Rd. Follow Round Top Rd., turning right onto Campground Rd. then left onto Chapman Way. Cross the inlet to Lowe Pond on a bridge at about 16.1 mi.

Turn right onto Boern Lane and left at junction 49 to the entrance of Chapman Way, which leads to Boxford center. Take Chapman Way to Georgetown Rd. Turn left (south) onto Georgetown Rd. and follow it to Depot Rd. Continue south about 0.25 mi. to Boxford Center at 16.9 mi. In Boxford center turn left onto Topsfield Rd. (BCT sign), follow it for 0.5 mi., turn right onto Cahoon St. (BCT sign), then right again into Boy Scout Park. Follow blazes onto Dana Rd., turning right onto this road and entering Lockwood Forest at 18.2 mi.

Follow the path to Fish Brook, turn left, and continue on the path with the brook on the right. Pass through a field and reach Lockwood Lane at 18.8 mi. Turn right onto Lockwood Lane, then left just before a second bridge. Follow trail markers to Middleton Rd. Cross the road and reach Bald Hill Reservation at 19.5 mi.

Bay Circuit Trail: Prospect Hill (Rowley) to Middleton Rd. (Boxford)

Distances from Prospect Hill

to US 1: 7.6 mi., 3 hr., 35 min.

to MA 97: 14.9 mi., 4 hr., 40 min.

to Bald Hill Reservation: 19.5 mi., 6 hr., 30 min.

Section 3. Boxford to Andover (15.2 mi.)

From the entrance to Bald Hill Reservation continue straight through the gate and past a pond on the left. At junction 13 turn left and gradually ascend to junction 12, where a side trail leads to the summit of Bald Hill (limited view in winter). The trail descends, turning right at junction 11 then right at junction 7, left at 6, and left at 2 before reaching an abandoned quarry. Rock cairns lead to Sharpner's Pond Rd. at 3.4 mi.

Turn right onto Sharpner's Pond Rd. and follow this for 0.8 mi., then turn right onto an old railroad bed. Leave left at the first BCT blaze and cross Salem St., then some power lines at 4.4 mi. Bear right at the fork, then right again at the next junction. Follow blazes to the road past the athletic fields, then turn left onto Berry Rd. Follow Berry Rd. to MA 114 at 5.4 mi.

Cross MA 114 to Harold Parker Rd. at the entrance to Harold Parker State Forest. The BCT enters the woods about 100 yd. down the road on the right. Be alert and follow blazes carefully for the next 1.25 mi. through the forest, especially at junctions. Note the relocation of the trail at about 0.9 mi. due to wet conditions. Cross Salem St. (parking) at 7.9 mi. (there is a picnic area on the right), then reach Berry Pond Rd. at 8.2 mi. Follow the road right for a short distance, then turn right onto a trail past old quarries to a footbridge. Cross Jenkins Rd. (parking) at 9.0 mi., reaching Skug River Reservation at 9.2 mi. Many trails in Skug River Reservation use white blazes; look for BCT logos at junctions.

The trail passes a former mill site then crosses an extended boardwalk before turning left onto Salem St. (parking here) at 10.0 mi. Follow Salem St. for the short distance to Hammond and Mary French Reservations. At 10.3 mi. the trail begins a long boardwalk section that crosses the Skug River twice and offers beautiful views of the wetlands. From the boardwalk continue to Korinthian Way, turn left and follow the road to Grey Rd., turn right onto Grey Rd., then almost immediately leave the road left through the woods to Tucker Rd. at 11.3 mi.

Quickly leave Tucker Rd. right, then bear left into Charles Ward Reservation. Continue along a grassy cart path along the edge of a field and into the woods. Gradually ascend through a field to a confusing junction—follow the wide, level path to the top of Holt Hill, where there is a beautiful view. Take a sharp left (BCT marker) and descend to a paved access road at 12.2 mi. Turn left onto the access road, then right onto the trail, and continue to Prospect Rd. Turn right onto Prospect Rd. at 12.8 mi. and parallel MA 125 briefly past a wetland, then enter the woods into the Phillip's Academy Sanctuary.

Follow a woods road and cross the field on the diagonal through a driveway to Salem St. Turn right onto Salem St., then immediately left onto Holt Rd., then right into the woods, passing athletic fields and tennis courts. Follow a driveway to Main St., where the trail turns right at a traffic light. Cross the street and continue north to Philips St. Turn left onto Philips St., cross both School St. and Central St., then turn left onto Lupine Rd. and reach Purdon Reservation at 15.2 mi.

Bay Circuit Trail: Boxford to Andover

Distances from Boxford

to MA 113: 5.4 mi., 2 hr., 10 min.

to Tucker Rd.: 11.3 mi., 3 hr., 50 min.

to Purdon Reservation: 15.2 mi., 5 hr., 20 min.

Section 4. Andover (Shawsheen River) to Lowell (National Park Visitor Center) (11.7 mi.)

The BCT is unblazed in the town of Tewksbury. In Lowell the BCT coincides with the Merrimack River Trail, which uses similar markings to the white blazes of the BCT.

From Reservation Rd. at the south end of Indian Ridge Reservation, follow the road uphill 0.1 mi., turn right and follow the trail up an esker to the Alice Buck Memorial stone, then climb a second esker that passes behind Andover High School. At 1.0 mi. follow a boardwalk to West Parish Reservation, where the trail crosses the meadow and proceeds down a boardwalk before turning right onto Reservation Rd. Follow the trail through West Parish Cemetery to MA 133 at 1.8 mi.

Cross MA 133 and enter Doyle Link. Follow the trail to High Plain Rd., turn left (west), and follow the road about 1.4 mi., crossing over I-93 and I-495 along the way. (*Note: At 3.6 mi. a woods road leaves to the left; this is the beginning of the proposed portion of the BCT that would lead east into Tewksbury.*) The trail enters Harold Rafton Reservation at 4.6 mi.; watch for the BCT logo at trail junctions. At 5.3 mi. the BCT crosses a brook, then passes through a field before reaching the junction of River and Chandler Rds. (parking) at 6.2 mi. Turn left onto River Rd. and quickly turn right onto Launching Rd. to reach Deer Jump Reservation.

Follow the trail toward the Merrimack River, turning left at the junction and descending toward the riverbank. Follow the river trail for 2.5 mi. to the Tewksbury pumping station. At the pumping station follow the driveway to River Rd., turn right (west) past the cemetery, and continue to a junction with MA 133. Turn right onto Burnham Rd. and walk toward the river, then turn left at the river onto the public river trail that runs through Lowell. Follow the trail along the river (BCT and Merrimack River Trail). Follow the trail closely, as some abutters have infringed on the right of way, making passage more challenging. At 11.2 mi. reach the confluence of the Merrimack and Concord

Rivers. Leave the trail, walk around the Lowell Memorial Auditorium, and turn right onto Merrimack St. Follow the Merrimack River Trail to the Lowell National/State Historic Park Visitor Center (11.7 mi.) on the corner of Market St. and Shattuck St. (parking).

This is the end of the marked trail in this area.

Bay Circuit Trail: Andover (Shawsheen River) to Lowell (National Park Visitor Center)

Distances from Shawsheen River

   to MA 133: 1.8 mi., 40 min.

   to Harold Rafton Reservation: 4.6 mi., 1 hr., 55 min.

   to National Park Visitor Center, Lowell: 11.7 mi., 4 hr., 15 min.

Section 5. Acton (MA 225–MA 27 Intersection) to Concord (Annursnac Hill Conservation Area) (6.2 mi.)

The Acton section of the BCT runs along the grade of an abandoned railroad line just southeast of the intersection of MA 225 and MA 27. Follow the railroad bed generally south, crossing MA 27 at 0.7 mi. opposite a gravel pit. The trail crosses Butter Brook, then Nashoba Brook at 1.1 mi. Turn left onto a driveway (permission to use the driveway has not formally been obtained) that leads to MA 27. Turn right (south) along MA 27 (Main St.) to Wheeler Lane on the left (east). Turn onto Wheeler Lane and follow it to the dead end, where a kiosk and parking area are located.

The trail soon enters Nashoba Brook Conservation Area and runs parallel to the brook. At 2.3 mi. cross a boardwalk, then cross Nashoba Brook on a wooden bridge. Turn left (east) at the junction and head uphill, entering Spring Hill Conservation Area. At 3.0 mi. come to a junction where the BCT splits into two routes, one going to Carlisle and the other to Concord. The Carlisle link is a proposed route at this time.

The Concord link begins by turning right (south) at the junction, traveling uphill, and crossing boardwalks at 3.7 mi. and again at 4.2 mi. The BCT now climbs through forest to the top of Strawberry Hill (4.6 mi.) with views to the south. The trail descends to Jay Lane (dead end) and out to Strawberry Hill Rd. (parking). Turn left (east) on a sidewalk, turn right (south) onto Pope Rd. at 5.2 mi., then turn left (east) onto Stoneymeade Way. Bear left and enter the Stoneymeade Conservation Area at 5.9 mi. At 6.2 mi. enter the area of a ruined wartime bunker and the Annursnac Hill Conservation Area.

Bay Circuit Trail: Acton (MA 225–MA 27 Intersection) to Concord (Annursnac Hill Conservation Area)

Distances from MA 225–MA 27 intersection

to Nashoba Brook: 2.3 mi., 55 min.

to Strawberry Hill: 4.2 mi., 1 hr., 45 min.

to Annursnac Hill Conservation Area: 6.2 mi., 2 hr., 55 min.

Section 6. Concord (Annursnac Hill Conservation Area) to Walden Pond (6.5 mi.)

The section begins at the Annursnac Hill Conservation Area astride the Acton–Concord line. The BCT crosses a brook and reaches Strawberry Hill Rd. (there is an information kiosk here) at 0.5 mi. Turn right (south) onto Strawberry Hill Rd. then quickly right (south) to College Rd., which in turn leads to Barrett's Mill Rd. Turn left (east) onto Barrett's Mill Rd., crossing Strawberry Hill Rd. and the ruins of the Barrett Mill (1.9 mi.). Cross Lowell Rd. and follow Barnes Hill Rd. as it merges into Eastabrook Rd. Cross Liberty St. (Muster Field on the right) and enter Minuteman National Historic Park and Visitor Center at 3.3 mi. (parking and restrooms).

Continue down a dirt track past the Minuteman statue and the Old North Bridge where the "shot heard 'round the world" occurred in 1775. Cross the restored bridge that spans the Concord River at 3.7 mi. Follow the trail to Monument St. and turn right (south), traveling about 0.25 mi. to an old railroad bed. Turn right, passing a lumberyard and crossing Mill Brook before reaching Lowell Rd. at 4.2 mi. Turn left onto Lowell Rd., cross Mill Brook once more, and reach Monument Square. Pass through the square, turn right onto MA 62 (Main St.), and continue down the road, turning left (south) onto Walden St. and left (northeast) onto Heywood. Cross Mill Brook and swing right onto the trail that enters Heywood Meadow at 4.9 mi.

Note: For the next 0.6 mi. traffic can be a great hazard; proceed cautiously. Turn right onto Lexington Ave., then quickly bear right onto the Cambridge Turnpike. Past the home of Ralph Waldo Emerson, cross the road to a sidewalk on the east side. Follow the sidewalk over the brook and recross the turnpike at 5.6 mi. (utility pole 26), then follow the trail into Hapgood Town Forest. The trail wraps around a hill, reaches Fairyland Pond at 6.0 mi., and continues around a portion of the pond. Turn left before crossing the pond's inlet and climb past a spring. At the crest of the hill turn right and descend to

Walden St. Turn left onto Walden St., which leads shortly to MA 2. Cross MA 2 (great caution is advised) and travel a short way down MA 126 to the entrance of Walden Pond State Reservation (6.5 mi.) on the right.

Bay Circuit Trail: Concord (Annursnac Hill Conservation Area) to Walden Pond

Distances from Annursac Hill Conservation Area

   to Barrett Mill: 1.9 mi., 50 min.

   to Haywood Meadow: 4.9 mi., 2 hr., 10 min.

   to Walden Pond: 6.5 mi., 2 hr., 55 min.

Section 7. Concord (Walden Pond) to Wayland (Great Meadows National Wildlife Refuge) (11.7 mi.)

The trail enters Walden Pond State Reservation and passes near the cabin (on the right) of Henry David Thoreau. The BCT follows the trail along Walden Pond, past the RR tracks on the right. Turn right and follow the Esker Trail past the Emerson's Cliff Trail, then turn right onto a fire road that leads out of the reservation and to MA 126 at 1.3 mi.

Cross MA 126 then follow beside the road (turn right, south) on a trail that parallels the highway. At the junction with Old Concord Rd. cross MA 126 to Old Concord Rd. and follow it 0.1 mi. to a dirt road on the left. Follow the dirt road into the woods and reach Mt. Misery at 1.4 mi. Follow the Kettle Trail (blazed blue) to an intersection where the BCT turns left on a path marked with blue bike blazes. The path continues past a small pond to the parking area at the end of the pond. Continue through the parking area to MA 117, then turn left and follow the trail (east) that parallels the road, reaching the canoe launch parking lot for Farrar Pond at 2.4 mi.

Cross MA 117 just past the parking area, go up a private driveway (numbers 17 and 19), and turn left through fences onto a trail that stays close to the fence line. The trail then reaches Farrar Pond, crosses a spillway, and heads uphill. Follow the trail, now pavement, to Birchwood Lane and turn right into the woods at 3.3 mi. The trail shortly exits the woods near Kettlehole Dr. Turn right onto Kettlehole Dr., which soon reaches Oxbow Rd. at the Wayland town line.

Note: Through Wayland there are BCT logos at trailheads. The remainder of the trail is not blazed. Follow Oxbow Rd. to Campbell Rd., turn right, and continue to a water department access road on the right. Turn left onto the access road and continue a short way to a trail on the right before the pumphouse. Enter the Trout Brook Conservation Area on a red-blazed trail that crosses the brook, then climbs uphill through an area with many kettleholes. Follow red blazes to the B junction, then follow yellow blazes (right turn) to the M junction. Continue on the yellow-marked trail to Sherman's Bridge Rd. and the main trailhead for the Trout Brook Conservation Area.

Cross Sherman's Bridge Rd. onto Alpine Rd. Continue a short distance to the Castle Hill Conservation Area and a colonial-style road on the left at 4.6 mi. The trail passes through wetlands east, then south, of Schoolhouse Pond and then east to MA 126. Turn right onto MA 126 and proceed to Moore Rd. This section of trail can be closed due to beaver activity flooding the trail. The bypass route is to travel 0.3 mi. east on Sherman's Bridge Rd., turn right onto MA 126, and travel to Moore Rd., where the route rejoins.

At Moore Rd. (6.0 mi.) turn right (northwest) and travel 0.4 mi. to a parking area for the Sedge Meadow Conservation Area on the right. Follow the trail through Sedge Meadow, passing fields and water company land along frequently wet paths. Pass Sedge Meadow Monument at 7.3 mi. before reaching Glezen Lane near Black Cat Farm (parking). Turn right (west) onto MA 27 (there is parking to the left at Cow Common Conservation Area).

Cross MA 127 and enter the Cow Common Conservation Area at 8.1 mi. The BCT heads across a field, turns right (south) into the woods and over a stream, coming to some community gardens and reaching MA 27 at 9.0 mi. Turn right onto MA 27, then bear left onto Bow Rd. to Concord Rd. (MA 126). Turn right onto MA 126 and pass through the town center. Turn right (west) onto US 20, then follow Pelham Island Rd. southwest across the Sudbury River on a narrow bridge. Turn left onto Heard Rd. and follow this to its dead end (parking). The trail enters a field and loops around Heard Farm to Erwin Rd. Turn right onto Erwin Rd. then quickly left onto Pelham Island Rd., which passes Heard Pond and enters Great Meadows National Wildlife Refuge at 11.7 mi. This is the end of this portion of the BCT. It resumes in Sudbury at the Weisblatt Conservation Land.

Bay Circuit Trail: Concord (Walden Pond) to Wayland (Great Meadows National Wildlife Refuge)

Distances from Walden Pond

   to Mt. Misery: 1.4 mi., 45 min.

   to Cow Common Conservation Area: 8.1 mi., 4 hr.

   to Great Meadows National Wildlife Refuge: 11.7 mi., 5 hr., 50 min.

For a description of the Bay Circuit route from Sudbury to its southern end on the coast in Duxbury and Kingston, see Southeastern Massachusetts and the Islands, Part VI, of this book.

Dogtown

The Dogtown area of Cape Ann, which occupies approximately 3 sq. mi. of undeveloped land between Gloucester and Rockport, was the site of an early village. In the 1600s it was "common land" where each settler in the village at the southern end of the cape had rights for cutting wood and pasturing; thus it was known as the Commons. When a village started to grow here in 1719, it was known as the Commons Settlement. By about 1741, 25 houses were at Dogtown, including those of some wealthy families. After the American Revolution, however, the more prosperous families began moving toward the harbor where opportunities for trade were better, and Dogtown slid into decline. Some trace the name *Dogtown* to the packs of animals that poor women and widows kept for protection. Others insist that the origin is lost in history.

Generations ago the upland plateau known as Dogtown resembled something out of *The Hound of the Baskervilles*, with rough moors and obtrusive boulders. Today the area is growing up into a thick coastal forest of oak and sumac, with the thorny tangles of greenbrier filling the swamps. It is easy to get lost—follow the trails and markers carefully. The cellars are designated by numbers carved on nearby rocks.

The city of Gloucester owns much of the Dogtown area, and the described trails explore land open for public use. Avoid venturing onto private land, and do not walk on or cross the MBTA high-speed RR tracks at the southeast end of Dogtown.

To reach Dogtown take MA 128 to the rotary in Gloucester (Exit 11). Turn left onto MA 127 toward Annisquam and continue 1.0 mi. to Reynard St., located on the right just after the Mill River crossing. Take Reynard St. east until it ends at Cherry St. Turn left (north) onto Cherry St. and drive for about 0.15 mi. to Dogtown Rd., the first right off Cherry St. Turn right to the parking area. The left gate is the continuation of Dogtown Rd.; the right gate is the entrance to the Cape Ann Sportsman's Club Rifle Range (gunshots are often audible). Don't block the gates when you park. The trails in Dogtown can be divided into fire roads, main trails, and secondary paths. Be cautious when venturing onto secondary trails, as it is sometimes challenging to keep to the paths.

Dogtown Trail

Follow Dogtown Rd. beyond the gate as it heads northeast. The Adams Pines Trail leaves left (north) for Common Rd. at junction 1. Dogtown Rd. continues past many cellar holes, each with a number chiseled on it for identification by Roger Babson, who made a directory of the families who once lived here. The trail reaches Dogtown Square, where a low rock on the right is marked D.T. SQ. Granny Day Swamp is to the left (northwest), with Wharf Rd. following the east side of the swamp to Common Rd. The Moraine Trail heads east from here. Dogtown Square is used as a common point to make circuits of the surrounding land.

Old Gravel Rd.

This trail heads southeast from Dogtown Rd. near the south end of the gravel pit. It crosses over fairly level, easy ground and through a maze of glacial boulders, the rocky remains of a glacial moraine left behind as the ice retreated thousands of years ago. The path now descends, tapering to a rugged, often wet trail that leads to the northern tip of Babson Reservoir. Just east of the reservoir, at junction 22, the Babson Boulder Trail heads north toward Dogtown Square and the Old Gravel Rd. ends.

Babson Boulder Trail

Whether you agree with his methods or even his sentiments, Roger Babson left his mark on Dogtown. Many of those marks are found along the trail that bears his name. The trail passes a number of boulders with words and phrases painstakingly carved into them. From the Old Gravel Rd. junction the trail begins to ascend the ridge, reaching a boulder (Truth) just before a side trail leaves left. The Babson Boulder Trail continues uphill, passing Work and Courage. The path now crests the ridge and cruises through the woods before climbing to a marshy wetland with blueberries. Nearby Loyalty makes us either feel good or guilty, and the trail reaches relatively level ground. Near Uncle Andrew's Rock the trail reaches Dogtown Rd. very near Dogtown Square.

Common Rd.

Common Rd. links Goose Pond Reservoir in the west to Squam Path Trail in the north. The trail begins off the service road, midway up the east side of the reservoir. From the Dogtown parking area it can be accessed by taking Dogtown Rd. to the Adams Pines Trail at junction 1, then turning left (north) onto the Adams Pines Trail to junction 2 just east of the trailhead. The trail passes through a swampy area with tangles of brier and summersweet. At junctions 4 and 5 Wharf Rd. leaves right (south) for Dogtown Square. Past the Wharf Trail is a large glacial boulder called Peter's Pulpit; then the path swings north and climbs over a small plateau. It then drops down to meet the Luce Trail at junction 16. Common Rd. coincides with the Luce Trail (orange dots) and reaches the signature feature of Dogtown—the Whale Jaw boulder.

Whale Jaw is a huge glacial boulder split in such a way as to look like a tremendous whale, mouth agape, breaking from the ground in search of hiker snacks. Generations ago when Dogtown was open country the stark boulder was chillingly impressive. Today the oaks and brush seem to be swallowing the rock rather than the reverse. The trail continues with the Luce Trail until Common Rd. ends at Squam Path at junction 19 at the far northern end of the reservation.

Ravenswood Park (TR)

This 600-acre wooded reservation, located in the Magnolia section of Gloucester, was the vision of Samuel Sawyer, who began to acquire and preserve land in the 1800s. When he died in 1889 he left an endowment and instructions to a group of trustees to turn the then 26 parcels into a park named Ravenswood, from the *Bride of Lammermoor* by Sir Walter Scott. Today the property consists of about 10 mi. of carriage roads and hiking trails, including a boardwalk through Great Magnolia Swamp where sweet bay magnolias grow. The park is located on MA 127 in Gloucester. From MA 128, take Exit 14 and follow MA 133 east for 3 mi. to MA 127. Go south on MA 127 for 2 mi.; the entrance and parking are located on the right.

The wide carriage roads are generally hard-packed and smooth enough to be used for wheelchairs. A broad carriage road (closed to vehicles) enters the park from the main entrance and is intersected by an extensive network of narrow woodland paths. New trail markers are now in place.

Valley Rd.

Also known as Gravel Rd., this broad carriage road runs north from the main entrance. It soon passes the southern end of the Ledge Hill Trail on the right. Shortly thereafter the Swamp Path leaves to the left and a cutoff to the Ledge Hill Trail leaves right. At 0.3 mi. another broad carriage road, Ridge Rd., leaves right. At 0.5 mi. Valley Rd. ends at an intersection with Old Salem Rd.

Valley Rd.

Distance from entrance

   to Old Salem Rd.: 0.5 mi., 30 min.

Old Salem Rd.

This trail begins on MA 127, about 0.3 mi. west of the main entrance. Because there is no parking here, most hikers approach this trail via Valley Rd.

   The trail enters the woods north of MA 127 as a narrow footpath, and soon crosses the Swamp Trail (to the left is the swamp, to the right is Valley Rd.). Shortly an unmarked link to the Swamp Trail is passed on the left. At 0.6 mi. the trail meets Valley Rd. and continues straight (northeast) on the carriage road. To the right Valley Rd. leads back to the main entrance. Also at this junction is another link to the Swamp Trail, leaving east past an old cellar hole.

   Old Salem Rd. continues on the carriage road, past a trail junction where the northern end of the Swamp Trail leaves left and an unmarked link to Ridge Rd. leaves right. At 1.0 mi. another carriage road, Evergreen Rd., leaves on the right, followed shortly by an unmarked link to Evergreen Rd., also on the right.

   At 1.6 mi. a stone with a plaque marks the former location of the old Hermit Shelter, once the home of Mason Walton, a naturalist who lived in a cabin here in the late 1800s. At this point the carriage road turns to the right and becomes the north end of Evergreen Rd. Old Salem Rd. reverts to a narrow path and continues straight. The Ledge Hill Trail departs to the right just before the Ravenswood property boundary. Old Salem Rd. continues off the property and ends at MA 127 a short distance north of Hough Ave.

Old Salem Rd.

Distances from MA 127 (Western Ave.)

  to Valley Rd.: 0.6 mi., 20 min.

  to southern end of Evergreen Rd.: 1.0 mi., 30 min.

  to northern end of Evergreen Rd.: 1.6 mi., 50 min.

  to MA 127 (Western Ave.): 1.8 mi., 1 hr.

Other Trails

Several smaller trails bear off from Old Salem Rd.

The Spring Trail leaves Old Salem Rd. to the right almost immediately after the trailhead. It leads past a spring to the Ledge Trail (0.8 mi.).

The Swamp Trail leaves on the left between two boulders, 0.2 mi. from the trailhead. After traversing huge flat ledges, it descends the western side of the moraine to a large swamp filled with ferns in spring and scarlet swamp maples in fall. After crossing the swamp the trail veers north for 0.5 mi. before rejoining Old Salem Rd. by an old cellar hole (1.5 mi.). The swamp can be impassable in spring but can be avoided by taking a shorter trail that runs north along the western side of the moraine before rejoining Old Salem Rd. by the cellar hole (0.8 mi.).

The Ledge Trail leaves Old Salem Rd. directly opposite the south junction with the Swamp Trail. It winds its way northeast past Otter Pond, around boulders covered with evergreen ferns, among tall hemlocks and oaks, and past views over a quarry and Buswell Pond. It ends at the north end of Old Salem Rd. (2.0 mi.).

Farther up Old Salem Rd. is the forked entrance to Ridge Rd., which leads northeast to connect with Evergreen Rd.

Halibut Point (DCR and TTOR) and Sea Rocks (Town of Rockport)

Halibut Point in Rockport is Cape Ann's northernmost headland, originally called "Haul-about Point" by mariners heading to and from Annisquam to the southwest. The protected land on the point includes a 56-acre state park (DCR) and an adjoining 12-acre property of The Trustees of Reservations, and features a stretch of rockbound coastline similar to that found farther north in Maine. Universally accessible restrooms are available. Sea Rocks is a narrow stretch of rocky headland owned by the town of Rockport and open to the public. It is located just east of the tract owned by TTOR.

From MA 128 take Exit 9 to MA 127 and continue north 3.0 mi. to Rockport center. Turn left onto Railroad Ave. (MA 127) and continue 2.4 mi. to Gott Ave. Turn right to the entrance and a large parking area.

The state park is dominated by a large, abandoned quarry. In the early 1900s, stone blocks of up to 40 tons were moved from here with the aid of steam drills, four hoisting derricks, and a railroad system. The Great Depression, along with the shift in construction from cut stone to concrete, led to the end of quarrying in 1929. The main quarry is now flooded and the deep green water looks inviting, but swimming is strictly forbidden due to danger from submerged rocks and equipment. The visitor center is located in the old fire-control tower at the edge of the Babson Quarry. Amazing views can be had from the top of the 60-ft.-tall structure. Most areas of the park are universally accessible, and assisted-listening devices are available for park tours.

Halibut Point offers some easy and well-marked walking trails leading to the rocky coast and overlooks of the Atlantic Ocean. Below the high-tide level, many tidal pools lie among the granite boulders; use caution, as the rocks can be slippery. A consistent ocean breeze blows over the point, and from the top of the "grout pile" (waste stone heap) a clear day offers a view extending to the Isles of Shoals in NH and beyond to Mt. Agamenticus in ME.

Maudslay State Park (DCR)

Once the elegant estate of the Moseley family, this 480-acre state park is a joy to visit. Located on the Merrimack River in Newburyport, the grounds are a blend of 19th-century gardens growing near tangles of mountain laurel and azalea. Towering pines and woodlands offer hiking and biking trails. Some of the features accessible from the many trails include the punch bowl, kettle pond, beech grove, Italian rose garden, and Rhododendron Dell.

Two attractive walks are the Castle Hill Trail, which leads to the highest point on the property and takes about 1 hr.; and the Merrimack River Trail, which takes about 1.5 hr.

To reach Maudslay Park from I-95 (Exit 57), take MA 113 east for 0.5 mi. and turn left onto Noble St. Continue to a stop sign and turn left onto Ferry Rd. Bear left and follow signs to the entrance. From the west, take Exit 55 off I-495 to MA 110 east. Travel 1.0 mi. to Merrill St., turn right at the second light, and continue for 1.5 mi. on Merrill and Spofford Sts. At a stop sign turn right onto Ferry Rd. and follow signs to the entrance.

Parker River National Wildlife Refuge (USFWS)

The Parker River National Wildlife Refuge on Plum Island, in Newbury, Rowley, and Ipswich, is operated by the U.S. Department of the Interior's Fish and Wildlife Service. The headquarters is located on Plum Island near the Newburyport Harbor Lighthouse, but is slated to move to an off-island site in the future. The refuge includes a 6.3-mi. beach and extensive salt marshes. The birdlife, especially shorebirds, is outstanding. Parker River is a nesting site for many shorebirds, including the endangered piping plover. The area is managed primarily as wildlife habitat; recreational use is limited accordingly. Beginning April 1 the entire 6.3 mi. of beach is closed to all public entry to protect the plovers and other birds such as least terns. Areas of the beach that are not being used by the birds may be reopened beginning July 1. The entire beach is usually reopened by mid-August. A limited deer-hunting season is allowed in fall, and at this time the area is closed to all other activities. Current information about closings can be obtained from the Fish and Wildlife Service (978-465-5753).

Nelson Island is accessible only by foot. Biting insects are troublesome throughout the refuge during the warmer months. Mosquitoes, greenhead horseflies, and ticks are common.

Universally accessible restrooms can be found at parking areas 1 (seasonal) and 4 (year-round). Potable water is available only at parking area 1.

To reach the refuge from the traffic light on MA 1A just south of Newbury center, turn right (northeast) onto the Plum Island Turnpike, continue 0.5 mi., and turn right (east) again. Proceed 2.3 mi. (passing the airport on the right) to a paved road on the right (south). Turn onto the paved road and enter the refuge in 0.5 mi.

The number of visitors is strictly limited; on busy days the entrance gate may close as early as 9 a.m. (*Note: The gate closing applies to cyclists as well as those arriving by car.*) Gate closings can last for several hours; an early arrival is recommended.

The 6.5 mi. of road that leads to Plum Island are designed for scenic enjoyment and not fast travel. Roadside parking is prohibited along the entire length of the road, and the speed limit is 25 mph throughout. The first 3.5 mi. of roadway are paved; the remaining distance is gravel. Various small parking lots provide access to boardwalks to the beach. The salt pans, just after lot 2, attract numerous and varied shorebirds. At lot 4 the Hellcat Swamp Nature Trail traverses a series of boardwalks over the marsh, passing a bird blind and observation tower. Other short trails are located at lots 5 and 6. The road ends at Sandy Point State Park, which includes more beach and a wooded hill.

Public access in the refuge is limited to the road, the beach, and the marked trails. Off-limit areas are clearly indicated by blue-and-white signs.

Crane Beach (TTOR)

Crane Beach consists of 1233 acres of white sand beach and dunes along both sides of Castle Neck, a finger of land extending into the sea. The area is one of the most important nesting sites for the endangered piping plover (dogs are not allowed between April 1 and September 30). An extensive pitch pine forest, carnivorous plants, and cranberries can all be found here. More than 5 mi. of marked trails explore the area, some on elevated walkways to protect the environment. The area is also known for its bird watching and fall foliage.

From MA 128 take Exit 20A and follow MA 1A north for 8 mi. to Ipswich. Turn right onto MA 133 east and continue 1.5 mi., then turn left onto Northgate Rd. Travel 0.5 mi., turn right onto Argilla Rd., and drive 2.5 mi. to the entrance at the end of the road (1300 cars).

During peak season (Memorial Day through Labor Day) Crane Beach is a popular albeit expensive swimming beach. (Admission fees are lower for cyclists.) Summer weekends can be particularly crowded.

Two trails start from the right side of the beach parking lot: a short, well-marked nature trail, and a longer, less well-defined "low-impact" trail marked by posts in the dunes. Take a pleasant round trip of about 5 mi. by following the posts up and down the dunes until the path emerges on the bank of the Castle Neck River. (Exact location of the posts may change occasionally to minimize the impact of foot traffic.) At the river turn left and follow the riverbank around the point to the barrier beach, and then follow the beach back to the parking lot.

(*Note: This area is ecologically fragile. The dunes, which prevent the land from being engulfed by the sea, are held together by the long, connected roots of plants. Stay on the marked trail and do not walk along the crests of the dunes, slide down the dunes, or step on the vegetation.*)

Near Crane Beach is the Crane Wildlife Refuge (TTOR), which consists of 697 acres of islands, salt marsh, and intertidal environments. More than 3 mi. of trails explore this area, where over 200 species of birds have been observed.

Bradley W. Palmer State Park (DCR)

Bradley Palmer was a high-powered lawyer in the first half of the 20th century who counted among his clients Sinclair Oil (Teapot Dome scandal) and Woodrow Wilson (the Treaty of Versailles). His estate is now a 712-acre park located in the towns of Hamilton and Topsfield. The park includes old farm and pastureland that have grown up to woods extending south from the Ipswich River. Carriage roads run across the property and are often lined with rhododendrons, providing spectacular scenery in June.

A universally accessible trail begins near the parking area by the main entrance on Asbury St. and runs roughly along the course of the Ipswich River. It ends near the footbridge that spans the river and leads to the Ipswich Rd. parking area. Unmarked trails of various lengths total more than 20 mi. Horseback riders use them extensively, as do cross-country skiers and snowshoers. Willowdale Hill (196 ft.), known locally as "Moon Hill," provides a good view north from its grassy top.

To reach the main entrance and park headquarters, follow Ipswich Rd. in Topsfield 1.25 mi. east from US 1 (state park sign) and turn right onto Asbury St. The park entrance is a short distance on the left.

Grassland Trail (DCR)

This trail begins on the paved road (closed to vehicles) leading northwest through a gate opposite the parking area. At 0.3 mi. the road curves left (heading toward the Ipswich River and the River Trail), while the Grassland Trail continues as a dirt road straight ahead. At a trail junction at 0.5 mi. the Willowdale Trail goes left (north) to a junction with the River Trail and the Fisherman's Trail, while the Bittersweet Trail goes right (south) toward Blueberry Hill. The Grassland Trail continues straight and shortly thereafter turns sharp right; the Winthrop Trail leads straight ahead from this junction to reach the Ipswich River in 0.3 mi. near Willowdale Dam and the remains of an old gristmill. (From the end of the Winthrop Trail, a return loop can be made via the Fisherman's Trail and the River Trail.)

Heading south, the Grassland Trail passes a short side trail to the right leading to the open field atop Willowdale Hill. Passing several other trail junctions but continuing straight, it ends near the recreation area at the eastern end of the park.

Grassland Trail

Distances from park headquarters

> *to* Willowdale Trail: 0.5 mi., 15 min.
>
> *to* Winthrop Trail: 0.6 mi., 20 min.
>
> *to* recreation area: 1.4 mi., 40 min.

Willowdale State Forest (DCR)

This 2400-acre forest in Ipswich is composed of three separate areas, each of which consists of mixed conifer and hardwood growth scattered amid swamps and meadows. The forest is traversed by 40 mi. of easily followed, but unmarked, woods roads. These travel on the ground that borders and separates the eastern and western sections of Willowdale Swamp, which occupies most of the central section of the area. Additional recreational opportunities exist at Hood Pond, a 100-acre lake within the forest. The eastern end of Willowdale also borders Bradley W. Palmer State Park along Ipswich Rd. Hikers at Bradley Palmer can walk across the footbridge near the end of the universally accessible trail, cross Ipswich Rd., and hike on the gravel carriage roads. The Bay Circuit Trail bisects the forest.

All three areas border on Linebrook Rd. in Ipswich, which crosses US 1 at a point 3.6 mi. north of the junction of US 1 and MA 97 in Topsfield. The smaller areas are on the right (north) and left (south) of Linebrook Rd., 1.5 mi. and 2 mi., respectively, west of its junction with US 1. The main entrance to the forest is through a gate on the right (south) side of Linebrook Rd., 0.8 mi. east of US 1 and 100 yd. west of Howe St. A woods road goes right (south) from the gate, reaches a fork at 150 yd., goes left, and continues to a second fork, where the Willowdale Circuit Walk begins. (A right turn at the first fork, continuing south at all intersections, leads to a point on Gravelly Brook Rd. a few hundred yards north of where Gravelly Brook Rd. joins Ipswich Rd. opposite the western entrance to Bradley W. Palmer State Park.) Refer to the USGS Georgetown quadrangle.

Willowdale Circuit Walk (DCR)

This walk begins 300 yd. south of the main entrance at the second fork. It turns left (east) along a woods road, passes a woods road on the left leading to Linebrook Rd., and, near a grove of red pines, turns right (south) along another woods road that follows along a glacial esker just north of Willowdale Swamp. The trail turns right (south) along a dirt road, continues through a cornfield, and crosses a causeway over a narrow neck of the swamp. After passing over Bull Brook at the swamp's northeast outlet. The trail continues east to a fork (the dirt surface ends here) and follows a woods road right (south). (Going left at the fork skirts the northern base of steep, twin-summited Bartholomew Hill [184 ft.] to end at Pine Swamp Rd., the eastern boundary of the forest.)

The trail continues south on the woods road and in 0.3 mi. descends a bluff to a woods road on the right. (This 0.4-mi. road connects the eastern and western parts of the circuit and can be used to shorten the walk by 1.5 mi.) The trail continues south from this junction, then turns right at a crossroads. (The woods road traveling northeast from here passes between the northern and southern summits of Bartholomew Hill. The woods road traveling southeast skirts the base of the southern summit. Both roads end at Pine Swamp Rd., 0.1 mi. apart.) The trail bears sharp right (west) along a 160-yd. causeway that crosses a narrow strip of swamp and Gravelly Brook (the south outlet of Willowdale Swamp), which between this point and the Ipswich River forms the eastern boundary of the forest.

The trail proceeds right at a fork to a grassy triangle, makes a sharp right turn (northwest), and soon bears right (north) at a wide triangle. (A left turn leads south to Gravelly Brook Rd., which in turn goes south to Bradley W. Palmer State Park.) The trail follows the woods road north between the eastern and western sections of the swamp, crosses the narrow northwestern end of Gravelly Brook, passes through a gravel pit, and reaches the western end of the shortcut. The trail then crosses an unnamed stream via a bridge and slightly more than 0.3 mi. farther north returns to the beginning.

Willowdale Circuit Walk

Distance from second fork in woods road

   to second fork (circuit): 3.5 mi., 2 hr., 30 min.

Discover Hamilton Trail

This 10-mi.-long, white-blazed loop trail begins and ends at the town hall in Hamilton's Historic District. It uses roads and trails to connect the many parks and reservations around the area, including Harvard Forest, Appleton Farms Grass Rides, Essex County Greenbelt Willowdale Mill Reservation, Bradley W. Palmer State Park, and Pingree Reservation. Trail maps and information are available at the Hamilton Town Hall on Bay Rd.

Ipswich River Wildlife Sanctuary (MAS)

This is Massachusetts Audubon's largest sanctuary, consisting of 2265 acres of unspoiled forest, wetland, and meadows in Topsfield. In addition to 10 mi. of trails the preserve also offers 8 mi. of canoeing on the Ipswich River. Camping is permitted on Perkins Island about 0.25 mi. upstream on the river, and a cabin is available for rent (MAS members only) near the office. Part of the sanctuary was once an old arboretum; the boulders and exotic plants are explored along the sanctuary's Rockery Trail. Specific features to enjoy include Great Wenham Swamp, Hassocky Meadow, Rockery Pond, and the drumlin called Bradstreet Hill.

From Boston and points south, follow I-95 north to Exit 50, turning onto US 1 north. At the junction of US 1 and MA 97, turn right onto MA 97 south (toward Beverly and Danvers). Take the second left onto Perkins Row. Continue on Perkins Row for 1.0 mi. to the entrance on the right.

From the north, take I-95 south to Exit 53 and follow MA 97 south to its junction with US 1 in Topsfield. Continue on MA 97 south and take the second left onto Perkins Row. Follow Perkins Row for 1.0 mi. to the entrance on the right.

Trails are well marked by numbered posts at junctions, keyed to a trail map available at the registration desk. Restrooms are available near the parking area and office.

Swamp Marsh Edge Circuit

This circuit route combines parts of several different trails to provide an interesting and varied walk.

Proceed south from the sanctuary headquarters to post 6 and follow the Bunker Meadows Trail for 0.4 mi. along a stone wall, crossing the Drumlin Trail at post 7. To the right is a wooden observation tower that offers a nice view of the Bunker Meadows marshes, notable for their magnificent expanse of waterlilies in summer. The Bunker Meadows Trail turns east to the Ipswich River. At post 10 continue northeast, picking up the South Esker Trail, which offers a resting bench with a view of Wenham Swamp and Fowler's Island. The South Esker Trail turns north through higher ground and ends at a wooden bridge (post 29). A few yards north a larger stone bridge with views of Mile Brook and Waterfowl Pond often offers sightings of painted turtles and colorful dragonflies.

At post 30 follow the signs to Averill's Island. The Averill's Island Trail splits at post 32 and comes together again at post 34, with both branches heading north. At post 38 stay left to pick up the White Pine Trail, and follow this trail west to the Mile Brook Trail. Turn left (south) onto the Mile Brook Trail, following the edge of a privately owned swamp. (*Note: The Mile Brook Trail may be very wet. Several paths to the right lead to the higher North Esker Trail, which can be used as an alternate route.*) Both the Mile Brook and North Esker Trails go south through forest to reach the stone bridge.

Cross the stone bridge and turn right at post 28 onto the Innermost Trail, a boardwalk through marshy woods that leads to a wide grass path back to the sanctuary headquarters.

Phillips Academy Bird Sanctuary

This sanctuary in Andover is especially beautiful in May and early June when the azaleas and rhododendrons are in bloom. Wild ducks and Canada geese often land on the artificial ponds, and many birds inhabit the woods. The trails are well-maintained gravel roads. The sanctuary closes at 6 p.m. Dogs are not allowed in the sanctuary.

Circuit Trail

This trail begins in Andover at the end of Chapel Ave., just beyond the Andover Inn at the parking area beyond George Washington Hall. The trail leads straight ahead on a continuation of Chapel Ave. past Phillips Academy dormitories on the left and George Washington Hall on the right. The trail passes Stimson House on the right (sign) and enters the Moncrief Cochran ornamental memorial gate. Soon after passing through this gate the trail leads through the right-hand door in the metal sanctuary fence. (*Note: Be sure that the gate is securely latched after you enter.*) The trail proceeds up a path among rhododendron bushes. At the crest of a rise it bears right at the fork.

A road soon enters left. This is the western end of a loop around two artificial ponds. The Circuit Trail continues straight ahead, crossing a bridge over a small brook in a short distance. It ascends a slight rise and passes the eastern loop road on the left. The trail continues straight ahead and soon reaches a log cabin at the crest of a hill. The trail continues on the road, which bears a sharp left downhill. It turns left at a fork at the foot of the first short descent, passes a trail on the right (a shortcut), and continues straight ahead. The eastern loop around the pond soon enters left. The trail then crosses a bridge over a pond outlet. Near the top of a steep rise, the western loop enters left. The trail bears right uphill and soon swings left, leading back to the crest of the rise.

Properties of Andover Village Improvement Society (AVIS)

AVIS is an open-membership, private society that acquires and holds land in Andover for conservation and recreational purposes. All its lands are kept in a natural state and are open to the public under suitable regulations. Total holdings are about 1000 acres, containing approximately 30 mi. of trails and divided into about two dozen reservations ranging from Harold R. Rafton Reservation at 233 acres to Mansour Reservation at 0.7 acre. For information about the other sections and trails not mentioned here, contact the Andover Conservation Commission, 36 Bartlett St., Andover, MA 01810 (508-470-3800), or the Andover Village Improvement Society, P.O. Box 5097, Andover, MA 01810. AVIS maps and guidebooks are on sale at the town library, town offices, and many local stores. (*Note: In the descriptions that follow, the I-93 exits cited are for travel heading north.*)

Rocky Hill Reservation (40 acres)

Part of the eastern section of this reservation is wetland, and the rest is hilly with rock outcrops. To reach the reservation, take I-93 to Exit 41, then follow MA 125 east for 2.9 mi. Just past the police barracks on the right, turn left and park west of MA 125 at the intersection with Gould Rd. Rocky Hill Rd. (unpaved) runs off Gould Rd. diagonally across the reservation from southeast to northwest.

Two places in the reservation are especially worth visiting: some rocky cliffs and an interesting view of a deep valley. To reach the cliffs, follow Rocky Hill Rd. north for 750 ft., turn right onto a woods road for about 500 ft., then turn left up a short, steep slope, following the white blazes to the upper part of Rocky Hill Rd. From here the trail gradually descends to a rocky knob with a good view into a deep ravine, and then continues on to complete the loop at the Gould Rd. parking lot. (Loop distance: 1.0 mi.)

Vale Reservation (45 acres)

Located between the commuter rail tracks and the Shawsheen River, this reservation consists of hillocks and wetlands. To reach it, follow I-93 to Exit 42, then take Dascomb Rd. east. Turn right onto Clark Rd. and continue 0.5 mi. Turn right onto Andover St., cross the railroad tracks, turn sharp left onto Dale St., and continue to the end of the dirt right of way (no sign) where the reservation begins. Parking is available here.

The marked trail begins on the right (east) and continues to the Shawsheen River. After about 0.25 mi. the trail crosses over an elevated platform and splits. The right fork follows the west side of the river downstream and then rejoins the left fork. (The right fork may be impassable during wet weather.) The left fork heads north through woods and open fields into Shawsheen River Reservation. (Loop distance: 2.0 mi.)

Shawsheen River Reservation (30 acres)

This reservation extends 0.5 mi. between the Shawsheen River and the railroad tracks. It is mostly woodland, with some grassy fields and some wetlands along the river. Take I-93 to Exit 43, go east on Dascomb Rd. for 1.3 mi., turn left onto Andover St., and go 0.7 mi. to the Horn Bridge. Park just beyond the bridge in an open space on the right.

Walk under the bridge onto Central St. and enter the reservation on the right. The trail leads across a meadow. In 0.1 mi. a marshy brook traverses the field. Cross the small bridge near the railroad tracks, then follow the river past some large granite blocks. At 0.5 mi. a path diverges across the meadow (possible short loop) and the trail continues south to Vale Reservation.

Indian Ridge Reservation (23 acres)

This reservation includes open pine woods, an esker, a swampy wooded area, and an open field. It lies between Reservation Rd. on the west and Red Spring Rd. on the east, with signs at the entrances on both roads. Both roads start at the intersection directly opposite the Horn Bridge (see Shawsheen River Reservation), with Reservation Rd. running northwest and Red Spring Rd. running north. The entrance on each road is 0.1 mi. from the Horn Bridge. Several unmarked woods roads crisscross the reservation. About 800 ft. along the ridge near the reservation entrance is a plaque mounted on a large rock commemorating Alice Buck, whose efforts more than 70 years ago helped preserve these woods.

Baker's Meadow Reservation (59 acres)

This bird sanctuary is remarkable for its migratory waterfowl. It consists of a marsh and a pond along with a bordering strip of higher ground. The entrance is located on Reservation Rd., 0.8 mi. northwest of the Horn Bridge (where parking is available), opposite the exit from Indian Ridge Reservation and the Esker Trail. The marked, 1.3-mi. trail begins at a sign for Baker's Meadow. It passes through hilly woods and then skirts the edge of a pond. At 0.7 mi. a marked spur trail on the right leads 0.3 mi. to Argilla Rd. The main trail, bearing left around the pond, crosses a dam and continues around the pond for 0.2 mi. It then leaves the pond, running 0.1 mi. northeast to Reservation Rd. It continues 0.3 mi. northwest on the road to the beginning. (*Note: Heavy beaver activity in this area may cause sections of the trail to become flooded.*)

Four Reservations Trail

This trail traverses Vale, Indian Ridge, Baker's Meadow, and Shawsheen River Reservations. Begin at the southern end of Vale Reservation (see the Vale Reservation description for directions). The trail proceeds north along the Shawsheen River, leaves Vale Reservation at the Horn Bridge, turns left under the bridge, then proceeds northwest on Reservation Rd. to the entrance to Indian Ridge Reservation. It continues through this reservation on the Esker Trail, emerging on Reservation Rd.

The trail crosses the road to the entrance to Baker's Meadow Reservation and continues through the reservation to Reservation Rd. Crossing the road, the trail follows the Indian Ridge Trail to the top of the slope. The trail then turns right and proceeds southeast to the entrance to Indian Ridge

Reservation. It turns left onto Reservation Rd. and continues southeast to the Horn Bridge. After passing under the bridge, it turns right into and through Shawsheen River Reservation and crosses town land into Vale Reservation. It continues across an open field and along the base of the railroad embankment to the beginning.

Four Reservations Trail

Distance from Vale Reservation

   to Vale Reservation (circuit): 6.3 mi., 4 hr., 30 min.

Harold R. Rafton Reservation (226 acres)

This reservation is bordered by High Plain Rd. on the west, I-93 on the east, and I-495 on the south and is bisected by a power-line right of way that runs west–east. Most of the terrain is rocky woodlands. The western section is high and hilly, while the eastern section is low, including a marsh through which Fish Brook passes from south to north. To reach the reservation, take I-93 to Exit 44, then take Lowell St. east for 0.3 mi. Turn left onto Greenwood Rd. and in 0.9 mi. turn left onto High Plain Rd. Cross over I-93 and I-495 and continue to the top of the hill. About 400 ft. beyond the top of the hill an AVIS sign is mounted high on a tree on the right. Parking is allowed on the roadside.

Bay Circuit Trail

The Bay Circuit Trail follows a well-trodden path called Harold's Trail for 1.9 mi. through Harold R. Rafton Reservation. It heads into the woods a few feet beyond the sign. At 0.2 mi. the trail turns parallel to a power line, continues through a stone wall, and divides. The left branch passes under the power line, enters the woods, and continues on fairly level ground. At 0.3 mi. it turns left, then descends about 1200 ft. to a wide water-line right of way running north–south. Cross Fish Brook on a bridge to the west of the right of way and continue 0.9 mi. to a field. Cross the field to the intersection of Chandler Rd. and River Rd. (To return by road to the starting point, turn left onto River Rd., left onto Forest Hill Dr., left onto Cross St., and left onto High Plain Rd.)

Deer Jump Reservation (160 acres)

This reservation lies between River Rd. and the Merrimack River in West Andover. It contains two large wooded areas, each with a 0.3-mi. frontage on the river, connected by a relatively narrow strip of shore varying from about 60 to 400 ft. wide and 2.3 mi. long. Some of the terrain is hilly, with several small gullies and brooks. It adjoins Spaulding Reservation on the west. Trails are blazed in white. The Merrimack River Trail, with white blazes similar to those used on the Bay Circuit Trail, follows the river along through the property.

To reach the reservation, take I-93 to Exit 45, then follow River Rd. west 1 mi. Turn right onto Launching Rd. and park in the small parking area just past the second cul-de-sac on the left.

The Goldsmith Woodlands (170 acres)

This lovely tract bordering Foster's Pond is accessible directly from MA 28, 0.1 mi. north of its intersection with MA 125. The major trail, a former dirt road for summer campers, runs the length of the reservation, with side trails to high points and views. Foster's Pond lies north of the main trail. Just inside the reservation, there is a posted map of all the trails, nearly 4 mi. of which are maintained.

Charles W. Ward Reservation (TTOR)

This 695-acre reservation in Andover and North Andover is owned and administered by The Trustees of Reservations. It includes Holt Hill (420 ft.), the highest point in Essex County, Boston Hill (385 ft.), and Shrub Hill, separated by Cat Swamp. The reservation has 17 mi. of stone walls and is an excellent place to see club mosses, ferns, and other flora. Another feature is the solstice stones, large blocks of cut stone arranged to mark the seasonal equinoxes and solstices. For the most part the reservation paths pass through wooded areas, but the hilltops have some viewpoints of Mt. Monadnock and the Temple Hills to the west, southern Kearsarge to the northwest, and Boston and Great Blue Hill to the south.

At the base of Holt Hill is Pine Hole Bog, an interesting quaking bog with an interpretive trail and 700 ft. of boardwalk. The entire reservation contains 14 mi. of hiking trails ranging from moderate to strenuous.

To reach the reservation from I-93, take Exit 41, go north on MA 125 for 5 mi., then turn right onto Prospect Rd. Trail information and maps are available at the parking area.

Bald Hill Reservation

Located in the towns of Boxford, North Andover, and Middleton, Bald Hill Reservation comprises three adjacent, protected properties: Boxford State Forest, the John Phillips Wildlife Sanctuary, and property owned by the Essex County Greenbelt Association.

To reach the forest, take I-95 to the Topsfield Rd. interchange. Follow Topsfield Rd. 1.3 mi. west to Boxford center and turn left onto Main St. Follow Main St. 0.3 mi. to Middleton Rd. Turn left onto Middleton Rd. and proceed 1.7 mi. to the Bald Hill Rd. entrance to the reservation.

A trail map is posted, and is also available from the Essex County Greenbelt Association, 82 Eastern Ave., Essex, MA 01929 (508-768-7241). Trail junctions are numbered and are keyed to the trail map. A volunteer group, Friends of Bald Hill Reservation, has been organized to assist with trail maintenance and land-use planning, and can be reached through the Greenbelt Association.

Sawyer Trail

This trail begins at trail junction 11 on the Bald Hill Rd. and proceeds generally south along a woods road to Peabody St. in Middleton. This woods road is referred to as Thomas Rd. on most maps and is a private drive into the Wissa Farm (formerly the Sawyer Farm) at the Peabody St. end. The trail is not marked but is very obvious for its entire length. Those wishing to use the trail at the extreme southern end should request permission at the farm.

After leaving Bald Hill Rd. the trail passes a small burial plot on the left at 0.25 mi., passes a narrow trail left at 0.35 mi., and then continues through fairly dense woodland to a junction with a woods road on the right (dead end) at 1.0 mi. The trail continues straight ahead at this junction and passes another trail junction on the left at 1.3 mi. After passing through some partially cleared land, the trail reaches the Wissa Farmhouse and Peabody St., just west of the Ipswich River.

Sawyer Trail

Distance from Bald Hill Rd.

   to Wissa Farm (Peabody St.): 1.6 mi., 50 min.

Weir Hill Reservation (TTOR)

This 194-acre property in North Andover, belonging to The Trustees of Reservations, is bounded by Lake Cochichewick and Stevens Pond (Lake Cochichewick is a public water supply—public access is prohibited). Pronounced *wire hill*, the reservation consists of a double drumlin—a long hill formed by glaciers—rising about 300 ft. over the valley. There are beautiful views from the meadow of the Merrimack Valley, 1 mi. of lakeshore, and 4 mi. of moderate woodland trails. The property is an ideal spot for hiking, cross-country skiing, nature study, picnicking, and photography.

From I-93 follow MA 125 north (Andover By-pass), merging with MA 114 west. At Merrimack College turn left (Andover St.), turn right at the traffic lights, bear right at the fork, and continue through North Andover center to Stevens St. Turn left onto Stevens St.; the entrance is 0.8 mi. ahead on the right.

A detailed trail map is posted at the Stevens St. entrance as well as at many of the trail junctions.

Harold Parker State Forest (DCR)

This 3000-acre forest located in Andover, North Andover, North Reading, and Middleton is open for a wide range of outdoor recreational activities. Hardwood, hemlock, and white pine forests predominate. There are 35 mi. of trails and forest roads and 11 ponds. The waterways amid the wooded terrain, and the abundance of birds and wildflowers, make for scenic hikes. Most of the forest ponds are the result of dams built in the 1930s. Universal-access facilities include restrooms, camping, and beaches. A nature center is located in the campground off Jenkins Rd. during the season, and nature walks and programs are run from forest headquarters on Middleton Rd.

The state forest is accessible from a number of roads, including Middleton Rd. (where the forest headquarters is located); the eastern section of Harold Parker Rd. (which runs south from MA 114 in North Andover); and the western section of Harold Parker Rd. (which runs east from MA 125 in Andover).

Stearns Pond Trail (DCR)

The Stearns Pond Trail is reached from a short trail that begins on the east side of the eastern section of Harold Parker Rd., 0.3 mi. from MA 114 or 0.8 mi. from Middleton Rd. Limited parking is available at this end of the trail; no on-street parking is available at the other trailhead on Marblehead St.

The trail begins as a gravel road (closed to vehicles) that enters the woods, leads to a footpath that follows the bank of a pond, and then crosses a brook below a spillway dam. Shortly thereafter a second trail diverges left to a second dam.

The trail runs into a paved road, from which other roads lead to a large parking lot, a swimming beach, and park headquarters. The trail soon passes through another gate and reaches Middleton Rd. Turning left onto Middleton Rd., the trail reenters the woods in about 25 yd. (marked by a sign, Upper Salem Pond Rd.). The trail winds around, climbing slightly, until it reaches Salem Pond and crosses a small footbridge over a narrow channel between parts of the pond.

The trail now continues past another section of the pond on the left to a fork, where it bears left. In about 0.3 mi. Salem Pond Rd. (a.k.a., the Sudden Pond Trail) diverges left. The Stearns Pond Trail continues straight past this junction, winds and climbs for a short distance, then descends straight past Bradford Pond on the right to its end at Marblehead St. A side trail that circles Bradford Pond diverges from the Stearns Pond Trail just before Marblehead St.

Stearns Pond Trail

Distances from Harold Parker Rd.

to Middleton Rd.: 1.2 mi., 45 min.

to Sudden Pond Trail: 2.5 mi., 1 hr., 15 min.

to Marblehead St.: 3.5 mi., 1 hr., 45 min.

Sudden Pond Trail (DCR)

This trail begins at the last fork in the Stearns Pond Trail, turning left at a sign marked Salem Pond Rd. The trail soon skirts the southern end of Salem Pond, crosses a bridge over the pond outlet, and bears sharp right. Shortly after crossing the pond outlet the trail bends left and almost immediately forks, with both forks leading quickly to Middleton Rd. The trail turns right onto Middleton Rd. and continues past the North Andover–North Reading boundary sign and the Forest Riding Academy (both on the left). It proceeds southeast on Middleton Rd. and turns left onto paved Sudden Pond Rd. just past the riding academy. This point is located about 1 mi. southeast of the forest headquarters.

The trail follows Sudden Pond Rd. briefly, then turns right off the paved road where the road turns sharp left. The trail follows a woods road leading north and soon crosses the pond outlet. It continues along the shore and soon branches right and then turns sharp left. Soon it turns left onto a woods road, then left again at a large rock. It follows this side path back to Sudden Pond Rd. (*Note: If you miss this path, just follow the shore of the pond and rejoin the trail on Sudden Pond Rd.*) Continuing west, the trail passes a path on the right and almost immediately passes between two posts and emerges on Middleton Rd. at a point a short distance southeast of where the Stearns Pond Trail crosses Middleton Rd.

Sudden Pond Trail

Distance from fork

to Middleton Rd.: 2.8 mi., 1 hr., 15 min.

Brackett Pond Trail

The Brackett Pond Trail begins at the main parking lot on the western section of Harold Parker Rd., 0.3 mi. east of MA 125.

From the parking lot, walk east along Harold Parker Rd.; Collins Pond will soon appear on the left, and Field Pond on the other side of the road. Fifty yards after passing the partially submerged fish-stocking structure below the Collins Pond dam, turn left into a smaller parking lot and head through the gate. This woods road leads along the eastern shore of Collins Pond and then Brackett Pond. About 200 yd. along this road a trail leaves to the left, crossing between the two ponds on a scenic route that leads almost directly back to the starting point.

For a longer hike continue north on the road along the eastern shore of Brackett Pond. Bear right at a fork leading away from the pond north on a woods road (Walker Rd.). (A left at this fork leads around Brackett Pond then back to Harold Parker Rd.) Soon reach a second fork; a left turn leads to another pond, while a right turn leads another 0.5 mi. to the trail's end at the forest boundary.

Brackett Pond Trail

Distance from parking lot

to forest boundary: 1.4 mi., 45 min.

Reading Town Forest

The Reading Town Forest and Well Fields comprises 290 acres in the northwest portion of Reading and is under the supervision of the Reading Town Forest Committee. One hundred thousand red and white pines as well as some spruce, balsam, and Scotch pines were planted by Boy Scouts and other townspeople beginning in 1930. The area includes several examples of hardwoods and many fine eskers, and the proximity of the Ipswich River makes it a good place for bird watching. The forest has vernal pools and is home to great horned owls, red foxes, and many varieties of wildflowers, including pink and showy lady's slippers. In winter cross-country skiing and snowshoeing are excellent. There are several forest roads and short trails that lead off these roads. Most are easy to follow, and many are paint-blazed. Camping is by permit only.

The forest can be accessed off Fox Run Lane (off Franklin St.) and Strout Ave. (off Grove St.), with additional parking off Roma Lane.

Big Pine Trail

This trail uses unpaved roads and short trails marked with bright yellow blocks and arrows. It begins immediately behind the trail sign and follows the path along the ridge of an esker to an overlook of the Point One parking area (the Ipswich River is on the left). Here the trail doubles back (south) along a smaller esker (a road runs parallel below). After a short distance the trail drops to the road, crosses it, and continues south along another esker until it is intersected by a road. The trail drops down right to the road junction, then goes left (northeast) along the well-traveled dirt road. It continues past the "Old Council Ring" on the right and a pumphouse on the left, emerging from the pines as the road descends to a fork.

On the right the road continues to Scrub Oak Hill; ahead on the left is the Ipswich River and the site of an old swimming hole. However, the trail immediately cuts back into the pine woods to the southeast along a well-worn path. (Look carefully on the right for the two yellow arrows and the continuation of yellow markings.) After about 200 yd., just before reaching a woods path, the trail follows the Garden Club Trail left (east). It continues 30 ft., crossing a damp area, then goes right (southwest) at a fork on an esker until reaching its end. (Watch along the left of the esker for a wide variety of spring wildflowers and dogwood.)

From the esker the trail continues to be marked with yellow blazes. It goes through a wet area, then up another esker, following it until arriving at the top of a cliff overlooking the junction of the well-traveled road. The trail drops down to the road, turns right at the fork, and then turns immediately left at the next fork in the road. After about 0.1 mi. the road arrives back at the Big Pine Trail sign.

Big Pine Trail

Distances from Big Pine Trail sign

    to Garden Club Trail: 1.1 mi., 45 min.

    to Big Pine Trail sign (circuit): 1.6 mi., 1 hr.

Willard Brook State Forest (DCR)

Located in Ashby and Townsend, this 2597-acre forest is hilly and rocky, with many large areas of mountain laurel. It is a scenic area, especially in the vicinity of Willard Brook. Trap Falls Brook, Trap Falls, and Pearl Hill Brook are other attractive features. Recreational activities include swimming, hiking, birding, and fishing.

The trails generally emanate from either the Damon Pond recreation and camping area or the Pearl Hill Brook Pond recreation and camping area. To reach Damon Pond from the junction of MA 119 and MA 124 in West Townsend, go 3.1 mi. west on MA 119 and turn left onto Hosmer Rd. To reach Pearl Hill, follow MA 119 west from West Townsend. Almost immediately after passing MA 123, turn left onto New Fitchburg Rd. and follow it 1.8 mi. to the recreation area. Parking, trail information, camping, swimming, and picnicking are available at both recreation areas; a parking fee is charged in season. Parking along the sides of the roads within the state forest is prohibited.

From Damon Pond two main hiking trails are maintained by the DCR that can be combined into an interesting 3.0-mi. loop. The north trail leaves Damon Pond and follows the south side of Willard Brook through hemlock forests while staying close to Townsend Rd. Leaving the brook, it climbs briefly, crosses two wet areas, and at 1.2 mi. reaches the Trap Falls Brook area and a gravel forest road a few hundred yards from the forest headquarters on Townsend Rd. (MA 119). From the road turn right (south) and follow the road past two intersections. Bear right each time. The road passes a small pond as it swings northwest. A south trail trailhead is about 600 ft. past the pond on the right. The path now climbs generally west, passing two connector paths that link to the north path. The trail passes a junction on the left that leads in about 0.2 mi. to Fort Hill Rd. The south trail ends as it reaches Hosmer Rd. just east of Damon Pond. (Loop distance: 3.0 mi., 1 hr., 40 min.)

Gulf Brook & Heald's Pond

This is the most scenic area of Pepperell, lying in the western part of town and crisscrossed by a series of blue-blazed connecting trails. Refer to the USGS Townsend quadrangle.

Jeff Smith Trail

The Jeff Smith Trail is about 4 mi. long and runs from Blood Brook Ravine on Jewett St. in Pepperell to Rocky Pond Rd. in Hollis NH. The path passes through protected natural areas including Heald's Pond, Gulf Brook Ravine, Stewart Brook, and Nashoba Conservation Area. The Jeff Smith Trail is blazed with blue paint dots throughout.

Blood Brook Ravine Trail

This trail runs from Jewett St. to Shag Rock on the west shore of Heald's Pond over Pepperell Conservation Commission land. To reach the trailhead take MA 113 northeast from its intersection with MA 119 near Pepperell. In 0.25 mi. turn left onto Shattuck St. and continue past Harbour St. to its end on Jewett St. Turn left (west) onto Jewett St. and follow it 0.6 mi. to a small pond or swamp on the left draining through a culvert into Blood Brook on the right.

The trail begins 200 ft. east of the culvert at a sign marking the Blood Brook Ravine Conservation Area. Watch carefully for the yellow blazes that mark the trail, as the footpath is not well worn. Most of the trail is clearly blazed with yellow triangles, except for a section along the shore of Heald's Pond, which is marked with a few faded blue blazes.

The trail passes the foot of the highest rock face in Pepperell and meets Heald's Pond at the mouth of Blood Brook. Here the trail turns left (north) and steeply upward to the face of Shag Rock, which slopes steeply down into the pond. Once over Shag Rock, the trail skirts the pond to its northern end on Heald St. (behind the Community Church on MA 113 in Pepperell center).

Blood Brook Ravine Trail

Distance from Jewett St.

 to Heald St.: est. 1 mi., 30 min.

Gulf Brook Trail

This trail leads through a gulf or gorge, following the brook from Heald St. to Chestnut St. Although scenic, the trail is not easy to follow; following the brook over rocks or fallen trees is necessary. Marked by occasional single blue blazes, the trail begins at Heald St. across from Heald's Pond—the end of the Blood Brook Ravine Trail. The trail follows a well-traveled cart path along the left (west) bank of the stream, which is littered with rocks and thick with beech trees. The cart path ends after several hundred yards, passing on the left the almost closed entrance to a pre-Revolutionary silver mine blasted out of solid rock. Several hundred yards farther on are the remains of a mill and dam in the middle of the gorge. The trail now crosses land owned by the Belmont Springs Water Company, and the walking becomes a little easier as it reaches its end at Chestnut St. To reach the trailhead from the Pepperell Town Hall drive about 2.0 mi. on Heald St. to the ravine on the right. Parking is on the side of the road.

Gulf Brook Trail

Distance from Heald St.

 to Chestnut St.: 1 mi., 40 min.

Groton Town Forest

This area is in the southwestern part of Groton, generally northwest of Ayer. It includes the Dead River, an old channel of the Nashua River through which the flow was supposedly north–south during the glacial period. The forest includes numerous woods roads, which are good for hiking. Refer to the USGS Ayer quadrangle.

Nashua River Walk

To reach the trailhead, follow MA 2A for 1.1 mi. northwest of its junction with MA 111 in Ayer. Turn right (east) at an unmarked road just before the Nashua River. Continue about 200 yd. to a railroad crossing just before the state-owned Ayer Pheasant Farm. Park on the road. The trail follows the tracks to the left (northwest) under a power line and across the river. (*Caution*: *Watch your step as you cross the bridge. The crossing may be uncomfortable for people with a fear of heights.*)

About 75 yd. after crossing the river the trail turns right (northeast), joins a woods road near the tracks, and follows the road on a winding but generally northerly course. The lower end of the trail affords views of the Nashua River on the right. (*Note: Avoid taking any of the intersecting trails; follow the main trail, which is the widest.*)

Continuing north, the trail passes an intersection marked by a utility sign. In a short distance is a bluff, with a view to the right of the old Dead River bed. The trail continues to an intersection marked with a Groton Town Forest memorial plaque to veterans of the "Great War." Here the trail turns into Town Forest Rd. and continues north to MA 225 (called W. Main St. or W. Groton Rd.). The trail turns right onto W. Main St., crosses the Nashua River, and turns right at a large brick gateway entrance to the private Groton School. Walk behind the gate and continue past a stone memorial to the Groton Hunt. The trail then bears right and follows a path along the river, heading south with the river on the right. At junctions, stay to the right along the river. The trail ends at Richard's Boat House (owned by the Groton School).

Nashua River Walk

Distance from railroad crossing

   to Richard's Boat House: 3.3 mi., 1 hr., 40 min.

Lowell-Dracut-Tyngsboro State Forest (DCR)

This 1000-acre preserve offers 180 acres of wetlands, including swamps and ponds. The forest has 6 mi. of trails for hiking, horseback riding, biking, skiing, and snowmobiling. The main entrance and parking area are on Trotting Park Rd. in Lowell. To reach the forest, take US 3 north to MA 113 in Tyngsboro. Head east on MA 113 and continue 3 mi. to Trotting Park Rd. Follow State Forest signs to the entrance.

Great Brook Farm State Park (DCR)

This unique destination in Carlisle combines more than 20 mi. of hiking trails with a working dairy farm. The mosaic of open fields and woods separated by stone walls is the epitome of New England scenery. There are lots of old cellar holes left behind by English colonists centuries ago. And once the hikes are done there are barn tours and an ice cream stand. Universally accessible restrooms are available, and recreation opportunities include hiking, canoeing, horseback riding, skiing, and mountain biking. A nature center is also on the grounds.

To reach the park take MA 128 to Exit 31B. Follow MA 225 west to Carlisle center, then travel north on Lowell St. to the entrance.

Some trails that offer good hiking include the multi-use Pine Point Loop, the Woodchuck Trail, the Garrison Loop, and the Litchfield Loop Trail. The Woodchuck Trail circles Meadow Pond and begins near the canoe launch at the eastern end of the lake. The trailhead parking area is off North Rd.

Just north of the Meadow Pond canoe launch and on the opposite side of the road is the trailhead for the Woodchuck Trail. This multi-use trail heads northeast, passing the Garrison Loop on the right, and the log cabin on the left. It then reaches the historic site called "the city," a cluster of cellar holes built during colonial times, a little farther on the right. After the city is past, the Garrison Loop enters. Turn right (south) onto the Garrison Loop to return to the earlier junction with the Woodchuck Trail. Then turn left (west) and return to the trailhead. (Loop distance: 0.5 mi., 20 min.)

The Litchfield Loop Trail circles the main farm complex, offering varied views of the fields, pastures, and barns as it explores the park. It is also close to the ice cream stand.

Old Town Hill (TTOR)

This 509-acre reservation of tidal creeks and salt marsh surrounds a drumlin called Old Town Hill. Three miles of moderate hiking trails wander through the upland woods that grow on the hilly terrain above the Little River, which snakes through the marsh. Years ago the marsh was cut for its salt hay.

The reservation is located off Newman Rd. in Newbury Old Town Hill. To reach Old Town Hill from I-95 take Exit 54 to MA 133 and travel east for 4.5 mi. Turn onto MA 1A north; just beyond the bridge over the Parker River turn left onto Newman Rd. The parking area and entrance are on the left in 0.2 mi.

Misery Islands (TTOR)

This 87-acre preserve in Salem Sound is much nicer than its name suggests. The preserve's two islands got their name when a winter storm stranded shipbuilder Capt. Robert Moulton for three days in the 1600s. Today a system of trails on Great Misery Island explores rocky shorelines, open grassy fields, and overlooks. Nearby Little Misery Island can be accessed during times of very low tide by walking the shallow channel between the two islands.

Access to Misery Islands is by canoe, kayak, or a rowed boat such as a dinghy. Landing sites are the three rocky beaches. Additional access is provided from Salem via Sun Line Cruises, which operates from Salem Willows Park. Public restrooms (composting toilets) are available.

Appleton Farms & Appleton Farms Grass Rides (TTOR)

Appleton Farms is a 658-acre working dairy farm with 4 mi. of easy trails over sweeping pastures and fields. The farm employs agricultural techniques that seek to work with the ecology of the area and demonstrate that dairy products can be produced in harmony with the environment. Some of the trails are part of the Bay Circuit Trail system; one path links Appleton Farms with nearby Appleton Farms Grass Rides. Offering more than 5 mi. of carriage paths lined by stately woods, Appleton Farms Grass Rides is unique because the carriage paths emanate from a central point, a clearing dominated by a granite obelisk once part of the Harvard Library. The name derives from the original use of the trails as bridle paths—so the intent was to ride the paths, not walk them.

To reach Appleton Farms and Appleton Farms Grass Rides from MA 1A in Hamilton, take Cutler Rd. to Highland St. Turn right onto Highland St., then quickly right again to reach the parking area.

Joppa Flats Wildlife Sanctuary (MAS)

This 54-acre sanctuary is located in Newburyport near the much larger Parker River National Wildlife Refuge. A treasure trove for birders, Joppa Flats features a newly restored salt marsh overlooking the Merrimack River estuary. Massachusetts Audubon Society staff conduct interpretive programs, and the kiosk at the entrance highlights program schedules as well as bird sightings. The Bay Circuit Trail (BCT) passes by the sanctuary.

To reach Joppa Flats from I-95, take Exit 57 and travel east on MA 113/1A for 3.3 mi. to Rolfe's Lane. Turn left (north) at the traffic light, go to the end of Rolfe's Lane, turn right, and continue 0.1 mi. to the parking area on the left.

Walks in the Vicinity of Ayer

Walks may be started at Woodford of Ayer, the former Ayer Hospital on Winthrop Ave. (a brick building on top of the hill east of the village). To reach Woodford of Ayer from Main St. (MA 111), go north on Washington St., then east on Highland Ave. to its end, and proceed south on Winthrop Ave. Woodford of Ayer is on the left. These walks visit Chapel Hill, Pingrey Hill, Snake Hill, and Tophet Swamp, the last being a deep gorge presumed to have been formed during the glacial period. They do not follow marked trails, so follow the directions carefully. Interesting variations on the walks described are possible with the aid of the USGS Ayer quadrangle. Take care when crossing private property.

Chapel Hill Walk

This walk begins in front of the Woodford of Ayer Nursing Home on Winthrop Ave. and ends at the corner of Old Ayer Rd. and Indian Hills Rd. in Groton. It goes north on Winthrop Ave. and continues generally north and uphill for 0.3 mi. through the woods to the Ayer water towers. The trail crosses the Ayer School grounds to the east, keeping right of all the buildings and left of the athletic field, then descends to Groton–Harvard Rd. The trail turns left onto Groton–Harvard Rd. (downgrade) and continues 0.3 mi. to the second power line. On the right an obscure path ascends the ledges on the left side of the power line. The trail follows this path about 500 ft., then goes left (leaving the power line) on a good path to a big hayfield with extensive views. (*Note: Do not cross the hayfield.*)

The trail goes northeast along the edge of the field next to the woods, then turns left onto Snake Hill Rd. and right onto Old Ayer Rd. It continues to the foot of the hill, turns right at the Chapel Hill sign, and continues 0.5 mi. to the top of the hill (views in all directions). The trail descends (no path) northeast to Indian Hills Rd. It turns left onto Indian Hills Rd. and continues a short distance to the junction with Old Ayer Rd.

Chapel Hill Walk

Distance from Woodford of Ayer Nursing Home

   to junction of Indian Hills Rd. and Old Ayer Rd.: 3.5 mi., 2 hr., 45 min.

Snake Hill Walk

Follow the directions for the Chapel Hill Walk to Snake Hill Rd. This trail turns right onto Snake Hill Rd. then descends under a power line to the telephone company's underground cable. It turns sharp left and continues to the top of Snake Hill (view west). The trail follows the cable line 1 mi. to a woods road, turns right onto the road, and proceeds 50 yd. to Wright Rd. It turns right onto Wright Rd. and continues 0.5 mi., passing several driveways on the left that lead to cottages on Sandy Pond. At the end of Wright Rd. the trail turns right onto Snake Hill Rd., passes the Ayer Gun Club on the right, and continues to the power line. After crossing the power line the trail immediately turns left onto a path to recross the power line.

   Following the path blazed with metal triangles through the woods, the trail continues 0.5 mi. to a brook, crosses on a broken-down dam, then bears left along a meadow and proceeds uphill past Balance Rock. It turns left onto a woods road, which leads to Groton–Harvard Rd. The trail turns left onto Groton–Harvard Rd., proceeds to the first house, then turns right onto a winding woods road. Ascending, the trail makes a sharp left to avoid another woods road on the right. Near the top of the hill this trail merges with the beginning of the Chapel Hill Walk. It passes a small swamp and turns right, then left onto Winthrop Ave., where the walk began.

Snake Hill Walk

Distance from Woodford of Ayer Nursing Home

   to Woodford of Ayer Nursing Home (circuit): 3 mi., 1 hr., 30 min.

SUGGESTED HIKES

Easy Hikes

Charles W. Ward Reservation

Bog Nature Trail [rt: 0.4 mi., 0:20]. A fascinating walk that includes 700 feet of boardwalk to Pine Hole Bog, one of the reservation's treasures.

Bradley W. Palmer State Park

Grassland Trail, Winthrop Trail [rt: 1.8 mi., 2:00]. A walk through fields and hills to interesting sites along the Ipswich River.

Moderate Hikes

Crane Beach

"Posted" Trail [lp: 5.0 mi., 2:50]. A trail leads up the beach and through dunes, passing the Castle Neck River midway.

Ashland State Park

Ashland Reservoir Trail [lp: 3.2 mi., 1:45]. A hike that offers excellent views of the reservoir.

Willowdale State Forest

Willowdale Circuit Walk [lp: 3.5 mi., 2:30]. A series of easy-to-follow woods roads provides a great forest walk.

Strenuous Hikes

Harold Rafton Reservation (AVIS)

Bay Circuit Trail [rt: 9.2 mi., 5:15]. A trip along the long-distance Bay Circuit Trail to Harold Rafton Reservation.

Old North Bridge

Bay Circuit Trail, Section 6 [rt: 7.4 mi., 3:45]. A trip through Revolutionary War history, this hike passes the Minuteman statue and ends at the restored Old North Bridge.

Hamilton

Discover Hamilton Trail [lp: 10 mi., 5:00]. This collection of paths links a number of parks and reservations around Hamilton.

Part V

Boston and Vicinity

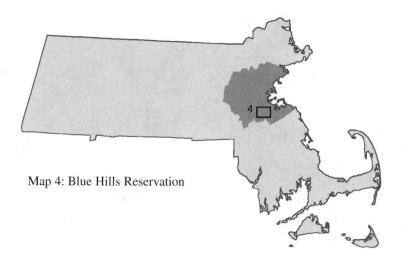

Map 4: Blue Hills Reservation

LIST OF TRAILS

LIST OF TRAILS

The area around greater Boston is framed by a number of remarkable natural areas. To the west of the city is a string of parks, forests, and reservations that wrap around the boundary of the metropolitan area like a necklace of natural gems. Among these are the Blue Hills, Rocky Narrows, and Noanet Woodlands. The rugged coastal areas offer adventures like no other place in the state, and include such destinations as World's End and the Boston Harbor Islands. Interlaced throughout the region are natural areas, from marshes to riverside forests, that are magnets to wildlife. These include Neponset River Marshes Reservation and Great Meadows National Wildlife Refuge.

While the landscape in this region is largely suburban and urban in nature, many destinations make the city feel far away indeed.

Blue Hills Reservation (DRC)

Blue Hills Reservation is located less than 10 mi. south of downtown Boston in the communities of Milton, Canton, Randolph, Braintree, Dedham, and Quincy. This mostly wooded, 7000-acre reservation—under the jurisdiction of the Department of Conservation and Recreation (DCR)—is the largest open space located within the inner metropolitan area. I-93 bisects the reservation. The larger, northern section includes a stretch of the Neponset River and the adjoining wetlands of Fowl Meadow; a series of wooded summits, the largest of which are Great Blue Hill (635 ft.) and Chickatawbut Hill (517 ft.); Houghtons Pond and several smaller ponds; and the Quincy Quarries Historic Site, now a popular rock climbing locale. Ponkapoag Pond, the largest body of water in the reservation, is the principal attraction south of the highway.

The reservation offers many outdoor activities in addition to hiking. Picnicking, fishing, boating, horseback riding, swimming, mountain biking, and rock climbing are all permitted in various parts of the park. In winter there is alpine skiing at the Blue Hill Ski Area on the western side of Great Blue Hill, ice skating at several ponds and artificial rinks, and cross-country skiing on many of the reservation trails and across the neighboring Ponkapoag golf course.

The Mass Audubon Society operates two educational facilities within the reservation. The Trailside Museum on MA 138, 0.5 mi. north of I-93, is open to the public (617-333-0690). The Chickatawbut Hill Education Center offers workshops and programs for organized groups by reservation only.

The AMC's Ponkapoag Camp, on the east shore of Ponkapoag Pond, has cabins available for rent. Reservations are required; contact the AMC's

Joy St. headquarters (617-523-0655) or go online at www.outdoors.org for information.

For the hiker the reservation offers 125 mi. of trails, woods roads, and old carriage roads that can be combined into trips of varying lengths. Trail difficulty generally ranges from easy to moderate. A large network of trails has been blazed. The blazing system uses circles to indicate a loop trail, with the color of the blaze—yellow, green, or red—indicating easier, moderate, or more strenuous terrain, respectively. Rectangular blazes indicate one of the two major trails that traverse the park: the 9-mi. Skyline Trail (blue blazes). Trail intersections have been marked with four-digit numbers keyed to the DCR's Blue Hills Reservation map, which is posted at many trailheads.

In addition to the marked trails, many unmarked paths beckon the adventurous. Although it is hard to become truly lost in the Blue Hills due to the proximity of roads and other major landmarks throughout the park, hikers on these paths will find a map and compass useful.

Trail information and maps are available at the Trailside Museum (see above) and at the reservation headquarters on 695 Hillside St., Milton, MA 02186, behind the state police station. Also refer to map 4, Blue Hills Reservation, included with this book.

Great Blue Hill Red Loop (DCR)

This 1.2-mi. loop trail (red circles) is the most popular route for climbing Great Blue Hill. It begins at the bulletin board behind the Trailside Museum and heads generally east and then southeast. After crossing paved Summit Rd. it becomes somewhat steeper and rockier. At the summit the Eliot Tower offers views of the Boston skyline and the surrounding area. Descending, the trail heads northeast from the summit, takes a sharp left at marker 1082, and follows a pleasant woods path back to the museum.

Great Blue Hill Green Loop (DCR)

This 2.8-mi. loop meanders through the Great Blue Hill section of the reservation. It generally follows the cols between the hills, never ascending to any of the summits.

It begins at the north parking lot at the Trailside Museum. Heading northeast, it soon reaches paved Summit Rd., where it turns right and immediately bears left onto a dirt road (Wolcott Path), which heads east through a stand of tall white pines. At marker 1085 the loop proper begins, with the return trail coming in from the right. Continue straight on the road for a few hundred feet to marker 1100, where the trail turns left onto Border Path and runs northeast along the edge of some wetlands.

At marker 1135 the trail turns right and heads southeast through the col between Wolcott Hill on the right and Hemenway Hill on the left. At marker 1141 it crosses a dirt road and the Skyline Trail. Continuing southward on Five Corners Path, the trail circles Wolcott Hill and turns north through Wildcat Notch on Wildcat Notch Path, which separates Wolcott Hill from Great Blue Hill. It passes two small swamps, and just after the second, the trail turns left and heads northwest to the dirt road (Wolcott Path) where the loop began. Turn left onto the dirt road to return to the parking lot.

Houghtons Pond Yellow Loop (DCR)

This easy, 1-mi. trail is a popular walk for families with small children. The trailhead is at the main parking lot for the Houghtons Pond swimming area. Take Exit 3 north from I-93, turn right onto Hillside St., and turn right into the parking lot in 0.3 mi. There is supervised swimming here in summer.

The trail proceeds to the left (east) past the beach, bearing right just after the bathhouse. It joins a dirt road for a short distance around the eastern end of the pond, and then turns right off the road just before reaching a playground. The trail continues along the southern edge of the pond, crosses the pond's outlet at the western end, and heads north past a field and playground. It then travels through a small swamp and bears left (east) up a hill past a pavilion to the starting point.

Houghtons Pond Green Loop (DCR)

This 2.8-mi. trail begins at Houghtons Pond and circles (but does not ascend) Tucker Hill to the northeast of the pond. It begins at the Houghtons Pond beach parking lot and follows the yellow loop trail along the north shore of the pond. After passing the bathhouse, the green loop bears left from the yellow loop, then turns left and heads due north on an old carriage road. At marker 2070 the loop proper begins. Traveling clockwise, the trail leaves the road and continues north on Tucker Hill Path, crossing the Skyline Trail (which leads right up to the summit of Tucker Hill).

Circling the north end of Tucker Hill, the trail approaches (but does not meet) Chickatawbut Rd., then heads south through Dark Hollow on Dark Hollow Path, again crossing the Skyline Trail. At marker 2096 it turns right onto a dirt road and heads generally west back to the starting point of the loop. Turn left at this intersection to return to the trailhead.

Ponkapoag Green Loop (DCR)

This 3.9-mi. trail starts at the small parking area just south of Exit 3 off I-93. It heads south for 0.3 mi. to a fire gate on the left where it splits, heading either east or west and returning to the same point. Traveling west (right), it follows a woods road (Redman Farm Path) for 0.4 mi. to the YMCA camp, where a mapboard and trail marker on the left indicate the entrance to the dead end Ponkapoag Bog boardwalks (a nice side trip). Ponkapoag Pond is slowly drying up, and the bog represents the first stage in the pond's transition to what will eventually be dry land.

From the YMCA camp, heading left (south), the trail proceeds along the eastern edge of the Ponkapoag golf course for 0.6 mi. to the fire gate at the end of Maple Ave., the paved golf access road. Turning left, the trail follows Acton Path along the south shore of the pond for 0.8 mi. to Fisherman's Beach on the left, where there is a scenic view of Great Blue Hill. Continuing east through wetlands and then turning north, the trail passes the AMC's Ponkapoag Camp (reservations required). At marker 5343 the Ponkapoag loop continues west on a bluff above the pond back to its starting point.

Skyline Trail (DCR)

This trail, marked by blue rectangular blazes, is the longest in the Blue Hills Reservation, extending from Fowl Meadow in Canton east to Shea Rink on Willard St. in Quincy. The trail can be accessed from any one of four major streets: (1) MA 138, at a parking lot on the west side about 0.5 mi. south of the Trailside Museum. (2) Hillside St., at the reservation headquarters. (3) Randolph Ave. (MA 28), where the closest parking is about 0.25 mi. south of the trail crossing. (4) Willard St. at the trail terminus at Shea Rink.

Section 1. Little Blue Hill (DCR)

This section of the Skyline Trail was established in 1979. From the parking lot on MA 138 the trail runs west through open woods along MA 138 for 1 mi. to Green St. The Skyline Trail officially ends in this area. However, it is possible (with some difficulty) to continue on various paths in a generally northwest direction, skirting an abandoned highway interchange to reach Burma Rd. This 2-mi.-long dirt road runs north through the Fowl Meadow wetlands bordering the Neponset River, eventually reaching a parking area at the intersection of Brush Hill Rd. and Neponset Valley Pkwy.

Section 2. Blue Hill Ave. (MA 138) to Hillside St. (DCR)

From the parking area on MA 138 the trail leads 0.5 mi. steeply up the southwest side of Great Blue Hill to the circular road and bridle path at the summit.

From the top of Great Blue Hill, two routes, the North Skyline Trail and the South Skyline Trail, lead east, joining at the reservation headquarters on Hillside St. The longer, northern branch crosses Wolcott, Hemenway, and Hancock Hills, while the southern branch crosses Houghton Hill. Blue blazes mark both.

The North Skyline Trail begins at marker 1063, to the east of the stone tower on the summit of Great Blue Hill, at the north end of the stone bridge. It descends steeply to Wildcat Notch and the junction with Wildcat Notch Path and the Great Blue Hill Green Loop at marker 1092. It follows the green loop left about 50 ft., then turns right across low ground and ascends the ridge of Wolcott Hill (470 ft.). It continues over the summit and down to a hollow, where it bears right for 50 ft., then left up a rise to the top of the ridge.

The trail continues down the ridge to Five Corners Path junction (marker 1141) in the Wolcott–Hemenway col, where it crosses the other side of the Great Blue Hill Green Loop. The trail goes straight across the junction and ascends, first gently and then steeply, to a ridge on the south side of Hemenway Hill. At 1.8 mi. the trail turns right over ledges with good views ranging from southeast to northwest. At 1.9 mi. the trail bears left across some ledges, then in 225 ft. turns sharp right around a large boulder. It descends left to a small col, crosses Breakneck Ledge Path, and ascends a rocky grade to the ridge of Hancock Hill (510 ft.).

After crossing an old bridle path, the trail climbs a short rise to the summit of Hancock Hill. From the top, the trail descends more gradually near a ledge on the left (with good views) and crosses Hancock Hill Path to meet a woods road, which it follows left to a gate. Turn right onto a gravel path to the DCR stables. With the stables on the left, the trail continues on a paved driveway to Hillside St. and the junction with the South Skyline Trail.

At the summit of Great Blue Hill the South Skyline Trail leaves east from the circular summit drive at marker 1066, about 200 yd. south of the stone bridge. The well-defined trail passes over ledges, with good views east and south. It descends Shadow Cliff via a steep, rocky path and continues on the right side of a wet-weather brook to a brook crossing on large stones. Continuing on the left side of the brook, it soon passes between large boulders. Leaving the brook, it crosses Five Corners Path and Houghton Path then ascends the slope of Houghton Hill. Crossing just south of the summit, the trail then turns right and descends steeply to Hillside St. Follow Hillside St. left (north) 200 ft. to meet the northern branch.

Skyline Trail: Blue Hill Ave. (MA 138) to Hillside St.

Distances from Blue Hill Ave.

to summit of Great Blue Hill: 0.5 mi., 30 min.

to summit of Hancock Hill (via northern branch): 2.2 mi., 1 hr., 20 min.

to Hillside St. (via northern branch): 2.5 mi., 1 hr., 30 min.

to Hillside St. (via southern branch): 1.9 mi., 1 hr., 15 min.

Section 3. Hillside St. to Randolph Ave. (DCR)

This section of the trail starts at the junction of the North and South Skyline Trails at the marker on Hillside St. across from the DCR stables. It bears right onto Bugbee Path, a well-worn woods road, for about 400 ft., then turns left into the woods at marker 2054. It bears right up a slope, crosses Tucker Hill Path, continues to the west ridge of Tucker Hill (499 ft.), and proceeds through scattered pine trees (care is needed here) to a ledge with fine views to the west and south. It continues along ledges and down a steep, rocky trail to the bottom of Dark Hollow and the Dark Hollow Path. Next it bears left, then right; it crosses low ground and climbs gradually on a rocky trail, passing through a wooded section over the north ridge of Boyce Hill (404 ft.) and crossing the Doe Hollow Path. Continuing eastward, the trail ascends a steep, rocky grade to the ridge of Buck Hill (496 ft.). From the summit the trail plunges down a steep, rocky slope, crosses Buck Hill Path and Forest Path, then continues down the hillside to Randolph Ave. (MA 28).

Skyline Trail: Hillside St. to Randolph Ave.

Distances from Hillside St.

  to summit of Buck Hill: 1.9 mi., 1 hr.

  to Randolph Ave. (MA 28): 2.2 mi., 1 hr., 10 min.

Section 4. Randolph Ave. to Willard St. (DCR)

After crossing Randolph Ave. the Skyline Trail quickly reaches a pipeline right of way then follows an easy route to a hemlock grove, where it turns right onto a bridle path. It continues through the grove about 100 ft. to marker 3042, where it turns left and proceeds up Chickatawbut Hill (517 ft.) on a steep, rocky path. It bears right at the top of the ridge and turns left into the woods within 100 ft. Soon ascending another steep ledge, the trail bears right uphill. At the top of the ledge the trail ascends gradually into the woods and over more ledges, passing a large puddingstone boulder on the left. The trail skirts the summit of Chickatawbut Hill, then descends into Slide Notch, climbs back up over Kitchamakin Hill, then heads down again over stone steps to Sassaman Notch. (Local rock climbers call the large boulder here the Grepon.)

From Sassaman Notch the Skyline Trail turns right for 50 yd., then turns left and follows the blue blazes up some stone steps. At the top of the steps the trail turns right, away from an intersecting trail, and ascends steeply to the ridge of Nahanton Hill, following ledges to the summit (480 ft.), where there are good views north and south. The trail bears right through scrub oak and over open ledges, some of which offer views of South Shore Plaza. The trail descends gradually through the Broken Hills and across several cols with short, steep descents and ascents until it reaches a fence around Blue Hills Reservoir.

The trail follows the fence to the right some distance, then proceeds over more ledges to Chickatawbut Rd. It crosses the road at a trail marker post, and at the Wampatuck Hill marker post it goes right up the slope and over the ledges of Wampatuck Hill (353 ft.), providing views of Boston and the bay. The trail turns right along ledges south of the summit and continues along the rim of a cliff with views of South Shore Plaza and Great Pond. The trail descends into scrub oak at the end of the ledges and soon crosses a DCR pipeline.

After crossing the pipeline, the trail descends and bears to the left. After 40 yd. it turns right up a steep, rocky trail to Rattlesnake Hill; bear left to skirt a smooth ledge near the top of the rock. At the top the trail turns right and crosses a trail to the right that leads to the top of Rattlesnake Hill and many views. The Skyline Trail descends rock steps, crosses an old trail, climbs briefly, and continues over a ledge and boulders to an old quarry. It continues around the quarry to a gravel path, which it follows to the right for about 140 yd., then forks left. It soon forks left again into pines and oaks, and after some distance reaches an old woods road, which it follows to the right a short distance to Wampatuck Rd. Cross this road and follow the trail between the ponds to Shea Rink on Willard St.

Skyline Trail: Randolph Ave. to Willard St.

Distances from Willard St.

> *to* summit of Chickatawbut Hill: 0.7 mi., 20 min.
>
> *to* summit of Nahanton Hill: 1.3 mi., 35 min.
>
> *to* Chickatawbut Rd.: 2.1 mi., 1 hr.
>
> *to* Willard St.: 3.6 mi., 1 hr., 45 min.

Stony Brook Reservation (DCR)

This 400-acre reservation is located between the West Roxbury and Hyde Park sections of Boston, and is crisscrossed by a network of easy—although generally unmarked—hiking paths. Although none of these paths can be considered a major hiking trail, Stony Brook is notable as a very large, publicly owned, undeveloped forest preserve within the city limits. As such, it provides Bostonians with the chance to do some easy forest walking without traveling farther. Despite its location, Stony Brook is relatively unknown. Visitors are unlikely to encounter the crowds normally found at other urban parks.

Stony Brook Reservation is located on both sides of the Enneking Pkwy. (formerly the Turtle Pond Pkwy.). The section to the east of the parkway is the larger of the two, and includes such points of interest as Stony Brook itself, Turtle Pond, and some excellent examples of glacial drumlins. On the eastern side of the reservation is Bald Knob, a rock outcrop with good views of Hyde Park and the Blue Hills. At the northeast tip of the reservation, at the corner of Washington St. and the West Roxbury Pkwy., is Bellevue Hill, the highest point in Boston. At one time this summit afforded an excellent panoramic view, but in recent years the view has become all but obliterated by trees.

There is some limited parking along Enneking Pkwy., although the parking areas may be closed at times due to DCR budget cutbacks. There is always parking available at the recreation complex at the very south end of the parkway, although this requires a short walk to reach the undeveloped part of the reservation.

Boston Harbor Islands National Park & State Park

Boston Harbor Islands National Park and State Park consists of 34 islands in Boston Harbor, just 45 min. by ferry from Boston. The Massachusetts Department of Conservation and Recreation manages 17 of the islands as Boston Harbor Islands State Park; six of these islands are staffed and open to the public during the warmer months. Recreational opportunities include island camping, hiking, fishing, and boating.

The harbor islands have experienced many commercial and public uses over the past 350 years, including forts, prisons, hospitals, lighthouses, sewage plants, a firing range, an airport, and even a glue factory. As some of these older enterprises faded, efforts began to convert some of the islands to recreational uses, which in turn led to the establishment of the state and national parks.

Most of the islands have easily followed walking paths, and many have interesting abandoned fortifications and historical ruins. Care should be taken, as these ruins, as well as the rubble left from other past uses, can create some hazards for walkers.

Most of the islands can only be reached by boat. Ferry service is available in season to Georges Island from Long Wharf at State St. and Atlantic Ave. in downtown Boston. Boston Harbor Cruises supplies the ferry service (617-227- 4321). Free water taxi (shuttle) service is available from Georges Island to other islands, including Lovells, Peddocks, Bumpkin, and Grape Islands. A shuttle schedule is available at Long Wharf and other departure points, including Hingham Shipyard off MA 3A.

Camping is permitted only on four designated islands: Grape, Bumpkin, Lovells, and Peddocks. Reservations are required, and a fee is charged. Potable water and food are not available. Campsite reservations on Grape and Bumpkin Islands can be made by calling 877-422-6762; for Lovells and Peddocks call 617-422-6762.

Islands accessed by ferry or shuttle service:

Lovells Island (62 acres) is separated from Georges Island by a waterway known as the Narrows. Just east of the Narrows is Bug Light. The shuttle from Georges Island docks at the pier on the southwest shore near Fort Standish. A trail leads from the pier past Fort Standish on the right, then traces a course northwest along the shore past a camping and picnic area.

Georges Island (28 acres) has a pier, restrooms, and ferry service to Boston. Trails diverge from the pier, with one heading north to Fort Warren at the northern end of the island, and the other exploring the south section. Fort Warren is constructed of granite and once housed prisoners during the Civil War.

Peddocks Island (113 acres). This large, elongated island is formed by five drumlins—large glacial hills. On the island are Fort Andrews (near the pier where the Georges Island shuttle docks), a camping area with 11 campsites (north of the pier), and a lighthouse northwest of the pier. A nest of paths covers the north part of the island, with fewer but longer trails heading south through the narrow neck of land at the island's center to West Head at land's end on the southwest shore. Black-crowned night herons as well as many other birds nest on the island. Restrooms are located on the south side of the island's north end.

Grape Island (50 acres) is due north of Hewitts Cove and close to the ferry dock at Hingham Shipyard. It is covered with roses, wildflowers, bayberries, and many species of birds. There are 10 campsites, including one group site, and picnic facilities. Easy walking trails cross the island.

Bumpkin Island (35 acres) in Hingham Bay is one of the more southerly of the harbor islands and offers slate beaches, 10 individual campsites, and one group site. A trail leads to the remains of a hospital for children and the ruins of a stone farmhouse.

Islands without public boat service include:

Great Brewster Island (23 acres), one of a group that make up the outer islands, has one of the highest hills (about 100 ft.) of the harbor islands, with vistas of Massachusetts Bay and the harbor. It was used for centuries to defend the harbor. Great Brewster Island is open for day use only. Visitor facilities include picnic tables, a self-guided trail, a composting toilet, and a small shelter for use in inclement weather.

Gallops Island (16 acres) is just west of the narrows between Lovells and Georges Islands and used to be served by shuttle from Georges Island. However, Gallops Island is presently closed to the public—debris containing asbestos was discovered there in 2000. The island will remain closed until it is again safe for use by the public.

Middle and Outer Brewster Islands (12 and 17.5 acres) were originally used for agriculture, but because of their impressive sea cliffs they have often been used for harbor defense.

Whitney & Thayer Woods Reservation (TTOR)

This property in Hingham and Cohasset comprises 824 acres of gently rolling glacial woodland with some marshy areas, brooks, and huge glacial boulders (erratics). More than 10 mi. of moderate cart paths and foot trails weave through a hemlock-pine-hardwood forest with scattered American holly trees. Clusters of azalea and rhododendron bushes bloom in spring next to wild-flowers and ferns. A highlight of the property is the Milliken Memorial Path, created in the late 1920s by Arthur Milliken in memory of his wife, Mabel. Stone walls running throughout the woods mark much of the land as having once been farms and pasture. The property contains a stretch of Brass Kettle Brook and a portion of Great Swamp. Turkey Hill, a 187-ft.-high glacial drumlin with a view of Cohasset Harbor is co-managed with the towns of Cohasset and Hingham. The remains of a radar installation dating from the Cold War are atop the hill. The trails are open for hiking, cross-country ski-ing, and snowshoeing. The property abuts 3500-acre Wompatuck State Park and is close to Boston Harbor Islands State Park.

The entrance to the reservation is on MA 3A opposite Sohier St. in Cohasset, 2 mi. south of the junction of MA 228 and 3A. Numbers in the descriptions below refer to numbered trail junctions. Detailed trail maps can be purchased at the service station across from the entrance on MA 3A.

Howe's Rd.

This cart path is one of the main trails through the south portion of the prop-erty. It starts at the north side of the Route 3A parking lot and goes southwest, crossing Brass Kettle Brook near the boundary with Wompatuck State Park. Bear right (west) at 19 onto the Milliken Memorial Path to head toward

Turkey Hill via One Way Path. At 21 turn left (south) onto the Bancroft Trail, which loops past Rooster Rock (on the left) and Ode's Den on the right. Here Theodore Pritchard lived in a boulder cave when he lost his home in 1830. This loop returns to Howe's Rd. at junction 20, north of Brass Kettle Brook.

Howe's Rd.

to Brass Kettle Brook: 0.8 mi., 50 min.

Whitney Rd.

This road exits right at 22 (northwest) from Howe's Rd., 0.5 mi. from the beginning of the latter. It passes several roads and trails, all of which are marked. The road ends at 15, Side Hill Rd., which can be followed north to MA 3A. Or follow Turkey Hill Lane northwest to Turkey Hill.

Whitney Rd.

Distance from Howe's Rd.

to junction 15: 1.1 mi., 45 min.

Bancroft Trail

This white-blazed trail begins at the Nature Trail sign in the grassy field near the entrance on MA 3A. It travels southwest across the reservation, passing along ledges and intersecting Howe's Rd. at 2. It then proceeds west to 3 at Bigelow Boulder, a 200-ton glacial granite boulder with a nearby smaller boulder. Turning south, the path crosses Whitney Rd. at 4, then climbs steeply through giant hemlock and white pine woods, crossing Howe's Rd. at 21. Rooster Rock, a glacial boulder supported on one side by a small stone, is on the left. The trail descends through hemlock woods to Ode's Den (where Theodore Pritchard once lived under a large fragment of the granite rocks). Swinging north, the trail crosses Howe's Rd. at 20, Whitney Rd. at 5, and Boulder Lane at 6, then circles eastward to end at Bigelow Boulder.

Bancroft Trail

Distance from Nature Trail sign

to Bigelow Boulder: 1.8 mi., 1 hr.

Boulder Lane

This road leaves Howe's Rd. at 1, 0.3 mi. from the parking area, and goes right (northwest) past Bigelow Boulder, ending at Whitney Rd. (7).

Boulder Lane

Distance from Howe's Rd.

   to Whitney Rd.: 0.8 mi., 25 min.

Milliken Memorial Path

This path, a continuation of Howe's Rd., begins at 19, 1.1 mi. from the parking lot. It continues to the junction of James Hill Lane and Ayer Lane at 18. Heavily used as a bridle path, it is popular because of its rhododendrons, azaleas, and other plants not commonly found in the area.

Milliken Memorial Path

Distance from Howe's Rd.

   to junction of James Hill Lane and Ayer Lane: 0.8 mi., 25 min.

James Hill Lane

This trail exits left (west) at 18 from the Milliken Memorial Path and continues 1.0 mi. to Leavitt St. in Hingham.

James Hill Lane

Distance from Milliken Memorial Path

   to Leavitt St. (Hingham): 1.0 mi., 30 min.

Ayer Lane

Ayer Lane is a connecting link from the Milliken Memorial Path (18) to Whitney Rd. (10), and is often used as a bridle path.

Ayer Lane

Distance from Milliken Memorial Path

   to Whitney Rd.: 0.4 mi., 15 min.

Thayer Trail

One of the main east–west trails, the Thayer Trail begins on Whitney Rd. at 8 and circles east, passing an abandoned well and turning west after Adelaide Rd. (12). Continuing west, the trail crosses an abandoned railroad bed, and turns left (west) at a T-junction. It then winds through a magnificent American holly grove. The trail then crosses One Way Lane at 16 and ends at Turkey Hill Lane, southwest of Turkey Hill.

Thayer Trail

to railroad bed: 0.7 mi., 40 min.

to holly grove: 0.8 mi., 45 min.

to Turkey Hill Lane: 1.5 mi., 1 hr. 30 min.

Turkey Hill Trail

Starting at the intersection of One Way Lane and the Thayer Trail (16), the Turkey Hill Trail climbs north on One Way Lane to Turkey Hill Lane (paved). The trail turns right and continues a short distance to pastureland on the left, from which there are views over Cohasset Harbor. Return via the same route, as the old Turkey Hill loop trail has been abandoned.

Turkey Hill Trail

Distance from junction 16

to pasture: 0.3 mi., 15 min.

World's End Peninsula (TTOR)

This 251-acre peninsula in Hingham was originally laid out by Frederick Law Olmsted and includes an interesting drumlin and beach. A number of cart paths snake through the reservation, with footpaths emanating from them to explore the meadows and hills. The peninsula is a large glacial drumlin roughly shaped like an hourglass; its "waist" is a slender neck of land about 500 ft. wide called the bar. The surface is mainly grassy with occasional granite outcrops. The upper peninsula, called World's End, is traced by three loop trails. The Rocky Neck section of the lower peninsula is laced with footpaths that explore Ice Pond and other natural features.

The pristine nature of World's End is now protected, but the land was once the proposed site of a nuclear power plant, and before that was the intended location of the United Nations headquarters.

To reach the peninsula from MA 3A in Hingham, turn onto Summer St. and continue northwest to a four-way intersection with Rockland St. Continue straight onto Martin's Lane and travel 0.7 mi. to the gatehouse and parking on the right. Parking is limited and often fills up, particularly on pleasant spring or fall weekends.

Cutler Park (DCR)

This park on the Charles River covers 700 acres of marsh and woods in the towns of Dedham, Needham, and Newton. Protecting the largest freshwater marsh on this portion of the Charles River, the park is known for its wide diversity of animal and plant life—especially birds, with more than 100 species. Popular activities include birding, hiking, canoeing, and fishing.

From I-95 take the Highland Ave. (Needham) exit, and turn left at the first light on Highland Ave. onto Hunting Rd., which parallels I-95. In about 0.5 mi. turn left onto Kendrick St., which immediately crosses the highway. The area shares a driveway with a Polaroid building at 140 Kendrick St. The Brook Farm Historic Site is best accessed from the parking area off Baker St. in Brookline. The marsh is at the south end of the property and can be accessed from Needham St.

Cutler Park Loop

This interesting loop through the park circles Kendrick Pond to the south of the parking area on Kendrick St. An extension of the trail runs from the south part of this loop to Powells Island. The path begins at the parking area and bears to the left of the pond, going east then swinging south through marshland. At 0.3 mi. it enters the woods and continues south, following the Charles River. At 0.5 mi. there is an open view of the opposite bank and a distant view of the Blue Hills. Also in view are some abandoned concrete bunkers, originally used by the DCR for water-control operations.

At 0.65 mi. the main path turns right and heads back toward Kendrick St. Heading north, the path passes a pond and side trail on the left. (This side trail ascends an esker for about 0.5 mi. and passes through a mature oak forest where lady's slipper orchids are abundant in early June. It then descends the esker and rejoins the main path about midway up Kendrick Pond.) The main path soon comes to another open view of the pond, including the Wells Industrial Park and the Gothic tower of the Gosman Jewish Community Center in Newton. The path finally ends back at the parking lot, having made a circuit of about 1.6 mi.

To reach Powells Island, leave the main loop trail at 0.65 mi. and head southeast. The path descends into a boggy area and crosses a streambed 0.25 mi. from the main path. It then ascends to an oak forest that extends southeast in a strip about 350 yd. wide between the wetlands and I-95. At 0.7 mi. the path crosses a short stretch of marsh to Powells Island, which still shows the scarred trunks and standing deadwood left from a forest fire in the late 1980s. (Powells Island is actually what southerners would call a hammock, surrounded on three sides by the Charles River and separated from the mainland by about 100 yd. of marsh.) At 0.9 mi. there is a meadow, and at the far end a path begins that circles around the island. Turn left at the first fork, and for the next 0.3 mi. the path runs along the embankment above the river, dropping down twice for boat landings. The reviving forest is an ideal bird habitat, and a bench along the path is a good place to watch and listen. At the next fork a triple-masted radio tower to the northwest serves as a landmark, and the right-hand path will return to the meadow in 0.1 mi. From there retrace the path to the main trail.

Cutler Park Loop

Distances from parking lot

> *to* Powells Island cutoff: 0.65 mi., 20 min.
>
> *to* marsh crossing: 1.5 mi., 45 min.
>
> *to* island circuit and return to mainland: 2.25 mi., 1 hr., 5 min.
>
> *to* return to main loop: 3 mi., 1 hr., 30 min.
>
> *to* return to parking lot: 4 mi., 2 hr.

Neponset River Marshes Reservation (DCR)
Lower Neponset River Trail (Dorchester and Milton)

This new trail, not yet completed, follows the path of an abandoned railroad grade that runs along the banks of the Neponset River. The path is designed to link the Neponset area with other DCR trails in order to offer more and varied opportunities for recreation in the region. The trail begins in the Port

Norfolk area of Dorchester, passes through Pope John Paul II Park, and proceeds across Granite Ave. and through the Neponset Marshes. It then continues through the Lower Mills to Central Ave. in Milton.

Eventual extensions of the trail will include a section from Port Norfolk to Commercial Point, designed to link with an existing trail that reaches to Castle Island, and from Central Ave. to Mattapan.

Webster Conservation Area

This 113-acre wooded area in the Newton Centre and Chestnut Hill sections of Newton is owned and maintained by the city of Newton. Adjoining the Webster Conservation Area to the west of Hammond Pond Pkwy. is the 14-acre woodland owned by Temple Mishkan Tefila and 38-acre Hammond Pond Reservation (DCR). (The reservation includes an easement granted by the DCR to the Mall at Chestnut Hill and the Chestnut Hill Towers condominium, which provides vehicular access to these two establishments.

The trails through the Webster Conservation Area are short and easy to follow, but it is helpful to consult the map available from the Newton Conservation Commission. Deer Park is a popular spot in the area. To reach Deer Park, park at the end of Suffolk Rd. (off Hammond St.) and walk along Lowell Lane to the Deer Park gate, where the deer shelter, feeding station, and watering trough are located.

Blue Trail

The Blue Trail meanders through Hammond Pond Reservation from the parking area at Hammond Pond, located just behind the Mall at Chestnut Hill on MA 9. The trailhead is unmarked, but the Blue Trail is the largest trail leading from the parking lot. The blue dots and directional triangles begin about 200 yd. up the trail, although they are at times difficult to follow.

At Hemlock Vale the trail continues across the culvert over Tarn Pond Brook, takes a sharp left just before the MBTA Green Line, and crosses Hammond Pond Pkwy. to the parking lot of the Temple Mishkan Tefila, where it follows the Temple Path. On the north side of the temple the trail turns right into the Webster Conservation Area woods, passes Cake Rock, and comes to Gooch's Caves, located on a high rock ledge. The trail then returns to Hammond Pond Pkwy., turns right along the fence (unmarked), and uses the same crossing and trail back to the parking lot.

Green Trail

To reach the Green Trail park in the gravel lot west of Temple Mishkan Tefila, then follow the Temple Path to the Green Trail on the right. When the Green Trail reaches Gooch's Caves, it turns left and continues to the Elgin Path. At the intersection with the Elgin Path, the Green Trail turns sharp left and continues 150 yd., then turns to the right for 200 yd. to reach the fence at the MBTA tracks. At the fence the trail turns sharp left and goes a short distance past a spur on the right. The spur leads to a sign identifying the undeveloped Webster Playground land, near the intersection of Warren and Elgin Sts. The main trail continues another 200 yd. and turns left onto the Temple Trail, which returns to the temple parking lot.

Orange Trail

The Orange Trail follows the Temple Path from the north side of the temple, passes the Green Trail on the right, then bears right into the woods. At a bend the Orange Trail turns right onto the Green Trail; both continue to Gooch's Caves. From the caves the Orange Trail follows the Blue Trail back to the temple.

Yellow Trail

The Yellow Trail meanders around the Houghton Garden section of the Webster Conservation Area near Lowell Crossing. Parking is available along the garden's Suffolk Rd. frontage.

Temple Path

The Temple Path starts at Hammond Pond Pkwy., passes the north side of the temple, and continues west to its junction with the Carlisle Path (left) and the Elgin Path (right) in the Charles Cohen Conservation Area (also known as Webster Vale). Many small paths bear right to large rock formations, including Gooch's Caves and Cake Rock.

Carlisle Path

The Carlisle Path is accessible from the westbound lane of Boylston St. (MA 9) by turning right onto Langley Rd. then right again onto Madoc St. to reach the gate and trailhead. From the gate take the Madoc Path to its junction with the Carlisle Path. Turn left onto the Carlisle Path, which continues between the Charles Cohen Conservation Area (Webster Vale), Hammond Pond Reservation, and the Temple Mishkan Tefila woods to the junction with the Temple Path (right). A short distance north of this junction the Carlisle Path becomes the unmarked Elgin Path, which ends at a fenced Green Line right of way over which there is no legal access. At this point hikers can take the Green Trail (right) to Gooch's Caves and back to the Temple Path, or switch to the Orange Trail or the Blue Trail at Gooch's Caves and follow either of these to the Temple Path. Alternatively, take the Blue Trail to Hammond Pond Pkwy. and pick up any of the trails on the east side of the parkway.

Elgin Path

The Elgin Path enters Webster Conservation Area from Hammond Pond Pkwy. (*Note: In the area north of the Green Line and west of the parkway, the DCR does not permit parking on the parkway berms or on the road. Parking is available, however, along the Houghton Garden frontage at the end of Suffolk Rd. To reach the Elgin Path, follow Suffolk Rd. 1 block to the intersection of Old England Rd. and Clovelly Rd., where a path enters the woods. Follow this along the north fence of Deer Park to Hammond Pond Pkwy. Cross the parkway and turn right to find the Elgin Path.*) The Elgin Path joins the Ledge Path (right), which skirts the base of some magnificent sandstone ledges and an old quarry area. The trail continues on log steps up to the ledges, runs along the rim of the ledges, then returns to the parkway.

Noanet Woodlands (TTOR)

Noanet Woodlands is a 695-acre tract of forest and hilltop in Dover. Named for a leader of the Natick Nation who once fished the waters of Noanet Brook, the reservation was the site of Samuel Fisher's profitable sawmill in the early 1800s. An iron company also once operated here—a 24-ft.-tall dam on the property is its most noticeable remnant. Today the peaceful woods are laced with 17 mi. of moderate hiking trails with some strenuous sections. One of the reservations most popular features is Noanet Hill and overlook, which provides a grand view over the forest to the skyline of Boston.

Visitors to Noanet Woodlands use the parking facilites at Dover's Caryl Park, which abuts the reservation. To reach the parking area from the center of Dover, follow Dedham St. 0.6 mi. east to the Caryl Park entrance on the right. Additional parking is available at the western end of the park.

Caryl Trail

From the parking area in Caryl Park, the yellow-blazed trail heads south, then turns right (west). It passes a trail on the left, turns left (south) at a second junction, and crosses a branch of Noanet Brook. The trail swings east, passing trail junction 2 before bending south and meeting the blue-blazed Peabody Trail at junction 3 (the red-blazed Larrabee Trail is just east of the intersection at junction 4). From the junction the trail climbs moderately to junction 6. To reach Noanet Hill turn left (southeast) and continue straight to the overlook at the top of the hill (387 ft.).

The path now heads west, turns left (southeast) at junction 7, and continues to the southern foot of Noanet Hill. The trail swings southwest, traverses a long level area, then traces a course between a low hill and a wetland. Turning left (east) at the southern property line, the trail then follows the boundary northeast. Turning north, the trail proceeds the short distance to the tri-junction of the Peabody and Larrabee Trails. The Caryl Trail ends at this junction. Both trails can be followed back to the Caryl Trail at junction 3 located about 0.5 mi. south of Caryl Park and the parking area.

Caryl Trail

to junction 3: 0.5 mi., 25 min.

to Noanet Hill: 0.9 mi., 55 min.

to Peabody Junction: 2.2 mi., 1 hr.

Peabody Trail

This blue-blazed path begins at junction 3 off the Caryl Trail, about 0.5 mi. south of the parking area at Caryl Park. From the trailhead the path climbs steadily, passes straight through a three-way junction, then follows the contour of the hill past junction 37 to reach another intersection just northwest of a small pond. The Old Mill site can be reached by following the side trail left (east) across the north shore of the small pond.

The Peabody Trail continues south past junction 36 and, passing to the west of a larger pond, traces a course between Noanet Brook and the foot of Noanet Peak. The path passes another small pond to the east as it continues down the Noanet valley. Just before junction 34 the path turns east as it follows the base of a low hill. It then turns southeast, crosses the brook, and ends at junction 18 where the Peabody, Caryl, and Larrabee Trails converge.

Peabody Trail

> *to* junction 37: 0.3 mi., 10 min.
> *to* junction 18: 1.2 mi., 40 min.

Larrabee Trail

The third major trail of Noanet Reservation begins at junction 4, a short distance east of junction 3 and about 0.5 mi. south of the parking area at Caryl Park. To reach the trail follow the Caryl Trail south from the parking area to junction 3, turn left (east), and continue the short way to junction 4. The red-blazed Larrabee Trail heads north, descending toward the brook to reach junction 33, where the path swings southeast and begins to trace a course over the level ground of the valley. The trail crosses the brook just beyond junction 29, then continues south, passing close to the shore of a pond before swinging left (east) around the base of a hill. Turning south again, the path stays close to the top of a low ridge and easily descends to the southern terminus at junction 18, where it meets the Caryl and Peabody Trails.

Larrabee Trail

> *to* pond: 0.6 mi., 20 min.
> *to* junction 18: 1.4 mi., 40 min.

Rocky Woods Reservation & Fork Factory Brook (TTOR)

These adjoining reservations in Medfield and Dover comprise 491 acres of beautiful woods, lovely ponds, and excellent views. Rocky Woods Reservation was once "common land," divided up into woodlots that were parceled to residents who didn't have enough fuel wood on their own properties. Today the 6.5 mi. of trails explore the reservation's abundant wetlands, ponds, and rocky cobbles.

To reach the reservation from I-95, take Exit 16B and follow MA 128 west for 5.7 mi., to Hartford St. Turn right on Hartford St. and proceed 0.6 mi. to the entrance on the left. To reach the reservation from the intersection of MA 109 and MA 27 in Medfield, follow MA 109 east to Hartford St. and turn left. The entrance is 0.6 mi. ahead on the left. There is a gatehouse and large parking area at the entrance. Farther up the road is a second parking area by the visitor center and restrooms. Trail maps are available at the visitor center.

Chickering Pond Trail

This short 0.5-mi.-long trail loops around Chickering Pond. Beginning at the visitor center the trail heads east, crosses the outflow brook, and then swings northeast. The path climbs a ridge to an overlook with a view of the pond. Nearby is junction 3, where the Noanet Trail leaves right (northeast). The trail now traces a path between the southern foot of Cedar Hill and the lake, reaching junction 4, where the Tower and Ridge Trails enter, at the north end of the lake. The trail now leaves the lake, bending west and reaching junction 5 with the Quarry Trail. Turning south, the path again approaches the lake, where the bridle trail leaves right. The path now stays fairly close to the shore as it returns to the visitor center.

Cedar Hill Loop

A moderate loop can be made by combining the Chickering Pond, Noanet, Cedar Hill, and Tower Trails. Take the Chickering Pond Trail to junction 3 and turn right (northeast) down the Noanet Trail. At the Cedar Trail turn left (west) and ascend Cedar Hill to the Tower Trail. At this junction the Tower Trail leaves left (south), while the loop trail heads north, then west at a fork, and reaches an overlook on Cedar Hill (435 ft.). The trail steeply descends from the overlook to rejoin the Tower Trail. The Tower Trail continues down Cedar Hill to junction 4, where it joins the Chickering Pond Trail and heads back to the visitor center.

Echo Lake Trail

This trail begins at junction 1 on the western side of the Loop Trail, which can be accessed from the lower parking area. The Echo Lake Trail initially heads west toward Echo Lake, reaches the east shore, then turns southwest and follows the shoreline. While the Echo Pond Trail continues straight to its end at the East West Trail, a side trail (the preferred route for scenery) makes a sharp right (west) turn and crosses the width of the lake on a footbridge. After reaching the far shore, the path follows the shoreline briefly, turns left (northwest), and joins a side trail to reach the Harwood Notch Trail south of junction 6.

Fork Factory Brook Trails

This property abuts Rocky Woods to the east of Hartford St. It is predominantly flat wetlands, with Mill Brook tracing a course through the property. A network of paths explores wetlands and low hilltops, eventually leading to an old mill site at the south end of the property. The single trailhead is on the east side of Hartford Rd., a few yards north of the entrance road to Rocky Woods.

Rocky Narrows Reservation (TTOR)

This 227-acre property is situated in the southeastern part of Sherborn. Called the "gates of the Charles" for its tall cliffs, it consists of rocky woodlands on the banks of the Charles River. The reservation sports 7 mi. of hiking trails, including a section of the Bay Circuit Trail. There are two parking areas. One is off South Main St. (MA 27) just north of the junction with MA 115. This parking lot serves the portion of the reservation southwest of the railroad tracks and includes the Green Trail. Railroad policy forbids pedestrian crossing of the tracks. The other area is at the corner of Forest and Goulding Sts. at the north end of the property. A canoe landing is on the northeast portion of the reservation.

Green Trail

From the South Main St. parking area, this white-blazed trail travels east to junctions 1 and 5, where footpaths leave left (north). The Green Trail turns south to reach the property boundary, then heads east along the boundary. After crossing a brook the path climbs easily to a small hill, where it splits into a loop that skirts the railroad tracks.

Red Trail

This red-blazed trail begins at the north parking area and heads south before turning slowly east to pass wetlands and upland hills. It then makes a sharp right (southwest) turn at junction 20 (0.6 mi.), followed shortly by a left (southeast) to reach junction 19 at 0.8 mi. From here, the canoe landing can be reached by a footpath that heads a short distance east to the river.

The Red Trail continues west over level ground, then climbs to junction 18 nearly due west of the river narrows. The trail heads south along the ridge to reach the Narrows Overlook at 1.4 mi. From the overlook the path heads southeast past junctions 17 and 16, to reach junction 15 at 1.7 mi. A side trail leads from here to King Philip's Overlook

From junction 15 the Red Trail swings around the ridge and descends, approaching the railroad grade before turning northwest to pass between the tracks and the base of the hill. The trail follows an easy course north, then turns west at the northern end of the hill. The trail bends back north and continues on to the parking area at 2.7 mi.

Red Trail

to junction 20: 0.6 mi., 20 min.

to junction 19: 0.8 mi., 30 min.

to junction 15: 1.7 mi., 55 min.

to parking area: 2.7 mi., 1 hr., 30 min.

Sherborn Town Forest

This forest occupies several irregular contiguous and nearly contiguous tracts in the eastern and northern parts of Sherborn. It is mildly hilly and is bordered on the west by higher hills. The section of the forest just north of the junction of Goulding, Lake, Forest, and Snow Sts. (a triangle with a small house in the middle) has many trails of various lengths and conditions, but these trails, with the exception of the Town Forest Trail, leave the forest and traverse the surrounding area, including Mt. Misery and the woodlands west of the forest. Refer to the USGS Natick and Medfield quadrangles.

Town Forest Trail: Pine St. School to Lake St.

This easy hike passes near two wooded summits with limited views. The trailhead is located at the Pine St. School in Sherborn, just off MA 16 (Eliot St.) near its intersection with MA 27. Parking is allowed in marked spaces in the school lot from dawn to dusk on nonschool days, but is not allowed on Lake St. The trail leaves the parking lot by the rear of the jungle gyms and is marked with single white blazes. Double blazes mark the frequent turns.

The trail turns left in about 0.1 mi. and climbs quickly to the summit of Pine Hill, keeping to the right at a fork just before the summit. At about 0.2 mi. the trail bears right at a second fork, passing a horse-jumping field on the right. Turning right again, the trail follows a pipeline right of way down to Farm Rd.

The white blazes continue on the south side of Farm Rd., as the Town Forest Trail joins the white-marked Bay Circuit Trail. The trail bears left and returns to the pipeline track in about 0.1 mi., follows the pipeline for about 0.2 mi., and enters the woods to the right. When the Town Forest Trail bears left in about 100 yd., a short side trail to the right leads to the summit of Mt. Misery (279 ft.). The remainder of the trail winds through the woods down to Lake St., just north of the intersection of Lake, Goulding, Forest, and Snow Sts. A green metal gate marks this end of the trail.

Town Forest Trail: Pine St. School to Lake St.

Distance from Pine St. School

    to Lake St.: 2.0 mi., 1 hr.

Girl Scout East–West Trail

This trail is one of two trails on Brush Hill (396 ft.) marked by the Girl Scouts, using painted can tops attached to trees.The east–west trail begins as a narrow, grassy path leading west off MA 27, 0.3 mi. north of its junction with MA 16. The road soon crosses a railroad track at 0.2 mi., passes through a clump of red pines, and reaches a former Girl Scout camp. From the camp the wooded path continues southwest, then west, rising sharp to the height-of-land, where it crosses the north–south trail. From this intersection unmarked but well-traveled trails lead 0.3 mi. north to Prospect St. and 0.3 mi. south and west to Hunting Lane. This trail is part of the Bay Circuit Trail.

Girl Scout East–West Trail

Distance from MA 27

    to intersection with north–south trail: 1.0 mi., 30 min.

Broadmoor Wildlife Sanctuary (MAS)

This Massachusetts Audubon Society sanctuary comprises about 624 acres off Eliot St. (MA 16) and South St. in South Natick and Sherborn and borders the Charles River. The area around Little Pond in Sherborn (262 acres) was given to the Audubon Society in 1962 by Henry M. Channing in memory of Katherine Minot Channing. The Broadmoor property (South Natick and Sherborn) was donated by Dr. and Mrs. Carl Stillman in 1968.

The entrance to the sanctuary is at 280 Eliot St. (MA 16), 1.8 mi. southwest from South Natick. Trail maps are available at the nature center. The visitor center is a 1911-era horse barn renovated in 1983 that features composting restrooms, solar heating, and other innovative, earth-friendly features.

Gorgeous boardwalks and 9 mi. of trails through peaceful wetands and forests are the signature of Broadmoor. A number of well-marked trails leave from the parking area. A nice loop hike is the Charles River Loop, which follows along the river bank. Trail information and maps are available at the information center.

Walden Pond State Reservation (DCR)

Walden Pond and its surrounding woodlands, the site of Henry David Thoreau's retreat, were given to the state in 1922 with the provision that the public be allowed to swim, canoe, hike, and picnic there. During summer Walden Pond is a popular swimming and picnic spot. In the off-season visitors find the pond and its environs a tranquil escape. Maps of the extensive trail system are available at the park office or at the parking entrance. Trails include the 1.8-mi. Pond Path circuit, paths to the original site of Thoreau's cabin, a trail up Emerson's Cliff, loop trails west of the railroad tracks around the "Andromeda" ponds, and trails that connect to adjacent conservation land in Lincoln and Concord.

Near the pond hikers are asked to stay on marked trails and off the steep slopes, where bank erosion has been a problem in recent years. Park staff conduct year-round programs about Thoreau's life and his stay at Walden. A small bookstore is located near the restrooms adjacent to the parking lot. A beach wheelchair is available for universal access to the swimming area.

The reservation is located in Concord at the intersection of MA 126 (Walden St.) and MA 2. There is a parking fee from May through October (space for 350 cars). The lot may fill up on summer weekends due to the popularity of the pond's beach. Cars parked on the state highway will be towed. Dogs and mountain biking are not permitted. For more information, contact the park supervisor (978-369-3254).

Great Meadows National Wildlife Refuge (USFWS)

Established to protect the habitat of migrating birds, this 3600-acre refuge is located 20 mi. west of Boston and encompasses 12 mi. of the Concord and Sudbury Rivers. This freshwater marsh area is divided into two large units (Concord and Sudbury) which provide habitat for a great diversity of migrating and nesting birds, including waterfowl, shorebirds, and songbirds. More than 220 species of birds have been observed here; the Concord unit is famous for being one of the best birding areas in Massachusetts. Great Meadows offers opportunities for wildlife observation, hiking, photography, and nature study.

Trails in the Concord unit include the Dike Trail (2.7 mi.), a loop path that circles a pool in the marsh; the Black Duck Creek Trail (about 1 mi.); and the Timber Trail (0.5 mi.). In 1998 additional property was added and a new trail, the O'Rourke Trail, was established. This portion of the refuge is accessed through the adjacent town of Carlisle conservation lands of Foss Farm off Bedford Rd. (MA 225) or Greenough Land off Maple St.

To reach the Concord unit follow MA 62 (Bedford Rd.) 1.4 mi. northeast of Concord center toward Bedford. After about 1 mi. turn left onto Monsen Rd. (refuge sign), then continue to the refuge entrance at a dirt road on the left. Parking, photo blinds, and a seasonal comfort station are provided.

The Sudbury unit offers the Weir Trail, a 0.75-mi. trail that weaves around marshes, woods, fields, a red maple swamp, and brooks. The trail begins at the visitor center (universally accessible), where a three-story building houses exhibits, the refuge headquarters, and facilities for seasonal interpretive programming. The visitor center is open weekdays year-round; closed holidays and weekends except during May and October. Another trail is under construction with a trailhead and parking off the east side of the MA 4 bridge in Billerica. When completed it will follow the river to Two Brothers Rock.

To reach the Sudbury unit, follow Concord–Sudbury Rd. about 1.7 mi. north from Sudbury center and turn right onto Lincoln Rd. (high school on corner). Proceed about 1.4 mi., and turn left onto Weir Hill Rd. (refuge sign), and follow signs to the visitor center. The Wood Duck Hollow Trail (0.5 mi.) is also located in the Sudbury unit. Follow US 20 west through Wayland and turn left onto Pelham Island Rd. Continue to a parking lot on the right side of the road, across from Heard Pond.

For more information contact Great Meadows NWR, 73 Weir Hill Rd., Sudbury, MA 01776 (978-443-4661).

Middlesex Fells Reservation (DCR)

This reservation, lying in Stoneham, Medford, Winchester, Melrose, and Malden, is maintained by the DCR. It contains 2575 acres of rough woodland, ponds, brooks, reservoirs, and granite outcrops traversed by fire roads, bridle paths, and footpaths. Stone towers on Pine Hill and Bear Hill, as well as numerous outlooks, offer good views. Middlesex Fells (*fell* is the Saxon word for "rocky place") is a very popular destination. Mountain biking is permitted on all fire roads as well as on the designated bike loop path (marked with red-and-white bike path markers). This loop circles the three reservoirs in the western tract and consists of mostly fire roads with some single-track.

From I-93 take Exit 33 to MA 28, travel north a short distance to South Border Rd., take a right onto the road, and proceed to the Bellevue parking area in the south portion of the western tract. To reach the reservation by Mass Transit take the Orange Line to Wellington Station, then MBTA bus 100 to Roosevelt Circle Rotary. From there walk south to the rotary and follow South Border Rd. (on the right) less than 0.25 mi. to Bellevue Pond.

Cross Fells Trail (DCR)

The blue-blazed Cross Fells Trail is a good connecting trail between the eastern and western sections of the Middlesex Fells Reservation, because it touches every major trail in the reservation. This trail uses sections of the Rock Circuit Trail, the Mini Rock Circuit Trail, the Virginia Woods Trail, the Skyline Trail, and the Spot Pond Trail. The eastern end of this trail is 0.6 mi. north of the Oak Grove terminal of the MBTA Orange Line. To reach the trailhead in the eastern section of the fells, follow Washington St. north to Goodyear Ave., then follow Goodyear Ave. west (left) to the trailhead in Melrose, near the Melrose–Malden line.

The trail climbs west along easy wooded grades to a high rocky ridge. Here it turns left (south) and follows the Rock Circuit Trail (white-blazed) and the Mini Rock Circuit Trail (orange-blazed) to Black Rock. The Cross Fells Trail continues some distance with the Rock Circuit Trail (but not with the Mini Rock Circuit Trail) before exiting right (west) to cross Black Rock Path (a bridle trail) and Fellsway East (paved). It continues west, skirting the south side of the high reservoir and picking up the Mini Rock Circuit Trail. Shortly the two trails come to the Virginia Woods Trail (red-blazed). The Mini Rock Circuit Trail exits right (north) with the Virginia Woods Trail, while the Cross Fells Trail continues west.

The trail crosses several bridle paths before passing south of Shiner Pool. After this pool it rejoins the Rock Circuit Trail and crosses a swampy section. It then leaves this trail and crosses Woodland Rd. (paved) just north of the hockey arena. It next joins the Virginia Woods Trail, passing the southern end of Quarter Mile Pond and heading west over the hills. In 0.3 mi. the Virginia Woods Trail exits left (south) to Wright's Pond, while the Cross Fells Trail continues west to Fellsway West (MA 28). The trail follows Fellsway West and the Spot Pond Trail (yellow-blazed) a short distance to an underpass of I-93, then crosses Fellsway West.

The trail follows Brooks Rd. (dirt) to a junction with the Skyline Trail (white-blazed). Here the Cross Fells Trail turns left (south) to go partway up a short hill with the Skyline Trail. Soon the Cross Fells Trail turns right (west) to follow a ridge above Brooks Rd. The trail bends left (south) and picks up a series of bridle paths before turning left (east) into the woods to rejoin the Skyline Trail on the summit of Wenepoykin Hill.

The two trails then head south together to East Dam Rd. (dirt). Here the Cross Fells Trail continues south downhill to a brook and on to rejoin another section of the Skyline Trail. The two trails continue west until the Cross Fells Trail turns left (southwest) to pick up a group of bridle paths. After crossing S. Border Rd. (paved), the trail climbs a hill to the site of the former Lawrence Observation Tower. Descending the hill, the trail follows bridle paths to the reservation's Whitmore Brook entrance on Winthrop St. in Medford, across from Playstead Rd. (the end of the MBTA Sullivan Square–West Medford bus line).

Cross Fells Trail

Distance from Goodyear Ave. (Melrose)

   to Whitmore Brook entrance: 4.3 mi., 2 hr., 30 min.

Rock Circuit Trail (DCR)

This white-blazed trail affords the best views in the Middlesex Fells. Living up to its name, it is very rocky and offers rewarding but rugged hiking. A convenient approach to this trail is from Woodland St. in Medford, opposite the northern end of the hockey arena parking lot (south of New England Memorial Hospital in Stoneham). Follow a woods road east for a short distance to the crest of a hill to pick up the Rock Circuit Trail.

Turning right (south), the trail climbs a nearby ridge overlooking sections of Medford. Here it joins the Virginia Woods Trail (red-blazed) for a few feet, then goes south along the ridge before turning left (east) to another ridge. The trail goes north before turning sharp right (east) to drop into a valley, crossing a bridle path and a brook.

At the brook the trail turns left (north) and soon rejoins the Virginia Woods Trail, again for only a few feet. The Rock Circuit Trail crosses a bridle path and climbs southeast up a ridge. In 0.1 mi. the trail turns right (south) and drops into a valley. The trail then makes a long, gentle climb southeast to Boojum Rock, where it picks up the Mini Rock Circuit Trail (orange-blazed) for 0.1 mi. Leaving fine views of the Boston area, the trail drops sharply and heads east to cross a bridle path and then Fellsway East (paved). It rejoins the Mini Rock Circuit Trail and climbs Pinnacle Rock, from which there are fine views. At Pinnacle Rock both trails turn north, almost doubling back on themselves, and pass a television tower enclosure, where the Mini Rock Circuit Trail exits.

The Rock Circuit Trail then follows a rough ridge north to Black Rock. At Black Rock, this trail combines first with the Cross Fells Trail (blue-blazed) and then with the Mini Rock Circuit Trail to surmount a fine viewpoint. The three trails continue north a short distance before the Cross Fells Trail turns sharp right (east) downhill to exit the fells. The two Rock Circuit Trails continue north along the top of the ridge to White Rock and Melrose Rock with many fine views.

At Melrose Rock the two trails separate, with the Rock Circuit Trail turning left (west) through the woods to recross Fellsway East (paved) and to skirt the eastern end of the high reservoir. The trail crosses Wyoming Path to enter some young tree growth and soon rejoins the Virginia Woods Trail and then the Mini Rock Circuit Trail. It ascends a ridge behind (east of) New England Memorial Hospital, from which there is a fine view north. The Virginia Woods Trail separates here, with the two Rock Circuit Trails turning left from the ridge. Soon the Mini Rock Circuit Trail exits left (south), and the Rock Circuit Trail goes right (west) through a fine pine grove to join the yellow-blazed Spot Pond Trail for 0.2 mi. while passing south of New England Memorial Hospital.

After leaving the Spot Pond Trail and crossing several bridle paths, the Rock Circuit Trail passes the northwest shore of Shiner Pool and soon joins the Cross Fells Trail to cross a swampy area. It then leaves the Cross Fells Trail, turning left (south) along a ridge adjacent to Woodland Rd. to complete the circuit.

Rock Circuit Trail

Distance from trailhead

   to trailhead (circuit): 4 mi., 3 hr., 30 min.

Mini Rock Circuit Trail (DCR)

The Mini Rock Circuit Trail is a shorter and smoother variation of the Rock Circuit Trail. This orange-blazed trail takes in the best high points of the Rock Circuit Trail and some fine sections of other trails but avoids many rough sections. On a clear day this trail affords spectacular views. The Mini Rock Circuit Trail is accessible from any of the other trails in the eastern section of the fells or from either of its two crossings of Fellsway East. For this approach follow the Cross Fells Trail (blue-blazed) from its eastern end on Goodyear Ave. in Melrose. The Mini Rock Circuit Trail turns right (north) from the Cross Fells Trail 0.1 mi. from Goodyear Ave.

    The Mini Rock Circuit Trail goes along a ridge with the Rock Circuit Trail (white-blazed) over White Rock and Melrose Rock. The trails then turn left (west) and separate, with the Mini Rock Circuit Trail following a bridle path to Fellsway East (paved). After crossing Fellsway East, the trail winds gently west and ascends to a high rock behind (east of) New England Memorial Hospital, where it joins the Rock Circuit Trail and the Virginia Woods Trail (red-blazed). The latter separates almost immediately at a fine viewpoint. The other two trails descend and separate shortly, with the Mini Rock Circuit Trail going left (south) through the woods to rejoin another section of the Virginia Woods Trail.

    These two trails soon come to Bent Rd. (dirt), which they follow right (west) until the fence on the left (south) turns left around the high reservoir. The trails also turn left, and in 0.1 mi. they leave the fence, heading right (southwest) to meet the Cross Fells Trail. Here the Mini Rock Circuit Trail leaves the Virginia Woods Trail and turns left (southeast) to join the Cross Fells Trail. The two trails work back to the high reservoir fence and continue down a ridge before separating. The Mini Rock Circuit Trail continues southeast a short distance along a fire road before turning right (southwest) to zigzag up a hill to rejoin the Rock Circuit Trail on Boojum Rock.

    The Mini Rock Circuit Trail turns left (southeast), and the two trails soon reach an excellent viewpoint of Boston, its harbor, and the surrounding land. At the viewpoint the trails separate, and both head for Pinnacle Rock. The

Mini Rock Circuit Trail bears left (northeast), crossing two bridle paths and Fellsway East (paved). The two trails remerge for a short distance at Pinnacle Rock and then almost double back. They go north, separating after passing a television tower enclosure. The Mini Rock Circuit Trail follows bridle paths north to Black Rock, where it joins the Rock Circuit Trail and the Cross Fells Trail at another fine viewing location. The three trails continue north a short distance to complete the loop for the Mini Rock Circuit Trail.

Mini Rock Circuit Trail

Distance from trailhead

   to trailhead (circuit): 2.8 mi., 2 hr.

Skyline Trail (DCR)

This trail is located in the western section of the Fells. Marked with white blazes, it circles the Winchester Reservoirs as it travels through Medford, Stoneham, and Winchester. A popular starting point is Bellevue Pond, off S. Border Rd. in Medford, a short distance west of I-93 (Exit 33) and MA 28. Quarry Rd. (dirt) goes east (right) of Bellevue Pond. The Skyline Trail follows Quarry Rd. to the first blaze near the northern end of Bellevue Pond.

The trail turns right up Pine Hill, at the top of which is Wright's Tower with commanding views of Boston, its harbor, and the Blue Hills. The trail continues north along a rocky ridge before turning west to drop into a valley. It climbs the ridge to the west and on top of the second ridge turns north for 0.3 mi., dipping once to cross a notch with a spur of Quarry Rd. (bridle path). At the northern end of the ridge is a good view north over I-93.

The trail descends northwest, passing the northern end of the next ridge before turning more west and dropping into a valley. It continues west, descending a hill. Near the summit the trail turns right (north) and joins the Cross Fells Trail (blue-blazed) for a short distance to the summit. The Skyline Trail follows high land north over several hills, including Silver Mine Hill. Soon after Silver Mine Hill, the Skyline Trail rejoins the Cross Fells Trail for a short distance as it descends to Brooks Rd. (dirt). The Skyline Trail continues north over Gerry Hill and on to Chandler Rd. (dirt) along the Winchester Reservoir fence, which detours the Skyline Trail with the Reservoir Trail (orange-blazed) to the right (east) a short distance and then left (north).

Very shortly the Reservoir Trail exits left (northwest), while the Skyline Trail goes uphill to the Sheepfold picnic area. The trail passes the eastern end of the parking lot, skirts the east side of the picnic area, then crosses a former soapbox derby track on the way north to Winthrop Hill, where there is a fine view of the Winchester North Reservoir. From here it continues along a ridge toward Bear Hill. About 0.2 mi. north of Winthrop Hill the Skyline Trail turns sharp left (west) downhill at a trail junction. (*Note: Straight ahead—north— uphill is the short Bear Hill Connector Trail, which connects with the Spot Pond Trail at the Bear Hill observation tower.*)

The Skyline Trail crosses Dike Rd. (dirt), where it joins the Reservoir Trail to cross a brook and continue through a former meadow and a pine grove to another dirt road. Here the Reservoir Trail exits left (southwest) on the dirt road, while the Skyline Trail continues straight over Money Hill. On the west slope of Money Hill the two trails remerge and descend, crossing N. Border Rd. (dirt) into a ravine north of the Winchester North Reservoir dam.

The trails cross a brook (leakage from the reservoir), then soon bend left (south) a short distance before zigzagging up the west slope of the ravine to pass north of the old firehouse. They continue to paved Alben St., on to Reservoir St., and finally on to Hillcrest Pkwy., where there is parking and access to the trail. Both trails very shortly leave the paved roads and go south via the West Dam Path. After crossing a dirt service road, they soon separate. The Reservoir Trail exits right, while the Skyline Trail continues straight over a couple of minor hills. The Skyline Trail crosses the Reservoir Trail and soon climbs steeply up Nanapashemet Hill, where there are limited views.

The Skyline Trail continues south over numerous hills to merge with the Reservoir Trail at the Winchester South Reservoir standpipe. The two trails continue south, then east around waterland property at the west reservoir dam. The trails almost reach S. Border Rd. before passing over a hill to the Middle Rd. Path. A dirt road on the right leads shortly to a parking area off S. Border Rd. and an access to the two trails. The trails soon bend left (north) to pick up the East Dam Path. They soon separate, with the Reservoir Trail going straight (north) and the Skyline Trail turning right uphill. At the top of the hill the trail bends right along a ridge before turning left to cross Middle Rd. (dirt) and soon joins the Cross Fells Trail for a short distance. The Skyline Trail turns right to head for Panther Cave, passing almost directly over the cave before dropping to cross the Red Cross Path and Straight Gully Brook. It then climbs Little Pine Hill on its way to Bellevue Pond, where it completes its circuit.

Skyline Trail

Distance from Bellevue Pond

  to Bellevue Pond (circuit): 6.8 mi., 5 hr.

Reservoir Trail (DCR)

This orange-blazed trail is a very pleasant circuit around the three Winchester reservoirs. Individuals using the trail should be aware that the adjacent water-lands are not for general public access and that the nearby No Trespassing signs should be observed. This trail avoids major hills and rocky terrain. The trail was designed to be a possible ski touring trail when snow is sufficient. It has many fine vistas.

The Reservoir Trail can be joined from several locations. It will be described here starting from the Sheepfold and going counterclockwise. The trail follows close to the fence on the southern and western boundaries of the Sheepfold picnic area. It leaves the fence, crosses the former soapbox derby track, and enters the woods on an old bridle path. Soon it leaves the path and winds under Winthrop Hill along gentle slopes to keep between the hill and waterlands property.

North of the municipal waterlands property the trail drops down to Dike Rd. (dirt). It follows this road north to meet the Skyline Trail (white blazes) coming down from the side of Bear Hill. Here the Reservoir Trail turns left (west) with the Skyline Trail, goes to Dike Brook, then goes straight ahead through a former meadow and a pine grove to a dirt road. The Skyline Trail goes over Money Hill, while the Reservoir Trail leaves left (southwest) down the road and then climbs to skirt Money Hill to rejoin the Skyline Trail. The two trails descend together to cross N. Border Rd. (dirt) and enter a ravine north of the North Dam.

The trails cross a brook formed by leakage from the reservoir. Shortly the trails bend left (south) a short distance before zigzagging up the west slope of the ravine to pass north of the old firehouse (which has water pumps in the basement) out onto Alben St. (paved) to Reservoir St./Hillcrest Pkwy. There is parking and access here for the two trails. The two trails very shortly leave the paved roads and go south via the West Dam Path. They cross a dirt service road and soon separate. The Skyline Trail goes ahead (south) while the Reservoir Trail goes right (southwest) to skirt a couple of marshes, crosses a brook, and then crosses the Skyline Trail before joining a dirt road southeasterly toward the Middle and South Reservoirs.

At the end of the road, the trail enters a bluff with fine views of the Middle and South Reservoirs and the causeway between them. The trail bends back and drops into a ravine. It crosses a brook and goes over one small hill and then over the shoulder of another hill to a dirt road. From here the trail goes south for nearly a mile, crossing Molly Spring Rd. (dirt), two brooks, and several stone walls and eventually rejoining the Skyline Trail adjacent to the South Reservoir standpipe. The two trails go south, then east around the waterlands property near the reservoir's West Dam. The trails almost reach S. Border Rd. before going over a hill to the Middle Rd. Path. (The dirt road to the right leads shortly to parking off S. Border Rd.—an access spot for the two trails.) The two trails go straight, then bend left (north) to pick up the East Dam Path, where they separate. The Skyline Trail turns right (east) up a hill, while the Reservoir Trail goes ahead (north).

As the Reservoir Trail approaches the South Reservoir it leaves the road and heads northeast, not far from East Dam Rd. (dirt). Adjacent to the small East Dam the trail descends into a ravine, then ascends it and continues parallel to the patrol road going north. After going over Silver Mine Hill, the trail passes close to the sealed shaft of a silver mine. (Note the concrete posts of a former fence around the mine shaft.) The trail continues north with more views of the reservoirs, not far from the patrol road, until it reaches Chandler Rd. (dirt) with a fence on its north side. The trail goes right (east) along Chandler Rd., joins the Skyline Trail, and heads for the Sheepfold to complete its circuit.

Reservoir Trail

Distance from Sheepfold

  to Sheepfold (circuit): 5.5 mi., 3 hr.

Elm Bank Reservation (DCR)

A recent acquisition, this 182-acre property in Wellesley is a conglomerate of historic sites, period landscaping, and woods and fields surrounded on three sides by the Charles River. Listed on the National Register of Historic Places, this reservation is especially attractive for family outings. Terrain and facilities are friendly to the needs of children, whether infants in baby carriages or teenagers.

To reach Elm Bank Reservation from Boston, take MA 9 west to MA 16 (Washington St.). Travel south along MA 16 through Wellesley and past Wellesley College. About 1 mi. beyond the college turn left onto the entrance road, which crosses the Charles River and then forks roughly north and south. Both roads take circuitous routes to the center of the reservation, where the parking area, ranger headquarters, and Massachusetts Horticultural Society are located. A hiking trail explores the river neck, that makes up much of the north and central parts of the reservation, and can be accessed by following the roads either north or west from the parking area. A canoe access is located northwest of the reservation entrance.

Breakheart Reservation (DCR)

The DCR's Breakheart Reservation, in Saugus and Wakefield, covers 640 acres of oak-hemlock-pine forest, with numerous hills, jagged rocky outcrops, two freshwater lakes, and a meandering stretch of the Saugus River. Several rocky hills provide views south toward Boston and north to NH. The swimming area on Pearce Lake (restrooms and first-aid station) is popular in summer, and fishing and birding are popular on both Silver and Pearce Lakes. A network of blacktop roads serves all areas of the reservation, although only Pine Tops Rd. is open to vehicular traffic.

Pine Tops Rd. is a one-way counterclockwise loop through the center of the reservation. It heads north from the reservation headquarters on Forest St. to the swimming area Pearce Lake, where swimming is allowed only when lifeguards are on duty. The road then turns south roughly parallels the shores of Pearce and Silver Lakes before returning to the reservation headquarters.

The other paved roads are Elm Rd. and Hemlock Rd., which connect to form another loop from Pine Tops Rd. near the Pearce Lake swimming area. This loop heads around the west side of the lakes and back to Pine Tops Rd., about 200 yd. before the exit at the headquarters. Elm Rd. and Hemlock Rd. meet at the Wakefield Vocational High School gate, where parking is allowed. Vehicular access to the reservation is prohibited here. Finally, unpaved Flume Rd. runs between Pearce and Silver Lakes, connecting Hemlock Rd. to Pine Tops Rd. at fire gate 11 in the middle of the reservation.

In addition to the roads, an extensive series of hiking trails crisscrosses the reservation. The Fox Run, Breakheart, Saugus, and Lodge Trails are all marked with yellow blazes as well as wooden trailhead posts.

Take the Lynn Fells Pkwy. exit off US 1, then continue southwest 0.4 mi. to Forest St. on the right. Follow Forest St. to the parking area at the reservation headquarters. Trail information is available at the headquarters building.

Fox Hill Trail (DCR)

This trail begins about 75 yd. north of the front gate and entrance onto Pine Tops Rd., after a wooden fence on the left. A gate and a wooden post mark the trailhead. It climbs steeply for a short distance and bears right (north) at a junction with the Breakheart Trail. The trail continues between the loop of Pine Tops Rd., then turns sharp left (southwest) at the junction with the Saugus River Trail. In about 100 yd. the path bends right toward an exposed rock ledge. It crosses a large rocky plateau overlooking Pearce Lake, and then descends steeply to the Pearce Lake swimming area at fire gate 9.

Fox Hill Trail

Distance from gate

   to Pearce Lake swimming area: 1.0 mi., 30 min.

Saugus River Trail (DCR)

This trail begins at the first gate on the right after entering the reservation on Pine Tops Rd. It heads east toward the river and connects with a spur on the right, which leads to the somewhat buried remains of a stone dam built in the early 1800s. (*Note: If you take the spur, stay to the right after a large opening before a small picnic area; otherwise you will just get to a small stream.*) The main trail stays to the left and follows the river, eventually turning west and crossing Pine Tops Rd. The trail reenters the woods about 50 yd. to the right on Pine Tops Rd. Shortly after this point the trail bears left at a fork, continues straight, and intersects with the Fox Hill Trail.

Saugus River Trail

Distance from gate

   to Fox Hill Trail: 0.8 mi., 25 min.

Lodge Trail (DCR)

The Lodge Trail is well marked by a wooden trailhead marker. It exits left from the Saugus River Trail a short distance from the trailhead and heads north, passing a rhododendron grove and then the scant remains of an 1800s hunting lodge built by the founder of the reservation. The trail continues on to Pine Tops Rd. at fire gate 4, 0.25 mi. from the reservation headquarters building.

Lodge Trail

Distance from Saugus River Trail

   to Pine Tops Rd.: 0.3 mi., 10 min.

Pearce Lake Trail (DCR)

This trail starts at the swimming area and circles Pearce Lake, hugging the shoreline, which varies from sandy beach to rocky outcroppings to dense hemlock groves. It is a well-traveled path marked with blue blazes, and passes the Flume Trail, which leads to the Silver Lake Trail. The trail heads south, leaving Pine Tops Rd. south of fire gate 9 and intersecting a dirt road on the left at a point nearly opposite Eagle Rock on the far shore.

   The path then stays close to the lake, coming close to Hemlock Rd. as the path swings around the south end of the lake. Heading north, the trail passes the Fern Trail on the left (north) and quickly comes to a jeep road and the Eagle Rock Trail, both leaving left. The Eagle Rock Trail leads to Eagle Rock which overlooks the lake, then rejoins the Pearce Lake Trail near the north bay. The Pearce Lake Trail continues to follow the shore, meeting the Eagle Rock Trail a short distance before reaching Elm Rd. Turn right (east) and continue the short way to the beach.

Pearce Lake Trail

Distance from Pearce Lake beach

   to Pearce Lake beach via Elm Rd. (circuit): 1.3 mi., 45 min.

Silver Lake Trail (DCR)

The Silver Lake Trail can be accessed from Flume Rd. south of fire gate 11 or from the dirt road that leaves Hemlock Rd. north of fire gate 18. From Flume Rd. the trail heads east to where the path splits and the loop begins. Proceeding clockwise (east), the path travels southeast, roughly follows the shore, and passes through the narrow area between the lake and Pine Tops Rd. near fire gate 12. The trail then heads west along the shore before bending south to trace the contour of the southern cove.

   Turning north, the path passes the dirt road on the left that leads to Hemlock Rd. Continuing north, the trail hugs the lake and closes the loop just east of Flume Rd. To return to the beginning, follow the shore of Silver Lake and continue past the Flume Trail, a short spur that connects the Silver Lake Trail to the Pearce Lake Trail.

Silver Lake Trail

Distance from Flume Rd.

> *to* Flume Rd. (circuit): 0.9 mi., 30 min.

Ridge Trail (DCR)

This trail, clearly marked with white blazes, begins on Pine Tops Rd. at fire gate 14 near the headquarters building. It initially heads southwest, then jogs left and right before turning sharp right (northwest). The trail crosses both parts of the Ash Path loop, a wide dirt road, and follows a series of ridges and valleys roughly parallel to Hemlock Rd. As the trail approaches a run of power lines, it passes a short spur trail on the left (west) that leads to the top of Castle Rock (good views). The Ridge Trail continues north and reaches the Spruce Path. Turn right (east) to reach Hemlock Rd. at fire gate 17.

Ridge Trail

Distance from trailhead

> *to* Hemlock Rd.: 1.7 mi., 50 min..

Ash Path (DCR)

This cart path starts on Hemlock Rd. at fire gate 13, approx. 200 yd. before its intersection with Pine Tops Rd. near the headquarters building. It loops around Ash Hill and ends on Hemlock Rd. at fire gate 18 a short distance west of the starting point.

Ash Path

Distance from Hemlock Rd.

> *to* Hemlock Rd. (circuit): 1 mi., 30 min.

Lynn Woods (Town of Lynn)

Located northwest of Lynn, this 2200-acre woodland reservation comprises the second largest municipal forest park in the United States. The park is bisected by Walden Pond (not to be confused with Thoreau's Walden Pond in

Concord). About one-quarter of the park (the wilder part) lies north of the pond, while the remainder lies south. The reservation is open to mountain biking, horseback riding, and hiking. Bikes are permitted only on official, blazed trails, and are not permitted on any trail marked Foot Traffic Only. Horses are allowed on the orange-blazed fire roads. Camping, fishing, ATVs, and dirt bikes are not permitted within the reservation. Picnicking is permitted, but grills, open fires, and stoves are *not* allowed due to the fire hazard in the woods. The Stone Tower atop Burrill Hill is presently closed for restoration.

The main entrance is located at the south end of the reservation just west of Breed's Pond; take Walnut St. to Pennybrook Rd. and turn north. The east entrance is located just southeast of the eastern tip of Walden Pond; follow MA 129 (Lynnfield St.) to Great Woods Rd.

The trail network is based on a web of fire roads that spread throughout the woods. These blazed roads are linked by trails at frequent intervals, providing the opportunity to create many different routes through the reservation. The official trail map contains a grid that corresponds to trail intersections, which aids in navigating through the forest. This map is especially useful for first-time visitors and is available at the Lynn town hall. Sanctioned trails are marked with paint blazes. Unblazed paths are either closed or are bootleg trails that should not be used.

Burrill Hill Rd.

This fire road exits Great Woods Rd. 0.3 mi. northwest of the east entrance. It turns southwest and strenuously climbs Burrill Hill. After cruising along the crest of the hill, the road meets Dungeon Rd. at 1.1 mi.

Mt. Gilead Trail

This trail begins with Dungeon Rd. off Great Woods Rd., 0.8 mi. northwest of the east entrance. Veering away from Dungeon Rd., the trail climbs the hill along a wide gully near the top and reaches the stone observation tower at 0.25 mi. (closed for renovations). Past the tower, it continues along the western ridge of Mt. Gilead to rejoin Dungeon Rd. at 0.4 mi.

Dungeon Rd.

This road begins off Great Woods Rd. 0.8 mi. northwest of the east entrance. It climbs Mt. Gilead, slabbing the north face to meet the Mt. Gilead Trail on the western ridge at 0.25 mi. It then descends the ridge, sweeping around the slopes to avoid the steepest places, and meets Pennybrook Rd. at 0.4 mi. Heading southeast, the trail regains the high ground and cruises over the ridges to meet Burrill Hill Rd. at 1.0 mi. The trail passes Dungeon Rock on the right before steeply descending to Breed's Pond. There it turns west and ends at Pennybrook Rd. at 1.9 mi.

Dungeon Rock

It is thought that pirates once came to hide their stolen treasures in Lynn Woods. One possible hiding spot was a cave on a hill above Breed's Pond. In the mid–17th century an earthquake closed the cave. A later treasure hunter wasted much time and effort reopening it in search of easy wealth. Of course there was no treasure, but today there is a sizable cave that descends into the rock and ends in a very dark rock chamber. The cave is open seasonally when a ranger is present.

Great Woods Rd.

This city road exits west from MA 129 (Lynnfield St.) about 3 mi. east of its junction with US 1. It enters the reservation through a gate and becomes a reservation road with the same name. Immediately past this gate, a paved road exits sharp left uphill to the Happy Valley Golf Club. Great Woods Rd. continues straight ahead to a parking lot with an athletic field on the right. This road (closed to automobiles) continues through a stone gateway at the far left corner of the parking lot. It runs parallel to the south shore of Walden Pond, but remains some distance away. Cooke Rd. enters left, and soon the Mt. Gilead Loop and Dungeon Rock Rd. enter left as well. Farther along is a picnic area on the right. Great Woods Rd. continues along the south and east shores of Walden Pond, parallels and then crosses Pennybrook, and ends at Pennybrook Rd.

SUGGESTED HIKES

Easy Hikes
Blue Hills Reservation
Houghtons Pond Yellow Loop [lp: 1.0 mi., 0:25]. This short path is a favorite among families with small children. The route circles the pond, passing a beach (swimming in summer) and a swamp along the way.

Whitney & Thayer Woods Reservation
Howe's Rd., Boulder Lane [rt: 2.2 mi., 0:45]. These carriage roads on a former estate lead to Bigelow's Boulder and back again.

Rocky Woods Reservation
Chickering Pond Trail [lp: 0.5 mi., 0:25]. This short path travels around Chickering Pond.

Moderate Hikes
Blue Hills Reservation
Great Blue Hill Green Loop [lp: 2.8 mi., 1:20]. This hike explores the reservation's Great Blue Hill area, starting and ending near the Trailside Museum.

Cutler Park
Cutler Park Loop [lp: 4.0 mi., 2:00]. This trail meanders through marshes and past a hammock of land called Powell's Island.

Rocky Narrows Reservation
Red Trail [lp: 2.7 mi., 1:25]. Sections of this trail travel along the rugged shoreline of the Charles River, passing viewpoints from ledges above the water.

Strenuous Hikes
Blue Hills Reservation
Skyline Trail [ow: 7.7 mi., 4:10]. This hike runs across the reservation from Blue Hill Ave. to Shea Rink on Willard Ave. Along the way the trail climbs numerous hills with views of Boston and the Bay.

Middlesex Fells Reservation

Cross Fells Trail [rt: 8.6 mi., 5:00]. This trail connects the east and west portions of the reservation, and intersects many other trails along the way.

Rock Circuit Trail [rt: 4.0 mi, 3:30]. This rugged and rocky trail offers the best views on the reservation, including those from White Rock and Melrose Rock.

Part VI

Southeastern Massachusetts and the Islands

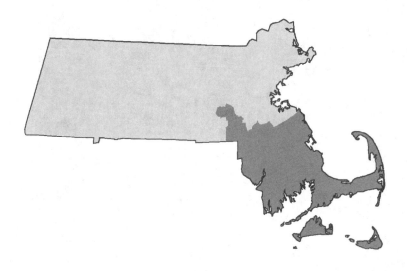

LIST OF TRAILS

This chapter includes areas south and southeast of the Boston metropolitan area. It extends from the Warner Trail corridor in the west to Cape Cod and the islands in the east. The landscape is composed of low rolling hills and level plains of seacoast sands and clays. There are no significant mountains, although a few scattered ridges and hills stand out against the level terrain. Along the coast are pine-oak woodlands, sand dunes, freshwater ponds, and many miles of sandy shoreline, including Cape Cod National Seashore.

The coastal areas seem to have more ticks than farther inland, and hikers in these areas should be particularly alert to the dangers of tick-borne illnesses such as Lyme disease (see Trip Planning and Safety in the front of this book). Mosquitoes and a number of biting flies also frequent this area; bring the bug dope. Poison ivy is abundant in many areas, and there is some poison sumac in the swamps.

Warner Trail (AMC)

The Warner Trail offers delightful and varied outdoor experiences as it stretches more than 30 mi. from Sharon MA, to Diamond Hill State Park in Cumberland RI. The possibility of establishing a woodland trail connecting the south fringe of the Boston area with the trail system in Rhode Island was first envisioned by AMC members Charles H. Warner and John Hudson prior to World War II. With the energetic assistance of Ron Gower and a number of other AMC members, the trail was slowly put together, one section at a time, starting at the AMC Ponkapoag Camp. By 1947 it extended south to High Rock in Gilbert Hills State Forest. By the early 1950s the trail had reached Diamond Hill RI, but development soon resulted in the loss of the stretch from Ponkapoag Camp to the Canton Junction Rail Station. This spurred Mead Bradner, another AMC member, to form the Friends of the Warner Trail in 1994 to protect the trail.

The basic philosophy in the development of the trail was to maximize the challenges while at the same time providing the greatest amount of enjoyment. As a result, the trail wanders considerably from elevated viewpoints to swamp crossings, brooks, and reservoirs. It connects a number of state and town forests, Audubon Society land, conservation areas, and other public land.

The trail is maintained by the Friends of the Warner Trail and AMC volunteers from the Boston, Narragansett, and Southeast Massachusetts Chapters. These individuals take care of blowdowns, marking, and relocations. If you would like to get involved in the stewardship of this trail, contact the Friends of the Warner Trail, P.O. Box 85, Mansfield, MA 02048. Maps and a guidebook are available by writing to this address. A small donation is appreciated with each request. Trail information can be obtained from the Moose Hill Audubon Sanctuary (781-784-5691) and the offices for the Gilbert Hills State Forest (508-543-5850)

This trail can be enjoyed as a series of day hikes, or it can be used for snowshoeing or to access paths to several lunch spots. Users are asked to respect the property of private landowners who have generously granted permission for the trail to cross their land.

The Warner Trail links many sections of public land with paths through private land. Public areas have varying rules and regulations regarding motorized and nonmotorized use of their properties, but only hiking is allowed on the Warner Trail when it passes through private property. No motorized vehicles or mountain bikes are allowed on these sections.

The Warner Trail is blazed with an array of markers, including old-style 2-in. metal disks that have probably rusted, newer stainless-steel 2-in. disks, and white metal 2-in. disks. White rectangular paint blazes are occasionally used, as are white plastic triangles with a dark green hiker in the center and Warner Trail on the bottom. A change in direction is shown by either stacked blazes with the top blaze offset in the direction of the turn, or, by having the top of the plastic triangle pointing in the direction of the turn.

Section 1. Sharon (Dedham St.) to Moose Hill Audubon Sanctuary Headquarters (Sharon) (3.8 mi.)

To reach the northern end of the Warner Trail, leave US 1 south of Boston near the Norwood Memorial Airport or take I-95 (Exit 11) to Neponset St. Follow Neponset St. 1.2 mi. east into Canton, turn right onto Walpole St., and continue for 1.5 mi. Turn left onto Dedham St. and proceed uphill 0.2 mi. to a pull-off on the left. The trail begins at the woods across from the pull-off.

The first 0.5 mi. of trail weaves through driveways and woods. It crosses a bog bridge and passes through a wet area before crossing Beaver Brook on a wooden bridge at 0.3 mi. The trail then reaches a woods road junction at 0.5 mi. and turns left (southwest). The trail continues roughly southwest through a pine grove and reaches a power line (0.9 mi.). The trail turns right (north) and follows the power line on the service road to Mt. Fern St. Turning left (southwest) onto Mt. Fern St. (gravel changing to pavement), reach Bullard St. (1.1 mi.) and turn right, following Bullard St. (watch for potential relocation here) the short way to Norwood St. (MA 27) at 1.3 mi.

The trail turns right onto Norwood St., then quickly enters the woods and follows a bridle trail through tall red pines to reach a power line at 1.7 mi. It turns right (west) and follows beneath the power lines a short distance, then turns left onto Everett St. (gravel). Following Everett St. onto Audubon land, the road tapers to a cart path, passes a large rock outcrop (left), and turns right onto a woods road just past a vernal pool (right). The path heads uphill then over level ground, turns left before a boardwalk, and reaches Moose Hill Pkwy. (paved) at 2.9 mi. Within Moose Hill Sanctuary the Warner Trail is also marked with the letter A.

After turning right onto Moose Hill Pkwy., the path quickly turns left (south), leaving the road and entering the woods. The trail wanders through the sanctuary, passing close to Moose Hill St. and through an old parking lot to Moose Hill St. at 3.7 mi. Turn right onto Moose Hill St. and continue the short distance to the sanctuary headquarters.

Warner Trail: Sharon (Dedham St.) to Moose Hill Audubon Sanctuary Headquarters (Sharon)

Distances from Dedham St.

   to power line: 0.9 mi., 25 min.

   to Norwood St.: 1.3 mi., 35 min.

   to Moose Hill Pkwy.: 2.9 mi., 1 hr., 25 min.

   to Moose Hill Audubon Sanctuary Headquarters: 3.8 mi., 1 hr., 45 min.

Section 2. Sharon (Moose Hill Audubon Sanctuary) to Foxboro (US 1) (9.5 mi.)

The trail (also marked with the letter A within the sanctuary) turns left through the parking lot gate and jogs slightly to the right to reach a gravel road passing between two stone posts. In about 50 yd. it turns right onto the Summit Trail, which it follows for 0.3 mi. to the fire tower atop Moose Hill. Proceeding left (southwest) from the fire tower, the trail comes out on a rocky knoll and drops down fairly steeply through the woods to a junction with a woods road. It turns right, then heads east on the Old Pasture Trail.

The trail now passes through an area with many side trails; watch for the Warner Trail blazes. Climb the northern slope of Bluff Head to the top, where there is a view to the south (1.5 mi.). The trail then heads southwest, slabbing down several rocky ledges, making one brief sharp climb past the chimney on Allen's Ledge, and reaching a woods road near the bottom of the slope. Turn left to head downhill to Walpole St. at 2.1 mi.

The trail goes left down Walpole St. for a few yards, then crosses the road and enters the woods, and climbs to the top of Pierce Hill (350 ft.) at 2.3 mi., where there are good views south and west. It then descends steeply at times to Old Post Rd. (once a main road, now a woods road), which it follows south for 0.3 mi. The path now follows a driveway for 200 yd. to Pine St. It turns left onto Pine St., continues to S. Walpole St., turns right (southwest) and follows S. Walpole St., as it goes over the northbound and under the southbound lanes of I-95. Beyond the interstate it passes a cranberry bog and turns left at telephone pole 46. The trail now follows Dudley Hill Rd., a thin path that is often overgrown and frequently hard to follow. *Note: In this section the trail is intentionally left overgrown and poorly defined to discourage misuse of the private property.*

Take care to go around the end of a blocking fence without damaging the bushes (intended to discourage all but pedestrians). Keep right of the blocking fence, passing along the edge of a backyard (white house). At the back corner of the yard the path begins again, bending right at a fork onto a smaller path through wetlands, and reaches a berm. The trail passes over the berm and crosses the swamp on bog bridging.

The trail now passes close to several houses as it comes to Beach St. Watch closely for blazes and take care to follow the trail. Turn right onto Beach St., continue for 50 yd., then turn left (south) onto a right-of-way just beyond a large pin oak (lower branches droop downward) and a wooden fence. The trail continues through a row of large rocks then turns left onto an old gravel road used by ORVs, which it follows a short distance to Edwards St. (parking) at 3.9 mi. *Note: The gravel road section may be relocated in the future.*

The trail turns right onto Edwards St., follows it for 0.6 mi., and turns left at telephone pole 27 to travel up an overgrown bank and through the woods to Camp Rd. (gravel). For the next 0.6 mi. take the following roads to Foxboro Conservation Property: McCasland Way (Whispering Pines), McKenzie Lane, and Munroe St. At the end of the cul-de-sac the trail reenters the woods onto Foxboro Conservation Commission land at 5.2 mi.

Heading to the south through open woods, the trail passes Neponset Reservoir on the left, then the dam at the reservoir outlet. It heads southwest to the railroad tracks, then runs parallel to the tracks over several bog bridges to Chestnut St. (parking). From Chestnut St. the trail turns right onto North St., then left onto Main St. (MA 140) and encounters a traffic light (look for a Dairy Queen and doughnut shop). Cross the road, turn left (south), and proceed the short distance to the Foxboro Conservation parking lot (right) at 6.7 mi.

From the back of the parking lot, the trail follows a lane to the west, then turns right at a trail junction. Continue through the woods toward Lakeview Rd. Near the road the path swings left and descends toward a brook, then follows the brook out to Lakeview Rd. The trail turns left and crosses the dam for Lakeview Lake. It then turns right, following the conservation lane along the side of the lake (lake on the right) and continues west until it comes to Upper Dam Pond, where it crosses the dam and swings southeast around the pond to Messenger Rd. (gravel).

The trail turns right (southwest) onto the road and begins a long climb toward High Rock in Gilbert Hills State Forest. As the road nears the top, the trail forks right (there is an emergency bad-weather shelter here) onto an old woods road and climbs almost to a fenced-in old radar test station. Here the trail turns left at the foot of a large boulder (High Rock) at 9.1 mi. and follows a short path over the rise to a gravel clearing at the foot of a large microwave relay tower and base building. A paved road, maintained by AT&T, leads to US 1, 0.5 mi. south of its intersection with MA 140.

Warner Trail: Sharon (Moose Hill Audubon Sanctuary) to Foxboro (US 1)

Distances from Moose Hill St. (Moose Hill Audubon Sanctuary)

to Bluff Head summit: 1.5 mi., 35 min.

to Pierce Hill summit: 2.3 mi., 1 hr.

to Edwards Rd.: 3.9 mi., 1 hr., 30 min.

to Foxboro Conservation Property: 5.2 mi., 1 hr., 55 min.

to Foxboro Conservation parking lot: 6.7 mi., 2 hr., 30 min.

to High Rock: 9.1 mi., 3 hr., 10 min.

to junction of US 1 and MA 140: 9.5 mi., 3 hr., 20 min.

Section 3. Foxboro (US 1) to Wrentham (Wampum Corner) (9.9 mi.)

To reach the northeast end of this section from the US 1 and MA 140 junction, follow US 1 south for 0.5 mi. to High Rock Rd., then follow High Rock Rd. to the gravel parking area of F. Gilbert Hills State Forest. Park only on the gravel area; do not park on the AT&T paved parking area, and do not block the fire lane gate.

The trail leaves the eastern end of the parking area near the barrier gate. At 80 yd. it turns left and follows a winding path, dropping down and passing under an overhanging cliff (Goat Rock—look for the tree growing out of the rock). The path swings right over a number of large rocks and an underground stream to reach a trail junction. Proceed up a series of rock steps built by the CCC to the junction with the Acorn Trail (sign for Warner Trail). The Acorn Trail is a rugged feeder path leading 2.2 mi. to the state forest headquarters on Mill St. in Foxboro.

From here the trail goes south a short distance to the top of a large rock slab (excellent view west). The trail descends southwest to the base of the slab, and after a short distance turns right (north-northwest) on a woods road and follows it 0.4 mi. Pass two towers before turning left onto a path that leads to US 1 at 1.3 mi. The trail crosses US 1 and proceeds on Myrtle St. in Wrentham. It follows Myrtle St. a few yards, then turns left just before a conservation area parking lot.

Following a path that parallels US 1 for a short distance, the trail jogs right and then left on a telephone-company-cleared way and into pine woods. It skirts a swamp and crosses over an extended bog bridge, eventually emerging on the cul-de-sac at the end of Davis Ave. The trail follows Davis Ave. 1 block to its end on Ames Ave., turns right onto Ames Ave. for 1 block, then turns left onto Dunn Ave. After 1 block the trail turns right onto Thurston St. and continues briefly to Warner Trail Rd., onto which it turns left and proceeds 0.2 mi. to a cul-de-sac. The trail continues straight on a 10-ft.-wide conservation restriction, then bears left, circles through a notch to the remains of the sealed-over Wrentham landfill, and passes through the gate to Madison St.

The trail crosses the street and enters Wrentham State Forest. It turns sharp left, and, after a short flat stretch, circles to the right and steadily climbs to the first of several peaks, with some views north to Boston. The trail descends to a woods road before making a short, steep climb to a ledgy crest, then proceeds over several other knobby peaks known as the Pinnacles.

From the Pinnacles the trail descends to a woods road, turns right, crosses a dirt bike trail, then bears left onto a dirt bike path. The trail leaves the bike path, passes some large boulders, and continues over a level, rocky area. Next, climb to a cliff, cross a dirt bike trail, and turn right onto a woods road. The trail follows this road and bears right at the next two junctions. It then weaves through dirt bike trails, paths, and woods roads (watch for blazing), finally climbing Outlook Rock at 4.6 mi.

From Outlook Rock the trail descends, crosses the brook, then traverses a wet area before climbing to a cliff overlooking Minnehaha Pond. Below and to the right are the remains of an old dam. Descending to Minnehaha Brook, the trail follows the eastern bank a short way before turning right (southwest) onto a woods road (the Red Fox Path). (A short bushwhack south about 200 yd. leads to the Minnehaha Falls rapids.)

The Warner Trail passes a number of trail junctions before winding under an impressive rock ledge to the right at 5.3 mi. The path passes more side trails, then follows a rutted dirt bike trail. After passing near some houses the trail emerges onto Taunton St. at 6.3 mi. and turns right (north).

After 0.1 mi. the trail turns left (west) into handsome pine woods and approaches the Wrentham Senior Center (parking). Cross the parking lot and reach the road that leads to the Wrentham Water Works and the Trout Pond Recreational Center. The trail follows a woods road roughly parallel to the DPW road and reaches the bottom of an abandoned ski lift. It then ascends the steep slope to the summit of Knuckup Hill at 6.9 mi. (extensive view north, including the Boston skyline).

The trail continues, following the gravel road left and down the hill, then branching right on a path that avoids the brick building. At the paved road it turns right and follows the gravel road along Trout Pond. At the far end of the pond the trail turns right onto another gravel road that runs past a second pond and reaches Beech St. The trail goes left (southeast) onto Beech St., bearing right at 170 Beech St. after 0.2 mi. onto Bear Swamp Rd. This private woods road (stay on the trail) then enters Wrentham State Forest.

The trail follows the woods road, nears I-495, turns right, passes beneath the cliffs of Wampum Rock, and approaches the highway twice more before curving to the right (north) and climbing slowly. It turns left, makes a long descent, a short sharp climb, and then drops through an area of abandoned autos and trucks to reach MA 1A (South St.). Turns right to reach Wampum Corner, the junction of MA 1A and MA 121, at 9.9 mi.

Warner Trail: Foxboro (US 1) to Wrentham (Wampum Corner)

Distances from US 1

    to Outlook Rock: 4.6 mi., 1 hr., 40 min.

    to Minnehaha Cliff: 5.0 mi., 2 hr.

    to Taunton St.: 6.3 mi., 2 hr., 35 min.

    to Knuckup Hill: 6.9 mi., 2 hr., 55 min.

    to Wampum Corner: 9.9 mi., 3 hr., 40 min.

Section 4. Wrentham (Wampum Corner) to Hancock St. (Wrentham) (2.9 mi.)

The trail leaves Wampum Corner on MA 121 (West St.), heads southwest for about 100 yd., then climbs a steep bank (left) and follows an old railroad grade for the next mile. The railroad bed passes under I-495 in front of the Wrentham Premium Outlet Mall, and by a pond (left). It then leaves the railroad bed to the right, follows a bike path, and climbs an embankment. The trail runs along some wetlands to the right, then turns sharp right before some power lines. It climbs to a mound above the mall, then descends to the mall's gravel emergency road. Turn left onto the emergency road and continue toward the cell tower, reaching Green St. at 1.8 mi.

Turn right onto Green St. then quickly turn left onto a gravel road used by dirt bikes and ATVs. Follow this worn track, ignoring the many side trails until the trail reaches a junction about 0.4 mi. from Green St. Turn right here, continue to another junction, and turn left to climb to the top of a ledge. The trail climbs 0.1 mi. to another outcrop, which affords limited views of Providence to the south and the High Rock microwave tower to the north.

The trail continues a few yards to a power line, where it jogs right 20 yd., then turns left into the woods. It proceeds to Sunset Rock, which offers excellent views west and southwest toward Diamond Hill in Rhode Island. Continuing southwest, the trail descends the ledge through the woods and soon emerges on Hancock St. at a point 0.7 mi. east of MA 121 in Sheldonville (a part of Wrentham).

Warner Trail: Wrentham (Wampum Corner) to Hancock St. (Wrentham)

Distances from Wampum Corner

    to Green St.: 1.8 mi., 35 min.

    to Hancock St.: 2.9 mi., 50 min.

Section 5. Hancock St. (Wrentham) to Diamond Hill (RI) (6.7 mi.)

Note: The Warner Trail between Hancock St. and Rhodes St. is closed until it can be relocated around the Wentworth Hills Golf Club. Follow the alternate route directions below until the relocation is completed.

Warner Trail Alternate Route: Turn right onto Hancock St., and follow it as it bears left at the fork. Continue about 0.5 mi. to Burnt Swamp Rd., turn left and travel about 1.6 mi. on Burnt Swamp Rd. to Reservoir Rd. and the Warner Trail.

Follow Reservoir Rd. southwest to Camp Ker-Anna, then turn right onto a path a short distance beyond the camp sign. For the next 2.4 mi. the trail cruises through the woods, circling Diamond Hill Reservoir on a woods road, and passing a brief cut-off to the left and another woods road. The trail continues generally west to a small brook, where it turns left (south) and goes through a swampy area. It then winds along the side of the reservoir, sometimes coming within a yard of the water. Climbing up to the right, the trail slabs along the side of a hill for about 0.5 mi. It then climbs west to a rocky ledge with an open crest and views of Diamond Hill Reservoir.

The trail goes generally south along a downsloping ridge, proceeds onto a woods road, and, just before the road goes underwater, turns right onto a path that leads up and over a rise. In 0.1 mi. the trail turns left (southwest) through some heavy brush, crosses a small stream, and climbs up a sharp rise. Descending the other side, the trail bears left (south) onto a woods road. It then bears right onto a path through many muddy, narrow spots along the side of the reservoir until it comes to Fisher Rd.

The trail turns sharp right and proceeds up the remains of the old road. The road becomes paved and enters Ski Valley Condominiums. Continue on the paved road for about 0.3 mi., then turn left onto a well-worn path up a slope and zigzag to the summit of Diamond Hill (481 ft.), where indistinct remains of the old ski operations can be seen. On the east side, below the summit, the Boston and Providence skylines are visible in good weather.

From here the trail passes a large water tank and wanders south along the ridge, emerging at the edge of several sheer drops, before finally coming to a steep dropoff on the right. At this point the trail descends to RI 114 in Cumberland (there are many unmarked trails through here). The trail continues, keeping the cliffs to the left. The trail travels north through woods at the bottom of an abandoned quarry, continuing straight ahead to reach the Diamond Hill parking lot.

Warner Trail: Hancock St. (Wrentham) to Diamond Hill (RI)

Distances from Hancock St. (approx.)

to Diamond Hill summit: 4.5 mi., 2 hr., 5 min.

to Diamond Hill parking lot: 5.6 mi., 2 hr., 45 min.

Bay Circuit Trail (Southern Sections)

The Bay Circuit Trail, the region's newest long-distance hiking trail, is still under development. When completed, it will stretch for almost 200 mi. in a great arc around the entire Boston metropolitan area, connecting now isolated parks and reservations into a continuous greenbelt. The northern trail is covered in Part IV of this guide. Described below are the sections of trail presently dedicated in this region, including the southern terminus at Bay Farm. The trail is blazed with vertical white rectangles supplemented with BCT logos at junctions, trailheads, and other locations where more clarity is required.

Section 8. Sudbury (Weisblatt Conservation Land) to Southborough (Pine Hill Trail) (9.4 mi.)

From the Weisblatt Conservation Land parking area of the Sudbury Conservation Commission follow the Salamander Trail to where it loops left; the BCT continues straight (BCT blazes begin here), entering the Nobscot Boy Scouts Reservation at 0.4 mi. Follow along a ridge and climb to Tippling Rock (426 ft.), a great split boulder at the south end of the ridge. The trail now descends the hill, following white blazes to Nobscot Conservation Land and reaching Brimstone Lane at 2.0 mi.

Cross the road and pass through a low wetland before climbing the hill to Wittenburg Woods in Framingham. Weave through the woods and over a stone wall to enter the Sudbury Valley Trustees' (SVT) Gross Tract property. Head downhill and cross a stream, reaching Wayside Inn Rd. Cross the road and enter Henry's Hill (SVT). Continue on the trail to again reach Wayside Inn Rd. Head south on Wayside Inn Rd., turn right onto Edmands Rd. at 3.7 mi., and continue to Welch Reservation (SVT). Follow the trail through the Welch Reservation, climbing the hill to Callahan State Park and reaching Edmands Rd. at 5.0 mi.

From the road climb the hill, following the Backpacker Trail up Gibbs Mtn. (504 ft.). Descend and reach Beebe Pond on the Pine Tree Trail and cross the dam at the south end of the pond. Continue to Nourse St., turn left (southwest) onto an abandoned road, and enter Sudbury Reservoir. After winding through the woods the trail emerges at Parmenter St. at 7.0 mi. Cross the road and follow the trail through pine and hemlock forests (DCR). The Pine Hill Trail ends at a gate by Nicholas Rd. and Clemmons Rd. at 9.4 mi.

This is the effective end of the BCT in this section. The next section of trail (disregarding walking along roads and highways) begins at Ashland Town Forest in Ashland.

Bay Circuit Trail: Sudbury (Weisblatt Conservation Land) to Southborough (Pine Hill Trail)

Distances from Weisblatt Conservation Land

to Brimstone Lane: 2.0 mi., 50 min.

to Edmands Rd.: 5.0 mi., 1 hr., 55 min.

to Pine Hill Trail: 9.4 mi., 4 hr., 35 min.

Section 9. Ashland (Ashland Town Forest) to Sherborn Town Line (7.0 mi.)

From the entrance of the forest (parking) follow the Turnberg Trail (white blazes) until it reaches Winter St. at 2.5 mi. Turn right (west) onto Winter St. and at 3.0 mi. turn right into the woods (this is private property; stay to the right of the hill). Follow the trail through a DPW yard and along Ponderosa Rd. to the Riverwalk. Turn left onto the Riverwalk and follow it downstream for 0.5 mi. At 3.9 mi. the Riverwalk ends at Sudbury and Birch Lanes. Take consecutive right turns onto Birch Lane, Birch Hill Rd., Pine Hill Rd., and Mill Pond Park (parking). Cross Myrtle St. and rejoin the Riverwalk for a short distance. Continue straight onto Concord Court, then make consecutive rights onto Concord St. and Front St. From here follow Main St. and Homer Ave. to MA 135. Cross MA 135 and continue on Chestnut St. to Wildwood Cemetery on the left at 5.0 mi.

Pass through the cemetery, staying far left, to an old cart path that reaches Cadorette Rd. Descend a hill to Grover St. at 5.6 mi. Turn left onto Grover St., cross Cedar St. onto Mulhall Dr. and then Wenzell Rd., reaching MA 126 at 7.0 mi.

Bay Circuit Trail: Ashland (Ashland Town Forest) to Sherborn Town Line

Distances from Ashland Town Forest

to Riverwalk: 3.4 mi., 1 hr., 35 min.

to MA 126: 7.0 mi., 2 hr., 30 min.

Section 10. Sherborn (Elevator Rock) to Medfield (Charles River) (6.0 mi.)

This section begins along MA 126 about 0.5 mi. south of the Market Basket Supermarket at a break in the east-side guardrail. No parking is available. The trail follows a dike through wetlands, passing Elevator Rock before running parallel to the railroad tracks to reach Whitney St. Use Whitney St. to safely cross the tracks. Return to the trail, which is near a rock ledge. It now passes through wetlands and beneath power lines, then swings south and reenters the woods. Cross Western Ave. at 1.1 mi. and follow Stevens St. to Harrington Ridge Rd. Turn right onto Harrington Ridge Rd., then left onto Oldfield Rd., left again onto Dexter Dr., and finally right onto the trail. Follow the trail across private land to Sherborn Conservation Land. Cross a brushy field and head north, crossing Brush Hill Rd. and following the trail through the woods to Perry St.

Cross the road and pass through a pleasant woodland that explores Sherborn Town Forest before reaching and following a pipeline. The trail now climbs up and over Brush Hill and crosses the railroad tracks before reaching MA 27 (N. Main St.). The path passes the Sherborn Highway Department and continues to follow the pipeline to MA 16 (Eliot St.) at 6.2 mi. Cross the road and pass through woodlands before reaching Pine Hill School. From the school the trail skirts Pine Hill Cemetery and follows the ridge uphill along an ancient fault line atop Pine Hill. The path descends the ridge to Farm Rd., which it follows to Farm Rd. Cross the road, remaining close to the pipeline, and make a series of road walks to Rocky Narrows Reservation at 7.5 mi.

Rocky Narrows Reservation is rugged and beautiful. Stay on the trail, as it is easy to get lost. The trail passes through woodlands and by the picnic and canoe area that serves the Charles River. It then ascends to a rocky ledge and on to King Philip's Overlook, with a stunning view of the river. Return to the parking lot. From the parking area follow Forest St. southwest, then take consecutive left turns onto Snow St. and MA 27. Pass the MA 27 parking area for Rocky Narrows Reservation, and cross the Charles River into Medfield at 9.0 mi.

Bay Circuit Trail: Sherborn (Elevator Rock) to Medfield (Charles River)

Distances from Elevator Rock

  to Rocky Narrows Reservation: 7.5 mi., 3 hr., 20 min.

  to Charles River: 9.0 mi., 4 hr., 5 min.

Section 11. Medfield (Charles River) to Sharon (US 1) (9.6 mi.)

Beginning at the Charles River, cross at MA 27 (parking) and travel east on MA 27 about 0.4 mi., then turn left (southeast) onto Hospital Rd. The trail leaves the road to the right, descending to a large field then climbing a hill past baseball fields before reaching West Mill St. Turn right onto West Mill St., then left onto Adams St., continue for 0.4 mi., then turn right onto West St. Follow West St. for a short distance to a dirt road along railroad tracks past a large landfill and the Medfield Town Garage, reaching MA 27 at 3.0 mi. Turn left onto MA 27, then left onto Dale St., then left again into a cemetery. Pass through the cemetery (the trail may have very few blazes here) to MA 109.

Turn right (southwest) onto Causeway St. and follow this for 1.6 mi., turning left (east) onto Noon Hill Rd. at 5.0 mi. Follow Noon Hill Rd. past the north end of Holt Pond and into the Noon Hill Reservation. The trail now loops through the reservation to again meet Noon Hill Rd., turns right (east) on the road, crosses a brook, and reaches South St. at 5.25 mi.

Turn right (south) onto South St., then left (east) onto Rocky Lane, left onto Henderson Way, left onto Granite St., right onto Forest St., and right onto MA 27 (High St.). Cross the road and proceed to the trail on the left before some power lines. The trail parallels the power lines then turns off into the woods, passing along access roads of town water wells. Continue along athletic fields near Wheelock School and follow the road to Elm St. Turn right (east) onto Elm St., reaching the Walpole town line at 2.3 mi.

Cross into Walpole and turn right onto a power-line path that blends into the Old Indian Trail, an undulating path that traverses an esker and follows Mine Brook. At the end of the trail turn left past the water treatment plant, then right onto Leonard Rd. and follow it to the end, taking the woods path south to Robbins Rd. Turn right onto Robbins Rd., then left onto MA 27 (Elm St.), then right on Glenwood Ave. to Main St. at 7.75 mi.

Cross Main St. and continue to Memorial Pond opposite the town hall. Follow the trail around the south end of the pond, turn right onto Diamond St., then turn left onto Stone St.; continue to the Clark Pond Conservation Area at 8.35 mi. Follow the trail around the west side of the pond, briefly follow Lake St. southwest, and pass through the parking lot of Walpole High School. At the back of the school pick up the trail that enters the Walpole Town Forest. Follow this river trail, which parallels the Neponset River. The BCT passes through forest—easy to follow with many blazes. Follow the trail up a Department of Public Works driveway, then cross Washington St. onto a trail that leads to the town forest. The trail heads south through varied terrain, reaching a gravel cart path. Continue southeast to the power lines, then turn left and follow the path beneath the wires to reach US 1 at 9.6 mi. Cross US 1 to Pine St. and travel about 0.2 mi. to the Sharon town line.

Bay Circuit Trail: Medfield (Charles River) to Sharon (US 1)

Distances from Charles River

  to Walpole town line: 2.3 mi., 1 hr., 5 min.

  to Main St.: 7.75 mi., 3 hr., 50 min.

  to US 1: 9.6 mi., 4 hr., 35 min.

Section 12. Sharon (Pine St.) to Borderland State Park (Sharon) (7.4 mi.)

Pine St. is called South Walpole St. in Sharon. Cross I-95 on South Walpole St. and follow the Warner Trail (triangle blazes) to Old Post Rd. Take a left onto Old Post Rd. and ascend Pierce Hill, descending on the northeast side. Cross Walpole St. and enter the Moose Hill Wildlife Sanctuary. Follow Trail A as it ascends easily to Bluff Head. Continue following Trail A to the summit of Moose Hill (3.4 mi.), then descend steeply at times to the visitor center.

From the Moose Hill Sanctuary Visitor Center (parking, restrooms) continue on Trail A, then turn onto Trail H (the Warner Trail stays on Trail A). Follow the left fork when Trail H splits, then rejoin it at 4.8 mi. Continue straight, reaching Moose Hill Pkwy. Turn right onto the paved road, which soon reaches the railroad tracks of the high-speed Acela express train. *Note: Approximately the next mile of trail runs parallel to and crosses active railroad tracks used by high-speed trains. In places the visibility up and down the tracks is poor.* It is advisable to pick up the trail again at Deborah Sampson Park (6.9 mi.) on South Main St. (parking).

Cross the park in an easterly direction, passing between old school buildings and through woodlands to Beach St. At Beach St. turn left and pass around the north end of Lake Massapoag to a five-way junction. Follow Massapoag Ave. south (east sidewalk) as it takes a course along the shore of the lake. Just before reaching Mansfield St. take the trail on the left that enters the trail system of Borderland State Park. The entrance to the park is approximately 1.0 mi. farther down Massapoag Ave., at 7.4 mi. This ends this portion of the BCT.

Bay Circuit Trail: Sharon (Pine St.) to Borderland State Park (Sharon)

Distances from Pine St.

to Moose Hill: 3.4 mi., 1 hr., 25 min.

to Deborah Sampson Park: 6.9 mi., 3 hr., 10 min.

to entrance of Borderland State Park: 7.4 mi., 3 hr., 25 min.

Section 13. Pembroke (Valley Rd.) to Duxbury (Bay Farm) (8.2 mi.)

From the Pembroke–Duxbury town line at Valley St. the BCT heads southwest on a cart path through woods, meadows, and a small marsh to reach Summer St. (MA 53) at 1.1 mi. The trail crosses Summer St. and enters the Trout Farm Conservation Area. The trail system here has numbered junctions. Turn right at junction 11, left at 10 and 9, continue straight at 8, cross the brook at 7, pass 6, cross the brook again at 5, then go left at 4 to reach Union Bridge Rd. at 2.1 mi. Turn right and follow the road briefly before crossing the street and entering the woods. Travel through woods, over a footbridge, and reach King Philip's Path (paved) at 2.3 mi. Cross the road, through the woods along a footpath, then a cart path, and reach Vine St. at 3.1 mi. Turn left and follow Vine St. to Chandler St., turn left onto Chandler St. and proceed to Mayflower St., and then turn right onto the cart path.

The BCT now passes along a dam and small pond, then past a cranberry bog to the east. Turn left onto East St. (4.4 mi.), cross over MA 3 at 4.9 mi., and follow cart paths until the trail approaches Mayflower St. The path turns right (there are both white and yellow blazes here) and runs to the east side of Round Pond. Follow the blazes as the trail wraps around the pond and comes to a cranberry bog. Continue between the cranberry bog and a small pond to a dirt road and Elm St. at 5.9 mi.

Cross Elm St. and proceed south on School St., which merges with Oak St. Cross MA 3A at 6.4 mi. and continue south on Park St., turning left onto Loring Ave. at 6.8 mi. Follow the mowed path left around the perimeter of Bay Farm meadow to a granite ledge (7.0 mi.) on the shore of Kingston Bay. This is the very beautiful end of the BCT. Pragmatically, the trail continues to the right toward the parking lot for Bay Farm, but enjoy the view first.

Bay Circuit Trail: Pembroke (Valley Rd.) to Duxbury (Bay Farm)

Distance from Valley Rd.

   to Summer St.: 1.1 mi., 25 min.

   to Union Bridge Rd.: 2.1 mi., 50 min.

   to Vine St.: 3.1 mi., 1 hr., 15 min.

   to MA 3: 4.9 mi., 2 hr., 5 min.

   to Elm St.: 5.9 mi., 2 hr., 35 min.

   to southern terminus at Bay Farm and Kingston Bay: 7.0 mi., 3 hr., 10 min.

Ashland Town Forest

This town-maintained forest occupies a 2-sq.-mi. section of northeastern Ashland. It is bounded on the west by Oak St., on the north by Oregon Rd. and Salem End Rd. (the latter in Framingham), on the east by Myrtle St. and Badger Rd., and on the south by Winter St., on which the main forest entrance is located. To reach the entrance, start from the intersection of MA 135 and Main St. in Ashland. Go north on Main St. for about 0.5 mi. and bear right onto Myrtle St. After about 100 yd. turn left onto Pine Hill Rd. At the road's end turn left onto Winter St. In about 200 yd. a roofed sign on the right says Ashland Town Forest. There is parking for about 5 cars.

The main trail from this entrance is smooth and well maintained, having once been a fire road. It bisects the town forest for 1.5 mi. from Winter St. to Oregon Rd. (also a trailhead, but no parking is available). The trail has many turns on slightly rolling terrain, rising gradually for its first two-thirds and then descending gradually to Oregon Rd. It crosses three small brooks. Eight unmarked side trails leave from the main trail to surrounding roads. At these trail junctions the main trail is marked by white blazes. The side trails are maintained, but they are rockier with steeper sections, so caution should be used. Side trails branching west from the main trail are generally less strenuous, although some are steep in places. Some of the trails branching east pass interesting rock formations and converge on top of Wildcat Hill (436 ft.). Refer to the USGS Framingham quadrangle. The main trail is excellent for cross-country skiing.

Ashland State Park (DCR)

This 470-acre state park in Ashland includes 157-acre Ashland Reservoir. Perhaps the most notable aspect of the park is its well-developed network of universally accessible recreation opportunities. These include UA swimming, beaches, picnicking, trails, and restrooms. There is even an accessible boathouse.

To reach Ashland State Park from I-495, take Exit 21A and travel east on MA 135 to the entrance on the right. A trail skirts the reservoir's wooded shore, offering interesting views of the water and shore as well as distant views of Ashland and the surrounding hills.

Ashland Reservoir Trail (DCR)

This trail is well worn and easy to follow. It begins right of the park bathing beach, follows the shore south for a short distance, then cuts through a wooded area to the Ashland Girl Scout Camp. It crosses the camp area to the left of the main camp building and continues south, staying close to the shore until it reaches a dirt road at the southern end of the reservoir. The trail then follows the dirt road left (east) across a bridge over an inlet to a boat-launching area, passes to the right of a small bathing beach, and continues north beside an old wire fence to within sight of the reservoir dam. The trail goes west across the top of the dam, turns left, and follows the shore south to the starting point at the beach.

Ashland Reservoir Trail

Distances from park bathing beach

   to Girl Scout camp: 0.5 mi., 20 min.

   to inlet bridge: 1.2 mi., 35 min.

   to dam: 2.5 mi., 1 hr., 20 min.

   to park bathing beach (circuit): 3.2 mi., 1 hr., 45 min.

Moose Hill Audubon Sanctuary (MAS)

This 1984-acre sanctuary is the oldest operated by the Massachusetts Audubon Society. Located 25 mi. from Boston, it includes mixed woods, open fields, and wetlands. The sanctuary's terrain, vegetation, and geology are diverse for this region. A red maple swamp, traversed by a boardwalk, is especially beautiful as the leaves turn in late summer.

Highlights include the summit of Moose Hill (534 ft.), with a panoramic view from its fire tower; Bluff Hill and Bluff Head (450 ft.), with precipitous granite ledges and spectacular views to the south and west; and geological formations, including drumlins, a kettle hole, a bog, and granite ledges and outcrops.

A network of trails and woods roads makes much of the property accessible. The Warner Trail (marked by white markers) passes through the sanctuary and over the summits of Moose Hill and Bluff Hill (see the description of the Warner Trail). The planned route of the Bay Circuit Trail also passes through the sanctuary. Trail maps are available at the information shelter by the sanctuary parking lot or at the sanctuary office.

To reach the sanctuary from the intersection of US 1 and MA 27 in Walpole, go east on MA 27 for 2.0 mi. and turn right onto Moose Hill St. The sanctuary is 1.5 mi. ahead on the right.

Summit Trail (MAS)

This trail travels north from the sanctuary headquarters, crosses a gravel road (Billings Way) in about 100 yd., then turns northwest and follows a fairly straight course. After crossing an old woods road, it continues to the summit of Moose Hill, where there is a fire tower with views in all directions. For most of its distance it coincides with the long-distance Warner Trail, and is marked with the Warner Trail's white blazes plus the letter A.

Summit Trail

Distance from parking lot

   to summit of Moose Hill: 0.5 mi., 20 min.

Bluff Hill (MAS)

This route is a combination of three separate trails and provides the most direct access to Bluff Hill from the sanctuary parking lot.

From the parking lot, start on the B (Billings/Boardwalk) Trail, and then bear right onto the C (Cistern) Trail. This leads through pine woods, past a wall of rocks on the right, and to a junction with the Warner (A) Trail in the col between Moose Hill and Bluff Hill. Turn left onto the Warner Trail, heading uphill past an old water cistern and a couple of small ponds to the summit of Bluff Hill.

Bluff Hill

Distance from parking lot via B, C, and A Trails

   to Bluff Hill summit: 1.5 mi., 45 min.

Stony Brook Wildlife Sanctuary (MAS)

This 122-acre reservation in Norfolk includes large areas of marsh, open fields, and woods. Highlights include Stony Brook; three interconnected ponds known collectively as Stony Brook Pond; adjoining marshes; and a narrow, wooded isthmus centrally located amid the three ponds. The northernmost and largest pond is called Kingfisher Pond.

The Stony Brook Nature Center, which includes the park's offices, is located a short distance south of the junction of North, Pond, and Needham Sts. in Norfolk. From Norfolk center follow MA 115 south for 1.0 mi. to North St. Turn right onto North St. to reach the sanctuary entrance on the right. Maps are available at the nature center.

Pond Loop Trail (MAS)

This loop trail starts from the rear (west) of the nature center. It leads west between stone walls and crosses a bridge between Stony Brook Pond on the right and Teal Marsh on the left. Muskrat houses are visible in the distance in Teal Marsh. The trail then climbs along the southern flank of a forested glacial knoll to the beginning of a long boardwalk. The boardwalk passes between Kingfisher Pond and Teal Marsh, provides great views all along the way, and ends at a small island forested with beech trees. At the western end of the island is an observation platform.

The trail loops around the island, then returns across the boardwalk. At the glacial knoll the path turns left and passes a boulder field called Rock Hollow. The trail continues to the north end of the knoll, crossing a bridge and wandering through woods of maple, birch, and dogwood to reach Stony Brook. The trail crosses the brook on a bridge; the ruins of an old mill and mill-race are nearby. The trail then heads south across an open meadow and past a butterfly garden to return to the starting point at the nature center.

Pond Loop Trail

Distance from Stony Brook Nature Center

   to Stony Brook Nature Center (circuit): 1 mi., 30 min.

Borderland State Park (DCR)

This 1600-acre state park was purchased in 1971 from the estate of Blanche Ames and includes wooded hills, ponds, and open fields. The name, given to the property by the Ames family, refers to the Easton–Sharon border on which the park lies.

Interesting features of the landscape include the many dams constructed in an attempt to transform swampland into ponds. The Ameses created a forest and wildlife preserve on the majority of the estate, while developing the land's potential for outdoor recreational activities such as hiking, canoeing, skating, and skiing.

The park contains a number of hiking trails, most of which are easy to follow and suitable for hikers of all abilities. There is a lovely trail over the Long Dam, which separates Lower and Upper Leach Ponds. Farther to the east lie more ponds and, at Mtn. St., the historic Colonel Israel Tisdale House, which was destroyed by fire in 1983.

More difficult trails include the Lower Granite Hills Loop and Upper Granite Hills Loop, both of which lie to the north of Upper Leach Pond. These interconnecting trails (a total of 3 mi.) wend their way through oak forests and large granite outcrops.

The ponds are great for fishing and non-motorized boating, and are most easily reached via the park road that leads in from the Bay Rd. entrance on the east side of the park. No open fires are allowed, and a strict no-alcohol policy is enforced.

To reach the park from Sharon center (MA 27 at N. Main St. and Depot St.), go south via Pond St. and Massapoag Ave., passing Lake Massapoag, for 4.4 mi. From the east, south, or west, use MA 106 or MA 123, which combine in this part of Easton. Opposite the Belcher Malleable Iron Co., turn north onto Poquanticut Ave. Follow this for 1.5 mi. to the second left, then turn northwest onto Massapoag Ave. and continue 2.0 mi.

Myles Standish State Forest (DCR)

At over 14,000 acres, Myles Standish State Forest in Plymouth and Carver is one of the largest reservations in the Massachusetts state park and forest system. The forest offers universally accessible restrooms, five camping areas (Fearing Ponds 1 and 2, Charge Pond, Barretts' Pond, and Curlew Pond), and 16 ponds. A portion of Charge Pond is set aside for equestrian camping. There are 15 mi. of cycling paths, 35 mi. of equestrian trails, and 13 mi. of hiking paths (blazed with blue triangles) that venture deep into this unique area.

Myles Standish State Forest contains some of the largest areas of pitch pine–scrub oak plant community in New England. The forest is also well known for its kettle ponds, created as huge chunks of glacial ice became partially embedded in the ground and then melted when the ice ages ended. The holes left behind filled with water and became round ponds. There are many fragile natural areas in the forest, such as the shores of the kettle ponds, and these are marked with signs—please stay on the trail in these areas. In summer interpretive programs include explorations of cranberry bogs, trips to ponds, and visits to fire towers.

The recreational opportunities here seem endless. In addition to hiking, the forest offers camping, bicycling, canoeing, and swimming. The terrain is excellent for mountain biking, and the sport is very popular here. Myles Standish State Forest is closed to all ATV and ORV use.

To reach the forest from the north, take MA 3 south to Exit 3. Turn right (west) onto Long Pond Rd. and travel about 3 mi. to the entrance on the left. Park headquarters is located on Cranberry Rd. To reach the headquarters from the west (I-495), take Exit 2 (South Carver) to MA 58. Turn north onto MA 58, continue straight on Tremont St. where MA 58 bears left, and proceed for a little less than a mile to Cranberry Rd. on the right.

Easthead Trail and Bentley Loop (DCR)

The original Easthead Trail is a 3.0-mi. loop circling Easthead Reservoir. In 1991 the 4.5-mi. Bentley Loop was added at the northern end of the original loop. Both the original trail and the Bentley Loop are clearly blazed with blue trail markers or blue paint slashes and are well maintained.

The Easthead Trail begins on the north side of Cranberry Rd., about 150 yd. east of park headquarters. A sign indicates the entrance to the East-head Nature Trail. Entering the woods, the trail proceeds north, roughly following the eastern side of the reservoir. In about 1.4 mi., the trail turns left onto a well-used bridle path that follows a gas pipeline. In a short distance the trail reaches two junctions. At the first, the original Easthead Trail loop turns left to begin its return to the starting point via the western side of the reservoir.

To continue on the Bentley Loop, walk a few yards right onto a paved road. Follow the paved road a short distance, then turn onto the first dirt road on the left (with a metal gate numbered 75). The trail continues a short distance along this dirt road and then turns right onto a woods road. At the end of this road, just before a meadow, is a trail junction where the Bentley Loop heads both left and right.

Turn left at the junction and follow the well-blazed trail. (Use caution, as there are many unmarked paths that cross the trail in this section. If no trail marker is seen after a short distance, retrace the route to the last intersection.) The trail skirts the edge of New Long Pond, bears right then left, and passes Three Cornered Pond on the left. Beyond the pond the trail traverses the first of several meadows. It proceeds almost straight across this meadow (there is a 5-ft. post in the middle), then turns left just before a second meadow and heads north toward College Pond.

The trail turns left at another meadow and continues some distance along its left edge. The path turns left into the woods at another marker and quickly reaches its northernmost point at a junction. The path heading north leads to the College Pond parking area, while the Bentley Loop turns right and proceeds south.

After about 50 yd. the trail turns left and descends the hill, turns sharp right, and comes to a meadow (the first since turning south). Traverse the meadow and exit left at the far end. Soon College Pond Rd. is visible on the left. The trail skirts the edge of a parking lot, then turns right into the woods.

Cross another meadow and the trail enters into the woods for a short time before proceeding straight across yet another meadow at the bottom of a hill. From here the trail takes a very winding course to arrive back at the loop's starting point.

To return to the Easthead Trail, walk down the woods road, turn left at the dirt road, and proceed to the gate at the paved road. Turn right onto the paved road, follow it to the bridle path, turn left onto the bridle path, and then make a quick right to continue on the second portion of the Easthead Trail. Follow it for about 1.5 mi. around the reservoir back to the starting point. At one point along this section, the trail follows the road for about 100 yd. and then reenters the woods.

Easthead Trail and Bentley Loop

Distances from Cranberry Rd.

   to start of Bentley Loop: 1.5 mi., 45 min.

   to end of Bentley Loop: 6 mi., 3 hr.

   to Cranberry Rd. (circuit): 7.5 mi., 3 hr., 45 min.

Stony Brook Valley (Cape Cod Museum of Natural History)

An interesting network of trails is located in the town of Brewster, on property belonging both to the town and to the Cape Cod Museum of Natural History. These trails are in the valley of Stony Brook, which flows down from a series of freshwater ponds, becomes a tidal estuary merging with a salt marsh, and has its outlet in Cape Cod Bay. There are 300 acres of town-owned conservation land abutting the museum, including Wing's Island on the north side of the shore road and many acres of salt marsh and beach. The Cape Cod Museum of Natural History owns an additional 80 acres, that include marshland and beech woods.

Three nature trails traverse salt marsh, sandy scrub, and woodland, with views over Cape Cod Bay. All of the trails are well marked and easy to hike. Park at the museum parking lot on MA 6A, located 1.7 mi. west of the junction of MA 6A and MA 137, and a short distance west of Paine's Creek Rd. Maps are available at the museum, which offers many exhibits and interpretive programs.

Nickerson State Park (DCR)

This 1900-acre state park contains 420 camping sites, an 8-mi.-long bike path that connects to the 25-mi.-long Cape Cod Rail Trail, and more than 15 mi. of excellent hiking trails. Universally accessible facilities include fishing, beaches, camping, picnicking, and restrooms. The park is also within walking distance of Cape Cod Bay. Although the trails are not blazed, they are easy to follow as they wind through the scrub pine around the various lakes and ponds. Trail access may also be gained at the end of Long Nook Rd. and at Fishermen's Landing, which can be reached by following the main park road 1.8 mi. to the parking lot on the left.

The park entrance is located on the south side of MA 6A in Brewster, about 1.5 mi. west of Exit 12 off the Mid-Cape Highway (US 6). The main parking lot is on the right just inside the entrance to the park. An easy access to some of the trails is at the end of Flax Pond Rd., the first road on the left after entering the park. Follow it to a parking area between Big Cliff Lake and Little Cliff Pond, where there is a boat ramp. Park maps are available at the entrance gate; also refer to the USGS Harwich and Orleans quadrangles.

Lowell Holly (TTOR)

This 135-acre property in Mashpee and Sandwich holds an array of attractions, all linked by a 4-mi.-long trail system. Two knolls overlook Mashpee Pond and Wakeby Pond, and offer fine views of the water. The donor of the property, Abbot Lawrence Lowell, planted many rhododendrons and mountain laurels, as well as more than 50 species and varieties of holly. During June, this is one of the most beautiful floral displays in Massachusetts. The trails range from paths to comfortable carriage roads.

To reach Lowell Holly from US 6 (Exit 2) follow MA 130 south for 1.5 mi. Take a left on Cotuit Rd., continue for 3.4 mi., turn right onto S. Sandwich Rd., and proceed for 0.1 mi. to parking on the right.

Sandy Neck Barrier Beach

Sandy Neck is a 6-mi.-long barrier beach bordering Cape Cod Bay. Managed by the town of Barnstable, it provides habitat for several endangered species, including piping plovers, diamond-backed terrapins, and spadefoot toads. The dunes are covered with wildflowers, wild cranberries, and hardwood trees. A choice of trails offers options ranging from a 1.6-mi.-long nature walk to a hike of more than 13 mi. along the protected marsh and 100-ft.-tall dunes to the open waters of Cape Cod Bay.

To reach Sandy Neck from US 6 (Exit 5), head north on MA 149, turn left onto MA 6A, then right onto Sandy Neck Rd. Follow Sandy Neck Rd. to the parking lot at its end. A fee is charged for parking in season. Four-wheel-drive vehicles are allowed in certain areas, and hunting is permitted during the appropriate season. Mileage is posted at all intersections. Check tide charts, as low-lying areas on the marsh side may be flooded at exceptionally high tides, especially in the area adjacent to the start of the Marsh Trail. The circuits below are described counterclockwise, but they can be walked in either direction. Hikers are not allowed to enter private property or areas marked Erosion Control and must stay off the dunes, crossing over only on designated trails. Because of the exposure, be sure to bring adequate water and sunblock; allow time for slow going in soft sand.

Sandy Neck Circuit

Begin this circuit on the Marsh Trail, the trailhead is located in the parking area opposite the check-in booth. The trail initially passes through an area of red pine and scrub oak, then opens up by the great marsh. Large square blue boxes line the marsh—these are traps to control the green fly. The dunes to the left obstruct the view of the ocean. Stay on the sandy trail to avoid ticks and poison ivy, and to avoid destroying the beach grass and other fragile dune plants. At 0.5 mi. a junction is reached. A left turn here leads 1.1 mi. back to the parking lot via the beach. Alternately, continue straight ahead to signpost 2 at 1.5 mi. Poverty grass displays its yellow blooms in early June, and pale purple patches of sea lavender grow prolifically along the trail.

As the trail approaches crossover 2, Scorton Creek comes into view meandering the bay. Turn onto crossover 2 to return to the trailhead and complete a 4.7-mi. hike. For a 9-mi. hike continue straight to signpost 4 (there is no 3). Along the way is a dune cottage with no less than 20 swallow houses! Watch for horseshoe crab molts and deer and coyote prints. The historic cottages on Beach Point and of the decommissioned Sandy Neck Light come into view as the trail approaches signpost 4. Turn left at crossover 4 to return to the parking area and to complete a 9-mi. hike, or continue straight for another 1.5 mi. to crossover 5 and turn left for a 12-plus-mi. hike.

A horse trail intersects trail 5. Cross straight over it to reach the shore. Private land lies between the path here and the tip of Sandy Neck. To extend the hike, continue east along the beach to the lighthouse before retracing the route and returning to the parking lot along the shore. Be aware that a trip to the lighthouse extends the mileage by a couple of miles.

Cape Cod National Seashore (NPS)

Established in 1961, Cape Cod National Seashore is maintained by the U.S. Department of the Interior's National Park Service. The seashore includes six beaches—Coast Guard Beach and Nauset Light Beach in Eastham, Marconi Beach in South Wellfleet, Head of the Meadows Beach in Truro, and Race Point Beach and Herring Cove Beach in Provincetown—plus extensive inland areas of scrub pine, salt marsh, and swampland.

There are two visitor centers—Salt Pond Visitor Center on the corner of Nauset Rd. and MA 6 in Eastham and Province Lands Visitor Center on Race Point Rd., about 1 mi. from Provincetown off MA 6. Province Lands Visitor Center has an observation deck with a 360-degree view, movies, and ranger-guided activities. The Salt Pond Visitor Center was closed for rehabilitation at the time of this writing: it will reopen sometime between 2004 and 2006. Temporary facilities including, a bookstore and restrooms, are available nearby during the closure.

There are a large number of hiking paths and nature trails in the Cape Cod National Seashore. Most are well marked and relatively easy to hike.

Great Island Trail

Great Island is open only to hikers and boaters; no vehicles are permitted. To reach the beginning of the Great Island Trail from the town pier in Wellfleet, turn right onto Kendrick Rd., then left onto Chequesset Neck Rd. The trail begins at the parking lot at the end of the road. The Great Island Trail is a scenic but somewhat strenuous loop through woods, dunes, and swamps. (*Note: The sections of trail along the marshes might be wet during high tide, especially during fall and winter.*)

From the parking lot the trail heads west on a sand path. Winding through a pitch pine forest, the trail heads toward the marshy neck of land that connects Great Island to the mainland. The loop begins on this neck of land. On reaching the island, turn left and proceed east-southeast, skirting the marshes and dunes along the northern edge of Great Island. Just before reaching the cliffs on the northeastern corner of the island, the trail turns sharp right. A side trail continues ahead to the edge of the cliffs, which offer scenic views across Wellfleet Bay.

The trail now winds through the woodlands that cover the interior of Great Island, heading generally west and south. As the terrain turns more to marshland, the trail heads to the south, and crosses over Great Beach Hill. At the southern end of Great Island is a trail junction, where a spur trail leads south along a sand spit toward Jeremy Point. (Due to encroachment by the sea, it is no longer possible to walk all the way to Jeremy Point.) The Great Island loop returns to the north, following the beaches along the western edge of the island. Ascending over some dunes via stairs and a boardwalk, the trail returns to the neck of land between Great Island and the mainland. Turn left to return to the parking lot.

Great Island Trail

Distance from parking lot

   to parking lot (circuit): 7.5 mi., 3 hr., 45 min.

Doane Loop Trail

This trail is a paved, universally accessible path on Doane Rd., located about 1 mi. from the Salt Pond Visitor Center (where directions are available). The trail wanders through a pine-oak forest and passes two unique features—Doane Rock and the site of the Doane Homestead. Doane Rock (a.k.a., Enoch's Rock) is a large glacial erratic and the largest exposed boulder on Cape Cod. Deacon John Doane settled here in 1644 along with six other Pilgrim families. The site of his home is marked by a granite marker just off the path.

Fort Hill Trail

This moderate 1.5-mi. trail offers grand views of the Atlantic Ocean and Nauset Marsh. It also connects to the Red Maple Swamp Trail. To reach the trailhead from MA 6 in Eastham, turn onto Governor Prence Rd. (brown sign for Fort Hill), and proceed to the parking area on the left.

Red Maple Swamp Trail

The boardwalk portions of this trail are universally accessible and can be reached via Hemenway Landing at Fort Hill. The trail connects with the Fort Hill Trail and wanders through a red maple swamp that is especially attractive during late summer and early fall. To reach the trailhead, follow the directions for the Fort Hill Trail.

Nauset Marsh Trail

This easy 1.0-mi.-long path begins at the Salt Pond Visitor Center and explores the edge of Nauset salt marsh and Nauset Pond, passing some gorgeous views along the way. The trail then wends its way through a young forest back to the visitor center.

Atlantic White Cedar Swamp Trail

This moderate 1.2-mi.-long trail begins at the Marconi Site and descends through pine-oak forest into a tall woodland. The path then comes to a boardwalk that winds through a swamp of beautiful Atlantic white cedar. From the boardwalk the path heads uphill and returns to its start via "Wireless Road," a path of loose sand that can be very tiring. To reach the trailhead from the Salt Pond Visitor Center, travel 6.0 mi. north on MA 6 to Wellfleet; watch for signs for the Marconi Site.

Cape Poge Wildlife Refuge (TTOR)

This 516-acre barrier beach is on the east shore of Chappaquiddick Island on the eastern side of Martha's Vineyard. The beach runs for 7 mi. from Wasque Point to the Gut beyond the Cape Poge Lighthouse. West of the beach are sand dunes covered in rugosa rose and beach pea that separate the ocean from Cape Poge Bay. The refuge contains 14 mi. of moderate trails. Portions of the refuge may be closed seasonally to protect nesting birds.

To reach the refuge from Martha's Vineyard, take the Edgartown–Chappaquiddick Ferry to Chappaquiddick Island, then travel east on Chappaquiddick Rd. for 2.5 mi. to Dike Rd. Continue on Dike Rd. (dirt) for 0.5 mi. to reach the Dike Bridge and parking area.

Menemsha Hills (TTOR)

This 211-acre reservation on Martha's Vineyard overlooks Vineyard Sound and offers about 3 mi. of trails across open bluffs and through oak and beech forest. The view from Prospect Hill encompasses the village of Menemsha, Gay Head Lighthouse, and the Elizabeth Islands. From the bluffs overlooking the sound is a view of the Great Sand Bank. The Harris Trail offers a pleasant walk through diverse plant communities.

To reach Menemsha Hills from West Tisbury, follow North Rd. west for about 4.7 mi. to the reservation entrance and parking are just beyond Tabor House Rd.

Coskata–Coatue Wildlife Refuge (TTOR)

This 1117-acre refuge protects a spectacular stretch of beach and rolling dunes on Nantucket Island. Jutting out into the waters of Nantucket Sound, the property is famous for its world-class fishing. More than 200 acres of dunes support varied plant communities, including bayberry, cedar barrens, and stunted oaks. About 16 mi. of trails offer a unique hiking experience. Harbor and gray seals are common at Great Point, and seasonal tours allow exploration of Great Point Lighthouse. Portions of the refuge may be closed seasonally to protect nesting birds.

To reach the refuge from the Nantucket town rotary travel east for 6.0 mi. on Polpis Rd., then turn left onto Wauwinet Rd. and follow it to its end.

SUGGESTED HIKES

Easy Hikes

Moose Hill Audubon Sanctuary

Summit Trail [rt: 1.0 mi., 0:35]. This short trail ascends to the spectacular views atop Moose Hill.

Stony Brook Wildlife Sanctuary

Pond Loop Trail [lp: 1.0 mi., 0:30]. Boardwalks, ponds, marshes…a fascinating walk for the whole family.

Cape Cod National Seashore

Nauset Marsh Trail [lp: 1.0 mi., 0:20]. This easy path travels by the Nauset Salt Marsh and pond. Grand views await.

Moderate Hikes

Cape Cod National Seashore

Fort Hill Trail [rt: 3.0 mi., 1:30]. A charming trail with views of the Atlantic Ocean and the Nauset Marsh.

Atlantic White Cedar Swamp Trail [lp: 1.2 mi., 0:55]. This trail passes a cedar swamp, woodlands, and over a boardwalk before returning along the Marconi "wireless road." This short hike earns a moderate rating due to the abundant loose sand that makes for a tiring walk.

Sandy Neck Barrier Beach

Sandy Neck Circuit [lp: 4.7 mi., 4:40]. This circuit visits beautiful shoreside environments. Turn onto crossover 2 for the 4.7-mile loop.

Strenuous Hikes

Kingston Bay

Bay Circuit Trail, Section 13 [ow: 7.0 mi, 3:10]. This hike covers the southernmost section of the Bay Circuit Trail, ending at Bay Farm by beautiful Kingston Bay.

Myles Standish State Forest

Easthead Trail and Bentley Loop [lp: 7.5 mi., 3:35]. A long hike past ponds and through forests and meadows.

Cape Cod National Seashore

Great Island Trail [rt: 7.5 mi., 3:45]. This hike crosses a narrow neck of land to explore Great Island.

Appendix A

Conservation and Recreation Organizations and Agencies

L isted below are various organizations that maintain open space and hiking trails in this region, or can provide information about hiking and recreational activities. Many of the publications and maps produced by these organizations are also available at outdoor recreation suppliers and bookstores, as well as at the AMC's Joy St. headquarters.

The Appalachian Trail Conference
The Appalachian Trail Conference (ATC) is a private, non-profit volunteer organization dedicated to the preservation, maintenance, and promotion of the Appalachian Trail. It is a membership-based organization partnered with 31 clubs (including the AMC) that maintain designated sections of the trail. The ATC holds general meetings every other year.

Various periodicals and books about the Appalachian Trail are available from the ATC. Among these is a series of 11 guidebooks, with maps, covering the entire length of the trail. *Appalachian Trail Guide to Massachusetts–Connecticut, Eleventh Edition*, 2000, covers the AT in Massachusetts.
P. O. Box 807
799 Washington Street
Harpers Ferry, WV 25425-0807
Phone: 304-535-6331
Fax: 304-535-2667
www.appalachiantrail.org

Bay Circuit Alliance
Since its founding in 1990 the Bay Circuit Alliance (BCA) has developed a partnership of volunteers and other organizations to realize the goal of completing and sustaining the Bay Circuit Trail, a long distance hiking trail around the perimeter of metropolitan Boston. Presently about 150 miles of trail are open with another 50 miles yet to be completed. Updated trail information is available on the BCA website.
3 Railroad Street
Andover, MA 01810
Phone: 978-470-1982
www.baycircuit.org

Berkshire Natural Resources Council (BNRC)

Headquartered in Pittsfield, the BNRC is a natural resource advocacy organization that works to preserve threatened lands in the Berkshires of western Massachusetts. The group presently owns and maintains more than 6000 acres with an additional 6000 acres protected by conservation restrictions. The hiking trails constructed to allow public enjoyment of these lands have a reputation of being both well-maintained and environmentally responsible. The BNRC publishes a number of high-quality maps for regions in the Berkshires, including Yokun Ridge, Mt. Greylock, and the South Taconic Range. Maps are available from the organization's headquarters in Pittsfield or online at their website.

BNRC Headquarters
20 Bank Row
Pittsfield, MA 01201
Phone: 413-499-0596
Fax: 413-499-3924
www.bnrc.net/index

Cape Cod Trails Conference

The Cape Cod Trails Conference is an informal organization of hiking enthusiasts that strives to improve the hiking experience on Cape Cod. Their website has information on many trails in the Cape Cod area.

www.cctrails.org

Housatonic Valley Association (HVA)

The HVA is a river conservation group dedicated to preserving and protecting the Housatonic River watershed from source to sea. The organization partners with businesses and the community to increase access to the river and waterside lands as well as improve the overall health of the watershed. Projects include greenway hiking trails, water quality monitoring, stream team surveys of the river, and storm drain awareness.

The Berkshire office of HVA is located at:
1383 Route 102
South Lee, MA
Phone: 413-394-9796
Fax: 413-394-9818
www.hvathewatershedgroup.org

Williams Outing Club (WOC)

An organization of Williams College in Williamstown, the Williams Outing Club is dedicated to making the outdoors more accessible to Williams students, as well as to others desiring to hike the trails maintained by the club. The WOC publishes a guide to north Berkshire Trails complete with maps.

WOC
Williams College
Williamstown, MA

Phone: 413-597-2317
Fax: 413-597-4449
www.wso.williams.edu./orgs/woc

Williamstown Rural Lands Foundation (WRLF)
The Williamstown Rural Lands Foundation is a non-profit, member-supported land trust that works with and within the community to protect lands around Williamstown in northern Berkshire County. Since its founding in 1986 the organization has helped protect about 3000 acres of land and maintains a number of trails in the northern Berkshires on land it owns or helps manage.
P.O. Box 221
Williamstown, MA 01267
Phone: 413-458-2494
www.wrlf.org

Midstate Trail Committee
This organization maintains and administers the Midstate Trail, a 92-mile-long hiking trail bisecting the state. The Midstate Trail Committee operates under the auspices of the Worcester chapter of the Appalachian Mountain Club. The work of the committee is augmented by a large group of volunteer trail maintainers. The organization's website has updated trail information.
Phone: 508-797-9744 (Voice Mail)
www.midstatetrail.org

Massachusetts Audubon Society
The Massachusetts Audubon Society (MassAudubon) manages 29,000 acres of land in 41 sanctuaries throughout the commonwealth. Dedicated to conservation, education, and research, this member-based organization is supported by 68,000 members and annually reaches 250,000 children and adults through educational programs. Many of the sanctuaries have trail networks, nature centers, and interpretive educational programs. Hours that the trails are open varies and some locations charge a modest admission fee.
208 South Great Road
Lincoln, MA 01773
Phone: 781-259-9500 or 800-AUDUBON
www.massaudubon.org.

Massachusetts Department of Conservation and Recreation (DCR)
The Massachusetts Department of Conservation and Recreation (DCR) includes the Massachusetts Division of Parks and Recreation and the Division of Urban Parks and Recreation.
www.state.ma.us/dcr

Division of Parks and Recreation

The DCR's Division of Parks and Recreation (formerly the Massachusetts Department of Environmental Management) operates the nation's sixth-largest system of state parks and forests, encompassing more than 250,000 acres. Many of the parks and forests have extensive recreational facilities, including a number that are universally accessible. Admission fees are charged at some locations. Many forests and parks have extensive hiking opportunities and many of the state's long distance trails, such as the Appalachian, the Metacomet-Monadnock, and Midstate pass through DCR properties.

Main Office and Region 6 (Greater Boston)
251 Causeway Street
Suite 600/700
Boston, MA 02114-2104
Phone: 617-626-1250
Fax: 617-626-1449
www.state.ma.us/dem/index.htm

Region 5 (Berkshires)
740 South Street
P.O. Box 1433
Pittsfield, MA 01202
Phone: 413-442-8928
Fax: 413-442-5860

Region 4 (Connecticut River Valley)
40 Cold Storage Drive
P.O. Box 484
Amherst, MA 01004
Phone: 413-545-5993
Fax: 413-545-5995

Region 3 (Central)
Route 110
P.O. Box 155
Clinton, MA 01510
Phone: 978-368-0126 or 508-792-7715
Fax: 978-368-0217

Region 2 (Northeast)
817 Lowell Street
P.O. Box 825
Carlisle, MA 01741
Phone: 978-369-3350
Fax: 978-369-1965

Region 1 (Southeast)
194 Cranberry Road
P.O. Box 66
South Carver, MA 02366
Phone: 508-866-2580
Fax: 508-866-7736

Division of Urban Parks and Recreation

The DCR's Division of Urban Parks and Recreation (formerly the Metropolitan District Commission) is a Massachusetts state agency that manages and maintains parkland and recreational facilities in the metropolitan Boston area. It was established in 1893 to oversee and maintain the Metropolitan Park System. The agency now manages about 20,000 acres as well as a 120,000-acre watershed that supplies water to 2.5 million people. The division's properties are divided into four districts.

Division of Urban Parks and Recreation Headquarters
20 Somerset St.
Boston, MA 02108
Phone: 617-727-5114 (General Information)
617-727-5114 ext. 501 (Charles and Neponset Districts)
617-727-5114 ext. 504 (Mystic and Harbor Districts)
www.state.ma.us/mdc

MassWildlife

The Massachusetts Division of Fish and Wildlife, known as MassWildlife, was founded in 1866 in response to the decline of salmon populations. Since its inception the agency has been dedicated to the protection, restoration, and management of the animals and plants of Massachusetts. The lands protected by MassWildlife are kept as wild and undeveloped as possible to serve as areas for wildlife restoration. These properties, called Wildlife Management Areas (WMA), total over 100,000 acres across the state. Past restoration successes include the wild turkey and bald eagle; the redbelly turtle, peregrine falcon, and piping plover are numbered among present projects. The recreational opportunities offered on MassWildlife lands include hiking and birding, as well as hunting and fishing. Hikers using these areas should be aware of open hunting seasons and take appropriate precautions. www.state.ma.us/dfwele/dfw

Contact the following District Offices for the most up-to-date WMA information.

Western Wildlife District
400 Hubbard Avenue
Pittsfield, MA 01201
Phone: 413-447-9789
Fax: 413-442-0047

Connecticut Valley Wildlife District
East Street
Belchertown, MA 01007
Phone: 413-323-7632; Fax: 413-323-9623

Central Wildlife District
Temple Street
West Boylston, MA 01583
Phone: 508-835-3607; Fax: 508-792-7420

Northeast Wildlife District
68 Harris Street
Acton, MA 01720
Phone: 978-263-4347; Fax: 978-635-0292

Southeast Wildlife District
195 Bournedale Road
Buzzards Bay, MA 02532
Phone: 508-759-3406; Fax: 508-759-0381

National Park Service (NPS)
Cape Cod National Seashore
The National Park Service operates a huge expanse of beaches and dunes along the
Atlantic shore of the Cape. Their website provides extensive updated information on the
many features and recreational opportunities on Cape Cod National Seashore.
99 Marconi Station Site Road
Wellfleet, MA 02667
Phone: 508-349-3785 (Headquarters), 508-255-3421 or
508-487-1256 (Visitor Information)
Fax: 508-349-9052
www.nps.gov/caco

U.S. Fish & Wildlife Service
The U.S. Fish & Wildlife Service operates a number of National Wildlife Refuges in Mass-
achusetts. Information on these facilities can be obtained through their headquarters or
website.
Headquarters – Great Meadows NWR
Weir Hill Road
Sudbury, MA 01776
Phone: 978-443-4661
Fax: 978-443-2898
www.northeast.fws.gov/ma/grm.htm

The Trustees of Reservations (TTOR)

The Trustees is a member-supported non-profit organization founded in 1891 by landscape architect Charles Eliot. The organization preserves for public use exceptional landscapes and special places across the commonwealth. TTOR presently protects over 35,000 acres in 89 reservations and numerous smaller parcels. Four of the reservations are designated National Historic Landmarks, one is a National Natural Landmark, and eight are listed on the National Register of Historic Places. Combined the reservations have 270 miles of trails. Sixteen properties contain links to long-distance trails, including the Appalachian Trail, Bay Circuit Trail, Metacomet–Monadnock Trail, Midstate Trail, and Tully Trail. Maps and guides are free at many reservations. www.thetrustees.org

Headquarters	978-921-1944 (Beverly)
Northeast	978-356-4351 (Ipswich)
Southeast/Cape Cod	781-821-2977 (Canton)
Islands	508-693-7662 (Vineyard Haven)
Central	978-840-4446 (Leominster)
Western	413-298-3239 (Stockbridge)

New England Cartographics

This private company publishes a series of excellent, full-color trail maps covering the major hiking areas of central and western Massachusetts, including Mt. Greylock, the Mt. Holyoke Range, Mt. Tom, Mt. Toby, the Quabbin Reservoir, and Wachusett Mtn.
P.O. Box 9369
N. Amherst, MA 01059
Phone: 888-995-6277 or 413-549-4124 Fax: 413-549-3621
www.necartographics.com

New York/New Jersey Trail Conference

This organization, a federation of 85 hiking clubs and environmental organizations (including the Appalachian Mountain Club) with a total membership of about 10,000, is dedicated to constructing and maintaining hiking trails in the New York/New Jersey area, including the South Taconic Trail of southeastern MA and eastern NY. The conference also publishes an excellent waterproof, tear-resistant map covering the trails in the South Taconic region of Connecticut, Massachusetts, and New York.
156 Ramapo Valley Road (Route 202)
Mahwah, NJ 07430
Phone: 201-512-9348 M-F 11:00 A.M.–5:30 P.M.
Fax: 201-512-9012
www.nynjtc.org

Town Conservation Commissions

Only a few towns have the resources to maintain municipal open space large enough to support trail systems. Where they exist, however, the recreational opportunities are often excellent. For information on trails and open space properties maintained by cities and towns contact the conservation commission, in care of the appropriate city or town hall. Many of these commissions also provide maps of their properties, either free or at a minimal charge.

Appendix B

Leave No Trace

The Appalachian Mountain Club is a national educational partner of Leave No Trace, a nonprofit organization dedicated to promoting and inspiring responsible outdoor recreation through education, research, and partnerships. The Leave No Trace Program seeks to develop wildland ethics—ways in which people think and act in the outdoors to minimize their impacts on the areas they visit and to protect our natural resources for future enjoyment. Leave No Trace unites four federal land management agencies—the U.S. Forest Service, National Park Service, Bureau of Land Management, and U.S. Fish and Wildlife Service—with manufacturers, outdoor retailers, user groups, educators, organizations such as the AMC and the National Outdoor Leadership School (NOLS), and individuals.

The Leave No Trace ethic is guided by these seven principles:
- Plan ahead and prepare
- Travel and camp on durable surfaces
- Dispose of waste properly
- Leave what you find
- Minimize campfire impacts
- Respect wildlife
- Be considerate of other visitors

The AMC has joined NOLS, a recognized leader in wilderness education and a founding partner of Leave No Trace—as the only sole national providers of the Leave No Trace Master Educator course through 2004. The AMC offers this five-day course, designed especially for outdoor professionals and land managers, as well as the shorter two-day Leave No Trace Trainer course, at locations throughout the Northeast.

For Leave No Trace information and materials, contact:
Leave No Trace Center for Outdoor Ethics, P.O. Box 997, Boulder, CO 80306
Toll Free: 800-332-4100, or locally, 303-442-8222; Fax: 303-442-8217
www.lnt.org

Appendix C

Accident Report

Incident Location:_____ **Date:**_____ **Time:**_____

Description of Lost or Injured Person:

Name_____ Age/Sex_____

Address_____ Phone_____

Reporting Person:

Name_____

Address_____ Phone_____

1. INCIDENT SUMMARY

_____

_____

2. PATIENT INFORMATION

Allergies_____

Medication_____

Previous Injury/Illness_____

Last 24 Hr. Food/Water Intake_____

MedicalConditions/Other_____

Experience_____

Physical/Mental Conditions_____

Patient Clothing (color/style/size):

Jacket_____ Shirt_____ Shorts/Pants_____

Hat/Gloves_____ Pack_____ Footgear_____

Patient Gear (circle all that apply):

Map	Sleeping Bag	Tent/Bivy	Rain/Windgear
Flashlight/Batts	Extra Clothing	Food/Water	Ski Poles/Ice Axe

3. PATIENT EXAMINATION
Problem Areas/Injuries (circle all that apply):

Head	Face	Eyes	Mouth	Neck
Shoulder	Chest	Stomach	Upper Back	Lower Back
Upper Leg (R)	Knee (R)	Lower Leg (R)	Ankle (R)	Foot (R)
Upper Leg (L)	Knee (L)	Lower Leg (L)	Ankle (L)	Foot (L)
Upper Arm (R)	Elbow (R)	Lower Arm (R)	Wrist (R)	Hand (R)
Upper Arm (L)	Elbow (L)	Lower Arm (L)	Wrist (L)	Hand (L)

4. VITAL SIGNS

	Essential			**Helpful**		
Time	Level of Consciousness	Breathing Rate	Pulse	Blood Pressure	Skin	Pupils

5. NOTES/PLAN

_____

_____

_____

Index

Note: Boldface type designates detailed descrition of trail. Trails marked with an asterisk are mentioned within descrptions of other trails.

Get Out & Get Active with the AMC

Since 1876, the Appalachian Mountain Club has promoted the protection, enjoyment, and wise use of the mountains, rivers, and trails of the Northeast. We encourage people to enjoy and appreciate the natural world because we believe that successful conservation depends on this experience.

Join Us!

With the AMC, you can participate in virtually every Earth-friendly outdoor activity there is. Connect with new people, learn new outdoor skills, and feel good knowing you're helping to protect the natural world you love. In addition to hundreds of adventures offered by your local AMC chapters, you'll also enjoy discounts on AMC skills workshops, lodging, and books.

Outdoor Adventures & Workshops

Develop your outdoor skills and knowledge! From beginner backpacking and family canoeing to guided backcountry trips, you'll find something for any age or interest at spectacular locations throughout the Northeast.

Destinations & Accomodations

From the North Woods of Maine to the Delaware Water Gap, AMC offers destinations tailored for every kind of traveler. Experience outdoor adventure at its best as our guest.

Books & Maps

AMC's hiking, biking, and paddling guides lead you to the most spectacular destinations in the Northeast. We're also your definitive source for how-to guides, trail maps, and adventure tales. Explore the possibilities!

Contact Us Today!

Appalachian Mountain Club
5 Joy Street
Boston, MA 02108
617-523-0636

www.outdoors.org

AMC Books

For the best walking, hiking, paddling, and more

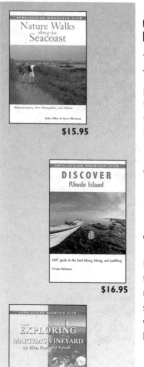

$15.95

$16.95

$14.95

Discover the Berkshires of Massachusetts

The latest addition to this popular series highlights 40 of the best hikes, mountain-bike trails, and paddles in the Berkshires.

Order # 1-929173-35-0 $16.95

WalkBoston

Here is the ultimate guide to Boston, its famous neighborhoods, and surrounding communities, written by the people who know them best.

Order # 1-929173-36-9 $14.95